LONE STAR PASTS

LONE STAR PASTS

Memory and History in Texas

EDITED BY

Gregg Cantrell *and* Elizabeth Hayes Turner

FOREWORD BY

W. Fitzhugh Brundage

TEXAS A&M UNIVERSITY PRESS

College Station

Gregg Cantrell, "The Bones of Stephen F. Austin: History and Memory in Progressive-Era
Texas," is reprinted, with minor revisions, from the *Southwestern Historical Quarterly* 108
(Oct. 2004): 145–78.

Library of Congress Cataloging-in-Publication Data

Lone star pasts : memory and history in Texas / edited by Gregg Cantrell and
Elizabeth Hayes Turner ; foreword by W. Fitzhugh Brundage. — first ed.
p. cm. — (Elma Dill Russell Spencer series in the West and Southwest ; no. 27)
Includes bibliographical references and index.
ISBN-13: 978-1-58544-563-9 (cloth : alk. paper)
ISBN-13: 978-1-58544-569-1 (pbk. : alk. paper)
1. Texas—History—19th century. 2. Texas—History—20th century. 3. Memory—Social
aspects—Texas. 4. Memorials—Texas. 5. Monuments—Texas. 6. Texas—Historiography.
I. Cantrell, Gregg, 1958– II. Turner, Elizabeth Hayes. III. Series.
F386.L78 2007
976.4'05—dc22
2006014551

For John B. Boles

Contents

Foreword

W. Fitzhugh Brundage

During the summer of 2005, cyclist Lance Armstrong's unprecedented effort to win his seventh consecutive Tour de France received extensive news coverage around the world. Few accounts of his performance failed to highlight that he was a Texan. Spectators along the race route honored his roots by routinely waving giant Lone Star flags when he rode past. It is hard to imagine that comparable attention would have been paid to Armstrong's birthplace if he hailed from, say, Nebraska or Delaware. But reporters and fans alike traced his remarkable resiliency and indomitable competitive spirit to his Texas origins.

The ubiquity of references to Armstrong and Texas is one example of the remarkable degree to which a mythic Lone Star identity has gained a hold on the national and international imagination. Along with California, Texas is unusual in the degree to which its recalled past is integral to its modern identity. Texas' identity, in many regards, is an exaggeration of purported American traits. Mythic Texas is loud, brash, extravagant, and rustic, like the pint-sized, fabulously rich, and mustachioed oil barons who drive immense Cadillacs (with cattle horns on the radiator) through Bugs Bunny cartoons. This version of Texas meshed perfectly with the enthusiasms of American popular culture during the twentieth century. To take one example, almost every decade of the last century seemed to warrant another film rendition of the battle for the Alamo. Indeed, the battle on the Texas frontier has been represented in more movies than the fight over Ft. Sumter, a siege of arguably much greater historical significance.

The enduring interest in Texas' mythic past warrants close scrutiny because it is suggestive of the confluence of history, memory, power, and identity that vexes our postmodern age. Scholars have adopted the conceit of "historical memory" to describe the amorphous and varied activities that groups have employed to recall the past. Recently, older notions of memory as a passive process of storing and retrieving objective recollections of lived experiences have given way to an understanding of memory as an active, on-going process of ordering the past. Similarly, collective or historical memory is not simply the articulation of some shared subconscious but rather the product of intentional creation. Collective remembering forges identity, jus-tifies privilege, and sustains cultural norms.

Although the impulse to compile collective memory is universal, it is manifest in ways that are specific to time and place. Different groups, as this collection demonstrates, have different resources and opportunities to fashion and perpetuate their version of the past. Elites typically enjoy a clear advantage in imposing their preferred past on their community, but, as sev-eral essays in this volume reveal, even the most disadvantaged communities often harbor alternative memories. By charting the persistence and shifting influence of both African American and Tejano counter-memories in Texas this collection draws welcome attention to the diversity of communities that harbor historical memories and their struggles to secure broader recognition of their recalled past.

The ambitions of architects of historical memory are never as simple as they appear at first glance. The Texas chapters of the United Daughters of the Confederacy (UDC), which are deftly treated in this collection, had an unambiguous goal: to commemorate Confederate valor and sacrifice. Yet the UDC simultaneously was a vehicle for women to accumulate power and exercise cultural custodianship, two goals that were seldom openly acknowl-edged. Similarly, the curious history of the exhumation and reburial of Ste-phen F. Austin's remains is a case study of struggles to weld memory to state-building and conventional politics. In both of these instances, campaigns to fashion history addressed, if sometimes obliquely, pressing political and cultural preoccupations.

Another fascinating dimension of the recalled past is the tenacity of some narratives and the evanescence of others. No enduring social memory can be entirely static. Each time a tradition is articulated, it must be given a mean-ing appropriate to the historical context in which it is invoked. For a histori-cal memory to retain its capacity to speak to and mobilize its intended audi-ence, it must address contemporary concerns about the past. Consequently, although the crafters of historical memory often resolve to create a version of the past that is impervious to change, their very success is dependent on its ongoing evolution. Here again, these essays clarify when and how each layer was added to the "Texas myth." Indeed, this collection offers numerous examples of the ways in which a "Texas" identity, rooted in the remembered past, has been perpetuated and intensified, rather than dissolved, by the forces of modernity. During the 1920s, for example, the Texas Ku Klux Klan espoused a reactionary ideology. But it also was a modern national organization that worked to assimilate both the nation's and the state's history into a seamless white identity. By reconciling these two strands of memory, the Klan ensured that white Texas identity would remain salient and relevant to twentieth-century circumstances. In sharp contrast, the waning of interest in Lyndon B. Johnson in his home state illustrates the speed with which shifting political and cultural currents can revise and even erase collective notions about historical figures and events. Neither Johnson's towering ambition nor his exceptional legislative achievements has been sufficient to earn Johnson the enduring status in Texas memory that either would seem to warrant.

Extraordinary political, economic, and cultural transformations in twentieth-century Texas unquestionably have broadened and complicated the collective memory of Texas. Apparently, the Texas of the Alamo, cattle barons, and oil wildcatters is resistant to the winds of time. But in recent decades Texas' position as a borderland, where cultural and economic exchanges are inevitable and frequent, seems to have fostered new awareness of inherited identities. At a time when the notion of "globalization" prompts anxieties about the erosion of everything from a sense of place to standards of living, the inclusion of new narratives about Texas is a reminder that communities can retain powerful identities even while they are irreversibly integrated into transnational networks. The new recognition of Tejano heritage, as well as African American heritage, demonstrates that collective memory can foster inclusion no less than exclusion. This more inclusive historical memory even exerts an influence beyond the boundaries of the state. The widening adoption of June 19—"Juneteenth"—as a national day to honor the abolition of slavery is an especially telling example. Emancipation Day ceremonies were a national phenomenon of the late nineteenth century, but advocates of the holiday could never agree on an appropriate date (because, after all, there was no single date on which all of America's slaves were simultaneously freed). The celebration of emancipation on June 19 was an idiosyncratic Texas tradition until Texas declared the date a state holiday; now even many communities that have long-established local Emancipation Day traditions have embraced Juneteenth.

Texas, at least as much as any state in the Union, cannot be understood without coming to terms with its collective memory. In the popular mind, at least, Texas history begins with one of the most famous appeals to memory in American history—"Remember the Alamo." As these gathered essays so eloquently reveal, the recalled past entails much more than the Alamo and its defenders. A fuller understanding of the ambitions and frustrations of Texas' architects of memory during the past two centuries may help us to better understand the responsibility that comes with the power to recall the past and fix it on the landscape. There are lessons in the surprising, complex, and, yes, colorful history of Texans and their past for all those who wield power over the past and all those upon whom that power is exercised.

Acknowledgments

By its nature, the writing of history is a collaborative enterprise, for historians depend upon librarians, archivists, colleagues, and family members for sources, criticism, advice, and moral support. In an edited work such as this one, this is particularly true. From the inception of this project, our editor at Texas A&M University Press offered enthusiastic support and sage advice, for which we are very grateful. The fine scholars who contributed essays accepted criticism from not one but two demanding editors, and they did it on tight schedules and with unfailing good humor. We would also like to thank our spouses, Brenda Cantrell and Al Turner, and our colleagues in the history departments at the University of North Texas and Texas Christian University for their support and encouragement. Thanks, too, go to the Dallas Area Social History Group for keeping historical discourse alive and for offering cogent advice on this book's prospectus. At an early stage of the project the Center for American History at the University of Texas graciously furnished a conference room that allowed the editors and authors to meet together and plan this book. The cost of illustrations was underwritten by the Center for Texas Studies at Texas Christian University, which allocated a portion of a larger grant from the Summerlee Foundation of Dallas; we are grateful to both organizations. Finally, we wish to acknowledge Dr. John B. Boles of Rice University, who served as friend and mentor to both of us in the formative stages of our careers as historians. Whatever skills we brought to this project as editors are in large measure due to his influence, and for that we dedicate this volume to him.

Introduction

A STUDY OF HISTORY, MEMORY, AND COLLECTIVE MEMORY IN TEXAS

GREGG CANTRELL & ELIZABETH HAYES TURNER

In May 2003, fifty-one Democratic members of the Texas legislature fled across the Red River to a Holiday Inn in Ardmore, Oklahoma, in an attempt to prevent a quorum and thus defeat a controversial Republican-backed redistricting bill. Responding to their action, House Speaker Tom Craddick invoked one of Texas' most cherished historical memories. "At the Alamo when Travis drew a line in the dirt, inviting those who wanted to leave, only one man, Moses Rose, climbed over the wall and fled," Craddick proclaimed in a press release. "It's not a disgrace to stand and fight, but it is a disgrace to run and hide."[1]

Craddick's statement stands as an example of the phenomenon explored in the following eleven essays. How did the Speaker come to know the story of Travis's line in the sand and Rose's alleged response to it? Craddick likely did not turn to the latest historical scholarship in order to find an appropriate example of cowardice to apply to the fugitive legislators; he didn't need to. Having lived in Texas since age eight, he simply *knew* the story of Travis's line in the sand and Rose's alleged response to it. As Texans might say, he had "grown up" with the story. He likely had been taught it in the public schools, seen it depicted in movies or comic books, or learned of it in visits to the Alamo. Why did he use it on this particular occasion? Clearly Craddick was making a political point, and he wanted to make it in a way that would resonate with large numbers of his fellow Texans. This was no occasion for discussing the historical veracity of the tale, the particulars of which are actually much disputed by modern scholars. Craddick's statement, then, was not so much a reference to history as it was an expression of a collectively remembered past.

Roland Barthes, in *Camera Lucida,* defined history as that time before an individual was born or before "we" were born. Hence memory, as opposed to history, becomes a person's recollection of the past after birth and cognizance.[2] Michel-Rolph Trouillot points out that "human beings participate in history both as actors and as narrators." Thus, history, or the events of the past, and memory have always been intertwined in the human mind. A simple explanation might be that history is the past and memory is what people remember about the past. American historian Carl Becker concluded that there are two histories: the actual events that once occurred and those that we remember. Individual memories, such as those of former slaves recorded by the WPA interviewers seventy years after the end of the Civil War, represent the remembrance of personal experience.[3]

Collective memory, by contrast, develops not only from the individual memories of those who witnessed an event but also from the "memories" of those who were not yet alive to experience the event. Societies, or groups within societies, derive their collective memories from a variety of sources. In preliterate societies, those memories were exclusively the product of stories passed down from one generation to the next. Such generational transmission of memory may still be important, but in modern times it is supplemented by a variety of other sources. Today, document-based historical research of the sort found in scholarly history books sometimes contributes to shaping collective memory, but a larger role is probably played by the history lessons taught in schools; visits to museums, monuments, historical sites, or public celebrations; and the viewing of historically themed art, television, and movies—to name a few. Since collective memory belongs to groups, it constitutes shared remembrances; it serves as a coordinator of identity and imbues meaning to past events of historic import. In the words of Maurice Halbwachs, "Collective memory . . . is a current of continuous thought whose continuity is not all artificial, for it retains from the past only what still lives or is capable of living in the consciousness of groups keeping memory alive."[4]

This rather simple rendering of the differences between history, memory, and collective memory does not speak to the more complicated so-called scientific or objective *written* examination of the past, especially when historians unearth records and documents that contradict memory or complicate human understanding of past events. Individual memory can change—be reshaped—in the light of historical writings on a given event. Collective memory may veer off into calculated struggles for dominance, as in the revered mythic memories surrounding Confederate "heroes." Thus, historians write history, sometimes using the tools of collective and individual memory, but they should do so with the same skeptical and trained eye that discerns the veracity of any primary source. When historical discourse—using evidence and interpretation—differs from memory, the ground for disagreement between what is the "truth" of the past and what is not leaves those with memories, even collective memories, often at odds with written history. What then are the paths through which one must travel to elicit a usable past?[5]

Concerns about historical fact and recalled memories are only part of the equation for understanding memory and its function vis-à-vis history. Historians also see, as a subject of immense importance, the way that collective memory has acted as a powerful shaping force in history. David Blight calls this the "*politics* of memory." That is, historians study the way groups behave, once they have grasped their identities through collective memory. "How cultures and groups use, construct, or try to own the past in order to win power or place in the present is why the broad topic of memory matters," he writes. How groups have used their collective memories to influence their paths to power is one side of the politics-of-memory question. Collective memories, as wielded by powerful groups, have had a tendency to shape and define that which is acceptable, that which should be remembered, that which should be forgotten, and who may be allowed entrée into positions of economic or political ascendancy. Hence societal norms related to power, class, gender, and race may be redefined through cultural hegemonic forces as seemingly benign as memories of the past.[6]

It is the historian's task to turn a trained eye to the veracity of individual or collective memories of events that have become accepted by a group or a society. A combination of human memory and human documentation must be present for historians to do the work of reinterpreting the past. Using documents other than remembrance, a construction of the recalled event may take on a very different interpretation. Written history becomes a record of the past interpreted through the "objective" skills of a historian; objectivity, detachment, the search for truth are goals historians seek when writing about past events. At the hands of the historian, the story of Travis's line in the sand—a story that went unrecorded until nearly forty years after the event—becomes too poorly verified to be considered a historical "fact." But in the collective memory of Texans it remains a factual depiction of what happened in 1836.[7]

Lest one believe, however, that scholarly histories are free of bias, omissions, judgments, or mistakes—accusations often leveled at collective memory—one need only look to the volumes of history now lying unread, gathering dust on library shelves. They are the product of revisions, reinterpretations, and historiographical change. Historians themselves concede that without revision and reinterpretation there would be no need for another written history, no point to the hours spent in research. Written histories are the product of the historian's environment, upbringing, education, sex, intelligence, nationality, ethnicity, and political persuasion. Where historical memory can be faulted for its reliance on the observations of a few whose voices may reveal bias, prejudice, or dominance, scholarly histories may be discredited for the omissions and bias of the author. Where then does truth reside?

One may argue that the sort of truth that attempts to recreate the reality of the past is not just elusive but impossible. No one can recreate an event from the past; the attempt to put words to actions is an abstraction. The best that human beings can do is to tell the story of the event, interpret its meaning, and record it for others to learn from. This process brings the reader full circle to the reconsideration of memory, its meaning, and its relationship to the past. Where memory and written history may converge is that place where the collective memory of a societal group influences the ideas or ideology of trained historians, or where historians adopt collective memory as historical "truth." In those cases—and it has happened most notably with southern history, including Texas history—a "distorted" version of the past may become the dominant one and be used to suppress other views of the past.[8]

Since the 1920s, the study of memory has gained wide acceptance in scholarly circles. Much is owed to the French sociologist Maurice Halbwachs, who explored the relationship between memory and history, creating the concept of "collective memory" and attaching it to cultural groups and the space they appropriated. Halbwachs emphasized the social contextualization of all individual memories. Halbwachs's work was followed by the seven-volume *Les Lieux de mémoire,* published between 1984 and 1992. Its principal editor, Pierre Nora, conceptualized "sites of memory," by which he meant not simply monuments to remind citizens of past valor but also paintings, writings, cuisine, or points of natural beauty that epitomize community or national character. Nora also characterized a shift from collective memory as shared, lived experience, *milieux de mémoire,* to sites of memory, *lieux de mémoire,* which represent self-conscious, deliberate attempts to preserve memory in historical ways. For Nora, memory and history exist in fundamental opposition to one another, with memory being the more authentic in the service of society because it accommodates only those facts that make the past relevant to the present. The relationship of a society to its past is central in constructing symbolic meaning and identity. Nora, and the many contributors to his massive study, scrutinized the meaning of national identity in post–World War I France. Others have illustrated the French drive to nationalize and thereby restore the idea of unification under a central nation-state by the symbolism inherent in the creation of World War I monuments.[9]

Stemming from studies surrounding World War II, the concept of memory continued as a help to survivors in understanding the meaning of the Holocaust and the war-ravaged continent—to cope with the greatest tragedy of the twentieth century. The scholarly journal *History and Memory* is devoted to understanding the Holocaust and the forces that led to it. Scholars in the western hemisphere took note of the value in the study of memory, not so much to heal deep scars and wounds caused by war or disaster—although that too has its place—but as a subject worthy of consideration in the light of national or regional history.[10]

Collective memory has generated as much debate over its definition as the original debate over history and memory. Although Halbwachs, Nora, and others have popularized the term "collective memory" to describe how a pattern of memory may unite groups and lead them to develop a national identity, different groups, tribes, or nations have differing experiences and, consequently, differing memories of a given historical event. Historians of the Holocaust observe that there is no such thing as a shared collective western memory of the horror. Auschwitz will never signify for Germans what it signifies for Jews. The same can easily be said of Texas, as the essays in this volume point out. While various groups of Texans may share some of the overarching myths of western civilization, they do not share one experience; rather, they share multiple "collective memories" of Texas' past.

The defining historical events in Texas history have been its successful war for independence from Mexico in 1836 and its unsuccessful bid to gain independence from the United States between 1861 and 1865. Both events constitute attempts at nation-building, and historians have long associated the power of common memories among a people as a contributor to the creation of statehood. For decades after the Civil War, however, defeat trumped victory in the collective memories of white Texans, while for African Americans another view of the past circulated quietly. At the turn of the century, a generation of Civil War veterans began to pass away, calling down the curtain on the humiliating defeat that C. Vann Woodward labeled the burden of southern history. Although redeemed in collective memory by the skillful turning of loss into noble valor by daughters, sons, and wives of Confederate veterans, the Lost Cause nonetheless brought none of the satisfaction that winning could provide. By the beginning of the twentieth century, then, Texans were turning to a more useful past, one that brought bravado and glory to their field of memories. Hence "Remember the Alamo" replaced the rebel yell, at least superficially.[11]

Women were particularly involved in the creation of these collective memories in Texas. White southern women, whose identities were tied to the military deeds of their men and the home-front sacrifices of their mothers—or of themselves—pushed to create cemeteries for the Confederate dead, hold patriotic celebrations and parades, and, finally, erect monuments in stone or bronze. These metaphors to a lingering identity recount a nation— a civilization in their minds—at once noble and just but forced to rebel against a materialistic and sordid Union. Gendered renderings of the romantic were seen everywhere in their symbolic tributes to the fallen Confederates. And as they amassed sums to buy the artwork—statues and monuments, plaques and tombstones—they asserted their cultural authority. With gloves and hats, members of the United Daughters of the Confederacy strode into the public sphere unobstructed by male "protection" or objection. Championing collective memories of a region devoted to its Lost Cause, white Texas women found a limited kind of power through their endeavors. Likewise, as memories of the Lone Star state's own days of nationhood took center stage on the grounds of the Alamo, Daughters of the Republic of Texas devoted themselves to its preservation, not with an eye to accuracy or to archaeological authenticity but to the re-creation of a dreamlike "national" shrine, imbued with the idyllic. The Alamo then and now had found its guardians. Texas women used gender power to gain authority over the symbolic representation of white collective memory. They, too, battled publicly and won the right to display a representation of the past that by 1910 had already come under scrutiny by scientists and historians.[12]

Although these collective memories still linger, as evidenced by Tom Craddick's denunciation of members of the Democratic Party in 2003, other remembrances of past historical events are demanding consideration. This book hopes to encourage an understanding of the power of the more established evidence of collective or cultural memory stemming from the nineteenth century and to elucidate the important twentieth-century events in the emerging light of memory studies. Historians' views of Texas in the nineteenth century and the understanding of the significance of the Alamo as a site of memory in architecture, art, and film across centuries constitute a major portion of this volume. In other cases, historical events analyzed here may also traverse both centuries, as in the construction of Civil War monuments by the United Daughters of the Confederacy, public and private Juneteenth celebrations, and the history of Mexicans in Texas culminating in a Tejano memorial. Exclusively twentieth-century chapters include collective memories and meaning attached to the Ku Klux Klan, the significance of the civil rights movement in the eyes of different generations of Texans, and the lasting (or not) memories of Texans toward Lyndon Baines Johnson. There are undoubtedly many topics that could and perhaps should have been included in this volume. For example, readers may raise an eyebrow at the omission of essays devoted exclusively to the Texas Rangers or to cowboys, both of which clearly play important roles in Texans' memories of their state's past.[13] The same could be said of a dizzying variety of other potential topics for a volume such as this. But as the great Texas novelist and journalist George Sessions Perry so aptly said, "It is manifest that nobody is going to write all about Texas in any one book." And that is the case here as well.[14]

For those dealing with the Anglo majority, several themes emerge. In "Early Historians and the Shaping of Texas Memory," Laura Lyons McLemore argues that Texas' collective memory has not changed much since the first Anglos came to the region. Since that time Anglo Texan memory has valorized noble Anglo sacrifices at the Alamo, ignored the history of Tejanos who fought against Mexican tyranny, validated Confederate heroism, vilified Reconstruction reformers including freed slaves, and, finally, exalted Texas Rangers who fought "perfidious Injuns and Mexicans." Early historians found the task of revising the deepening Anglo collective memory to be exceedingly difficult, and those who did were roundly ignored. This situation was complicated by the fact that the Texas public largely ignored the state's history. Historians, as a consequence, had little influence on the shaping of a Texan identity. Only after Reconstruction did an identifiable collective memory emerge, and then, as McLemore notes, historians "did not shape Texas memory so much as they affirmed it." Professor McLemore's research seems to substantiate the notion, evident in many of these essays, that memory is often a more powerful force than written history.

McLemore is not alone among our authors in identifying the early twentieth century as a time when collective memory underwent significant change. Gregg Cantrell in "The Bones of Stephen F. Austin: History and Memory in Progressive-Era Texas" (reprinted from the *Southwestern Historical Quarterly* [October 2004]) introduces the guardians of historical memory in Texas in the first two decades of the twentieth century. Progress, modernity, and the image of Texas were at stake in this battle, which took shape over the reintroduction of Stephen F. Austin to public memory, the reestablishment of the Texas Revolution as the sine qua non event in Texas history, and the restructuring of the Alamo of old—from mission, fort, liquor warehouse, and ruin—into a site for public adulation and memory. Professor Cantrell demonstrates that Gov. Oscar Colquitt had taken on a formidable opponent in the dispute concerning the future of the Alamo. He found himself embroiled with the Daughters of the Republic of Texas (in what might be called a gender controversy) over who would reconstruct the site and in what manner. The fact that the DRT won the contest and imbued the Alamo with a shrinelike atmosphere in a parklike setting suggests that there is much to learn from events such as this. Although Texans found a more usable past in the very un-southern memories of the frontier pioneers and the Texas Revolution, the interpretation of those memories became the province of those who held the surest connection to collective memory.

While acknowledging the complexity of Texan memory as it developed in the twentieth century, all of these essays are quick to emphasize that memory serves contemporary interests and helps to reinforce a desired common identity. Those who succeed in molding collective memory wield real power. In his essay "Memory, Truth, and Pain: Myth and Censorship in the Celebration of Texas History," James E. Crisp explores how two seemingly different graphic representations of Texas history—the widely read comic book series *Texas History Movies* from the 1920s and the monumental historical paintings of Robert Jenkins Onderdonk and Henry McArdle from an earlier era—reflected the hardening racial attitudes of the Anglo majority in the early twentieth century. The negative depictions of African Americans and Mexicans in these sources reinforced white supremacy and served the interests of those who benefited from segregation and racial oppression. Although representations of Texas collective memory in cartoons and in paintings addressed the Alamo in particular as "a fiercely contested Texan symbol," they did so in a manner that excluded and ridiculed nonwhites. Yet Professor Crisp makes a plea for saving—and explaining—Texas' "embarrassing" memories.

In "'Memories Are Short but Monuments Lengthen Remembrances': The United Daughters of the Confederacy and the Power of Civil War Memory," Kelly McMichael demonstrates the importance of the UDC of Texas, in the movement to commemorate Confederate "heroes." In the decades after 1890, white women assumed the tasks of raising funds, hiring sculptors, or purchasing ready-made statues to honor the dead and the living who fought for the vanquished southern nation. In doing so, these women became the principal bearers of and official guardians of the state's Civil War memories. In their long-running efforts to build Confederate monuments across the state, Professor McMichael argues, the women of the UDC recognized "the cultural power potential" that would accrue to them as the creators of shared public values and identity. They used memories of the Civil War in an attempt to further their own interests. However, unlike the white males who successfully recreated collective memory in that era, that power "proved elusive" for the Confederate Daughters, as materialistic, male-dominated values triumphed over the "feminine" ideals of self-sacrifice and domesticity. Hence, the power of Civil War memory and the Daughters' work toward shaping it were usurped by men who ultimately drew their own material benefits from it.

Walter L. Buenger's essay, "Memory and the 1920s Ku Klux Klan in Texas," likewise explores how groups within society used (and misused) memory to achieve their own ends. Buenger examines the career of the 1920s-era Ku Klux Klan, showing that Klansmen sought to manipulate both southern and American memories in order to spread their ideology and further their political agenda. They "transformed themselves and their society from southern to American," but in the end the Klan became a victim of its own strategy, as anti-Klan forces mustered the same set of shared memories to convince Texans of the un-American and un-Texan nature of the hooded order. Whereas some have opined that collective memory has served as an agent for entrenched power, Professor Buenger asserts that "the Texas example suggests that memories also served as agents of transformation."

Several of the essays in this book discuss both the dominant chord of Texas memory—identifying the power that lies within these remembrances and their "official" adoption—as well as the construction and uses of memory by groups outside the dominant Anglo Texan culture. In "Juneteenth: Emancipation and Memory," Elizabeth Hayes Turner explores the phenomenon of Juneteenth celebrations from the initial emancipation of Texas slaves in 1865 to our own time, showing how former slaves first used Emancipation Day celebrations to fashion a "counter-memory to those who could not or would not bow to power represented by white memories and commemorations." Using national symbols, such as Abraham Lincoln's Emancipation Proclamation and the Goddess of Liberty, and proclaiming their rightful place as citizens, African Texans kept alive their version of the meaning of emancipation. This version often differed in extreme ways from the views and memories held by white Texans. Clashes over the use of physical space to express their counter-memories and disparagement from the white press leading to violence did not diminish the desire by African Americans to keep the flame of liberty alive, at least symbolically. Juneteenth celebrations changed in the late twentieth century, and Professor Turner explains how Juneteenth was transformed in modern times into a wider celebration of culture and the arts in which people of all races can share.

In a similar vein, Andrés Tijerina studies the means by which Texans of Mexican ancestry have fashioned a collective "Tejano" memory as a counterweight to the suffocating power of the dominant Anglo Texan memory. His essay, "Constructing Tejano Memory," illustrates how memories, long confined to oral tradition and to largely forgotten pioneering scholarly works, can be resurrected by a group in order to claim its rightful place in modern society. Professor Tijerina argues that Tejano memory serves to connect Mexican Americans to a past full of founding pioneers, diplomats, members of the 1820 Mexican Revolution, the 1836 Texas Revolution, the establishment of an independent republic, and a proud tradition of education and labor in Texas. Yet, whereas Tejano history may have been silenced, forgotten, or distorted by early-twentieth-century Anglo historians and by Anglo memory, Tejano counter-memory has managed to survive. Tejano memory will be honored in a long-overdue monument on the grounds of the state capitol that gives tribute to the heritage of Mexican Americans. As such, it will constitute a lasting site of memory for those whose history is inextricably intertwined with the founding of the region, the republic, and the state of Texas.

Yvonne Davis Frear's essay, "Generation versus Generation: African Americans in Texas Remember the Civil Rights Movement," examines how the civil rights movement of the 1950s and 1960s has passed into the collective memory of African Americans in Texas. She argues that utilitarian design influences memories of the civil rights movement according to patterns of generational status. First-generation civil rights movement activists construct their memories of the events based on actual experience; second- and third-generation legates derive their "memories" of the movement through movies, histories, and current news events. Although both cohorts have constructed a "formidable social memory of the civil rights movement," the two groups disagree about the continuing significance of the movement and its legacies. Both groups have structured their social memory on a utilitarian framework; they base their beliefs on how the movement affected them. First-generation cohorts believe the movement was a success, with assurances of equality under the law; second- and third-generation cohorts view the movement either as a failure or as passé. The civil rights movement in Texas is a story that is beginning to make its way into scholarly accounts; Professor Frear provides an important challenge to the notion that the memories shared by African Texans are cohesive or even "collective."

Ricky Floyd Dobbs's essay, "Lyndon, We Hardly Remember Ye: LBJ in the Memory of Modern Texas," reminds us of the volatility of collective memory. Probing the place of this larger-than-life figure in the minds of modern Texans, Dobbs demonstrates that what we remember, as well as what we choose to forget, can be molded by rapidly changing political and ideological agendas. By examining textbooks, the Texas Assessment of Knowledge and Skills (TAKS) examination, surveys of college students' knowledge, and attendance at the LBJ Library and Museum and the LBJ ranch, Professor Dobbs found that LBJ is receding from memory. When polled, students identified LBJ with the assassination of John F. Kennedy, the Vietnam war, and a section of Interstate 635 in Dallas known as the Lyndon B. Johnson Freeway. What accounts for LBJ's disappearance from the radar of younger Texans can be summed up in a single sentence: "Lyndon Johnson doesn't fit Texas anymore."

In "Mission Statement: The Alamo and the Fallacy of Historical Accuracy in Epic Filmmaking," film historian and critic Don Graham scrutinizes Hollywood's most recent (2004) Alamo film. He finds that excessive attention to historical accuracy in a movie not only makes for poor cinema but also renders the film irrelevant as a reflection of collective memory. The film had been touted as a boon to the political right in its search for a national symbol after 9/11, yet its fair treatment of Mexicans and native Americans made it appealing to the liberal left. In the end, critics on all sides found the film flawed, called it an "expensive reenactment," historically inaccurate (despite all attempts to the contrary), and lacking in pathos, heroes, and melodrama. It suffered from divided loyalties, bad acting, and slow pacing. But its most probable cause of failure was that it "clashed with everybody's collective memory of the Alamo siege." Texans may want to remember the Alamo, but they do not want to remember it in a way that tries to present all sides of the story or that renders its heroes as complex, fallible humans.

Finally, if Texans—or at least most white Texans—have clung tenaciously to their memories of the Texas Revolution, the frontier, the cowboy, and their twentieth-century counterparts, the oil wildcatter and tycoon, this is not to say that Texans have entirely turned their backs on their southern heritage. In this volume's final chapter, "History and Collective Memory in

Texas: The Entangled Stories of the Lone Star State," Randolph B. Campbell provides a critique of Texans and their collective memories by emphasizing the selective nature of memory. Indeed, as he points out, memory often is as much about forgetting as it is about remembering. Campbell demonstrates how modern Texans cling to certain popular interpretations of their southern past, such as the belief that slavery was relatively benign and unimportant in Texas and that Reconstruction was a dark era of carpetbagger domination and corruption. These memories coexist, with no apparent contradiction, alongside the belief in the heroic pioneer and revolutionary past, as symbolized most dramatically by the Alamo. Campbell takes issue with Pierre Nora by arguing that the tendency of memory to be selective does society a disservice and can lead to its inability to deal with the real problems confronting it, because it allows people to view themselves as they would like to be rather than as they are, or rather, it allows some Texans to view their past as they would like to remember it rather than as historians today interpret it. As he points out, too often memory trumps history. Yet Professor Campbell recognizes the value of historians' study of memory and collective memory, as it has shaped and molded our understanding of the past.

The essays in this book, then, open a window onto an approach to history that has been sorely neglected by Texas historians. With each passing year, with the publication of dozens of academic books and articles, we learn more about the events that have shaped the history of the Lone Star State. But only now are we beginning to probe the questions of how Texans-at-large—the vast majority of whom don't read our scholarly monographs and articles—comprehend that history. This book should be considered a starting place, rather than a final destination, on the road to studying how Texans remember and understand their past.

NOTES

1. Statement by House Speaker Tom Craddick, Texas House of Representatives, May 12, 2003, available from http://www.house.state.tx.us/news/release.php?id=311 (accessed Apr. 25, 2005). The editors wish to thank Laura Lyons McLemore for her contribution to this introductory essay.

2. Roland Barthes, *Camera Lucida: Reflections on Photography* (New York: Hill and Wang, 1981), 64.

3. Michel-Rolph Trouillot, *Silencing the Past: Power and the Production of History* (Boston: Beacon Press, 1995), 2; Carl Becker, "Everyman His Own Historian," *American Historical Review* 37 (Jan. 1932): 222.

4. W. Fitzhugh Brundage, ed., *Where These Memories Grow: History, Memory, and Southern Identity* (Chapel Hill: University of North Carolina Press, 2000), 4; Halbwachs quoted in John Bodnar, *Remaking America: Public Memory, Commemoration, and Patriotism in the Twentieth Century* (Princeton, N.J.: Princeton University Press, 1992), 11. See also Kirk Savage, *Standing Soldiers, Kneeling Slaves: Race, War, and Monument in Nineteenth-Century America* (Princeton, N.J.: Princeton University Press, 1997), 6–7.

5. Mieke Bal, Jonathan Crewe, and Leo Spitzer, eds., *Acts of Memory: Cultural Recall in the Present* (Hanover, N.H.: University Press of New England, 1999), vii, x; Richard R. Flores, *Remembering the Alamo: Memory, Modernity, and the Master Symbol* (Austin: University of Texas Press, 2002), 17. For a discussion that explores the notion of myth in a Texas context see Robert F. O'Connor, ed., *Texas Myths* (College Station: Texas A&M University Press, 1986). Many sociologists and historians equate memory and collective memory with myth, but the two terms are not really synonymous. Myths constitute the realm of the "collective subconscious," the sphere dominated by factors beyond our control, and collective memory belongs to the "collective conscious," that sphere susceptible to new ideas and thus to conscious choices.

6. David W. Blight, *Beyond the Battlefield: Race, Memory, & the American Civil War* (Amherst: University of Massachusetts Press, 2002), 191 (emphasis in original). To rephrase Michael Kammen, scholars are fascinated by the phenomenon of a group in society—ethnic, gendered, or regional—becoming its own historian (Michael Kammen, *Mystic Chords of Memory: The Transformation of Tradition in American Culture* [New York: Knopf, 1991], 17).

7. For a discussion of the tools of objectivity see Jacques Le Goff, "History as a Science: The Historian's Craft," in *History and Memory*, trans. Steven Rendall and Elizabeth Claman (1977; New York: Columbia University Press, 1992), 179–99; Flores, *Remembering the Alamo*, 17–19. See also Stephen L. Hardin, *Texian Iliad: A Military History of the Texas Revolution* (Austin: University of Texas Press, 1994), 136; and William C. Davis, *Lone Star Rising: The Revolutionary Birth of the Texas Republic* (New York: Free Press, 2004), 219.

8. For a discussion of the use of words to narrate the past see Trouillot, *Silencing the Past,* 4. For southerners' continuing adherence to memory see David Goldfield, *Still Fighting the Civil War: The American South and Southern History* (Baton Rouge: Louisiana State University Press, 2002), 4–5.

9. Maurice Halbwachs, *Les Cadres sociaux de la mémoire* (Paris: Presses universitaires de France, 1925); Halbwachs, *La Mémoire collective* (Paris: Presses universitaires de France, 1950); Halbwachs, *The Collective Memory*, trans. Francis J. Ditter Jr. and Vida Yazdi Ditter (New York: Harper & Row, 1980), 78; Halbwachs, *On Collective Memory* (Chicago: University of Chicago Press, 1992); Pierre Nora, *Realms of Memory: Rethinking the French Past,* 3 vols. (New York: Columbia University Press, 1996–98); Nora, "Between Memory and History: Les Lieux de mémoire," *Representations* 26 (Spring 1989): 12. See also Daniel J. Sherman, *The Construction of Memory in France* (Chicago: University of Chicago Press, 1999), 4–5.

10. Noa Gedi and Yigal Elam, "Collective Memory—What Is It?" *History and Memory* 8 (Spring/Summer 1996): 30; David Thelen, "Memory and American History," *Journal of American History* 75 (Mar. 1989): 1117–29. Several of the most important studies of American history, southern history, and memory are Kammen's *Mystic Chords of Memory* and David W. Blight's *Race and Reunion: The Civil War in American Memory* (Cambridge, Mass.: Harvard University Press, 2001); W. Fitzhugh Brundage's *The Southern Past: A Clash of Race and Memory* (Cambridge, Mass.: Harvard University Press, 2005); and Brundage's *Where These Memories Grow.*

11. C. Vann Woodward, *The Burden of Southern History* (Baton Rouge: Louisiana State University, 1968); Flores, *Remembering the Alamo,* 157–60; Walter L. Buenger, "Texas and the

South," *Southwestern Historical Quarterly* 103 (Jan. 2000): 309–24; Buenger, *The Path to a Modern South: Northeast Texas between Reconstruction and the Great Depression* (Austin: University of Texas Press, 2001), xxiv, 227, 258–60. See also James E. Crisp, *Sleuthing the Alamo: Davy Crockett's Last Stand and Other Mysteries of the Texas Revolution* (New York: Oxford University Press, 2004).

12. See Kelly McMichael Stott, "From Lost Cause to Female Empowerment: The Texas Division of the United Daughters of the Confederacy, 1896–1966" (Ph.D. diss., University of North Texas, 2001); Elizabeth Hayes Turner, *Women, Culture, and Community: Religion and Reform in Galveston, 1880–1920* (New York: Oxford University Press, 1997), 178–82; Holly Beachley Brear, "We Run the Alamo, and You Don't: Alamo Battles of Ethnicity and Gender," in *Where These Memories Grow,* ed. Brundage, 299–317; and Holly Beachley Brear, *Inherit the Alamo: Myth and Ritual at an American Shrine* (Austin: University of Texas Press, 1995).

13. In this volume, Andrés Tijerina's essay on Tejano memory examines the Rangers, and Gregg Cantrell, Tijerina, Don Graham, and Randolph B. Campbell all allude to the importance of the cowboy as an element of Texan memory (see chapters 2, 7, 10, and 11). While hundreds of books have been written on Rangers and cowboys, curiously, neither topic has been examined in the context of collective memory in more than a cursory fashion. Several modern works provide revisionist views of the Rangers (some more revisionist than others), but they tend to concentrate on debunking popularly held "myths" about the Rangers rather than exploring the actual sources of modern memories about the legendary agency; see, for example, Robert M. Utley, *Lone Star Justice: The First Century of the Texas Rangers* (New York: Oxford University Press, 2002); Benjamin Heber Johnson, *Revolution in Texas: How a Forgotten Rebellion and Its Bloody Suppression Turned Mexicans into Americans* (New Haven, Conn.: Yale University Press, 2003); Julian Samora, Joe Bernal, and Albert Peña, *Gunpowder Justice: A Reassessment of the Texas Rangers* (Notre Dame, Ind.: Notre Dame University Press, 1979); Charles M. Robinson III, *The Men Who Wear the Star: The Story of the Texas Rangers* (New York: Random House, 2000); Charles H. Harris III and Louis R. Sadler, *The Texas Rangers and the Mexican Revolution: The Bloodiest Decade, 1910–1920* (Albuquerque: University of New Mexico Press, 2004). The same has largely held true for cowboys; numerous works compare "real" cowboys with their popular image, but few specifically explore how collective memories of the cowboy were constructed. The best work on the subject is still probably Joe B. Frantz, *The American Cowboy: The Myth and the Reality* (Norman: University of Oklahoma Press, 1955); also see Paul H. Carlson, ed., *The Cowboy Way: An Exploration of History and Culture* (Lubbock: Texas Tech University Press, 2000), especially the essays by Carlson ("Myth and the Modern Cowboy") and Lawrence Clayton ("Today's Cowboy: Coping with a Myth"). More narrowly focused, but also useful in exploring the sources of modern memories of the cowboy, is Don Graham, *Cowboys and Cadillacs: How Hollywood Looks at Texas* (Austin: Texas Monthly Press, 1983).

14. George Sessions Perry, *Texas: A World in Itself* (New York: McGraw-Hill, 1942), vii.

Chapter 1

EARLY HISTORIANS AND THE SHAPING OF TEXAS MEMORY

LAURA LYONS MCLEMORE

Shaping society's understanding of the past or some aspect of the past is the goal, the "noble dream," of every modern historian. Therein lies the impetus behind historical revision: to correct, to clarify, to interpret the past in light of new information and insight in order to provide a society with more accurate knowledge about itself. "If I can correct the misperception about the route of this expedition," a colleague once confided, "I will have achieved something worthwhile in my career." "Shaping" implies some kind of molding or transforming that goes beyond simply reinforcing an existing form. Historians have found the task of shaping or revising collective memory difficult. Frequently, they have found their adherence to evidence and efforts at objectivity no match for the selective and self-serving memories of the dominant culture. In Texas, as elsewhere, the question arises as to whether historians have succeeded in shaping society's memory of the past or have themselves been shaped by it.[1] One might fairly conclude that Texas memory, more often than not, shaped early historiography rather than the other way around.

To what extent the historians of Texas, during its formative years as a colonial province, an independent republic, and a southern state, helped to shape Texas' collective memory is the subject of this chapter. The purposes for which Texas historians wrote changed between the late eighteenth century, when Juan Agustín Morfi penned his *History of Texas,* and the end of the nineteenth century, when history became a discipline at the University of Texas and the Texas State Historical Association was founded. Exploring how and why the early purveyors of Texas history failed or succeeded in influencing Texans' memory of their collective past may enable Texans to close or, at least, understand the gap between the historical past and their "memory" of it.

If one assumes the validity of the premise that "collective memory" is the self-conscious, deliberate attempt to preserve memory in historical ways by accommodating only those facts that make the past relevant to the present, then identifying Texas' "collective memory" is not difficult, because it has not changed dramatically since the arrival of the first Anglo Americans in the region.[2] Prior to that time, Texas memory, such as it was, consisted of the lived experiences of Spanish missionaries in search of souls and conquistadores in search of gold and the mixture of Iberian legend and Judeo-Christian mythology they brought with them across the Atlantic—legends of riches and myths of a New World Eden. *Texas Observer* writer Debbie Nathan has defined the Anglo Texan collective memory as succinctly as anyone: "You know the tale: noble Jim Bowie against the evil Santa Anna, greedy Yankee Carpetbaggers versus vanquished and suffering Confederates, valiant Rangers fighting perfidious Injuns and Mexicans."[3] But another *Observer* contributor, Cathy Corman, probably more poignantly expressed the challenge Texas memory presents to historians and the problem it poses for present and future generations of Texans. In describing the experience of introducing her Massachusetts-born children to the Texas capitol, Corman wrote, "Before we'd even left the ground floor, [the kids had learned] that Mexico was an easily conquered nation and that the two most important figures in early Texas history were both white men. No mention in our guide's recounting of the important roles Tejanos played in the events of the Texas revolution. Nothing about the disempowerment of an entire group of people when the United States and Mexico signed the Treaty of Guadalupe Hidalgo. Our guide said nothing—not one word—about the presence of African Americans in Texas, not as slaves, not as soldiers, not as cowboys, field hands, civil rights crusaders, business owners, or legislators. Missing, too, from his spiel was an appreciation of the stories of native peoples." Few would argue that Texas memory is overwhelmingly nostalgic, but nostalgia, Corman observed, is "necessarily predicated on the illusion of a rosy past. Horseback riding and bluebonnets are things to savor; racism and cultural amnesia are not."[4] While Texas memory has not always been nostalgic, it has often been selective and expedient. Early Texas historians found that even the mildest attempt at revision met with stubborn resistance from the dominant culture. Thus, if they shaped Texas' collective memory at all, they did so by reinforcing the memory of that culture. Those who challenged Anglo Texans' "collective conscious" were soon forgotten.

The perception that Texas history writing prior to the Civil War was entirely literary and romantic seems pervasive, and hence the assumption that these characteristics explain the nostalgic quality of Texas memory. In fact, those who wrote during and about that era in Texas history had, in retrospect, very little hand in the shaping of Texas memory among their contemporaries or future generations of Texans. This circumstance might be attributable largely to the fact that most of these writers were less concerned with their legacy to posterity and more concerned with persuading a contemporary audience for immediate financial gain or political ends. The earliest histories of Texas as a distinct geographical entity, compiled by highly educated members of the Catholic clergy in Mexico, Juan Agustín Morfi and José Antonio Pichardo, represented attempts to bring historical facts to bear on specific arguments.[5] Morfi, chaplain to Teodoro de Croix on his tour of inspection in 1777, turned to history writing to dispute Antonio Bonilla's blaming of Franciscan missionaries for the failure of Spain's colonization efforts in Texas. Pichardo, reputed to be one of the most educated men in Mexico at the dawn of the nineteenth century, undertook the research and writing of a history of the boundary between Texas and Louisiana in 1808 at the command of the viceroy of Mexico in order to clearly establish Spain's territorial claims in view of the Louisiana Purchase. Both produced thoroughly rational, secular histories. Their work exhibited a self-conscious effort at objectivity, a search for cause-and-effect relationships in the actions of humans and the evidence of physical science, an inductive method, abundant sources, and a critical, direct style. This effort did not prevent either of them from perpetuating or attempting to corroborate New World mythology, such as the legend of Quivira or Texas as the New World Eden. In doing so, they affirmed existing myths, possibly because they thought it was what their audiences expected or in the hope that the inclusion of these legends would heighten the interest of officials looking for return on Spanish investment in Texas. While both Morfi and Pichardo were respected and regarded as authoritative by later historians, their work had little effect among their contemporaries. There is scant evidence that Morfi's writing deterred the Spanish plan to abandon or secularize the Franciscan missions in Texas, and his work was not translated into English until many years later. Morfi's chief legacy was to provide later historians with a valuable source of facts about Spanish Texas. With the Adams-Onís Treaty in 1819, the boundary between Louisiana and Texas was settled, Pichardo's *Treatise* notwithstanding. For years, Pichardo's work also

was available only to readers of Spanish. Its twentieth-century editor and
translator, Charles Wilson Hackett, maintained that Pichardo's greatest contribution to the historical record was the detailing of significant and little-
known events that occurred in the Spanish province of Texas during the last
three-quarters of the eighteenth century.[6] However, contributing to the historical record did not equate with contributing to the collective memory. As
many historians and sociologists have pointed out, history and memory are
not synonyms; historical memory and collective memory are different kinds
of memory.[7]

Possibly more widely read, certainly by American audiences at the time,
was journalist William Darby's short history of the ill-fated Gutiérrez-Magee
expedition to Texas in 1813.[8] By the time Darby published his account in
August 1819, Cuban and Mexican relations were among the leading political
topics in contemporary periodicals. *Niles Weekly Register,* which reprinted
Darby's article, had a reputation for printing chiefly facts, statistics, speeches,
and documents covering both sides of political and economic issues of the
day. It was influential in its own time and has remained a prime source for
historians up to the present.[9] Darby based his assessment of American relations with Spain on his personal observations as both a scientist and a
journalist. He condemned what he saw as the selfish and ignoble motives
responsible for the Gutiérrez-Magee debacle and the unwillingness of Americans to educate themselves about the culture and perspective of the Spanish
Mexican population with whom they shared the continent. His admonitions
had little apparent effect on his compatriots. American nativist attitudes had
appeared in print as early as 1810, when Zebulon Pike's narrative spawned
serious American interest in Texas, and were incorporated into perceptions
of it. Such nativism stemmed from American antipathy toward Catholicism,
combined with suspicion and distaste for monarchy and the impulse toward
expansion following the Louisiana Purchase. One study of political nativism
in Texas noted that American dislike of the foreigner and hatred of the Catholic Church could be ascribed to the strong spirit of nationalism that characterized English settlers from the first.[10] Though more accurately described as
impressions than as "memories," these sentiments were what Darby sought
to counter. While it would be difficult to say how many Americans actually
read Darby's account, in light of subsequent events they clearly did not heed
its message. Less than fifteen years after his report appeared in *Niles,* Texans
declared their differences with Mexico irreconcilable and broke with the government to which they had sworn their allegiance. Nearly a century later,
Texans' "collective memory" of Mexico and Mexicans did not appear to have

changed significantly, as is evident in the title *Texas: A Contest of Civiliza-tions,* a book by Texas' first professional historian, George P. Garrison.

Romantic, literary histories ultimately fared little better than Darby's journalistic effort, despite their proliferation and appeal to contemporary audiences. Their failure to alter popular notions may have been attributable to the fact that most histories or quasi-histories written in the first half of the nineteenth century promoted either self-interest or some larger cause. The romantic era of the 1830s and 1840s was the heyday of the grand narrative as the dominant paradigm. In the case of writers such as Mary Austin Holley, financial gain and promotion of her family's real estate ventures provided the motivation for a combination of history, travelogue, and immigrant guide adorned with the trappings of romantic literature: classical references, nature metaphors, romantic heroes and villains, elevation of the common man, and idealized frontier agrarianism.[11] Holley's *Texas: Observations Historical, Geo-graphical and Descriptive* (1833) made no pretense of being anything other than promotional. It received critical acclaim and was influential enough that other writers plagiarized it. With the 1836 revision, *Texas,* she intended to further the Texas cause in the United States. Holley's correspondence with family members indicated that she expected the book to appeal to the public, and it did. Mary Austin Holley became possibly one of the best-known women in America in the early nineteenth century.[12] Perhaps her greatest contribution to Texas history was her translation and publication of a number of key documents of the Texas Revolution, including the Texas Declaration of Independence, the Constitution of the Republic of Texas, and Travis's famous victory-or-death letter from the Alamo, as well as the Mexican Constitution of 1824 and the colonization laws. One could certainly argue that she greatly influenced Texas memory. But one might also argue that Mary Austin Holley simply affirmed Texans' perceptions of themselves or, at least, the perceptions they wished to project to the rest of the world, especially since her "primary source" was the empresario Stephen F. Austin.

The image of Texas that Holley portrayed did not go unchallenged. Others, for example, David Barnett Edward, expressed quite a different view of the Texas Revolution. He espoused a decidedly pro-Mexican stance sharply critical of slavery, Indian oppression, and speculators. Writing just prior to the Texas Revolution, he claimed to be writing for the purpose of setting the record straight about Mexico in relation to Texas, arguing that "no country or people, so nearly allied with the republicans of the North, have ever been less impartially considered; or when spoken of, more unwarrantably exposed to the extremes of *calumny* and *panegyric:* each in its turn creating no little excitement in the breasts of those who are anxious to know of things *just as they are,* before a movement should be made which might bring disappointment, if not ruin, in its train."[13] His book created quite a stir but certainly contributed little to inculcating his views in Texas society except insofar as he aroused defensive ire so heated that Texas' first "revisionist" historian found it necessary to leave Texas for good. The reaction of prominent Texans to Edward was illustrative of the resilience of Texas memory to attempts to alter it. John T. Mason, a land agent whose business was almost wiped out when the revolutionary government of Texas canceled some large land grants, called the book "a slander on the people of Texas." E. M. Pease warned his father, L. T. Pease, then engaged in writing a geographical and historical account of Texas himself, to "be cautious of using Edward's *History of Texas.* There is little in his work that can be relied on."[14]

Frenchman Frédéric LeClerc also provided something of a contrast to narratives such as Holley's. He represented the European observer writing for an audience other than Texans. Like the works of many other such observers, his writing may have been of consequence to potential European immigrants to Texas but probably had little effect on most of its inhabitants. LeClerc's *Texas and Its Revolution* refrained from treating Texans as larger than life. He was among those who interpreted the Texas Revolution as a land grab. "Texas," he observed, "offered an almost limitless field to slave labor, one practically boundless both in area and in types of agriculture which might prove profitable," and in addition, "by extending its frontier to the Rio Grande, the United States would have drawn considerably nearer to the great mining regions. . . . Finally, one step more would have been taken, and a very important step, towards the Sea of California and the Pacific Ocean."[15] LeClerc's assessment of Poinsett's mission to Mexico confirmed the rumor in the United States that negotiations were under way in 1829 for the cession of Texas. A translation of his short history appeared in the *Southern Literary Messenger* shortly after its publication in the French periodical, *La Revue des deux mondes,* in 1840, but there is little or no evidence that it had any particularly lasting influence on Texans. John H. Jenkins described LeClerc's observations on the physical and political scene as useful; no doubt he meant "useful to twentieth-century historians."[16]

Other works by Americans and Europeans appeared in the years between 1812 and 1840 that took advantage of the intense public interest in Texas, its revolution, and its bid for annexation. Most combined historical narrative with immigrant guides or travelogues such as those of Detlef Dunt and Amos Andrew Parker or of Edward Stiff, whose *The Texan Emigrant* (1840) portrayed the Texas revolutionaries as nobly motivated and worthy of respect "by all who espoused the cause of freedom" and post-revolutionary Texas as the Promised Land.[17] The writers of all these tomes had practical motives. Their appeal to public interest stemmed mostly from the promotion of self-interest or political agendas outside of Texas. They were concerned with affecting immediate outcomes, not making lasting impressions. Their work, aside from promoting immigration to Texas, was of interest to later historians, but if it affected Texas memory at all, it was largely to confirm it.

The same was true of historians of Texas in the 1840s. William Kennedy and Henry S. Foote were both encouraged and employed, respectively, by Mirabeau Lamar, president of the Republic of Texas, to promote Texas interests in Britain and America.[18] William Kennedy, in the diplomatic service of Britain, produced the most thorough, comprehensive account of Texas history up to the time of its publication in 1841. Kennedy's influence was profound outside of Texas, his book proving to be a critical factor in England's ultimate recognition of Texas independence. American critics called it "a fuller and more satisfactory answer" to the question of the recognition of Texas as an independent republic than any other to their knowledge. Editors for the *New York Review* expressed confidence that it would "do more to correct the erroneous impressions in regard to Texas, which are prevailing amongst us, than could be done by any other means."[19] Kennedy's research was unquestionably the most thorough since the work of Morfi and Pichardo, and while he was generally sympathetic to the Texas cause, he was relatively objective in his assessments. He did not lionize Austin, Houston, or the Alamo defenders but rather examined the probable motives for their behavior as well as that of General Martín Perfecto de Cos, and he pointed out discrepancies and exaggerations in the accounts of other writers such as Chester Newell. Kennedy's account was sympathetic to Texans for a number of reasons. He was concerned for British interests in Texas and might have written his pro-Texan history to encourage and hasten the signing of commercial treaties between England and Texas. He was British consul to Texas, and it is possible that he wrote to generate interest abroad in anticipation of his own colonizing effort in 1842. Kennedy's history set a standard for histories of Texas at least until Henderson K. Yoakum's was published in the 1850s. Kennedy's history had a much greater effect on perceptions of Texas outside the state than it had on Texan collective memory, however. To the extent that it confirmed Texans' perceptions of their history, it was well thought of. Any departures were deemed errors by Texas critics. Kennedy's work exhibited themes of liberty and the superiority of Anglo Saxons. "With the degenerate races of the South," he wrote, "liberty was but a poetical abstraction . . . with the Anglo-Americans it was a substantial inheritance—dear to them as the memory of their ancestors—essential to their social progress as the air of heaven to their physical existence."[20] Influenced by personal interests as well as the expectations of President Lamar (his benefactor), Kennedy did not challenge Texans to reexamine their memory of their history; ultimately, he served to reinforce it.

If William Kennedy at least made some efforts at objectivity, Henry S. Foote's *Texas and the Texans* was unabashedly biased, solicited as it was by Mirabeau Lamar and his supporters to vindicate Lamar's administration. Foote elevated William Travis, Branch T. Archer, and Ben Milam to epic stature while maligning the character of Sam Houston, Lamar's rival in politics. He protested his *impartiality* (Foote's emphasis) too much, and it seems clear that contemporaries saw Foote's history for the propaganda it was. Editors of the *New York Review,* who were effusive in their praise of William Kennedy's work, summed up their reaction to Foote in a single sentence: "We have not particularly adverted to the work of Mr. Foote as it is, in great measure, occupied with earlier historical details than have engaged our attention, and as, also, we wished rather to present our readers with the impressions [of a traveler from abroad] than those which have been made upon one of our own citizens, who might, perhaps, be supposed to have a stronger personal interest in speaking favorably of it."[21] Foote was hired to present a version of Texas history flattering to Texans and particularly supportive of Lamar's agenda. According to his version of the history of the war in Texas, *all* Texans were unblemished heroes and *all* Mexicans were "vulgar tyrants" and "demoniacal" agents and their cohorts, "unprincipled renegades." It not only confirmed but exaggerated Texas memory of the revolution, and it appears that contemporary Texans as well as modern ones were aware of its bias, which robbed it of any serious value in shaping Texas memory.

One bias deserved another. The 1840s also produced at least one would-be "revisionist" in the person of Nicholas Doran P. Maillard, a bitterly frustrated British investor in Mexican bonds who wrote a scathing indictment of all things Texan. Maillard's history was revisionist in the sense that it presented an interpretation of Texas history thoroughly different from Texans' memory of themselves and their past. He challenged several well-documented lapses in Texas memory, including the origins of their rebellion against Mexico, their treatment of "Negroes" and Indians, and their aggressive policy toward Mexico. His extreme bias failed to convince any Texans of his interpretation of Texas history because it insulted them and because it contained many errors, but Texans were not his target audience in any case. John H. Jenkins called it "the most vitriolic denunciation of the Republic of Texas, written with absolutely no regard for the truth."[22] Ashbel Smith wrote Anson Jones that "in the interest of the persons hostile to our country a book styled a *History of Texas* has been published, characterized by a most extraordinary disregard for decency and of truth. J. Doran [sic] Maillard is the avowed author." Maillard's interpretation did nothing to impress anyone outside of Texas either. In the words of one English reviewer, Maillard's *History of Texas* was "as wholly anti-Texan as it is possible for any man [to be]." Upon its release, Arthur Ikin, British consul for the Republic of Texas, wrote to Anson Jones that "a book has also lately issued from the press under the auspices of the Mexican and Colonial interests attacking Texas and the Texians in a manner the most false and virulent."[23] Granted, Maillard was his own worst enemy, but the reaction to his alternative to the dominant Texan interpretation of the history of the revolution illustrated the fate of challenges to that interpretation.

The first history of Texas and its revolution from a Mexican perspective appeared in the 1840s as well. General Vicente Filisola's *Memorias para la historia de la guerra de Tejas,* published in September 1848, brought the entire history of Texas colonization to bear on the Texas Revolution and its outcome. The editors of this work assured their readers that they would find in it "the truth of the matter set straight and made manifest." They were convinced that knowing the history of Texas would enable present and future generations to benefit from the faults and errors that led to the loss of Texas and the potential compromise of Mexico's independence and national existence. While Filisola's honesty and insight may have contributed to the Mexican memory of its loss of Texas—and, by the time 1848 was over, much of its territory in North America—it had no obvious effect on Texan or American understanding of the event, undoubtedly because it was published in Spanish and, also, possibly because of a lack of interest in the Mexican view.

Thus, the historians of Texas in the first half of the nineteenth century did not represent a completely uniform interpretation of Texas' past. They were not all Americans, and, significantly, they were mostly not Texans either. They represented sometimes drastically different perceptions of Texas history, yet none could be said to have significantly altered the memory of the dominant culture. Many were more influenced by collective memory than they were shapers of it. Their romantic narrative style was a product of their milieu, dictated by popular tastes. Even those with a strongly pro-Texan bias merely perpetuated existing myths about the superiority of Anglo Saxons, the triumph of liberty and progress, and the heroism of the revolution; they did not originate them. Whatever position they espoused, they had an immediate interest in doing so and were seeking immediate results rather than immortality. Those who reinforced Texans' memory of the past could be said to have done so because they sought the goodwill of Texans. In that sense, their historical interpretations were influenced by their audience. Those, like Filisola, Edward, and Maillard, who presented opposing views—in some cases more objective or complete views—failed to significantly affect Texas memory because they were rejected, ignored, or simply not read by many Texans, as in Filisola's case.

In the 1850s some historians focused on specific topics in Texas history that they considered to have been slighted or neglected by previous histories. William M. Gouge's *The Fiscal History of Texas* and José Antonio Navarro's series of newspaper articles on Texas' Tejano heritage were examples.[24] Gouge, an accountant, U.S. Treasury Department agent, and former editor of *The Journal of Banking,* published a financial history of the Texas Revolution and the Republic of Texas in 1852. Gouge had a reputation for his opposition to banks, corporations, and paper money, and his bias was evident in his writing. He laid claim, at least, to a genuine desire to effect change. "History," he wrote, "is of importance only as it illustrates principles; and principles may be as strikingly illustrated in [small communities] as in larger ones."[25] Gouge appealed to his readers to heed the warning he saw in the operation of general laws of finance, as evidenced in history. His assessment of Texas' handling of its public credit did not please Texans like Sam Houston, who accused him of writing specifically for the purpose of sabotaging Texas' credit reputation.[26] His effort to shape Texas memory with regard to its financial history met with immediate resistance. Texans generally reacted defensively to Gouge's book when it appeared and were bitterly critical of his views long afterward, although it was no more biased than any other early-nineteenth-century Texas history and it illuminated an aspect not previously examined in any depth.

José Antonio Navarro also sought specifically to reshape the memory of Texans to include the contributions of Tejanos to the history of their state. Writing in response to contemporary Anglo American renderings of Texas history that portrayed the Tejano population as morally and intellectually destitute and dependent on Anglo American influence, Navarro attempted to set the historical record straight. In doing so, he tried to establish a "collective memory" by drawing parallels between Anglo Texans and the revolutionary struggles of the Tejanos of San Antonio. He translated his writing into the language of the dominant culture, making reference to its most sacred myths and symbols: Tejanos, too, were "guided only by an instinct for their liberty, against enemies so superior that they may be placed alongside the most free and fortunate nations of all mankind—such as the nation with the flag of stars."[27] Navarro based his arguments on not only his own eyewitness but also historical manuscripts. Particularly noteworthy, too, is the fact that Navarro, unlike the majority of Texas historians up to that time, was a native Texan—born on Texas soil and a lifelong citizen of that country. Nevertheless, he had no appreciable effect in changing the predominant view of Tejanos' role in Texas history.

In fact, the first historian to figure prominently in Texas memory was Henderson Yoakum. With his two-volume *History of Texas,* published in 1855, he literally became a part of the collective memory. When he died in 1857, he was remembered as "the father of Texas History," who laid "in the wilderness the foundation for a vigorous quest for truth."[28] The "vigorous quest for truth" alluded more to Yoakum's method than his content. He meticulously researched and documented his work. The reference to "wilderness" suggested that his interpretation was not a dramatic departure from prevailing notions of what Texas represented to Anglo Americans. Yoakum, frequently praised for his objectivity if not his style, was himself something of an ideologue. A staunch Jacksonian, he endorsed agrarian republicanism, Indian removal, and the imperial expansion of the United States. He saw the displacement of the "savage" as the will of God. When Whig ideas of industrialization and centralization began to threaten his political career in Tennessee, he moved to Texas, where he found a climate of opinion more nearly like his own. In this sense, he confirmed existing beliefs rather than modifying them or effecting new interpretations. He was criticized by contemporaries for his sympathetic treatment of Sam Houston, but the influence of his work undoubtedly later contributed to a softening of Texans' memories about the general, and he probably deserves credit for shaping the image of Stephen F. Austin as the pioneer and builder. Yoakum spent years collecting and preparing his history. He recognized and acknowledged the relative quality of various sources, yet he was no less romantic and no less biased than any of his predecessors. What he did that others, like Kennedy, had been unable to do, was, more or less, to institutionalize Texan ideology. His research impressed readers and provided a justification for their views about Anglo Saxon superiority and manifest destiny.

Yoakum's history also represented a significant milestone in Texas memory because it survived the furnace of Civil War and Reconstruction.

Yoakum's *History of Texas* was more highly regarded after the Civil War than it had been before it. Immediately after the release of the first edition in 1855, the *Dallas Herald* criticized Yoakum's inability to escape his biases and sympathies "so as to give an impartial and unprejudiced narrative." If his account of San Jacinto was a sample of his work, the public would have to "look to some future historian beyond the influence of living actors" to present "a faithful and unbiased account of them."[29] Articles in 1859, 1860, and 1861 leveled even stronger criticism. Ashbel Smith called Yoakum's *History of Texas* "a burlesque of history," and Peter W. Gray, to whom the work was dedicated, had but faint praise for it, criticizing Yoakum's style as "too unpretentious for his subject" but probably a standard for the future.[30] In these comments, the term "future" is most revealing. Henderson Yoakum dealt with not only the remote but also the recent past, as had other historians of Texas up to the middle of the nineteenth century. In doing so, he confronted lived experience and the living memory of that experience. Criticism of his work suggested that anything contradictory to what Texans chose to remember would meet with resistance no matter how well documented. Revealingly, post–Civil War historians were much more admiring. Hubert Howe Bancroft called Yoakum's work "one of the best, if not the best history of Texas." Dudley Wooten printed Yoakum's *History of Texas* in its entirety in his own book, *A Comprehensive History of Texas,* stating that it could not be superseded. C. W. Raines and Z. T. Fulmore both hailed it as the "standard" for the period it covered, and in the mid-twentieth century it was still being hailed as such.[31] It is difficult to explain conclusively why Yoakum's history survived the Civil War to become more famous and influential than others with similar themes, but a few explanations seem reasonable. For one thing, Yoakum's was the last comprehensive history to be published prior to the Civil War. When the war ended in defeat for the Confederacy (and for Texas by association), Yoakum's history was a reminder of triumphant Texas. Yoakum's book took Texas history nearer the present than other similar histories written before it, which were current only up to their own year of publication, and Yoakum's research was more extensive, owing not only to his diligence but to the fact that more information was accessible than had been previously. It was the most complete history of Texas available at the end of the Civil War.

Reflecting upon how antebellum historians fared provides insight into the dynamic of Texas history and memory. Those, like Gouge and Navarro, who made an effort to change or reshape Texans' understanding or memory of lived events met with resistance or were simply ignored. Yoakum, whose themes reflected the basic assumptions about patriotism, God, morality, and

Anglo American progress that had guided Americans since the late eighteenth century, may have done little to affect lived memory except to affirm it. Following the Civil War, those lived memories began to fade, and those basic assumptions began to change as Texans grappled with the defeat of the Confederacy and the challenge (or threat) to rural agrarianism posed by industrialization and urbanization. The surge of nostalgia in the United States as it entered the Gilded Age has been well documented. Historiographer Michael Kammen defined nostalgia as a concept that tended to deny the notion that progress or change was necessarily for the better. He observed that it was especially likely to occur in response to dramatic changes such as revolution or civil war, rapid industrialization, or the crumbling of a venerated value system, all of which were present following the Civil War.[32] Yoakum's influence increased precisely because his ideology embodied and embalmed those former assumptions. Reality might have pointed in a different direction, but Texas memory clung to those pre-war assumptions so well articulated by Yoakum.

The Civil War had as chilling an effect on historical writing in Texas as it did throughout the South, but the reactions to some of the attempts by historians to shape the collective memory during the third quarter of the nineteenth century are instructive. DeWitt Clinton Baker typified the changes occurring in the second half of the nineteenth century in America as well as in Texas. Baker was a lifelong devotee of public education, and he was sometimes described as an urban progressive. He was appointed to the state school examining board by Gov. E. J. Davis in 1872 and became involved in efforts to institute a public school system. In 1873, he published *A Brief History of Texas from Its Earliest Settlement,* intended for use in schools, and the state board of education adopted it. But revisions in the public school law, over Davis's veto, began dismantling the public school system and effectively doomed the textbook. Texans complained that it expressed anti-southern views, though no such bias is apparent. Baker actually mentioned slavery only once, when he observed that the tensions that long existed between North and South on the question spilled over into Texas politics and increased in intensity yearly between 1857 and 1860. He characterized Houston as calm and rational in his stand against secession, but that was the extent of anything that could be construed as anti-southern, suggesting that any anti-southern bias would have to have been inferred by a blindly prejudiced reader.[33] It is more likely that the book's adoption by a Republican school board rendered it unacceptable no matter what was in it. It was distinguished as a casualty of "collective memory." Baker then produced a second book in an effort to recoup some of his losses and those of his publisher, A. S. Barnes and Company. In *A Texas Scrap-Book,* which appeared in 1875, he abandoned traditional history for a compilation designed for the casual reader. Like countless other volumes produced in the decade following the Civil War, it reflected a bent for "embalming the memory of the past" and "enshrining it in the present." *A Texas Scrap-Book* included anecdotes, poems, speeches, statistics, descriptions of climate and natural history, long lists of individuals, and biographical sketches of war dead, veterans of San Jacinto, and others who played some role in Texas' past. It did not include interpretation or conclusions that might be construed as political bias that cast Texans in less than a positive light. In fact, it included very little original writing by Baker at all except for blatantly promotional material for immigrants and the biographical entries, which seldom exceeded a paragraph in length. He did not compose all of those. *A Texas Scrap-Book* was exactly what its title implied: a compilation of snippets from various sources, including newspapers, the *Texas Almanac,* official documents, and the histories of Holley and Yoakum. It could not be characterized as a history. Presumably, it was an attempt to sidestep any possible controversy in the hope of selling enough copies to break even. As Robert Calvert concluded in his introduction to the Texas State Historical Association's reprint of the book in 1991, "The prose in *A Texas Scrap-Book* represents much of what Texans were like at the time: patriotic, maudlin, colorful, and insensitive about race and ethnic groups. Moreover, as Baker hints in the preface, with the passing of the Republic and the population growth after the Civil War, white Texans were anxious to romanticize and glorify their past. Baker attempted to compile selections that captured nostalgia for an older pioneer life many Texans thought was ending."[34]

Baker's *A Texas Scrap-Book* failed to fully redeem the publisher's losses, and Barnes sold the plates to another publisher who used them in *A Pictorial History of Texas, from the Earliest Visits of European Adventurers, to A.D. 1879,* by Homer S. Thrall, a Methodist minister and educator. Thrall, too, produced a textbook, *A History of Texas,* which was published in 1876 and later expanded and reprinted. Thrall offered little original research, relying primarily on earlier histories. For the most part, he avoided controversial subjects such as slavery and Indians, devoting only two paragraphs to slavery and three pages to native tribes and Indian relations. By contrast, he devoted six pages to the siege of the Alamo, in which he specifically rejected Filisola's report, and another three to the battle at San Jacinto. Thrall's *A Pictorial History of Texas,* designed to appeal to a popular audience, like Baker's *A Texas Scrap-Book,* provided an example of late-nineteenth-century historians who attempted to acquiesce in, rather than mold, Texas memory. Nevertheless, it drew scathing criticism from Temple Houston, son of Sam Houston, including a charge that Thrall slighted individuals whom he (Houston) considered more worthy than those included in the section devoted to "Biographical Sketches of Distinguished Characters in Texas." Houston's passionate, some might say hysterical, denunciation provided an example of the potency of Texas memory: "It matters not in my eyes what faults these brave men may have had, or how bitterly they hated my father, they loved Texas, and that single fact throws a halo of brightness around their memories. . . . I denounce [Thrall's] work as a stigma on the name of history." Houston's tirade revealed Texans' sensitivity and intolerance to any perceived criticism of or deviation from their memories.[35]

One veteran of the Texas Revolution who came to Thrall's defense was Reuben M. Potter. "Mr. Thrall deserves great credit for his efforts to keep alive the names of so many of the pioneers and veterans," he told M. A. Bryan in 1883, suggesting that Thrall's history was no less accurate than Houston's memory.[36] Potter himself did quite a bit of writing after the Civil War, primarily for eastern newspapers and periodicals such as the *New York Times* and the *Magazine of American History.* Potter undertook to correct the historical record with regard to the final assault on the Alamo, observing that "wild exaggerations" had taken the place of historical details in popular legend. "The reason will be obvious when it is remembered that not a single combatant . . . survived to tell the tale," he explained of his purpose.[37] Potter also recognized the contributions of Mexicans in the Texas Revolution and dealt with racial myths perpetuated by Anglo American and European historians. He made explicit in his series of articles his intention to reshape Texans' memory of the revolution. He was one of the first to treat Texas history as American history and assert its role in shaping that history, but he is far better remembered for his sentimental poem, "Hymn of the Alamo," written in 1836, than for his later historical writing.

The attitude toward these first post–Civil War histories of Texas signaled the fading of the "Revolution generation." At the same time, the professionalization of history was giving rise to a new chapter in American and Texas historiography. The intersection of these two events, combined with the continuing need to cope with defeat, led to the cementing of what is so frequently identified as Texas' "collective memory." Hubert Howe Bancroft's *History of the North Mexican States and Texas,* in two volumes, in the 1880s provided an example of this nexus between the professionalization of history and what has come to be known as Texas' national myth. Bancroft was widely criticized, of course, for his "history-factory" approach, but that had little relevance to the importance of his accomplishment. The history of Texas he produced resulted from the most impressive accumulation of sources ever amassed on the subject, dating from the explorations of Hernan Cortés. His history focused on institutions in an attempt to convey a sense of Texas' growth beyond its revolutionary epoch toward a more cosmopolitan future. The two volumes comprised unquestionably the most comprehensive and critical treatment of Texas ever to be written, but they made little impression on Texans. Too much attention focused ón his perceived lack of ethics, stemming from his publishing under his own name the compiled work of his staff of paid assistants. His influence on the *professional* study of Texas history would be profound: Texas history ever after would have to be thought of in its relation to the history of Spanish North America. But his effect on Texas *memory* was questionable. Certainly there appears to be little evidence that Mexican Texans were accorded a greater presence in the national memory because of it. By the time Bancroft's works appeared, the professional study of history had begun a gradual withdrawal from the popular forum to an academic one. At most he won the grudging admission that historians of the future would have to work upon the foundation he laid.[38]

A much more powerful influence than Bancroft's brand of critical history emerged in the last two decades of the nineteenth century. Many historiographers in recent years have described the phenomenon that took place in the final quarter of the nineteenth century, owing in part to the trauma of the Civil War and in part to increasing industrialization. Here one may recognize the shift, described by Pierre Nora, from *milieux de mémoire,* or natural collective memory, to *lieux de mémoire,* or sites of memory that represent self-conscious, deliberate attempts to preserve memories by historical means. The Civil War was a transforming event in American memory. Between 1861 and 1907, American memory began to take form as a self-conscious phenomenon.[39] While most states reached back to the American Revolution for a defining identity, Texans looked back to the Texas Revolution for theirs. Texans became more self-conscious in the last quarter of the nineteenth century, and those who had living memories of the revolutionary era became the leaders in shaping a Texas identity from it.

Memoirs, memorials, and "vanity" histories became the paradigm for writing the history of Texas between 1883 and 1899. Dudley G. Wooten's massive two-volume effort, *A Comprehensive History of Texas,* was a memorial to the events of Texas history and those who participated. Wooten began with a reprint of Yoakum's *History of Texas* in its entirety, which he insisted could not be substantially improved upon. The remainder consisted of chronologically arranged essays and memoirs ranging from the founding of Austin's colony to 1897 and concluded with a summary of the last fifty years of the century and statistical tables. Though it was praised for its scholarship and objectivity, C. W. Raines's review of Oran M. Roberts's contribution on the Civil War and Reconstruction was telling: "Reconstruction was the hideous nightmare worse than war for Texans. The tyranny of the Davis administration does not escape recital and condemnation." This pervasive belief about Reconstruction was an example of self-conscious memory, not historical facts.[40] Roberts, who had been chairman of the secession convention, a former Confederate colonel, and the governor of Texas, was one of the few remaining Texans with a lived memory of the Texas Republic. Just as earlier historians had had their uses for particular versions of Texas' past, so, too, did Oran Roberts. Memorialists characteristically cast themselves in a favorable light. Personal journals and reminiscences were printed in record numbers. John Henry Brown, also a veteran of the republic, was another example of self-conscious memory. One reviewer wrote that his work could "be scrutinized in vain to find a deliberate utterance antagonistic to public or private virtue or unfaithful to the glory of Texas." But, in general, Brown's *History of Texas,* like Wooten's, was praised for its thoroughness, impartiality, and accuracy.[41] "Accuracy," in this case, was relative to memory. These works focused primarily, like earlier histories of Texas, on the revolution and the republic. They differed significantly in that they were more years removed from those events, and they incorporated more recent events, specifically Reconstruction. They seemed to demonstrate that distance made the memory grow stronger, and there seemed to be fewer and fewer challengers.

Widespread calls for history instruction in schools and universities inspired the production of several Texas history books in the 1890s. Their purpose, according to Anna J. Pennybacker, whose *A New History of Texas for Schools* was printed in four editions between 1888 and 1900, was to present "varied and romantic scenes" that would "cultivate true patriotism." Mary M. Brown's book, *A Condensed History of Texas for Schools,* was meant to help the teacher "kindle the fire of patriotism in the breast of the pupils."[42] Dudley Wooten and John Henry Brown both produced school histories during the same period. These became the sources of historical memory for Texas schoolchildren for the last decade of the nineteenth century and into the twentieth, only to be replaced by the pseudo-history, *Texas History Movies,* in the 1920s. These textbooks presented perhaps the greatest opportunity of the nineteenth century for their authors to actually shape Texas' collective memory, because theirs was a captive audience of impressionable young Texans decades removed from the events they read about and with no lived memory of them. Yet they presented the same Anglocentric version of Texas history that had dominated Texas history writing for nearly a century. Mrs. Brown devoted seven pages in her textbook to the Civil War and Reconstruction but twenty-two pages to Sam Houston. Pennybacker devoted six pages in her book to Reconstruction and mentioned slavery only once in more than four hundred pages.

The twilight years of the revolutionary generation inspired a preservation movement and a surge of monument building concurrent with similar activity all over the United States in the Gilded Age. The "sites" of memory, as described by Pierre Nora, became key in the preservation and perpetuation of public memory. The Daughters of the Republic of Texas organized to memorialize the veterans of the revolution and republic, and efforts by women such as Adele Looscan and Adina De Zavala to preserve historical sites drew much public attention. This group of women worked energetically, constantly, and tirelessly to preserve Texas' memory of its creation story. The greatest part of their efforts focused on the Alamo and the San Jacinto battlefield. Both of these shrines are the result of their labors. Not only the monuments themselves but also the very public, and at times acrimonious, battles over them impressed the events they represented on the popular mind. The women organized history clubs, promoted Texas history in public libraries, researched and published articles in magazines, and furnished Anna Pennybacker with information for her textbooks. It is reasonable to conclude that they had a greater hand in shaping Texas memory than any historians who preceded them, but their story was essentially the same: Anglo Texans were heroes. Mexicans and Indians were villains. Slavery was seldom or never mentioned, and Reconstruction was too painful to talk about.[43] Perhaps, due to the involvement of Adina De Zavala and her sisters, the granddaughters of Lorenzo de Zavala, the role of Tejanos in Texas history received somewhat more sanguine treatment, but it was still far from a balanced one.

Many of these same patriotic club women and amateur historians were instrumental in locating and collecting important documents of Texas history. A concerted effort to collect the sources of Texas history and to promote its study resulted in the organization of the Texas State Historical Association, which brought amateur and professional historians together in an effort to encourage a systematic and objective approach. Previous attempts to form a historical society, such as that of Henderson Yoakum in Huntsville in the early 1850s, had failed. In 1897, O. M. Roberts, F. R. Lubbock, John H.

Reagan, Dudley G. Wooten, A. J. Rose, Dr. George T. Winston, president of the University of Texas, and Prof. George P. Garrison, head of the Department of History at the University of Texas, succeeded. In its early years, the association focused its efforts on securing testimony from living witnesses of past events. The work of the association in gathering together the sources of Texas history was truly impressive. Officers and fellows worked diligently to start local history organizations around the state, with mixed success. They encouraged individuals to contribute articles to the *Quarterly*. But for all of these efforts, the public's collective memory remained essentially unchanged. The Texas State Historical Association was a third step in the institutionalization of Texas memory along with the publication of school textbooks and the teaching of history as a discipline in the university.

The establishment of the Department of History at the University of Texas seemed a major step forward for Texas history and an opportunity for historians to have an impact on the historical memory of a new generation of Texans. George P. Garrison, the department's first chair, had been trained at the University of Chicago in scientific methods, but he shared most of the same beliefs and prejudices typical of white Americans in Texas. H. Y. Benedict, former president of the University of Texas, recalled, "In Garrison, the scientific historian was ever subordinate to the patriotic citizen. He firmly believed that history revealed an unceasing moral purpose running through the ages and that the experience of the past could profitably be brought to bear on the problems of the future."[44] Garrison was demonstrative of the realization that much of what has been referred to as Texas' "collective memory" is American myth writ small. In his most important local study, *Texas: A Contest of Civilizations,* Garrison revealed the influences of nationalism, social evolution, manifest destiny, and the racial superiority of Anglo Saxons, themes that marked a century of writing about Texas. He opened the chapter on Austin with a paragraph that echoed Yoakum: "The military hero, and especially he that takes the lead in moments of national peril, playing his more dramatic part with the eyes of his countrymen fixed upon him, will never fail of his due need of glory; but he that plants in the wilderness, 'in labours more abundant' and 'in deaths oft,' the germ of a new civilization, is but rarely remembered as he should be."[45] By comparison, Yoakum begins his chapter on the Austins this way: "If he who, by conquest, wins an empire, and receives the world's applause, how much more is due to those who, by unceasing toil, lay in the wilderness the foundation for an infant colony, and build thereon a vigorous and happy state! Surely there is not among men a more honorable destiny than to be the peaceful founder and builder of a new empire."[46]

This remarkable similarity might be construed as evidence of Yoakum's influence on Garrison. It could easily be interpreted as evidence of similar ideologies. Garrison's potential influence in shaping Texas memory by applying scientific principles to its study was further mitigated by pressure from conservative Texas political sentiment. In June 1897, the Texas legislature adopted a resolution demanding an investigation into teaching at the University of Texas that purportedly failed to emphasize support for southern traditions. Faced with destruction of the history department, Garrison capitulated. Texas' first professional historian was constrained by Texas' so-called "collective memory" even as he strived to shape a more accurate historical memory. The academy, as Walter Buenger and Robert Calvert observed in their collection of historiographic essays, *Texas through Time* (1991), squandered its opportunity to really shape the collective memory of Texans and acquiesced in it. "The academy's provincialism remains," they wrote. "Clinging to past ways and past ideas offers a simpler choice to those who write about Texas. They can comfortably ignore the rest of the historical profession rather than challenge the mind-set of the homefolk." "By a curious paradox," Marc Bloch has noted, "through the very fact of their respect for the past, people came to reconstruct it as they considered it ought to have been."[47]

Until the Civil War, histories of Texas were written by visitors with a variety of perspectives, motives, and audiences. By the end of Reconstruction, Texas historians were writing for one audience of which they were themselves a part. Perhaps Maurice Halbwachs was correct in his assertion that true history can never be totally disengaged from social memory or serve as the corrective for its flaws. As Michael Kammen and others have observed, not enough people pay attention to scholarly history; they never have and probably never will. What people believe to be true about their past is usually more important in determining their behavior and response than truth itself. As early historians of Texas demonstrated, historians are members of society whether they are "unloving critics" or "uncritical lovers of their cultures." They are shaped and controlled by that society's memory as much as they are shapers of it.[48] The early historians of Texas demonstrated that shaping the collective memory of a society must involve more than either reinforcing popular views or presenting facts that contradict them; it must involve persuasion. It must involve challenging the public to think about its history in new ways. Their experience demonstrated that those who "challenge[d] the mind-set of the homefolk" were at best ignored, at worst publicly renounced, and at last forgotten. By the end of the nineteenth century, when they had the opportunity to shape the memory of schoolchildren, they did so by perpetuating the same romantic, Anglocentric, patriotic views that had characterized Texas memory for more than a century. In that respect, they did not influence Texas memory as much as they were influenced by it. They fell short of any fundamental reinterpretation of Texas history or memory. They failed to establish any historical memory that incorporated the diversity of lived experience in Texas. The early historians of Texas, particularly in the latter nineteenth century, did not shape Texas memory so much as they affirmed it.

NOTES

1. Anita Shapira, in her article "Historiography and Memory: The Case of Latrun 1948"(*Alpayim* 10 [1994]: 9), claims that modern historical research, despite improved methods, has no effect on the shaping of "collective memory"; on the contrary, "collective memory" actually affects the work of professional historians (quoted in Noa Gedi and Yigal Elam, "Collective Memory—What Is It?" *History and Memory* 8 [Spring/Summer 1996]: 41).

2. See Pierre Nora, "Between Memory and History: Les Lieux de mémoire," *Representations* 26 (Spring 1989): 8, 12.

3. Debbie Nathan, "Lone Done Gone," *Texas Observer* (Jan. 16, 2004): par. 1, available from http://www.texasobserver.org (accessed Mar. 10, 2005).

4. Cathy Corman, "Take Me Back to Texas," *Texas Observer* (May 12, 2000): pars. 6, 9, available from www.texasobserver.org (accessed Mar. 10, 2005).

5. Juan Agustín Morfi, *History of Texas, 1673–1779*, trans. Carlos Eduardo Castañeda, 2 vols. (Albuquerque, N.Mex.: Quivira Society, 1935; reprint, New York: Arno Press, 1967); José Antonio Pichardo, *Pichardo's Treatise on the Limits of Louisiana and Texas*, trans. and ed. Charles Wilson Hackett, 4 vols. (Austin: University of Texas Press, 1931).

6. Pichardo, *Pichardo's Treatise*, xx.

7. See for example Maurice Halbwachs, *The Collective Memory*, trans. Francis J. Ditter Jr. and Vida Yazdi Ditter (New York: Harper & Row, 1980), 78, and Carl Becker, "Everyman His Own Historian," *American Historical Review* 37 (Jan. 1932): 222.

8. William Darby, "Province of Texas," *Niles Weekly Register*, supplement to 16 (Aug. 7, 1819): 42–46. Darby's account first appeared in the *New York Columbian* on August 3, 1819.

9. See Frank Luther Mott, *A History of American Magazines, 1741–1850* (New York: Macmillan, 1947), 1:161–62, 268; and John William Tebbel, *A History of Book Publishing in the United States* (New York: R. R. Bowker, 1972), 1:121.

10. Sister (Paul of the Cross) McGrath, *Political Nativism in Texas, 1825–1860* (Washington, D.C.: Catholic University of America, 1930), 23.

11. Mary Austin Holley, *Texas: Observations Historical, Geographical and Descriptive* (Baltimore: Armstrong & Plaskitt, 1833), and *Texas* (Lexington, Ky: J. Clarke and Co., 1836).

12. J. P. Bryan, "Introduction," *Mary Austin Holley: The Texas Diary, 1835–1838*, ed. James Perry Bryan (Austin: University of Texas Press, 1965).

13. David B. Edward, *The History of Texas; or, The Emigrant's, Farmer's, and Politician's Guide to the Character, Climate, Soil and Productions of That Country: Geographically Arranged and from Personal Observation and Experience* (Cincinnati, Ohio: J. A. James and Co., 1836), viii.

14. John T. Mason to Stephen F. Austin, July 5, 1836, Stephen F. Austin Papers, Center for American History, University of Texas at Austin; Pease quoted in John H. Jenkins, *Basic Texas Books: An Annotated Bibliography of Selected Works for a Research Library,* rev. ed. (Austin: Texas State Historical Association, 1988), 140.

15. Frédéric LeClerc, *Texas and Its Revolution,* trans. James L. Shepherd III (Houston: Anson Jones Press, 1950), 67.

16. Jenkins, *Basic Texas Books,* 326.

17. Edward Stiff, *The Texan Emigrant: Being a Narration of the Adventures of the Author in Texas, and a Description of the Soil, Climate, Productions, Minerals, Towns, Bays, Harbors, Rivers, Institutions, and Manners and Customs of the Inhabitants of That Country; together with the Principal Incidents of Fifteen Years Revolution in Mexico: and Embracing a Condensed Statement of Interesting Events in Texas, from the First European Settlement in 1692, down to the Year 1840,* iii–iv.

18. William Kennedy, *Texas: The Rise, Progress, and Prospects of the Republic of Texas, in One Volume,* 2d ed. (1841; Fort Worth: Molyneaux Craftsmen, 1925); Henry S. Foote, *Texas and the Texans; or, The Advance of the Anglo-Americans to the Southwest; Including a History of Leading Events in Mexico, from the Conquest by Fernando Cortes to the Termination of the Texas Revolution,* 2 vols. (Philadelphia: Thomas, Cowperthwaite and Co., 1841).

19. Both quotations from a review of *Texas: The Rise, Progress, and Prospects of the Republic of Texas* by William Kennedy, *New York Review* 9 (July 1841): 188.

20. Kennedy, *Texas,* 517.

21. Review of *Texas and the Texans* by Henry S. Foote, *New York Review* 9 (July 1841): 208.

22. Jenkins, *Basic Texas Books,* 363.

23. Ashbel Smith to Anson Jones, May 17, 1842, *Diplomatic Correspondence of the Republic of Texas,* pt. 3, ed. George P. Garrison, vol. 2, pt. 2 of *Annual Report of the American Historical Association for the Year 1908* (Washington, D.C.: GPO, 1911), 957; review of *The History of [the Republic of] Texas* by N. D. Maillard, *Monthly Review* 157 (1842): 174; Arthur Ikin to Anson Jones, Mar. 15, 1842, in *Diplomatic Correspondence of the Republic of Texas,* 951.

24. William M. Gouge, *The Fiscal History of Texas, Embracing an Account of Its Revenues, Debts, and Currency, from the Commencement of the Revolution in 1834 to 1851–52 with Remarks on American Debts* (Philadelphia: Lippincott, Grambo, and Co., 1852); David R. McDonald and Timothy M. Matovina, eds., *Defending Mexican Valor in Texas: José Antonio Navarro's Historical Writings, 1853–1857* (Austin, Tex.: State House Press, 1995).

25. Gouge, *The Fiscal History of Texas,* v.

26. Sam Houston, "Remarks on the Texas Debt, and for the Issue of Certain Certificates of Stocks to Texas in Payment Thereof," Mar. 1, 1853, in Amelia W. Williams and Eugene C. Barker, eds., *The Writings of Sam Houston, 1813–1863,* 8 vols. (Austin: University of Texas Press, 1939), 5:409.

27. Navarro quoted in McDonald and Matovina, *Defending Mexican Valor,* 63.

28. Yoakum obituary in *Bar and Bench* (Huntsville, Tex.), Apr. 28, 1857, 292.

29. *Dallas Herald* quoted in Bowen C. Tatum Jr., "A Texas Patriot," *Texas Bar Journal* 53 (Sept. 1970): 722.

30. Ashbel Smith to Hon. C. Anson Jones, Nov. 11, 1878, Ashbel Smith Papers; P. W. Gray to Col. H. Yoakum, Feb. 18, 1856, Henderson King Yoakum Papers, both in Center for American History, University of Texas at Austin.

31. Hubert Howe Bancroft, *History of the North Mexican States and Texas, 1801–1889,* vol. 16 of *The Works of Hubert Howe Bancroft* (San Francisco: History Company, 1889), 384;

Dudley G. Wooten, *A Comprehensive History of Texas, 1685 to 1897,* 2 vols. (Dallas: William G. Scarff, 1898; reprint, Austin: Texas State Historical Association, 1986), 1:xxiii; C. W. Raines, review of *A Comprehensive History of Texas 1685 to 1897* by D. G. Wooten, *Quarterly of the Texas State Historical Association* 2 (July 1898): 87–93; Z. T. Fulmore, *The History and Geography of Texas as Told in County Names* (Austin: Steck, 1935), 151; see also Herbert Gambrell, "Scholars of the Past Find Our History a Rich Field," *Dallas Times Herald,* Oct. 7, 1945, and Eugene C. Barker, "Professor Barker Considers Growth of Our Historians," *Dallas Morning News,* Oct. 7, 1945.

32. See E. R. A. Seligman, "Economics and Social Progress," *Publications of the American Economic Association,* 3d ser., no. 4 (1902); Dorothy Ross, "Historical Consciousness in the Nineteenth Century," *American Historical Review* 89 (Oct. 1984): 921; Michael Kammen, *Mystic Chords of Memory: The Transformation of Tradition in American Culture* (New York: Knopf, 1991), 295–96.

33. DeWitt Clinton Baker, *A Brief History of Texas from Its Earliest Settlement* (New York: A. S. Barnes and Co., 1873), 116–20.

34. Robert A. Calvert, introduction to *A Texas Scrap-Book: Made up of the History Biography, and Miscellany of Texas and Its People,* compiled by D. W. C. Baker (Austin: Texas State Historical Association, 1991), xxii.

35. See Temple Lea Houston, "Thrall's *History of Texas*," *Galveston News,* Sept. 28, 1880.

36. Reuben M. Potter to M. A. Bryan, Aug. 15, 1883, Reuben Marmaduke Potter Papers, Center for American History, University of Texas at Austin.

37. Reuben M. Potter, "The Fall of the Alamo," *Magazine of American History* 2 (Jan. 1878): 14.

38. "Book Reviews and Notices," *Quarterly of the Texas State Historical Association* 8 (July 1904): 88–89.

39. Susan Crane, "Writing the Individual Back into Collective Memory," *American Historical Review* 102 (Dec. 1997): 1379; Pierre Nora, "Between Memory and History: Les Lieux de mémoire," *Representations* 26 (Spring 1989): 7–24; Kammen, *Mystic Chords of Memory,* 100. Nora's article details this shift from natural collective memory to the deliberate hallowing of historic sites in order to preserve memories.

40. "Book Reviews and Notices," 87; see Randolph B. Campbell, *Gone to Texas* (New York: Oxford University Press, 2003), 268–89, for a concise summary of the historical facts of Reconstruction in Texas.

41. Anonymous reviews quoted in Jenkins, *Basic Texas Books,* 54.

42. Anna J. Hardwicke Pennybacker, *A New History of Texas for Schools,* rev. ed. (Austin, Tex.: Mrs. Percy V. Pennybacker, 1900), vi; J. M. Fendley, "A Note to Teachers," in *A Condensed History of Texas for Schools,* by Mary M. Brown, prepared from the general history of John Henry Brown (Dallas, Tex., 1895), 12.

43. "The present generation knows absolutely nothing of that period in our history, because it was so extremely painful to those who passed through it, that their pens refused to write of it, their tongues were silent from excessive emotion at the mere thought of trying to relate its humiliating experiences" (Adele B. Looscan to Charles Ramsdell, Apr. 4, 1916, Texas State Historical Association Records, Correspondence, Center for American History, University of Texas at Austin).

44. H. Y. Benedict, "George Pierce Garrison," *Quarterly of the Texas State Historical Association* 14 (Jan. 1911): 175.

45. George P. Garrison, *Texas: A Contest of Civilizations* (New York: Houghton-Mifflin, 1903), 137.

46. Henderson [King] Yoakum, *History of Texas from Its Earliest Settlement in 1865 to Its Annexation to the United States in 1846,* 2 vols. (New York: Redfield, 1855; reprint, Austin: Steck, 1935), 1:209.

47. Walter L. Buenger and Robert A. Calvert, eds., *Texas through Time: Evolving Interpretations* (College Station: Texas A&M University Press, 1991), xxxiii; Bloch quoted in Kammen, *Mystic Chords of Memory,* 31.

48. Kammen, *Mystic Chords of Memory,* 37–39.

Chapter 2

THE BONES OF STEPHEN F. AUSTIN: HISTORY AND MEMORY IN PROGRESSIVE-ERA TEXAS

GREGG CANTRELL

On a perfect October morning in 1910, a crowd of one hundred politicians, reporters, and family members gathered around a grave in a small churchyard cemetery in Brazoria County, Texas. The occasion was not a funeral but rather the disinterment of a body that had been buried there seventy-four years earlier. As the bystanders looked on, laborers began to dig. Their task was made difficult by the roots of a large oak tree that had grown into the gravesite, but when the workers reached the six-foot level, they began to encounter pieces of a rotted wooden coffin, and then human remains. The first bone lifted from the grave was the perfectly preserved skull of Stephen F. Austin, the "Father of Texas."[1]

The first Anglo American colonizer of Mexican Texas, Austin had been buried there in December 1836, just weeks into his tenure as the Republic of Texas' first secretary of state. The cemetery adjoined Peach Point Plantation, which the bachelor Austin had secured for his sister Emily and her family. This was a family burial plot, holding the remains of many members of the large Austin-Bryan-Perry family. A reporter for the *Galveston Daily News* described the disinterment in what today we would consider lurid detail. The coffin had disintegrated and filled with soil, but Austin's entire skeleton was found. "Loving hands collected the immortal relics and tenderly placed them" on a clean white cloth, which was then laid in a new metal casket. The skull, which was "almost perfectly preserved," was lifted from the grave and placed in the hands of Hally Bryan Perry, the forty-two-year-old grandniece of Austin and daughter of Guy M. Bryan. The skull elicited intense interest. "The teeth were in perfect condition," according to the Galveston reporter, "and so lustrous and deep was the natural enamel on them that when the skull was held up to the light the sun shone through them as though they were made of crystal." The *News* correspondent waxed poetic, noting that "the great brain cavity of the illustrious colonizer and diplomat was filled with the soil for which he suffered and endured and pleaded and it seemed appropriate that the clear and prophetic brain which once planned, organized, nurtured, directed and preserved this state should in the process of time be supplanted by some of its rich, warm earth." When the skull was emptied of that rich Texas soil, onlookers concluded that it was "a perfect specimen of cranial development, and an examination with a view of discovering distinctive characteristics would convince anyone versed in cranioscopy that Austin had every desirable quality that a human should have. The extremely thin portion of the brain covering, itself an indication of intelligence, was firm and white and hard."[2]

By the time the exhumation was finished, "every one present" pronounced the day "to have been one of the most profitable and satisfactory they ever spent; nothing happened to mar the occasion in the slightest." The casket was placed on a wagon for the twelve-mile trip to Brazoria, where the first of several memorial services was conducted. The chain of events that followed was part of the larger story of how Texans transformed the way they would remember their history.[3]

This essay will attempt to answer several questions about changing historical memories of Texans in the early twentieth century. First, it will work to identify when, how, and why the memory of the Texas Revolutionary era began to inform public life in Texas. Next it will examine who was responsible for the new awareness of the state's frontier and revolutionary past. Finally, it will suggest what this new awareness meant for public perceptions of Texas history down to our own time. In exploring these questions, this essay confirms and expands upon the recent work of historian Walter L. Buenger, who has suggested that beginning around 1910 there was an upsurge in interest in the period of Anglo American colonization and the Texas Revolution, as Texans began distancing themselves from the memories of the Civil War era—memories associated with slavery, defeat, military occupation, and poverty.[4]

Furthermore, the period marked a change in who took an interest in commemorating the deeds of the 1820s and 1830s, as male politicians, professionals, and other proponents of progressivism sought to take the roles of guardians and promoters of historical memory away from nostalgia-focused women's groups. The result was a new public view of Texas history that emphasized Texas as both a western and a quintessentially American state whose identity sprang from the hardy pioneers who tamed the wilderness and defeated the Mexicans in the Texas Revolution. It was a viewpoint that emphasized progress and modernity and marked a turning-away from Texas' retrograde southern heritage.[5]

In recent years there has been a virtual explosion in scholarly writing on how societies collectively remember their histories. One scholar defines collective memory as "the ways in which people construct a sense of the past." Another notes that it "comprises that body of reusable texts, images, and rituals specific to each society in each epoch, whose cultivation serves to stabilize and convey that society's self-image." In other words, at a given point in time, a society remembers its past by constructing a version of history that serves current needs. Collective memory, constructed through such activities as the writing and teaching of history, the celebration of holidays, the creation of art, the building of monuments and museums, and the preservation of historical sites, gives a society its identity and helps to define its values. Necessarily, different generations respond to changing times by remembering their past in different ways. Studying how a society remembers its history, therefore, usually tells us much more about that society's present identity and values than it does about the historical events being remembered. As another leading student of history and memory explains, "For a historical memory to retain its capacity to speak to and mobilize its intended audience, it must address contemporary concerns about the past." The following study of how Progressive-era Texans chose to remember the state's revolutionary past does not tell us much about the Texas Revolution or its heroes, but it does tell us a great deal about the concerns and needs of Texans in the early twentieth century.[6]

To say that Stephen F. Austin and all that he represents had been forgotten by Texans prior to 1910 is an exaggeration; after all, the state's capital city was named for him, and history buffs certainly knew of his role in the Anglo colonization of Texas. But memorializing Austin and other revolutionary heroes had not been a very high priority for most of the three-quarters of a century after 1836. Part of this neglect stemmed from the late-nineteenth-century preoccupation with the Confederate "Lost Cause." In Austin's case, this neglect might also be attributed to Austin's fall from grace in the eyes of Texans in the year just preceding his death. Austin had been implicated, probably unfairly, in the infamous Monclova Speculations of 1835, and his leadership of the so-called Peace Party in the pre-revolutionary years had earned him a reputation as being too pro-Mexican. Moreover, he had been absent from Texas during most of the revolution on a diplomatic mission to the United States and thus could not claim the military laurels that Sam Houston and others earned. Seventy-five years after his death, there was still no biography of the great empresario, and published histories of Texas at best gave mixed coverage of his career.[7]

Efforts at public recognition of Austin's life met with equally under-whelming results. Austin's family led the efforts to enhance their kinsman's image in public places. In 1875 Austin's nephew, Guy Bryan, a former con-gressman and Speaker of the Texas House, donated a portrait of his uncle to the state for placement in the governor's office.[8] At about the same time another nephew, Moses Austin Bryan, suggested to painter Henry McArdle that he execute a work on Austin. The result was one of the best-known and most interesting depictions of Austin, *The Settlement of Austin's Colony,* bet-ter known as *The Log Cabin.* The painting shows Austin issuing land titles in 1824 when a scout arrives to warn of impending Indian attack. Austin holds the Laws of Mexico in one hand, symbolizing his love of the rule of law and his fidelity to his adopted country, while reaching for his gun with the other, an indication that he would fight for the interests of his colonists. This image was exactly the sort that Austin's family wanted to present of their illustrious forebear—that he was a man of peace who would not shy away from war. Obviously they believed that the public image of Austin still needed consid-erable burnishing.[9]

Moses Austin Bryan had pledged to pay for the painting and donate it to the state, but he was unable to fulfill his financial obligation. The paint-ing hung in the capitol on loan from the artist for several years, and in 1888 McArdle lobbied the government to purchase it. The legislature refused to purchase the "'fancy' painting of Austin" (as the legislative committee termed it), an act that upset Austin's family.[10]

By the 1890s there were only modest signs that Texans were growing more interested in the history of revolutionary-era Texas in general and of Austin in particular. In 1892 a group of women calling itself the Board of Lady Managers (later renamed the Women's World's Fair Association) com-missioned sculptor Elisabet Ney to create statues of Stephen F. Austin and Sam Houston for the following year's World's Fair in Chicago. However, the project soon encountered financial difficulties. Ney, who was struggling to establish herself in Texas, had to agree to sculpt the statues for free, charg-ing only for the cost of materials. Ney failed to complete the Austin statue

FIG. 2.1. Stephen F. Austin statue by Elisabet Ney, carved in marble and placed in the state capitol in 1903. Courtesy Texas Parks and Wildlife Department.

in time to be displayed in Chicago, and when the Board of Lady Managers failed to raise sufficient funds to pay the contractors who built the Texas pavilion at the World's Fair, the Houston statue was seized by the creditors. Ney had continued to work on the Austin statue, though, because the board's members had told her that they intended to have both statues cut in marble and placed in the state capitol. Friends of the artist called on both the Daughters of the Republic of Texas and the general public for financial contributions to the project, but the pleas fell on deaf ears. Ney eventually got the Houston statue back from Chicago, but the two plaster works remained "buried" in her studio for several more years. In 1897 Ney herself renewed the effort to have the statues carved and placed in the capitol. She approached an unidentified state legislator who was to introduce a bill to appropriate state funds for the project, but the legislator let her down, and she could find no other politician interested in the undertaking.[11]

In 1900 Ella Dibrell, a founding member of both the Daughters of the Republic of Texas (DRT) and the United Daughters of the Confederacy, joined with Elisabet Ney in mounting another campaign to have the state acquire marble copies of the two statues. Dibrell's husband was an influential state senator, and after a year of lobbying they succeeded in having the legislature appropriate funds to have the statues carved in marble and placed in the capitol. The statues were finally unveiled in January 1903.[12]

The Ney statues notwithstanding, in the hearts and minds of the Texas public Stephen F. Austin's memory largely continued to languish. Twice in the nineteenth century the idea had been raised of removing the empresario's remains from their bucolic resting place at Peach Point to a more appropriate public location. Both times the effort failed, either through lack of public support or opposition from Austin family members.[13] Finally, in 1910 the legislature passed a bill providing for the removal of the remains and their reburial in the State Cemetery, the cost of which was to be paid from the legislature's "contingent fund."[14]

The exhumation of October 18, 1910, marked the beginning of an extraordinary three days. The remains were first brought by wagon to Brazoria, where the local schools had been dismissed for the occasion. Before the casket was loaded on a waiting train, the schoolchildren were lined up and marched by the casket, with "each one dropping a white flower on the casket as they passed, until the casket was covered with flowers." Not to be left out, the local "colored children did the same," after which a Dr. W. L. Weems delivered an address comparing Austin to the biblical Moses. "Like Moses," Weems intoned, "he was only allowed a glimpse of the promised land to which he had led his people." A similar ceremony, complete with children and flowers, was conducted when the train stopped at nearby Angleton.[15]

The train's next destination was Houston, where elaborate plans had been made for honoring the Father of Texas the following day. The *Houston Post* promoted the event by placing a portrait of Austin, adorned with state symbols, in the center of page one of the October 19 issue. The ceremonies began promptly at 8 A.M. that morning. The casket was brought to the Rice Hotel (built on the site where the capitol of the Republic of Texas once stood). A funeral cortege then was formed and made its way to the Stephen F. Austin School, where the main services were held. Schoolchildren once again formed into lines and dropped roses onto the casket, which was draped with Texas flags. Houston's superintendent of schools made brief remarks, as did state senator J. E. Kauffman, who had been a member of the legislative committee that had been responsible for the bill. The children sang "America" and "The Texas Flag Song," and more flowers were placed on the coffin. This performance was followed by an address by a seventh-grader, Alma Neurath, who recounted Austin's life and sufferings in dramatic fashion. Congressman Joe H. Eagle then delivered the day's principal address, speaking on the "life and achievements" of Austin. "It was a historic event," reported Austin family member Beauregard Bryan: "A wave of interest about the founding of Texas swept over the state, as Stephen F. Austin . . . was the very incarnation of the spirit that made it possible." As we shall see, Bryan's comment about the "wave of interest about the founding of Texas" was no exaggeration.[16]

Following the Houston ceremonies, Austin's bones were placed aboard a car of the Houston & Texas Central Railroad and taken to the capital city. The train was met in Austin by a band, a military honor guard, and an impressive list of dignitaries, including Gov. Thomas M. Campbell and former governor Joseph D. Sayers. Pallbearers included the state treasurer, the chairman of the Railroad Commission, the mayor of Austin, the president of the University of Texas, and incoming governor Oscar Branch Colquitt.[17] Amidst much pomp and circumstance, the remains were taken to the state capitol, where they would lie in state. The DRT handled many of the arrangements. That night three thousand spectators crowded the senate chamber for a memorial service. With the military honor guard standing at attention beside the flower- and Lone Star flag–draped casket, elder statesman Alexander Watkins Terrell delivered the evening's principal oration, which "with wonderful perception of detail brought to light historical incidents in that connection which vividly revived memories of which Texans and Americans are proud." Musical numbers included a choir singing "How Firm a Foundation" and a soloist's rendition of "Infinite Love." Dr. R. J. Briggs, minister of the First Congregational Church, delivered the closing eulogy, in which he called Austin a "God-chosen and God-inspired man."[18]

The concluding act in the three-day drama occurred the following afternoon, October 20. At 3:30 P.M., a crowd gathered once more in the senate chamber. Following the reading of scripture and a prayer, the children present filed out of the chamber and lined the way from the capitol grounds as the funeral cortege left the capitol for the short trip to the State Cemetery. The highest point on the "Hill of the Heroes" had been chosen as the site for the reburial. After graveside services officiated by minister Briggs, the Father of Texas was lowered to his final resting place. Rebecca J. Fisher, president of the DRT, placed a flag on the grave on behalf of her organization and the Texas Veterans Association, and the ceremonies were finished.[19]

Several significant aspects of these events stand out. First was the ritual use of children in the proceedings. At every stop along the path, the citizens responsible for planning the events not only included children in the

FIG. 2.2. Remains of Stephen F. Austin lying in state in the Texas senate chamber, 1910, before reinterment in the Texas State Cemetery, Austin. Photograph from Prints and Photographs Collection, CN 04123, courtesy Center for American History, University of Texas at Austin.

ceremonies but also gave them central roles. Young children were present at the disinterment. They were released from school, and they ceremonially placed flowers on the casket at Brazoria, Angleton, and Houston. They were included in the capitol memorial service, and they lined the route from the capitol to the cemetery. The Houston services were held in a schoolyard and featured a young girl reading her own essay. Several of the adult speakers at the various events prominently voiced the object lessons that Austin's life offered to contemporary children. In his oration at Houston, Congressman Eagle prefaced his remarks by saying, "If I talk to you older people, some of these little ones will be unable to understand me, but if I talk to them, all of you can understand." According to the *Post* reporter covering his speech, Eagle "drew a moral from the life of the early statesman, and urged the children to follow his example by answering the call of their country, no matter what it required in sacrifice or effort." In his closing address in the senate chamber,

Reverend Briggs specifically addressed the "young men and women" present, telling them that "this heritage is now descending to you from the hands of those who have so faithfully guarded it through the generations now passing from the stage of action. Will you be faithful to it? And how? The best way is by imitating their spirit." He exhorted the younger generation to "renew the fires of your enthusiasm," and he urged his listeners "to baptize the coming generations in the glorious traditions of your history." Finally, hundreds of schoolchildren participated in the actual reburial, forming a phalanx through which the casket was carried from the capitol to the cemetery. This pageantry was no exercise in romanticizing idyllic days gone by; it was all about furnishing the current generation (and generations to come) with a usable past that pointed the way to a better future. As state legislator John T. Curry had remarked just prior to the passage of the disinterment bill, Austin's new grave would be a place "where the brainy boys of Texas can come and kneel at his grave and think of the glorious achievements of earth's greatest men and be made strong and patriotic by the study of the teaching and heroic acts of the men who gave the republic of Texas to the world as one of its greatest commonwealths." If there were any doubt that honoring Austin was an exercise with practical utility, Curry also added that "around this grave our legislature may gather when in doubt as to any policy." Significantly, in the entire three days' commemoration, there was not one mention of the Civil War or the Confederacy or any attempt to link the history of the Texas Revolutionary era and its heroes with that of the Lost Cause.[20]

It also should be noted that when the remains were brought to Brazoria the day of the exhumation, the "colored children" of that town's segregated school system were released from classes along with the white children and played a prominent role in the ceremonies. Texas in 1910 may still have been a very southern place by most cultural and economic standards, but the planners of these events clearly seemed to be using Austin's memory to reinforce a view of a New South that they wished to promote—a New South that included harmonious (albeit paternalistic and unequal) race relations. On a related note, the *Galveston Daily News*'s correspondent at the exhumation included a separate portion of his report under the headline, "Negroes Manifested Interest." The story focused on an elderly former slave of Austin's late nephew Guy Bryan who was present at the exhumation, identifying him as "a capitalist among the Brazoria County negroes, being worth about $12,000." This account then digressed into a discussion of the economic development of the sugar-producing lower Brazos Valley area, with the observation that "land values are increasing, and the atmosphere seems charged

with the activity which betokens a new era of prosperity on the old plantations." Implicit in all of this verbiage was the idea that Stephen F. Austin
and the revolutionary heroes had laid the foundations for a South that was
embracing modernization, both in economics and race relations. No tears
were being shed over the passing of slavery or the traditional Old South way
of life.[21]

As if to underscore this idea, the *Houston Post* published, in conjunc-
tion with the other stories concerning Austin, a curious essay by one S. P.
Etheridge entitled, "Stephen Fuller Austin, a Business Man." If ever there were
a proponent of modernization and progress, it was Etheridge. He began
his essay by explaining that the standards by which we judge heroes have
changed. "It is true," he explained, that "the sentimental are with us yet
whose mind, in depicting a hero, would take his measure by the strength
of his armor, the keenness of his sword, and the number of knights or 'hea-
thens' he had sent home on their shields." But today our heroes are judged
by their "business acumen," Etheridge declared. Reminding his readers that,
in the modern world, "nothing succeeds like success," he explained that "to
be a real modern hero, a man must not only 'corner May wheat,' but be
able to realize handsomely on the venture." Etheridge then reviewed Austin's
business career and pronounced a four-word verdict on the Father of Texas
that would resonate with the chamber-of-commerce mentality of 1910: "Austin, a modern hero." Now, here was a usable past![22]

Throughout the three days of commemorative events, speakers had gone
out of their way to stress the American (as opposed to southern) qualities of
Stephen F. Austin and the Texas that he created. In the ceremony at Houston, schoolchildren sang both "America" and the "Texas Flag Song." For
the memorial services in Austin, Texas symbols were augmented by an "immense American flag on either side of the chamber," which "added to the
patriotic decorative effect." Alexander W. Terrell's featured oration conspicuously placed the Texas Revolution in the context of the Enlightenment and
drew parallels between the Texas and American Revolutions. In one place
the parallel was particularly striking; Terrell likened Austin to Thomas Jefferson, "the greatest diplomat and statesman of them all," and explained that
just as Jefferson had been passed over for the first presidency by the military
hero Washington, so the incomparable Austin had been supplanted by the
wartime chieftain Sam Houston in the political affections of Texans. Terrell,
himself a former Confederate officer, could easily have found ways to include
the revolution of 1861 and its heroes in his extended history lesson, but he

chose not to. That late unpleasantness, and all the baggage that came with it, had no place here.[23]

As extraordinary as those three days in October had been, the final chapter in the story of Austin's reburial had not been written when he was lowered into his grave on the Hill of the Heroes. Next would come the effort to erect a suitable monument to be placed over the grave. The wait would not be long; the Thirty-second Legislature convened in January 1911, and the issue was high on its list of priorities. Early in the session Rep. Andrew Todd McKinney of Huntsville introduced House Bill 27, entitled "An Act for the erection of a monument over the remains of General Stephen F. Austin in the State cemetery at Austin, Texas, to make an appropriation therefor and to declare an emergency." The bill called for the legislature to appropriate ten thousand dollars for an appropriate monument for the grave, the work to be done "under the supervision of the Governor and the Superintendent of Public Buildings and Grounds." McKinney's father had been president of Austin College, before that institution's move from Huntsville to Sherman. The language of the bill communicates something of the enthusiasm of its sponsor for the project: "The fact that seventy-four years have elapsed since the death of General Austin and no suitable expression of the love and gratitude of the people of this State, for his services to Texas, having yet been made, and that the monument herein provided for should be erected without delay, create an emergency and an imperative public necessity that the constitutional rule requiring bills to be read on three several days be suspended and that this act take effect and be in force from and after its passage and it is so enacted." The bill was referred to the Committee on Public Buildings and Grounds, which soon reported back with a favorable recommendation. The bill passed the house quickly and apparently without controversy. It similarly flew through the senate by unanimous vote, and Governor Colquitt soon signed it into law.[24]

It is hard to imagine a legislature and governor of an earlier generation so enthusiastically approving this sort of extravagant expenditure for something as frivolous as a statue (remember the response of an earlier legislature to the proposed purchase of the McArdle painting of Austin). Ten thousand dollars in 1911 was the equivalent of nearly two hundred thousand dollars today. Although members of Austin's family had certainly pushed the effort, the key figure in making it a reality was the new governor, Oscar Branch Colquitt. Colquitt was not a particular political favorite of the Bryans, who had long promoted the undertaking, so his support cannot be attributed to any political favors owed them. At first glance, in fact, Colquitt might seem like an unlikely champion of such projects. Although he had long been a supporter of Gov. James S. Hogg, Colquitt is not usually identified as a particularly "progressive" governor—mainly because he was a dedicated "wet" in the prohibition battles that dominated Texas politics of that era. His predecessor, Thomas Campbell—widely regarded as the most progressive of the Progressive-era governors—had signed the bill that moved Austin's remains to the State Cemetery and had also promoted several Texas Revolution–related memorials just before leaving office, but it would be up to Colquitt to continue pushing the movement to commemorate the revolution and its heroes.[25]

Colquitt was a no-nonsense sort of man. Born in Georgia in 1861, the son of a Confederate officer, he grew up poor in northeast Texas and reached adulthood with only a few years of education and little money. After working as a tenant farmer, he learned the newspaper business from the ground up and eventually became editor and owner of the *Terrell Star-Times*. From there he studied law and entered local politics, winning a seat in the state senate and later the Railroad Commission. In his drive to the top of Texas politics, Colquitt used hard work, intelligence, and tenacity to compensate for his lack of money and social connections. Blunt and outspoken, he did not suffer fools gladly, and these qualities generated his share of political enemies. But in politics, Colquitt was a modernizer. As state senator, state revenue agent, and member of a special state tax commission, he established himself as an expert on taxation policy and a reformer in that area. As governor, he championed major improvements in both public and higher education. He pushed successfully to reform the way in which county governments were financed. He devoted particular attention to improving and enlarging the state's eleemosynary institutions and reforming the prison system, and he signed a child-labor law. Always a realist and a pragmatist, he seems to have seen prohibition as a paternalistic, visionary distraction that interfered with the pursuit of more serious matters. He loved driving the state's expanding highway system in his new Cadillac motor car. In ways large and small, then, Colquitt embodied the spirit of entrepreneurship and modernization that characterized Progressive-era America. He was little interested in nostalgia or sentimentality and thus not the type one might expect to have much interest in history. Yet he took a keen interest in historical preservation, and, as we shall see, he surpassed all previous governors in his determination to have the state government play an active role in promoting public commemoration of Texas history.[26]

On closer examination, though, it should not surprise us that Colquitt was so interested in shaping (or reshaping) historical memory in Texas.

As W. Fitzhugh Brundage, one of the leading scholars of memory in the South, has explained, "Representations of history are instruments of, and may even constitute, power. . . . The depth and tenacity of a historical memory within a society may serve as one measure of who exerts social power there." Paraphrasing Michel Foucault, Brundage reminds us that "the interpretation of history . . . is a conspicuous form of domination." And as historian David Blight explains, "The stakes in debates over social memories are quite real; material resources, political power, and life chances may all be at stake." Progressive-era political leaders in Texas—led most conspicuously by Colquitt—seem to have understood that instilling in the public a particular collective memory of Texas history could serve their own needs and further their political agendas.[27]

Colquitt took a hands-on approach to the matter of the Austin statue and to almost everything else he did as governor. Early in his administration he met and befriended the Italian-born San Antonio sculptor Pompeo Coppini, and the two men, so different in background and temperament, developed something of an artist-patron relationship, if not a true friendship. Coppini, the stereotypical temperamental artist, had already established a record as a prominent producer of monumental statues, and Colquitt would steer almost all of the state's commissions to Coppini during his administration. The enabling legislation for the Austin memorial gave the governor, along with the superintendent of public buildings and grounds, the ultimate authority to decide on the design and execution of the piece. Members of the Austin family were told that their wishes would be taken into consideration, although the governor would make final decisions. Colquitt soon announced that the state would conduct a competition for designs for the monument. Early on, the Austin family decided that a mausoleum would be the best memorial, but Colquitt clearly wanted a statue. Wanting to avoid the appearance of favoritism toward Coppini, the governor decided to solicit formal design proposals from the public, and he appointed a committee to review the proposals and make a recommendation for the one to be chosen. Although the committee consisted of reporters from five of the state's major newspapers, plus Colquitt and A. B. Conley, the state superintendent of public buildings and grounds, the records leave no doubt that the decision would be the governor's. Indeed, Colquitt virtually dictated the design of the statue to Coppini, much to the sculptor's private distress, leaving Coppini the additional unenviable task of persuading the Bryans that the bronze statue of Austin was a far more suitable monument than the mausoleum that the family had first envisioned.[28]

FIG. 2.3. Stephen F. Austin grave monument at the Texas State Cemetery, sculpted by Pompeo Coppini, 1913. Courtesy Texas State Cemetery, Austin.

In June 1912 Coppini finished modeling the statue in clay, and the following month Colquitt made the trip to the artist's San Antonio studio to view the work. According to Coppini, the governor pronounced it the sculptor's greatest work yet. By the end of the year Coppini had made a plaster cast and shipped it to Chicago, where the nine-foot bronze statue would be cast. He personally traveled to Chicago to oversee the casting, and in the spring of 1913 the monument was completed and shipped to Austin to take its place over Austin's grave.[29]

If the three-year saga of the disinterment, reburial, and creation of the statue of Stephen F. Austin had been the only events commemorating the

Texas Revolutionary era and its heroes in the years around 1910, they might be written off as an isolated tribute to a long-neglected pioneer father, and little more. But Beauregard Bryan's previously quoted comment about the "wave of interest about the founding of Texas" that "swept over the state" is reinforced by a remarkable list of other, similar events taking place during a very brief span of time.

The very same day as Austin's reinterment (October 20, 1910), ceremonies were held in the public square at Gonzales to dedicate another Coppini statue, this one to commemorate the first military engagement of the Texas Revolution. The legislature had paid Coppini five thousand dollars for that monument, which is a bronze statue of a frontier militiaman in a defiant pose, with a rifle in one hand. That same fall, one of the most popular attractions at the 1910 state fair in Dallas was a full-scale replica of the Alamo chapel. The *Dallas Morning News* reported approvingly that "many children have visited the replica" since the opening of the fair, "and the interest these young Texans evince in their State's history has been a subject of commendatory remark by many older visitors."[30]

Early the following year, shortly after Colquitt took office, elaborate ceremonies were held in Huntsville to mark the unveiling of Coppini's monument at Sam Houston's gravesite. Although Beauregard Bryan pronounced the marble bas-relief of Houston on horseback "an outrage upon the people, and a travesty upon art," the ceremony attracted an even greater keynote speaker than the Austin ceremonies—none other than the famous Democratic politician William Jennings Bryan of Nebraska.[31]

In the wake of his involvement with the Stephen F. Austin statue, Colquitt now seemed determined to make the State Cemetery a showplace for the heroes of the Texas Revolution. As the Austin memorial neared completion in 1913, the governor was approached by the family of Joanna Troutman, who wanted her remains removed from her obscure grave in Georgia and reinterred in Austin. Troutman, as a seventeen-year-old girl in 1835, had sewed one of the first Lone Star flags, which was carried to Texas by the Georgia Battalion and flown by Fannin's garrison at Goliad, thus earning her the appellation, "the Betsy Ross of Texas." Colquitt enthusiastically embraced the idea, but realizing that a state appropriation for a statue of Troutman might be a somewhat harder sell than it had been for Austin, he personally mounted an ambitious campaign to raise the funds by private subscription. Using the resources and influence of his office, he blanketed the state with subscription forms, and the money flowed in from groups of schoolchildren, civic groups, and private individuals. He again awarded Coppini the contract

FIG. 2.4. Joanna Troutman monument at the Texas State Cemetery, sculpted by Pompeo Coppini, 1914. Courtesy Texas State Library and Archives Commission, Austin.

for a bronze likeness of Troutman, and the statue now stands over her grave not far from that of Stephen F. Austin.[32]

Perhaps the most unusual of the state's monument projects during the Colquitt administration was the effort to memorialize Elizabeth Crockett, the second wife of Davy Crockett. Elizabeth (whom Crockett had abandoned when he came to fight at the Alamo) had moved to Texas in 1854 with her son Robert and claimed a land grant in her late husband's name in present-day Hood County, where she died in 1860. Pierce Ward, the state senator who sponsored the 1911 bill to build a monument at her gravesite, delivered a long, impassioned speech in the 1911 legislature in favor of the bill. After giving a biographical account of the lives of Davy Crockett and his family, Ward made the case for the monument. There was no physical monument at the Alamo to commemorate the sacrifices of the 1836 heroes, he explained. But "look around us and see what monuments are erected to those noble martyred spirits," he urged. Ward then identified those "monuments" as the University of Texas and the other "schools and universities, [from] which the educated thousands of the sons and daughters of Texas and generations yet unborn will receive blessings and advantages." He went on to rhapsodize about "the many million acres of land now in cultivation and the great industries of our State," which he believed stood as further evidence of the fruits of the Alamo heroes' planting. Elizabeth Crockett had moved to the Texas frontier to "continue the struggle for independence" that her husband had begun, so that future generations could enjoy the blessings of liberty and prosperity. In short, Ward was making the case that the Texas Revolution and the sturdy pioneers of the frontier were the harbingers of progress—a progress that included education, industry, and economic development. As improbable as it might sound, the Elizabeth Crockett monument would be a monument not to death nor even to domesticity but rather to the state's rising greatness and modernity. Following his appeal, the legislature appropriated two thousand dollars for the monument and statue to be placed on her grave, and Governor Colquitt signed Ward's bill into law.[33]

Colquitt's interest in honoring the revolutionary past was not limited to reburials and the placement of statues over Texas heroes' graves. During his administration the state spent five thousand dollars to build a new cement-block wall around the State Cemetery and to make other significant improvements, such as new water mains and landscaping. By 1914 Superintendent Conley could report with pride that "the present condition of the State Cemetery is better than it had ever been before. It is well kept, and due regard has been paid to the sacredness of the ground." Colquitt also signed a bill in 1913 expanding the scope of the Texas State Library and Historical Commission.[34]

Preserving and improving several of the major battlefields of the Texas Revolution also preoccupied the governor. His predecessor, Thomas M. Campbell, had signed legislation in 1907 adding fourteen acres to the state-owned San Jacinto battleground. Colquitt subsequently took pride in improving the grounds and building "a splendid pavilion" that cost the state eight thousand dollars. He supported a bill in 1913 that authorized the state to acquire the Presidio La Bahía and Fannin battleground near Goliad, at the cost of ten thousand dollars. That same legislative session the state accepted,

Fig. 2.5. Elizabeth Crockett monument, Acton, Texas.

from the city of Gonzales, title to the land where the first shots of the Texas
Revolution were fired and appropriated seventy-five hundred dollars for improvements to the state park that was planned for the site. It is difficult to
judge how much political capital Colquitt had to expend in pursuit of the
aforementioned projects; most of them appear to have enjoyed broad support
from the taxpayers and the legislature—an indication of the newfound value
that Progressive-era Texans were placing on their state's revolutionary past. In
any case, Colquitt took great pride in his self-appointed role as the leading
promoter of Texas history. But not all of the governor's history-related causes
were free from political risk. Near the end of his first year in office, Colquitt

crossed swords with an unlikely foe over the state's most important historical site. That opponent was the Daughters of the Republic of Texas, and the site in question was the Alamo.[35]

At the close of the nineteenth century the Alamo had seemed almost forgotten. The ancient mission lay in ruins; even the small monument to the Alamo heroes that had stood near an entrance to the state capitol had not been replaced until a decade after it was destroyed in the 1881 capitol fire. The state did purchase the Alamo chapel in 1883, granting custodianship of it to the city of San Antonio. However, the city did little to improve the crumbling church for the next twenty years. In 1886 the fiftieth anniversary of the 1836 battle passed with no formal ceremonies in San Antonio. Moreover, the portion of the Alamo where much of the 1836 fighting actually took place—the *convento,* or "Long Barracks," as it was popularly called—had not been included in the 1883 purchase. That part of the structure had passed into private hands and was being used as a wholesale grocery and liquor warehouse. The building had been altered considerably during the seventy years since the battle, but beneath a rather dilapidated wooden exterior the thick stone walls of the two-story Long Barracks still stood, although nobody knew for certain just how much of the original structure survived. In 1903 the legislature passed a bill to purchase the property, but Gov. S. W. T. Lanham vetoed it. Two years later, when it became known that the owners of the property, the firm of Hugo & Schmeltzer, were considering selling the building to commercial developers who planned to build a hotel on the spot, a wealthy young woman named Clara Driscoll stepped in and mounted a campaign to purchase the site. Driscoll footed the $500 bill for an option on the property that forestalled its sale for a month, assuming that a public appeal would quickly bring in the $4,500 needed to extend the option for a year. The statewide appeal netted barely over a thousand dollars. Subsequent fundraising efforts proved equally deficient. Only when Driscoll finally wrote a personal check for $14,333.77 and promised to pay another $50,000 over the next five years was the state finally shamed into reimbursing her. The state of Texas authorized the governor to purchase the Hugo-Schmeltzer property on January 26, 1905, with the provision that when the purchase was completed, the DRT would become the custodian of the entire Alamo.[36]

What happened next is well known to historians and Alamo buffs. A bitter dispute arose within the ranks of the Daughters over what should be done with the site. On one side was a faction led by Clara Driscoll, who wanted to demolish the unsightly Hugo-Schmeltzer building and leave only the Alamo chapel, which would be surrounded by a landscaped park featuring

Fig. 2.6. The Alamo, ca. late 1800s. The two-story wooden façade of the Hugo & Schmeltzer grocery and liquor warehouse conceals the ruins of the original two-story Alamo *convento* (or Long Barracks) walls. Courtesy University of Texas Institute of Texan Cultures, San Antonio.

some sort of monument to the fallen heroes. "It is the desire of the Daughters of the Republic to convert this property into a beautiful Park," Driscoll explained, "filled with swaying palms, tropical verdure and native flowers, enclosed by a low wall, with arched gateways of Spanish architecture." Opposing her was a group led by Adina De Zavala, a local schoolteacher and granddaughter of revolutionary figure Lorenzo de Zavala. Adina De Zavala, a dedicated student of history, insisted that the original walls of the Long Barracks should be saved, since they were an integral part of the Alamo and were actually more historically significant than the chapel, which had been a ruin even before 1836. The dispute led to litigation and a nasty, long-running public controversy that finally left the Driscoll faction in control of the DRT and, presumably, the Alamo itself. There was, however, one crucial provision in the 1905 law: The Alamo was "to be maintained or remodeled upon plans adopted by the Daughters of the Republic of Texas, and approved by the Governor of Texas; provided that no changes or alterations shall be made in the Alamo Church proper . . . except such as are absolutely necessary for its preservation." In his final months in office, Gov. Thomas M. Campbell quite reasonably interpreted the law as prohibiting the Daughters from demolishing any of the Alamo's original structures; Driscoll's plans for razing the Hugo-Schmeltzer building would require new legislation. Thus matters stood when Colquitt took office in January 1911.[37]

Given his deep interest in such matters, it comes as no surprise that Colquitt followed the unfolding events closely. When the new legislature met, he asked for a seventy-five-hundred-dollar appropriation to begin improvements on the Alamo, to be directed by the governor. Although he got only five thousand dollars, it was enough to begin making specific plans. Adina De Zavala soon was writing to Colquitt, impressing on him the need to preserve the Long Barracks. Concerned about an erroneous newspaper report that Colquitt meant to tear down the structure, she received assurances from the governor that he intended no such thing. "The governor who restores the Alamo will bind the hearts of the people to him indissolubly," De Zavala gushed, "and historians will write his name high in the lists of those worthy of the Hall of Fame."[38]

Colquitt decided to travel to San Antonio and hold a public meeting of all interested parties in the controversy. Although he sympathized with De Zavala's position on the matter, the governor refused to take sides in the DRT's internal conflict. "I shall give the women who are interested in this a hearing before I do anything," he told De Zavala, "but I shall decline to become a partisan to either faction of the Daughters of the Republic. After I hear them I will act upon what I think is the best information in [an] effort to restore the Alamo to its original appearance, so far as the small appropriation at my disposal will permit." The meeting took place on December 28, 1911, and both sides in the dispute were well represented.[39]

Colquitt opened the meeting by stating his position in unequivocal terms. As reported by the *Dallas Morning News,* the governor declared "that he regarded both the chapel and the Hugo & Schmeltzer Building as parts of the Alamo; that he desired information showing what was the condition of these buildings before the battle; announced his purpose to restore the buildings to such condition, and declared with emphasis that he meant to assume the entire responsibility." The Alamo, Colquitt reminded the gathering, "was the common heritage of Texas, not peculiarly the property of the Daughters of the Republic."[40]

Colquitt's performance was, in many ways, a tour de force that modern historical preservationists would applaud. Paraphrasing the governor, the *Morning News* reporter wrote that "he will be guided in determining what shall be done with the walls and as to restoration by what shall be disclosed by the uncovering of the masonry and by excavation; by historic data and by such reports as may be obtained from the archives of the Republic of Texas and the Federal Government at Washington." When the Driscoll faction argued that the Hugo-Schmeltzer building in its entirety postdated 1836 and was constructed by the U.S. Army, Colquitt replied that he intended "to have the records ransacked to see if any such construction was done by the United States Government." Although Driscoll at one point made a tactical retreat and disclaimed any intention of demolishing any of the Alamo's original structure, it was clear that her faction wanted the Hugo-Schmeltzer/ Long Barracks structure gone. Daughter Sarah Elizabeth Eager, whom the Driscoll faction had appointed as the DRT's actual custodian of the Alamo, engaged Colquitt in debate at one point. She would admit only that perhaps one eight-foot-high wall of the *convento* fence (not a wall of the actual Long Barracks) actually survived beneath the Hugo-Schmeltzer exterior, to which the governor responded, "Do you think that wall ought to be torn down?" Eager replied that she supposed she would not object to leaving it, but added, "I have no love for the old eyesore." Colquitt reiterated his position: "If I can find out how this building looked when Travis lost his life, I will spend every dollar at my disposal to make it look like it looked then. I want information. Then I am going to assume the responsibility, and no power can budge me from my determination. (Applause.)" Eager restated the Daughters' desire to have the Hugo-Schmeltzer building torn down and replaced with a "park" in which a monument would then be built. Colquitt replied, "Texas could build a monument 7,000 feet high, and it wouldn't commemorate their deeds like these buildings. (Applause). . . . You might talk to me a thousand years and you couldn't change my opinion about tearing those parts down. . . . I want to restore it as it was before Travis defended it, and will do so if it takes $50,000, and I can get the money. If you have information as to how it looked then, I would like to have it. If not, this meeting will be adjourned."[41]

The escalating dispute between the governor and the Driscoll-led Daughters involved more than simply competing visions of how the Alamo should be preserved for future generations. Progressive-era women had inherited from their nineteenth-century counterparts a view of their societal role as the chief guardians of domestic virtue. Teaching children moral lessons about their heritage was a key component of this role. Organizations like the DRT, then, were an extension of this domestic role into the public arena. Mrs. Anson Jones, one of the DRT's founders, explained the Daughters' self-appointed mission clearly: "Let us leave the future of Texas to our brothers, and claim as our province the guarding of her holy past. . . . Let us love to study Texas history and teach it to her children." One of the DRT's founders, Betty Ballinger, expressed her organization's mission even more explicitly. "The material welfare of Texas is secure," she declared, "her future is in the hands of her sons. Daily they go forth to achieve great things, and we must blame them if, strong in their own strength, dazzled by the splendor of the present, they have somewhat forgotten . . . the past." That being the case, women's groups such as the DRT appointed themselves as the guardians of that "holy past."[42]

The Daughters' conflict with Colquitt operated on several levels. First, their vision of what the Alamo should be ran counter to the governor's vision. Colquitt wanted a restored Alamo that would capture the gritty, desperate battlefield conditions that existed when Travis, Bowie, and their men retreated to the old mission compound upon the arrival of Santa Anna's troops in February 1836. As anthropologist Holly Beachley Brear has pointed out, the Alamo-as-battlefield would have "none of the usual domestic characteristics of historic properties typically under the care of women's groups." As a consequence, the Daughters were horrified that Colquitt's restored Alamo, instead of being a parklike setting where children would learn reverence for the fallen heroes, would instead (as Colquitt explained it) enable people to "come here from all parts of the world" and "point out the place where Santa Anna made his assault, the place where Travis fell, etc." In short, Colquitt's mindset—a progressive, masculine mindset—led to his desire to wrest the Alamo away from the female amateurs of the DRT and place its fate in the hands of modern, professionally trained, male archaeologists, architects, and historians. Thus, the lushly landscaped garden that the Daughters wanted to create on the site of the Hugo-Schmeltzer "eyesore" was a nostalgic and thoroughly feminine undertaking, and Colquitt wanted no part of it.[43]

Whatever the competing visions of the governor and the Daughters may have been for restoration of the site, the very fact that the governor would presume to take away one of the few outside-the-home prerogatives that women claimed for themselves outraged the women of the DRT. Conversely, Colquitt was exasperated that the DRT, whom he considered to be a bunch of sentimental ladies with no training or expertise in such affairs, would presume to meddle in the serious business of maintaining and operating important state-owned assets. Although he did not explicitly state it during the Alamo controversy, Colquitt—always keenly interested in the economic development of Texas—undoubtedly understood the potential of the Alamo as a tourist destination, just as he did when he spent taxpayer funds to improve the roads and facilities at the San Jacinto battleground. The Daughters, on the other hand, saw themselves as defenders of the state's historical legacy against crass entrepreneurialism, as represented by Colquitt. Neither the Daughters nor the governor were about to surrender without a fight what each believed to be their rightful roles.

Driscoll and her fellow Daughters soon interjected politics into the dispute with Colquitt. In the December 1911 showdown with the governor in San Antonio, Driscoll, referring to the Hugo-Schmeltzer building, had stated that the Alamo should not be "disgraced by this whisky house." Of course, prohibition was the burning political issue of the day, and being a moral issue that affected children, families, and homes, women of that era felt free to take a leading public role in agitating the question. In doing so, Progressive-era woman were pushing the boundaries of women's activism. Denied the right to vote and shut out of most serious public-policy debates, they made common cause with male prohibitionists who also generally supported woman suffrage. Colquitt, an outspoken anti-prohibitionist as well as an opponent of woman suffrage, replied matter-of-factly to Driscoll's whisky-house complaint by stating that "the fact that these walls have been used for commercial purposes is not the fault of the present Executive: the fact that they were used for a whisky house is not his fault." Later in the debate, when Sarah Elizabeth Eager refused to accept the contention that a building that was a whisky house could ever be a "sacred" space, Colquitt responded by saying that "its use does not detract from the sacred character of the monument." Clearly, in the Daughters' feminized vision of the Alamo, the former use of the Hugo-Schmeltzer building as a whisky warehouse permanently stained the site that should, in their eyes, be a place for reverent contemplation and moral instruction of children. For the governor, the fact that a business—of whatever nature—had operated there was immaterial. For Colquitt, what mattered was what would happen to the Alamo in the future, not what had been done there in the years since 1836.[44]

The DRT's willingness to enter the public arena in order to claim their "domestic" prerogatives did not stop with the fight over the Alamo. When Colquitt's pet project of the Joanna Troutman monument was finished, the Daughters raised a furor over the nearly completed Coppini statue on the grounds that Troutman did not really design the first Lone Star flag. The Daughters' ire was exacerbated by the fact that Colquitt had decided (along with Coppini) that the statue should not be "hidden in the State Cemetery" as the Stephen F. Austin statue had been. Instead, the governor wanted to place it in "one of the parked circles in University Avenue" or on Congress Avenue at the front gate to the capitol, where the people of Austin and visitors to the capital city could all "see and admire it daily." The Daughters almost certainly were looking for any excuse to embarrass Colquitt after his stance on the Alamo, but it is hard to escape the conclusion that they also resented his campaign to memorialize a woman, no matter how noble (and domestic) she may have been. Such undertakings were the business of women, and woe be to the man who sought to deprive them of that right, even if he was the governor of Texas. Likewise, the fact that Colquitt seemed fond of celebrating women (e.g., Joanna Troutman, Elizabeth Crockett) who stayed in their cabins doing domestic things like sewing flags and raising children rather than getting involved in the manly world of politics or business was a point that would not have been lost on at least some of the Daughters.[45]

It is beyond the scope of this essay to follow in detail the subsequent history of the Colquitt-DRT fight over who would control the Alamo. Suffice it to say that Colquitt and the state did assume control in 1913 and begin rebuilding the two-story Long Barracks according to historical documents, only to have the work interrupted when the five-thousand-dollar appropriation was exhausted and, later, by litigation from the DRT. In the midst of the controversy, Clara Driscoll publicly declared her intention to stump the state against Colquitt if he should run for the U.S. Senate in 1916 (a threat upon which she apparently did not follow through). In the end the Daughters won their "war" with the state government, regaining custodianship of the Alamo in late 1913. The completed portion of the Long Barracks restoration was torn down by San Antonio officials with permission from the lieutenant governor when Colquitt was out of the state on business; only a section of the first-floor wall was retained and incorporated into the Daughters' long-sought garden landscape. A quarter-century later the Daughters' dream of adding an impressive artistic monument to the Alamo Plaza was also realized. Ironically, the sculptor of the Alamo Cenotaph would be none other than Pompeo Coppini, the erstwhile ally and supporter of Oscar B. Colquitt and Adina De Zavala.[46]

The public furor over the Alamo in 1913 overshadowed the concluding act in the story of the reburial of Stephen F. Austin. Indeed, the story in the April 29, 1913, *Austin Statesman* announcing that Colquitt had accepted, on behalf of the state, the completed Coppini bronze of Austin, appeared beneath the article in which Driscoll announced her intention to campaign against Colquitt in his upcoming Senate race. Moreover, just eleven days later, a new controversy erupted involving the governor and public historical memory. The *Statesman* reported that Colquitt had decided to evict the United Daughters of the Confederacy from the prominent ground-floor room in the capitol that they had used as a Confederate museum and meet-

FIG. 2.7. The Alamo, ca. 1913. This view is taken from behind the *convento* (or Long Barracks) walls, looking out toward Alamo Plaza. It was taken after the removal of the Hugo &
Schmeltzer façade but before the demolition of the upper story of the *convento*. The Alamo
chapel can be seen on the far left. Courtesy University of Texas Institute of Texan Cultures,
San Antonio.

ing place for their organization since 1905. Although Colquitt's stated reason
for the decision was that the government simply needed more office space,
the press did not fail to notice that the act once again placed him at odds
with a hereditary society run by women. Whatever his motives, it seems clear
that the governor had little use for the UDC and its shrine to the Lost Cause,
at least in the halls of government. Like the DRT, the Confederate Daughters would also take him to court, and once again Colquitt would lose. The
UDC would remain in possession of its room in the capitol until Colquitt's
successor, James Ferguson, persuaded them to vacate the capitol in favor of
new quarters in the old state Land Office building—quarters they would
share with the DRT.[47]

Colquitt's bitter disputes with both the DRT and the UDC underscore
the change in how Texans—at least white male Texans—used historical
memory in the early twentieth century. Throughout the Progressive era the
UDC struggled to interest the Texas public in its efforts to memorialize the
Lost Cause. As the leading scholar of the Texas UDC, Kelly McMichael
[Stott], has pointed out, "Texans were basically disinterested in erecting
Confederate monuments." Why? Because the values that the UDC was seeking to inculcate were antithetical to the progressive ethos, which looked to
the future rather than the past. If instilling patriotism alone had been the
main thrust of the UDC's efforts, perhaps its members would have had more
success in their various efforts. But as McMichael notes, the Confederate
Daughters "considered the lesson of resignation" and "the rejection of materialism" to be at least as important as the lesson of patriotism. Texans such
as Colquitt turned a deaf ear to the UDC's efforts to raise money for Confederate monuments because such monuments "either did not reflect a col-

FIG. 2.8. The United Daughters of the Confederacy room at the Texas state capitol, ca. 1913. Photograph PICA 23880, courtesy Austin History Center, Austin Public Library.

lective memory that most Texans wanted to identify with or they simply wanted to forget the past all together." McMichael's observations regarding the UDC hold equally true of the DRT; with their desire to commemorate the sacrifices of the Alamo martyrs by making the Alamo a gardenlike shrine to death, the DRT—many of whose members also belonged to the UDC— seemed no more relevant to the present or the future than the UDC. It was no coincidence that the DRT focused most of its energies in the early twentieth century on commemorating the 1836 siege of the Alamo, a battle that, after all, was a "Lost Cause" in itself. The Daughters of the Republic were far more interested in preserving a feminized Alamo than in celebrating the violent, bloody, masculine victory at San Jacinto. Like the UDC, the DRT was interested in rejecting or at least tempering materialism, not praising it.[48]

Of course it would be a mistake to read all of the evidence presented in this essay and conclude that in 1910 all Texans suddenly abandoned their maudlin devotion to the Lost Cause and instead embraced a progressive, entrepreneurial, usable version of the Texas Revolutionary past. Confederate reunions continued to attract large crowds in Texas after 1910, mostly for their entertainment value. And groups like the UDC and the United Confederate Veterans could still command press attention and, at times, influence politics. Certainly the Texas public did not cease to be essentially southern in many of its racial, political, and cultural values. But by the second decade of the twentieth century, as we have seen, the sentimentality of the Lost Cause, with its reminders of slavery, defeat, military occupation, and poverty, held little appeal for the forward-looking leaders who wanted to build a progressive future for Texas.[49]

In 1913, the same year that Colquitt was supporting appropriations for the Goliad and Gonzales battlefields, memorializing Joanna Troutman, and enlarging the scope of the State Library, a bill appropriating funds for the construction of monuments to Texas Confederates arrived on his desk to be signed into law. Colquitt issued a barbed response, claiming that since the legislature had refused to appropriate funds for "taking care of the helpless, the insane and caring for the living who need the aid of the State's charity," he was vetoing the bill. An attempt to override his veto failed in the senate.[50]

That same year, the John Bell Hood Chapter of the United Confederate Veterans mounted a public campaign to ban any use in the public schools of textbooks that contained an "anti-southern" bias. As evidence they pointed to an American history text that contained a picture of Abraham Lincoln. The state textbook board sided with the veterans, leading Colquitt to issue the following statement: "So far as I am concerned, I want the truth of history taught. . . . I had rather resign the Governor's office of Texas than to have my children studying a textbook in the public schools of Texas with Abe Lincoln's picture left out of it, and I am the son of a Confederate soldier."[51] Colquitt may have lost this skirmish in the culture wars of the Progressive era, as he likewise lost his fight with the DRT over the Alamo. But the trend was unmistakable. If Texas were to become the modern state that boosters like Oscar Branch Colquitt envisioned, it needed to shed the burden of southern history and pick up the sword of Texas history—not just any old Texas history, but a version of the revolutionary past that would reflect the progressive values and aspirations of modernizing society. The cogent observations of the German scholar Jan Assmann are applicable to the conflicting historical visions of groups like the UDC and DRT versus progressive male leaders like Colquitt: "One group remembers the past in fear of deviating from its model, the next for fear of repeating the past."[52]

In the end, however, we should remember that Colquitt's progressive, entrepreneurial vision of Texas history was still bound by his own cultural values and assumptions. He may have been more faithful to today's standards of historical preservation in his ideas on how the Alamo should be restored, but his version of the Texas past was very much a white, male, elitist version. For example, he pointedly dismissed any suggestion that the Alamo should also commemorate the colonial Spanish mission system, and the role of Tejanos in the Texas Revolution would go unacknowledged in all of the various acts of historical commemoration conducted by his administration. (The so-called "third" Battle of the Alamo—the movement to include Hispanics and Indians in the official interpretation of the Alamo site—would not be waged until our own time.) Colquitt may have wanted his fellow Texans to forget about slavery, the Civil War, and Reconstruction, but he also wanted them to remember a whites-only version of the Texas Revolution, a version in which Hispanics or Indians appear only as the enemy. It is no coincidence that throughout his term in office, when he was not memorializing the Texas Revolution or pursuing his legislative agenda, he was dealing (often in a very heavy-handed way) with the violent spillover of the 1910 Mexican Revolution into South Texas. Given those circumstances, Colquitt's enthusiasm for the Texas Revolution of 1835–36 could serve yet another contemporary political purpose: propagandizing against Mexicans.[53]

The Progressive-era version of Texas history quickly came to dominate the collective memory of Texans in the twentieth century. It found expression in the scholarly writings of Eugene C. Barker (who also made Stephen F. Austin the pivotal figure in Texas history) and of several succeeding generations of Texas historians. While this version may have been a very "usable" past, at least for progressive Anglo male elites, the triumphalism of the heroic revolutionary past also left Texans with a highly sanitized collective memory, in which Texas' Hispanic past was largely forgotten and the state's subsequent stake in slavery, secession, and racial injustice was glossed over. Texas emerged in the public consciousness of the Progressive era as a quintessentially western and American state. Even today, as academic historians include these overlooked aspects of the state's past in their scholarly writings, the dominant symbols—and hence the dominant public memories—of Texas history continue to be western symbols: the pioneer (symbolizing self-sufficiency), the Alamo (valor), the cowboy (rugged individualism), and the wildcatter (entrepreneurial spirit).[54]

We can only speculate whether Texans a century from now will still find a usable past in a version of Texas history fashioned by Oscar B. Colquitt's generation. In the meantime (to borrow a line from the Civil War), Stephen F. Austin's bones may lie a-mouldering in the grave, but his "truth"—as interpreted by early-twentieth-century Texans—keeps marching on.

NOTES

1. *Austin Statesman,* Oct. 19, 1910; *Galveston Daily News,* Oct. 19, 1910. Following the disinterment and reburial of Austin's remains, Guy Bryan Jr. privately published a pamphlet entitled *Account of the Removal of the Remains of Stephen F. Austin from Peach Point Cemetery in Brazoria County, Texas to State Cemetery, Austin, Texas, October 18 to 20, 1910* (Houston: Gray, Dillaye & Co., ca. 1911). It contains the following documents: the report of the joint legislative committee's official 1910 report on the event; the *Galveston Daily News's* coverage of Oct. 19, 1910; the *Houston Post's* coverage of Oct. 20 and 21, 1910; the *Austin Statesman's* coverage of Oct. 20, 1910; the addresses of Alexander W. Terrell and Rev. R. J. Briggs in the senate chamber on Oct. 19, 1910; the account of services held at Austin College in Sherman on Oct. 17, 1910; S. P. Etheridge's essay, "Stephen F. Austin, a Business Man," originally published in the *Houston Post,* Oct. 16, 1910; and the legislative reports pertaining to the appropriation of state funds for the statue by Pompeo Coppini that was commissioned for the gravesite. For convenience, all citations to the newspaper sources that are reproduced in this pamphlet will be cited hereafter as *Account of the Removal.*

2. *Account of the Removal,* 7–8.

3. Quotations in ibid., 8; Hally Bryan Perry to Alexander W. Terrell, Oct. 23, 1910, Alexander W. Terrell Papers, Center for American History, University of Texas at Austin (cited hereafter as CAH). Family members had predicted that since Austin was buried in a simple pine coffin, there would be nothing left of the body, and they were pleasantly surprised to find the skeleton intact (see Hally Bryan Perry to Alexander W. Terrell, Oct. 10, 1910, Terrell Papers, CAH).

4. See Walter L. Buenger, "Texas and the South," *Southwestern Historical Quarterly* 103 (Jan. 2000): 309–24; and Buenger, *The Path to a Modern South: Northeast Texas between Reconstruction and the Great Depression* (Austin: University of Texas Press, 2001), esp. 130, 258–60. In support of his thesis, Buenger cites such things as the upsurge in the observance of Texas Independence Day and San Jacinto Day in the years after 1910 and the elaborate celebrations of the centennial of the revolution in 1936. Buenger's evidence is limited mainly to the section of northeast Texas that was the focus of his research. The present chapter expands Buenger's analysis to other parts of the state and particularly to events transpiring in the state capital and the halls of government.

5. Like Frederick Jackson Turner, I view the terms western and American as essentially interchangeable. The idea of the West in American culture—unlike the idea of the South—has enjoyed lasting appeal precisely because the West and the frontier have seemed to embody quintessential American values such as courage, individualism, entrepreneurialism, and unrestrained freedom. Thus, to say that Progressive-era Texans embraced a western past is to say they also embraced an American past—and vice versa.

6. Quotations from Alon Confino, "Collective Memory and Cultural History: Problems of Method," *American Historical Review* 102 (Dec. 1997): 1386; Jan Assmann, "Collective Memory and Cultural Identity," *New German Critique* 65 (Spring/Summer 1995): 132; W. Fitzhugh Brundage, "No Deed But Memory," in *Where These Memories Grow: History, Memory,*

and Southern Identity, ed. W. Fitzhugh Brundage (Chapel Hill: University of North Carolina Press, 2000), 9–10. See also John Bodnar, *Remaking America: Public Memory, Commemoration, and Patriotism in the Twentieth Century* (Princeton, N.J.: Princeton University Press, 1992), esp. chap. 1. Terminology for this concept remains in flux. Of the scholars cited above, Confino and Brundage use the term "collective memory," Assmann prefers "cultural memory," and Bodnar writes of "public memory."

7. Henderson Yoakum's two-volume history, published in 1855, respectfully acknowledges Austin's importance as the first empresario but essentially stops there. In his one-paragraph summation of Austin's services to Texas, Yoakum argues that the empresario laid "the foundation of a great state," but this assertion is a far cry from the hero worship that would characterize twentieth-century accounts (Henderson Yoakum, *History of Texas from Its First Settlement in 1685 to Its Annexation to the United States in 1846,* 2 vols. [New York: Redfield, 1855], 2:202–203). Jacob De Cordova's *Texas: Her Resources and Her Public Men* (1858) combined almanac-like information with ads for land and biographical sketches of seventeen of Texas' "leading men." At the hands of De Cordova, Austin receives no mention at all. See De Cordova, *Texas: Her Resources and Her Public Men* (Philadelphia: E. Crozet, 1858), 127–87. In his well-known two-volume *History of Texas* (1892), John Henry Brown argued that Austin was not deserving of the "Father of Texas" title. Portraying Austin as simply one of many empresarios, Brown states that Austin's biographers "have attributed to him merit that he did not possess" (Brown, *History of Texas, 1820–1895,* 2 vols. [Saint Louis, Mo.: L. E. Daniell, 1892], 114–17). An extreme example of the lack of respect for Austin can be found in a curious literary work by one Victor M. Rose, entitled *Stephen F. Austin in the Balances* (ca. 1890). Born in 1842, Rose served in the Confederate army and later became a newspaper editor, poet, and historian. *Stephen F. Austin in the Balances* is a ten-page poem that viciously castigates Austin as a rapacious, pro-Mexican coward. Rose appends anonymous letters from "Old Texians" testifying that Texas would have lost the revolution if Stephen Austin had remained in command and that Austin saved all the best lands in Texas for himself. "Austin was a selfish, narrow-minded and jealous-hearted man. He lacked the essential elements of greatness in character," one of these letters reported (Rose, *Stephen F. Austin in the Balances* [n.p., ca. 1890], n.p.). The source of Rose's spleen cannot be stated with any certainty; see Craig H. Roell, "Victor Marion Rose," in *The New Handbook of Texas,* ed. Ron Tyler et al., 6 vols. (Austin: Texas State Historical Association, 1996), 4:678–79. For a discussion of the fate of Austin's public reputation in the decades following his death, see Gregg Cantrell, *Stephen F. Austin, Empresario of Texas* (New Haven, Conn.: Yale University Press, 1999), 367–79.

8. Richard Coke to Guy M. Bryan, July 22, 1875, Guy M. Bryan Papers, CAH. This portrait was later destroyed by fire, and when the new capitol was built in the 1880s, the Bryans donated a new portrait of Austin to the state. See "Extract from the Journal of the House of Representatives, Relating to the Presentation to the State of Texas of the Portrait of Stephen F. Austin," Twenty-first Legislature, 1889, CAH.

9. The state did not acquire the painting until forty years later. See Sam DeShong Ratcliffe, *Painting Texas History to 1900* (Austin: University of Texas Press, 1992), xx, 14–15, 103. Also see "The Settlement of Austin's Colony" and accompanying correspondence, typescripts in Guy M. Bryan Papers, CAH.

10. Ratcliffe, *Painting Texas History to 1900,* xx, 14–15, 103; quotation from "The Settlement of Austin's Colony" and accompanying correspondence, typescripts in Guy M. Bryan Papers, CAH.

11. Emily Fourmy Cutrer, *The Art of the Woman: The Life and Work of Elisabet Ney* (Lincoln: University of Nebraska Press, 1988), 126, 132, 137, 139–42, 147 (quotation), 181–84.

12. Ibid., 185, 194–96. Following their success with the state capitol statues, Dibrell and

the DRT mounted a second campaign to have the two statues reproduced for placement in the National Statuary Hall at the Capitol in Washington, D.C. This campaign also encountered difficulties, particularly from senior statesman John H. Reagan, who objected to the Houston statue, ostensibly on the grounds that Houston was depicted in "Indian apparel," but more likely because Reagan still bore bitterness toward Houston for opposing secession in 1861. Despite Reagan's opposition, the Daughters succeeded in their campaign, and the new pair of statues was completed in 1904. See Cutrer, *The Art of the Woman,* 197–99 (Reagan quotation, 198), 205–206. See also "The Stephen F. Austin Statue Fund," *Quarterly of the Texas State Historical Association* 5 (July 1901): 68–69.

13. The first of these efforts came in 1852, when the state legislature actually passed a joint resolution providing for the removal of Austin's remains to the State Cemetery. It appears that opposition from the Austin family prevented the action from taking place. See Fourth Legislature, Joint Resolution No. 15, Jan. 15, 1852 (Texas State Archives, Austin); Martha Doty Freeman, "History of the Texas State Cemetery," in *Confederate Veterans at Rest: Archeological and Bioarcheological Investigations at the Texas State Cemetery, Travis County, Texas,* ed. Helen Danzeiser Dockall et al. (Austin: Texas Parks and Wildlife Department, 1996), 25. The second effort came at the very end of the nineteenth century, in 1899, when Guy Bryan wrote to the governor, again seeking to have the remains moved to Austin. Bryan again apparently incurred the wrath of his Brazoria County relatives, who objected to his contention that the "Peach Point graveyard may be neglected in the future." Whether or not the relatives' objections or some other obstacle prevented the reinterment this time, it did not take place. See Guy M. Bryan to "Jimmy," Apr. 25, 1899, copy of typescript letter in the author's possession. I am grateful to Paul Gervais Bell of Houston for sharing a copy of this family letter with me.

14. Quotation in *Account of the Removal,* 2. Guy Bryan died in 1901, and the effort to have Austin reburied in Austin languished until the end of the decade. His son, Guy M. Bryan Jr., apparently renewed the effort. Bryan was assisted by elder statesman Alexander W. Terrell, an aficionado of Texas history and personal friend of the Austin-Bryan family. Although Terrell had stepped down from the legislature in 1905, he still had great influence in the halls of the state government. See Hally B. Perry to Alexander W. Terrell, Sept. 7, 1910; Beauregard Bryan to Alexander W. Terrell, Sept. 9, 1910; and Guy M. Bryan Jr. to Alexander W. Terrell, Sept. 15, 1910, all in Terrell papers, CAH.

15. *Account of the Removal,* 10.

16. *Houston Post,* Oct. 19, 1910; *Account of the Removal,* 11, 14–17; quotations from *Galveston Daily News,* Oct. 18, 1910; and Beauregard Bryan to Alexander W. Terrell, Oct. 25, 1910, Terrell Papers, CAH.

17. Colquitt had won the Democratic nomination for governor three months earlier and would win the general election three weeks later against token opposition. Busy assembling his administration and preparing for the upcoming legislative session, he appointed his son and campaign manager, Rawlins M. Colquitt, to represent him in the funeral cortege from the train station to the capitol. It is unclear whether he was present for the main services on the night of the nineteenth or the burial on the twentieth. See *Account of the Removal,* 18–19.

18. First quotation from *Galveston Daily News,* Oct. 20, 1910; *Account of the Removal,* 6, 13–14, 18–21, 36–38 (Briggs quotation, 37).

19. *Account of the Removal,* 6, 14.

20. Ibid., 5, 9, 10, 11, 14–17, 38 (Eagle quotations, 17; Briggs quotations, 38); Curry quoted in *Austin Statesman,* Sept. 11, 1910.

21. *Account of the Removal,* 11–13.

22. Ibid., 41–48.

23. Ibid., 15, 20 (flag quotations), 31, 32 (Terrell quotation).

24. Texas House of Representatives, House Journal, 32d Leg., reg. sess., 1911, 87–88, 204, 256, 623, 724, 774–75. Quotations from the full text of the bill in *General Laws of the State of Texas*, 32d Leg., reg. sess, 1911 (Austin, Tex.: Austin Printing Co., 1911), 24.

25. The most comprehensive source on Colquitt is George Portal Huckaby, "Oscar Branch Colquitt: A Political Biography" (Ph.D. diss., University of Texas, 1946). Huckaby concisely summarizes Colquitt's progressive achievements and the role that prohibition played in perceptions of those achievements (476). See also Lewis L. Gould, *Progressives and Prohibitionists: Texas Democrats in the Wilson Era* (Austin: University of Texas Press, 1973), 86–88.

26. Colquitt summarized the achievements of his administration in his farewell address to the legislature in January 1915, an address that ran forty-six printed pages. See House Journal, 34th Leg., reg. sess, 1915, 35–81. For a catalog of his achievements in historical preservation, see 68–69.

27. Brundage, "No Deed But Memory," 11, citing Michel Foucault, *Language, Counter-Memory, Practice: Selected Essays and Interviews,* ed. Donald F. Bouchard (Ithaca, N.Y.: Cornell University Press, 1993), 150; David W. Blight, "W. E. B. Du Bois and the Struggle for American Historical Memory," in *History and Memory in African American Culture,* ed. Geneviève Fabre and Robert O'Meally (New York: Oxford University Press, 1994), 68n16.

28. On the Colquitt-Coppini relationship, see Pompeo Coppini to O. B. Colquitt, July 25, 1911, June 26, 1912, Feb. 28, 1913; Pompeo Coppini to J. H. Kirkpatrick, Aug. 29, 1911; Pompeo Coppini to A. B. Conley, June 20, July 16, 1912; Pompeo Coppini to J. T. Bowman, July 16, 1912, all in Coppini-Tauch Papers, CAH.

On the role of Guy M. Bryan Jr. and other Austin family members, see A. P. Wooldridge to Pompeo Coppini, July 19, 1911; Beauregard Bryan to A. P. Wooldridge, July 31, 1911; Guy M. Bryan Jr. to Pompeo Coppini, Sept. 2, 1911, June 6, 1912; Pompeo Coppini to A. B. Conley, Sept. 12, 1911, June 20, 1912; Pompeo Coppini to Guy M. Bryan Jr., Sept. 19, Dec. 8, 1911, June 8, Aug. 23, 1912, all in Coppini-Tauch Papers, CAH; Lewis R. Bryan to A. W. Terrell, Sept. 28, Nov. 24, 1911, Jan. 26, 1912, Terrell Papers, CAH; and Guy M. Bryan Jr. to O. B. Colquitt, Jan. 6, 1912; O. B. Colquitt to Guy M. Bryan Jr., Feb. 13, 1912; O. B. Colquitt to J. P. Bryan, Oct. 28, 1912, all in Records of the Governor, O. B. Colquitt, Archives and Information Services Division, Texas State Library and Archives Commission, Austin (cited hereafter as Colquitt Papers, TSLAC).

On the process of choosing a design for the statue, see "Conception for the Stephen Austin Monument by P. Coppini sculptor," undated typescript; A. B. Conley to Pompeo Coppini, Nov. 28, Dec. 9, 1911, June 25, July 17, Aug. 3, 1912; Pompeo Coppini to A. B. Conley, Dec. 12, 1911, June 20, 1912, all in Coppini-Tauch Papers, CAH; Pompeo Coppini to O. B. Colquitt, Jan. 28, Mar. 2, 10, 20, 1912; O. B. Colquitt to Clarence Ousley, Feb. 16, 1912; O. B. Colquitt to Pompeo Coppini, Mar. 5, 11, 21, 27, 1912, all in Colquitt Papers, TSLAC; *San Antonio Express,* Mar. 27, 1912; Pompeo Coppini to O. B. Colquitt, June 26, Aug. 6, 23, 1912; J. T. Bowman to Pompeo Coppini, July 1, 1912; O. B. Colquitt to Pompeo Coppini, Oct. 9, 1912, all in Coppini-Tauch Papers, CAH. The governor's advisory committee on the statue consisted of John R. Lunsford of the *San Antonio Express,* C. L. Lombardi of the *Dallas Morning News,* R. M. Johnson of the *Houston Post,* Clarence Ousley of the *Fort Worth Record,* and George Robinson of the *Waco Herald.* See Pompeo Coppini, *From Dawn to Sunset* (San Antonio: Naylor, 1949), 200.

29. Pompeo Coppini to O. B. Colquitt, June 26, 1912; Pompeo Coppini to Guy M. Bryan Jr., Aug. 23, 1912; Pompeo Coppini to A. B. Conley, Aug. 23, 1912; William J. O'Connor to Pompeo Coppini, Dec. 5, 1912, all in Coppini-Tauch Papers, CAH; Coppini, *From Dawn to Sunset,* 200.

30. *San Antonio Express,* Oct. 20, 21, 1910; Coppini, *From Dawn to Sunset,* 173; quota-

tions from *Dallas Morning News,* Oct. 20, 1910; Joe Tom Davis, *Historic Towns of Texas,* 3 vols. (Austin, Tex.: Eakin Press, 1992), 2:67. The formal title of the Coppini statue is *The Texas Heroes Monument.*

31. Lewis Bryan, admittedly not an impartial observer, opined that "the ceremonies were not as impressive as those at Austin last October, nor were they as interesting and instructive in the matter dealth [*sic*] with by the speakers" (text and note quotation, L. R. Bryan to A. W. Terrell, May 1, 1911, Terrell Papers, CAH). The "Program of Exercises" for the April 21, 1911, event can be found in the collection of the Sam Houston Memorial Museum, Huntsville, Tex.

32. Message of Gov. O. B. Colquitt to the Legislature, Feb. 25, 1913, House Journal, 32d Leg., reg. sess., 1913, 650–51; Pompeo Coppini to O. B. Colquitt, Feb. 28, 1913, Coppini-Tauch Papers, CAH; O. B. Colquitt to Pompeo Coppini, Nov. 20, 1914, Colquitt Papers, TSLAC. For Colquitt's fundraising efforts for the Troutman statue, see various drafts of letters from O. B. Colquitt addressed to "Dear Sir," ca. 1913, in Colquitt Papers, TSLAC.

33. For Ward's speech, see Texas Senate, Senate Journal, 32d Leg., reg. sess., 1911, 421–24. The text of the final bill can be found in *General Laws of the State of Texas,* 32d Leg., reg. sess., 1911 (Austin, Tex.: Austin Printing Co., 1911), 26.

34. Quotation from Freeman, "History of the Texas State Cemetery," 3; *Austin Statesman,* Apr. 6, 1913; Senate Journal, 34th Leg., reg. sess., 1915, 68.

35. Message from the Governor, Jan. 12, 1915, in Senate Journal, 34th Leg., reg. sess., 1915, 68 (quotation), 69; *General Laws of the State of Texas,* 32d Leg., reg. sess, 1911 (Austin, Tex.: Austin Printing Co., 1911), 112; *General Laws of the State of Texas,* 30th Leg., reg. sess. (Austin, Tex.: Austin Printing Co., 1907), 104–106; James Wright Steely, *Parks for Texas: Enduring Landscapes of the New Deal* (Austin: University of Texas Press, 1999), 208. The legislature's Goliad bill erroneously referred to the "LaBahia Mission property near Goliad, where Colonel Fannin and his men were imprisoned." Fannin and his men were imprisoned not in a mission but rather in the Loreto Chapel at the Presidio La Bahía. Colquitt visited the presidio personally and met with officials of the Catholic Church, which owned the site, but they declined to sell it to the state. The state did accept the donation of the Fannin battlefield from its private owner, and Colquitt spent five thousand dollars in state funds to fence and improve the property. In the case of the Gonzales site, in 1958 the state deemed it "unsuitable for a state park" and returned the property to the city of Gonzales. See Land Conservation Program, Acquisition Files, "Gonzales State Park," Texas Parks and Wildlife Department, Austin. I am grateful to Cynthia Brandimarte of the Texas Parks and Wildlife Department for furnishing me with these documents.

36. Buenger, "Texas and the South," 315; Randy Roberts and James S. Olson, *A Line in the Sand: The Alamo in Blood and Memory* (New York: Free Press, 2001), 206–209; L. Robert Ables, "The Second Battle for the Alamo," *Southwestern Historical Quarterly* 70 (Jan. 1967): 377–82. Driscoll married Henry H. Sevier in 1906 and henceforth was generally referred to as "Mrs. Hal Sevier" in the documents cited in this essay. However, since she later divorced and reclaimed her maiden name (by which she is remembered today), I have chosen to refer to her by that name. On Driscoll, see Dorothy D. DeMoss, "Clara Driscoll," *The New Handbook of Texas,* ed. Tyler et al., 2:702–703.

37. Roberts and Olson, *A Line in the Sand,* 209–12, 213 (Driscoll quotation); Ables, "The Second Battle of the Alamo," 382–409 (legislation quoted on 382n42).

38. Adina De Zavala to O. B. Colquitt, Aug. 21, 25 (quotation), 1911, Adina De Zavala Papers, CAH.

39. O. B. Colquitt to Adina De Zavala, Sept. 20, Dec. 1 (quotation), 1911, De Zavala Papers, CAH.

40. *Dallas Morning News,* Dec. 31, 1911.

41. Ibid.

42. Holly Beachley Brear, "We Run the Alamo, and You Don't: Alamo Battles of Ethnicity and Gender," in *Where These Memories Grow: History, Memory, and Southern Identity,* ed. W. Fitzhugh Brundage (Chapel Hill: University of North Carolina Press, 2000), 299–317, esp. 300–304 (Jones quotation, 301); Ballinger quotation from Elizabeth Hayes Turner, *Women, Culture, and Community: Religion and Reform in Galveston, 1880–1920* (New York: Oxford University Press, 1997), 170. Turner's book (see esp. 168–83) gives an excellent summation of the ideologies of women's patriotic societies, including the DRT, for this era. For an account that places these societies in the broader context of women's history in the postbellum South, see W. Fitzhugh Brundage, "White Women and the Politics of Historical Memory in the New South, 1880–1920," in *Jumpin' Jim Crow: Southern Politics from Civil War to Civil Rights,* ed. Jane Dailey, Glenda Gilmore, and Bryant Simon (Princeton, N.J.: Princeton University Press, 2000), 115–39.

43. Brear, "We Run the Alamo," 304; subsequent quotations from *Dallas Morning News,* Dec. 31, 1911.

44. Quotations from *Dallas Morning News,* Dec. 31, 1911.

45. *Austin Statesman,* Nov. 17, 1914 (quotations); *San Antonio Express,* Nov. 19, 1914; *San Antonio Light,* Nov. 19, 1914. The Daughters' protest was technically correct, inasmuch as there were several flags of various designs all featuring one five-pointed star in use in the fall of 1835; Troutman's was merely one of these. Furthermore, the James Long filibustering expedition of 1819 had flown a flag with thirteen stripes and a lone star fifteen years prior to the Texas Revolution. None of these flags was the design that would later become the modern state flag of Texas. See Robert Maberry Jr., *Texas Flags* (College Station: Texas A&M University Press, 2001), 21–33.

46. *Austin Statesman,* Apr. 29, 1913; Olson and Roberts, *A Line in the Sand,* 213–14; Ables, "Second Battle of the Alamo," 411–12. The litigation between the DRT and the state can be followed through a series of clippings from various newspapers in the Oscar Branch Colquitt Papers, Box 2E199, CAH. For another valuable source of information, see "Alamo Property" folders dated Oct. 4, 1905, through June 17, 1913, in the Colquitt Papers, TSLAC. These folders include court documents and Colquitt–De Zavala correspondence. Colquitt himself submitted a lengthy compilation of documents pertaining to the Alamo as a message to the legislature. See *Message of Governor O. B. Colquitt to the Thirty-third Legislature Relating to the Alamo Property* (Austin, Tex.: Von Boeckmann–Jones, 1913).

47. *Austin Statesman,* Apr. 29, 1913; various clippings, dated 1913, in the UDC Scrapbook, CAH; *Catalogue of the Confederate Museum Maintained by the United Daughters of the Confederacy, Texas Division, 1935,* CAH; Retta Preston, "Texas Confederate Museum," *The New Handbook of Texas,* ed. Tyler et al., 6:308. Colquitt's public dispute with the UDC becomes even more striking when we realize that his wife Alice was president of the UDC's Austin chapter. The *Austin Statesman* commented on this fact, noting that Mrs. Colquitt's prominence in the organization "has added a delicate and complicating phase to the entire matter." She prudently recused herself from the group's deliberations on the controversy. See *Austin Statesman,* May 1, 1913.

48. Kelly McMichael Stott, "From Lost Cause to Female Empowerment: The Texas Division of the United Daughters of the Confederacy, 1896–1966" (Ph.D. diss., University of North Texas, 2001), 116, 121 (1st quotation), 126, 133 (subsequent quotations). Two works that consider the Lost Cause and its values in the South as a whole are Charles Reagan Wilson's *Baptized in Blood: The Religion of the Lost Cause, 1865–1920* (Athens: University of Georgia Press, 1980), esp. chap. 4; and Gaines M. Foster's *Ghosts of the Confederacy: Defeat, the Lost Cause, and*

the Emergence of the New South, 1865 to 1913 (New York: Oxford University Press, 1987), esp. chap. 12.

49. Stott, "From Lost Cause to Female Empowerment," 95–98.

50. House Journal, 33d Leg., reg. sess., 1913, 1913–1914, 1967–1968, 1973; quotation from *San Antonio Express,* Apr. 2, 1913.

51. Colquitt quoted in Huckaby, "Oscar Branch Colquitt," 292. For the movement to censor textbooks with an "anti-southern" bias, see Fred A. Bailey, "Free Speech and the 'Lost Cause' in Texas: A Study of Censorship and Social Control in the New South," *Southwestern Historical Quarterly* 97 (Jan., 1994): 433–78.

52. Assmann, "Collective Memory," 133.

53. For a perceptive look at how anti-Mexican attitudes affected collective memory in Progressive-era Texas, see James E. Crisp, "An Incident in San Antonio: The Contested Iconology of Davy Crockett's Death at the Alamo," *Journal of the West* 40 (Spring 2001): 67–77. For Colquitt's aggressive policies in dealing with the Mexican Revolution, see Don M. Coerver and Linda B. Hall, *Texas and the Mexican Revolution: A Study in State and National Border Policy, 1910–1920* (San Antonio: Trinity University Press, 1984).

54. In a provocative critique of the Bob Bullock Texas State History Museum, which opened in Austin on April 21, 2001, Buenger argues that the Progressive-era mindset still dominates public depictions of Texas history. See Walter L. Buenger, "'The Story of Texas'? The Texas State History Museum and Forgetting and Remembering the Past," *Southwestern Historical Quarterly* 105 (Jan. 2002): 481–93.

Chapter 3

MEMORY, TRUTH, AND PAIN: MYTH AND CENSORSHIP IN THE CELEBRATION OF TEXAS HISTORY

JAMES E. CRISP

What should we do when we are embarrassed by our history? Before we can begin to answer this question, we must untangle its many possible meanings. There are events in the past that are so painful to contemplate—deeds that are so sordid—that our first impulse is to turn our heads away in revulsion and shame for the human race. But if the philosopher George Santayana's warning has merit—if we are indeed condemned to repeat the past if we fail to remember it—then we must turn our gaze back toward the unwanted truths and face the facts. But the word "history," and thus our initial question, has a double meaning. Sometimes it is not so much the actual events of the past but the narratives that have been crafted about those events that are the source of our embarrassment. Historical narratives, in Texas as elsewhere, contribute to the collective memories by which the very identity of an "imagined community" is established and maintained.[1]

Teaching Texas history is a way of answering the question: "What does it mean to be Texan?" When Texans in the twenty-first century contemplate the historical narratives produced in the previous century and a half, the result is sometimes more than merely embarrassing. For those who discover that they and their ancestors have been virtually written out of Texas history or portrayed in ways that effectively deny their identity as "Texans," the effect can be quite painful. More often than not, that loss of "full historical citizenship" results from their membership in an ascribed category defined by race, nationality, or ethnicity. Through explicit statements, and implicitly by the omission of essential information, the assumptions and interpretations embedded in many traditional Texas historical narratives can raise in particularly uncomfortable ways the question of what we should do when we are embarrassed by our history. This question becomes especially pointed when those narratives are written in stone.

Written in Stone is the apt title chosen by Sanford Levinson, professor of law at the University of Texas at Austin, for his 1998 book subtitled *Public Monuments in Changing Societies.* Though Levinson pauses long enough in the vicinity of the fallen communist states to wonder whether it is "Stalinist" to tear down a statue of Stalin, most of his analysis focuses on the American South and particularly upon the struggles over public monuments (and of course, flags) that commemorate the Confederacy, its heirs, and its defenders.[2]

Levinson's two most prominent case studies come from Louisiana and Texas: "officially privileged narrative[s]" written in stone on the Liberty Monument in New Orleans and on the Memorial to the Confederate Dead on the grounds of the state capitol in Austin.[3] The Liberty Monument, a gleaming obelisk that once bore a plaque celebrating the return of white supremacy, was erected in 1891 to celebrate a battle fought in New Orleans in 1874 between members of the so-called White League and the supporters (both black and white) of the Republican Reconstruction government of Louisiana. After the fall of the Republican administration, the New Orleans City Council authorized in November 1882 the erection of a monument in honor of the eleven members of the White League "who fell in defense of liberty and home rule." A little more than a century later, following strenuous but unsuccessful efforts in the 1980s by two African American mayors of New Orleans to remove the offending obelisk, the Liberty Monument was moved to a less prominent location and its text revised to honor "both sides" of "a conflict of the past which should teach us lessons for the future"—though the nature of this conflict and its lessons were left unexplained.[4]

Unlike the Louisiana example, there is a studied avoidance of racial themes (including any reference to slavery) in the narrative engraved in 1901 on the Memorial to the Confederate Dead in Austin, which asserts that the honored Confederates, "animated by the spirit of 1776," had "died for state rights guaranteed under the constitution." The inscription explains that when "the North resorted to coercion, the South, against overwhelming numbers and resources, fought until exhausted." Above the pedestal of the monument are statues of four Confederate servicemen (from the artillery, infantry, cavalry, and navy). Between these figures, rising from the center, is the commanding seven-and-one-half-feet-tall form of Confederate president Jefferson Davis.[5]

Professor Levinson, provoked by a public monument that obfuscates the racial realities of the past even while challenging the racial sensibilities of the present, has outlined nine possible solutions for dealing with this problematical Memorial to the Confederate Dead, ranging from doing nothing at all to blowing it to smithereens. Though he has considered the options of sandblasting and/or revising the tendentious text using methods similar to those employed in New Orleans, Levinson's preferred solution is to balance the memorial's message with other monuments on the capitol grounds that would commemorate both the sufferings and the accomplishments of African Texans.[6]

Considering the question strictly as a legal matter, Levinson concludes after a lengthy examination of the implications of the Fourteenth Amendment that no one's constitutional rights are violated by such public Confederate monuments, nor even by the flying of Confederate pennants or neo-Confederate state flags on government buildings. But Levinson argues that as a matter of "political decency" such banners should be relegated to museums and to appropriate historic sites, where their display will not suggest the state's approbation of the policies or the beliefs of the past.[7]

In a review of Robert Maberry's superb book, *Texas Flags,* Prof. Robert E. Bonner of Michigan State University claims that "one can hardly ignore the whiff of conflict in the Confederate flags displayed in [Maberry's] book or fail to recognize the potential for controversy inherent in a Lone Star emblem that was also born in bloodshed." Without answering the question that he raises, Bonner notes that "it is worth considering why Texas symbols have not evoked protests against Anglo hegemony and violent territorial expansion."[8]

Professor Bonner should perhaps take another look at the twentieth-century history of the Alamo as a fiercely contested Texan symbol, but I will leave it to my anthropologist colleagues Richard Flores and Holly Brear to educate him on this particular point.[9]

As to the relative innocuousness of the Lone Star flag that was adopted by the Texas Republic in 1839 and serves as the state flag of Texas today, one important difference from the Confederate case may be especially relevant. Though the point has often been obscured in popular histories of the Texas Revolution, "Anglo hegemony" did not play the central and monolithic role in the birth of the Texas Republic that "white supremacy" did for the Confederacy.[10]

It is worth remembering that sitting in the 1839 Texan congress that adopted the present state flag as the official flag of the republic was one of the few Texans who was a veteran of both the Alamo's defense and the victory over Santa Anna at San Jacinto—Senator Juan N. Seguín of San Antonio (who was at the time chair of the republic's Senate Committee on Military Affairs, though he did not speak English). Despite recent claims—much overblown—of thousands of armed "black Confederates" aiding the South's military effort during the Civil War, the idea of an African American sitting as a member of the Confederate congress would have been considered both appalling and ludicrous to the secessionists. Yet Seguín and other Tejanos—Texans of Mexican ancestry—played important military and political roles in the both the Texas Revolution and the Republic of Texas.[11]

All this is not to say that Texas has been spared efforts to suppress or revise embarrassing versions of its early history, especially where racial matters are concerned. A case in point is a Texas icon that, like the Memorial to the Confederate Dead in Austin, combines both narrative and art. I am referring to *Texas History Movies,* a cartoon version of the state's past that Larry McMurtry once described as "the weirdest western [history] textbook ever published" and that *Texas Monthly* magazine called "the second most influential Texas book of the twentieth century." McMurtry, author of the book that topped the magazine's list of Texas books of the century (his Pulitzer Prize–winning novel *Lonesome Dove*), stated that "the ranking was clearly wrong." He argues that *Texas History Movies* deserves first place instead because its memorable images "stopped two generations of Texas public school students dead in their tracks where history is concerned." Half a century after encountering these cartoons in the schools of his native Archer City, says McMurtry, he still "can't shake the conviction that Sam Houston, Santa Anna, and other luminaries of Lone Star history must have looked just as they appeared in *Texas History Movies.*"[12]

The strange career of *Texas History Movies* may be one of the most vivid examples of what Walter Buenger and Robert Calvert have identified as the unusually long "shelf life of [historical] truth in Texas." This whimsical and engaging comic-book narrative of the Texan past was created by two young staffers of the *Dallas Morning News*—with Jack Patton drawing the cartoons and John Rosenfield Jr. providing the brief captions. Patton and Rosenfield, both born in 1900, each went on to long and distinguished careers with the *Dallas Morning News.* Patton illustrated stories in the newspaper until his retirement in 1961. Rosenfield served as the newspaper's music and drama critic for forty-one years, from 1925 until 1966, becoming in that capacity (according to *The New Handbook of Texas*) "the recognized cultural spokesman for the Southwest."[13]

The hundreds of original cartoon panels, which first appeared in serialized form in 1926 in the *Dallas Morning News,* were published as an oversized book in 1928. They were an instant hit with both teachers and students of Texas history, and from that time until the early 1960s a small paperback edition of *Texas History Movies* was made available each year to seventh-graders all over the state by the Magnolia Petroleum Company. According to Larry McMurtry, "The effect, not to mention the irreverence, of those comics would be hard to overstate."[14]

Texas History Movies did not linger over awkward subjects. In my own now-battered seventh-grade copy totaling 128 pages, secession and the Civil War got a page apiece, and the end of Reconstruction, half a page. (There was nothing at all on the substance of Reconstruction.) Given that the American annexation of Texas does not occur until page 123, the canonical meaning of "Texas history" becomes clear. Seventy-five pages were allotted to the settlement and winning of Texas by Anglo Americans between 1821 and 1846, and of the preceding fifty pages, well over half were devoted to various French and American explorers, pirates, and filibusterers.[15]

Spaniards and Mexicans overall got very short shrift, except where cruelty and butchery were involved. Fig. 3.1 portrays the violent suppression of domestic opposition to Mexican president Santa Anna in 1835, just prior to his march into Texas. Fig. 3.2 shows the cruel fate of the members of the 1841 Texan Santa Fe Expedition.[16]

FIG. 3.1. Portrayal of Mexican opposition to Santa Anna, *Texas History Movies.* Courtesy Texas State Historical Association, Austin.

FIG. 3.2. 1841 Texan Expedition to Santa Fe, *Texas History Movies.* Courtesy Texas State Historical Association, Austin.

Native Americans were essentially used for comic relief, as Fig 3.3 will attest.[17]

FIG. 3.3. Images of native Americans, *Texas History Movies.* Courtesy Texas State Historical Association, Austin.

African Americans received much the same treatment. The only such person identified by name in my copy of *Texas History Movies* was Richmond (see Fig. 3.4), the slave who accompanied Moses Austin on his first trip to Texas in 1820–21.[18]

FIG. 3.4. Treatment of African Americans, *Texas History Movies*. Courtesy Texas State Historical Association, Austin.

As shown by the energetic bayoneting of Mexican and Indian enemies of the Texas Republic in Fig. 3.5, *Texas History Movies* did not shy away from graphic violence. But it was the heavy-handed racial stereotyping in drawings and dialogue in a publication sponsored by a corporation that had become national—even global—in its reach and responsibilities that most likely brought about the book's demise. In 1961 the company that had be-

FIG. 3.5. Violence as a theme, *Texas History Movies*. Courtesy Texas State Historical Association, Austin.

come Mobil Oil stopped printing the book and turned over the paperback copyright to the Texas State Historical Association (TSHA).[19]

It was not long, however, before Texans demanded a return of their cartoons. Various firms that had gained the rights to the hardback edition brought out both unexpurgated and clumsily revised versions, neither of which were deemed suitable for the public schools. In 1974 the TSHA brought together a multiracial advisory board, which spent three months reviewing every single panel. In the words of TSHA editor George Ward, "Anything that was found to be offensive . . . was deleted or changed." Even the unfortunate feline, which had suffered a swift kick from an angry Spanish governor in the original *Texas History Movies,* had disappeared in the new edition (see Fig. 3.6).[20]

FIG. 3.6. Spanish governor's anger, before and after, *Texas History Movies.* Courtesy Texas State Historical Association, Austin.

Many panels were omitted altogether in the TSHA edition. Ironically, in this new version reviewed and approved by a multiracial board, virtually every image of an African American is gone. One or two survive with the individual's features literally "blacked out"—compare the original image of Moses Austin's slave Richmond with the "edited" version in Fig. 3.7. The cleaned-up TSHA edition contains less than a quarter of the original materials from the *Dallas Morning News* and fewer than half of the panels from my already-abridged seventh-grade paperback edition.[21]

Nevertheless, over the next decade, with the assistance of the Texas Educational Association, one hundred thousand copies of the radically revised cartoon book were sold and distributed under the title *Texas History Illustrated*

FIG. 3.7. Moses Austin's provider, before and after, *Texas History Movies*. Courtesy Texas State Historical Association, Austin.

by the TSHA. When the original title (though not the original content) was restored with a new printing in 1986, editor Ward happily announced that so far not a single complaint about the TSHA-sponsored booklet had been received.[22]

But in 1988 a complaint, or at least a lament, came from the prolific Texan historical cartoonist Jack Jackson, who felt that "much of the gusto— if not the essence—of the original" had been sacrificed in order to keep the book in the schools and, as he put it, "to bring it into line with modern ethnic perceptions." Certainly there is a loss of credibility as well as gusto when General Santa Anna's cry of "Yah! And they call themselves soldiers!" as his troopers are pushed back by the Alamo's defenders is replaced in the new version by the lame "OK! Let's try again!" (Fig. 3.8).[23]

There is a similar false note in the panel depicting fraternization (in the form of a game of horseshoes) between Spanish and American soldiers during the November 1812 siege of Goliad by the Gutiérrez-Magee expedition. When a Spaniard calls out, "Watch this ringer, Señor Bill," the politically correct American of the TSHA edition says, "I'm all eyes, friend." Patton and Rosenfield were closer to the intended message of male camaraderie when *their* brash Yankee rudely called back, "You're full of prunes, Pedro!" (Fig. 3.9).[24]

It is important to note that the creators of *Texas History Movies* spoke openly of their willingness to use "slang, colloquialism, modernisms, and

FIG. 3.8. Santa Anna's defiance, before and after, *Texas History Movies.* Courtesy Texas State Historical Association, Austin.

FIG. 3.9. Two versions of fraternization between soldiers, *Texas History Movies.* Courtesy Texas State Historical Association, Austin.

deliberate anachronisms" to capture what they believed to be "the spirit of an episode."[25]

Racial insult, however, rather than mere rudeness was the chief target of the TSHA reformers. In an analysis published in the January 1988 issue of *The Comics Journal,* Jack Jackson found that a comparison of the original *Texas History Movies* and its revisions revealed "not only the racism of the 1920s but [also] our present concern with expurgating all such tell-tale vestiges." Sometimes he found the results merely amusing; more often, they were for Jackson "closer to a nagging indictment of how squeamish we have become as a society, lest we give offense to anyone about anything." For Jackson, it was "difficult to view the modern product without a touch of sadness." From his perspective, the old version "told things much as they were, not as they should have been." The original version, he claimed, was "unvarnished history, not an exercise in progressive race relations."[26]

Here is where I part company with my friend Jack Jackson. No, despite their avowed desire to capture the spirit of early Texas history, Patton and Rosenfield were not simply producing "unvarnished history" that "told things as they were." One of the most valuable aspects of the original *Texas History Movies* is its utility in demonstrating how the racial ideologies and popular culture of the early twentieth century came together to produce a historical narrative every bit as tendentious and selective as the Memorial to the Confederate Dead—and as Larry McMurtry has suggested, one that has been far more influential than narratives written in stone.

In my own view, even the most galling of the old cartoons should be brought back into the classroom, not with the false promise of complete verisimilitude but as vivid examples of how our constructed "histories" both shape and reflect our collective identities. There are few documents that can show as vividly as the original *Texas History Movies* what most Anglo Texans took for granted with regard to race and ethnicity (and thus the "Texan" identity) in the first half of the twentieth century.[27]

Even the four outrageous panels depicting the nature of slavery in the early Texan colonies (Fig. 3.10) can be useful as a window into the casual assumptions of a century ago, when many academic as well as popular histories carried a strong dose of defense for the South's peculiar institution.[28]

The inquisitive student who attempts to document the account of humane legislation protecting slaves in Rosenfield's captions to these four panels will find that such provisions had been written into law by the legislature of the Mexican state of Coahuila y Tejas but were totally ignored by Anglo Texan slaveholders. On a more basic level, students who learn from their other texts about the skills and accomplishments of black Texans such as Nacogdoches linguist and businessman William Goyens may experience a moment of double awakening when they see that African Americans were routinely portrayed as buffoons in their grandparents' schoolbooks.[29]

To bring the point home, a reexamination of these once immensely popular cartoon panels from the *Dallas Morning News* of the 1920s might best proceed in tandem with a fresh look into the origins of two of the most

FIG. 3.10. Slavery in the early Texas colonies, *Texas History Movies*. Courtesy Texas State Historical Association, Austin.

racially problematic but currently "privileged" visual narratives of Texas history. These are the well-known early-twentieth-century paintings of the fall of the Alamo that hang today at the very heart of power and influence in the state: the Grand Foyer of the Texas Governor's Mansion and the senate chamber of the Texas capitol. One could easily argue that either one of these images has had a greater impact on the collective Texan memory (and thus on the Texan identity) than any textbook or academic history ever published in the state.

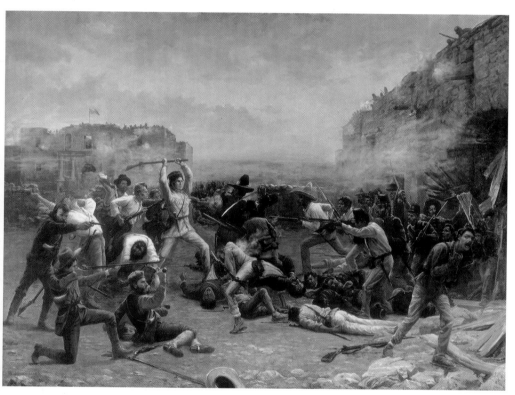

PLATE 1. *Fall of the Alamo,* by Robert Jenkins Onderdonk. Courtesy Friends of the Governor's Mansion, Austin.

PLATE 2. *Death of Dickinson,* by Theodore Gentilz. A Yanaguana Society gift, courtesy Daughters of the Republic of Texas Library.

PLATE 3. *Custer's Last Fight,* by Cassilly Adams, 1896 chromolithograph. Courtesy Amon Carter Museum, Fort Worth.

PLATE 4. *Dawn at the Alamo,* by Henry Arthur McArdle. Photographer Perry Huston, 8/3/94, Post Conservation, CHA 1989.81. Courtesy State Preservation Board, Austin.

When the artist Eric von Schmidt began research for his own enormous painting of the Battle of the Alamo—completed for the Texas Sesquicentennial of 1986—he found that the work of one of his predecessors had achieved a kind of "quasi-official" status in the state: *The Fall of the Alamo,* by Robert Jenkins Onderdonk (Plate 1). This canvas, originally known as *Crockett's Last Fight,* has since 1981 commanded the entrance hall of the Governor's Mansion in Austin.[30]

In 1999 I discovered from documents only recently made available to scholars that Onderdonk's painting had caused a near-riot among the Tejanos who viewed it when it was first displayed in San Antonio in 1903, where it also became the target of a surreptitious slasher who gashed several feet of the canvas. The specific area of the painting that was attacked (the lower right quadrant) depicts the Mexican soldiers pouring into the Alamo as a dark, menacing horde—an image very unlike renderings of the Mexican army done by most nineteenth-century Texan artists, who more often portrayed a neatly uniformed, light-complexioned, well-disciplined Mexican force.[31] (See, for example, Theodore Gentilz's *Death of Dickinson* [Plate 2].)

In addition to its frightful depiction of the Mexicans, Onderdonk's painting also contains a direct visual allusion, in the defiant central figure of Davy Crockett, to Gen. George Armstrong Custer's "last stand" against the Sioux at the Little Bighorn. Most viewers in San Antonio would have recognized Onderdonk's Crockett as a virtual mirror image of the doomed figure of General Custer in the battle scene that was at the turn of the twentieth century one of the most famous images in America. Cassily Adams painted *Custer's Last Fight* in the 1880s, and it had been lithographed in the late 1890s by the Anheuser-Busch Brewing Company and distributed to virtually every saloon in the country as an advertisement for Budweiser beer (see Plate 3).[32]

Perhaps not every visitor to the San Antonio gallery in 1903, however, would have realized that the beer company's lithograph also links Onderdonk's Alamo to yet another alleged instance of civilization's heroes overwhelmed by savagery: the destruction of British forces at Isandhlwana in the Anglo-Zulu war of the 1870s. In a bizarre anachronism, the lithographer Otto Becker added several Zulu warriors to *Custer's Last Fight.* Three or four of these Zulu fighters may be seen rushing, weapons drawn, toward General Custer's back.[33]

Onderdonk's painting of *Crockett's Last Fight* was an instant popular success, and soon his cross-town rival in San Antonio, the artist Henry A. McArdle, responded with his own version of the fall of the Alamo—one that matched the emotional power, if not the artistic subtlety, of Onderdonk's

FIG. 3.11. Preliminary sketch for *Dawn at the Alamo* (1874), by Henry Arthur McArdle. Courtesy Texas State Library and Archives Commission.

iconology. The Mexican soldiers in McArdle's massive 1905 *Dawn at the Alamo* (which now adorns the state capitol's senate chamber) have been described by one art historian as "plasticene, psychotic murderers" and by another as reflecting the artist's "Manichean vision of the combatants" as "two races that represent opposing forces in the painter's mind" (see Plate 4).[34]

One might also argue that the Mexican soldier who is about to drive a bayonet into the spine of the commanding figure of William Barret Travis atop the Alamo's rampart in McArdle's painting is closer to the artistic style of Jack Patton than to that of Robert Onderdonk. In researching the background of this painting, I was startled to learn that in McArdle's first version of this work (an extensive sketch done in the 1870s and now lost except for a photograph in the Texas State Archives), the figure of the menacing Mexican with the bayonet did not appear at all (see Fig. 3.11).

Capt. Reuben M. Potter, who wrote a very favorable critique of this first version in 1874, noted that "Travis is seen in a death grapple with a Mexican standard bearer, a struggle in which both are going down along with the banner which its bearer had vainly attempted to plant." In the original drawing, it is difficult to tell which figure is the Mexican standard bearer and which is Travis (see Fig. 3.12).[35]

Moreover, the attacking Mexicans in McArdle's original rendition of *Dawn at the Alamo* are neither bestialized nor dramatically darkened, unlike

FIG. 3.12. Detail of Travis and Crockett from preliminary sketch for *Dawn at the Alamo* (1874), by Henry Arthur McArdle. Courtesy Texas State Library and Archives Commission.

the brutes whose assault on Crockett and Travis now greets visitors to the Texas senate chamber. The face of the Mexican soldier who is struggling with the white-shirted David Crockett, just below and to the left of the Travis figure in the finished 1905 painting (see Plate 4), is, in the words of art critic Emily Fourmy Cutrer, "almost apelike in its ferociousness and stupidity."[36]

Why had McArdle's portrayal of Mexicans undergone such a drastic change in the intervening years? Could the evolving portrayal of Mexican soldiers in Texan historical art as shown by the contrasting works of Gentilz and Onderdonk (Plates 2 and 1, respectively)—or by the very different styles revealed in McArdle's two attempts to capture on canvas the essence of the Alamo's meaning (Figs. 3.11 and 3.12 and Plate 4)—reflect a deterioration of relations between Anglos and Mexicans in Texas as the nineteenth century gave way to the twentieth?[37]

This conclusion is bolstered by the research of anthropologist Richard Flores and historian David Montejano into the development (and manipulation) of Texan historical narratives, both written and symbolic, during precisely these years. Flores and Montejano have argued that a "great transformation" accompanied the arrival of railroads and the introduction of commercial agriculture (and with the latter a high demand for cheap seasonal labor) into the border regions of Texas in the late nineteenth century. These rapid changes, writes Montejano, assumed "a sharp racial character" that culminated in a culture of segregation that was not seriously challenged until the World War II era.[38]

Images of the past often served the immediate needs of powerful interests, so that by the early twentieth century, characters such as Juan Seguín had been "purged" from the story of the Alamo and the Texas Revolution and the fact that "Mexicans and Anglos had often fought on the same side" was conveniently forgotten. As policies of segregation and disfranchisement were being carried out in South Texas to restrict the rights of Mexican Americans (paralleling the restrictions faced by blacks in Texas and other southern states that were also undergoing economic transformations), Montejano writes, "Texan historical memories played a part similar to Reconstruction memories in the Jim Crow South" in justifying these measures.[39]

Historical narratives can take many forms, including visual images—from the complex artistic representations of Robert Onderdonk and Henry McArdle to the simple cartoons of *Texas History Movies*. Moreover, as we have seen, when such images become a part of the popular culture, they can have a powerful and lasting effect on a community's collective memory, despite their inaccuracies.

As we have also seen, many of the implicit propositions of *Texas History Movies*—as is equally the case with the heroic scenes composed by Onderdonk and McArdle—collapse when subjected to comparison with primary sources documenting actual conditions in early Texas. Most importantly, both the paintings and the cartoons depict a racial division in early Texas between Anglo and Mexican that is grossly exaggerated and that virtually erases the role of Tejanos in the social, political, and military affairs of Texas during the revolution and the republic.

Yet for historians of collective memory, the problematical productions of Patton and Rosenfield—like the mythic images of Onderdonk and McArdle—can become important evidence if these works of art are examined and interpreted in the contexts of their production, rather than being dismissed as examples of "embarrassing history" to be censored or, perhaps even worse, thoughtlessly celebrated as accurate or "unvarnished" pictures of the past.

So what should we do with our embarrassing history? Like Professor Levinson, I would rather add to our icons than subtract. I prefer to drop *nothing* down the Memory Hole—the more that we can responsibly reveal, the better. Historians should not be in the business of erasing even the most repellent evidence from the past, especially when it takes the form of such telling—albeit embarrassing—historical narratives. Papering over the racial ideas that helped to shape our world—pretending that they did not exist— produces bad history and bad education.

So let us continue to see the "unvarnished" *Texas History Movies* of Patton and Rosenfield, as well as the controversial paintings of Onderdonk and McArdle. But let us see them for what they are, and use them to better understand the conditions in Texas at the time of their creation. We need to take these images—and the historical memories deriving from them—seriously. And we need to remember that "history" is made with the pen—and the paintbrush—as well as with the sword.

NOTES

1. A penetrating analysis of these two different meanings of "history" and the tangled relationship between the two may be found in Michel-Rolph Trouillot, *Silencing the Past: Power and the Production of History* (Boston: Beacon Press, 1995).

"Collective memory" is a complex concept that lies at the heart of most of the essays in this volume. While historical narratives can take many forms, historian W. Fitzhugh Brundage has suggested that the terms "historical memory" and "collective memory" can apply to "any organized, explicitly public representation of the past" (W. Fitzhugh Brundage, ed., *Where These Memories Grow: History, Memory, and Southern Identity* [Chapel Hill: University of North Carolina Press, 2000], 24n7). See also Benedict Anderson, *Imagined Communities: Reflections on the Origin and Spread of Nationalism,* rev. and ext. ed. (New York: Verso, 1991).

2. Sanford Levinson, *Written in Stone: Public Monuments in Changing Societies* (Durham, N.C.: Duke University Press, 1998). For a fascinating account of "disappearing" historical figures in the communist world, see David King, *The Commissar Vanishes: The Falsification of Photographs and Art in Stalin's Russia* (New York: Holt, 1997).

3. Levinson writes that a plaque explicitly celebrating the return of white supremacy to Louisiana, which was added to the Liberty Monument in 1934, "might be called, in our postmodernist times, the officially privileged narrative of the events" (Levinson, *Written in Stone,* 48).

4. Levinson, *Written in Stone,* 45–52 (first quotation, 47; subsequent quotations, 50).

5. Ibid., 53–55 (all quotations, 55).

6. Ibid., 114–29.

7. Ibid., 90–113 (quotation, 111).

8. Robert E. Bonner, review of *Texas Flags* by Robert Maberry Jr., *Journal of Southern History* 69 (Aug. 2003): 751, 752 (quotations). Robert E. Bonner is the author of *Colors and Blood: Flag Passions of the Confederate South* (Princeton, N.J.: Princeton University Press, 2002). See also Robert Maberry Jr., *Texas Flags* (College Station: Texas A&M University Press, in association with the Museum of Fine Arts, Houston, 2001).

9. Richard R. Flores, *Remembering the Alamo: Memory, Modernity, and the Master Symbol* (Austin: University of Texas Press, 2002); Holly Beachley Brear, *Inherit the Alamo: Myth and Ritual at an American Shrine* (Austin: University of Texas Press, 1995). See also Randy Roberts and James S. Olson, *A Line in the Sand: The Alamo in Blood and Memory* (New York: Free Press, 2001).

10. For a revealing analysis of the role of race and slavery in the secessionist cause, see Charles B. Dew, *Apostles of Disunion: Southern Secession Commissioners and the Causes of the Civil War* (Charlottesville: University of Virginia Press, 2001).

11. Maberry, *Texas Flags,* 39–40; Jesús F. de la Teja, ed., *A Revolution Remembered: The Memoirs and Selected Correspondence of Juan N. Seguín,* 2d ed. (Austin: Texas State Historical Association, 2002), 33; Tony Horwitz, "The Black and the Gray: An Interview with Tony Horwitz," *Southern Cultures* 4 (Spring 1998): 5–15; see also John David Smith, "Armed, Confederate, and Black? Not Likely," *News & Observer* (Raleigh, N.C.), Feb. 4, 2005.

12. Larry McMurtry, *Sacagawea's Nickname: Essays on the American West* (New York: New York Review Books, 2001), 92 (first, second, third, and fourth quotations), 93 (fifth quotation); see also Anne Dingus, "Book of the Century," *Texas Monthly* 27 (Dec. 1999): 184.

13. Walter L. Buenger and Robert A. Calvert, "Introduction: The Shelf Life of Truth in Texas," in *Texas through Time: Evolving Interpretations,* ed. Walter L. Buenger and Robert A. Calvert (College Station: Texas A&M University Press, 1991), ix (first quotation), x; Jack Jackson, "Learning Texas History the Painless Way," *Comics Journal* 119 (Jan. 1988): 97; Ronald L. Davis, "Rosenfield, John, Jr., in *The New Handbook of Texas,* ed. Ron Tyler et al., 6 vols. (Austin: Texas State Historical Association, 1996), 5:684 (second quotation).

14. Jackson, "Learning Texas History," 97–99; John Rosenfield Jr. with Jack Patton, *Texas History Movies* (Dallas: P. L. Turner Company, 1928); McMurtry, *Sacagawea's Nickname,* 93.

15. *Texas History Movies,* rev. ed. (n.p.: Magnolia Petroleum Company, 1954).

16. Ibid., 95 (Fig. 3.1), 119 (Fig. 3.2). The captions on the original cartoons in Fig. 3.1 contain a factual error—it was General Santa Anna himself, not General Cos, who led the attack on Zacatecas in 1835. For the best available account in English of this campaign, see Roberts and Olson, *A Line in the Sand,* 5–27.

17. *Texas History Movies,* rev. ed. (1954), 4, 38 (Fig. 3.3).

18. Ibid., 55 (Fig. 3.4).

19. Ibid., 112, 118 (Fig. 3.5); Jackson, "Learning Texas History," 99; George B. Ward, "Introduction," *Texas History Movies* ([Austin]: Texas State Historical Association, 1986), [4].

20. Jackson, "Learning Texas History," 99–100; Ward, "Introduction," [4] (quotation); *Texas History Movies,* rev. ed. (1954), 12 (first panel, Fig. 3.6); *Texas History Movies,* TSHA ed. (1986), 11 (second panel, Fig. 3.6). The 1974 TSHA edition was identical to the 1986 TSHA edition of *Texas History Movies,* except for the fact that the former bore the title *Texas History Illustrated.*

21. For the "blacked-out" Richmond, see *Texas History Illustrated* (TSHA, 1974), 54, and *Texas History Movies* (TSHA, 1986), 54 as well as the second part of Fig. 3.7 of this chapter. Compare both the image and the dialogue attributed to Richmond with the original Patton and Rosenfield panel, which may be found in the first part of Fig. 3.7 of this chapter, on page 76 of the original (1928) edition of *Texas History Movies,* and on page 55 of the 1954 "revised" edition which I used in the seventh grade.

There were 217 pages of material in the original 1928 edition of *Texas History Movies.* A facsimile edition of this work was published as *Texas History Movies* (Dallas: PJM Publishers, n.d.). According to Jack Jackson, "The hardcover rights . . . were acquired in 1981 by Pepper Jones Martinez, Inc. of Dallas (PJM)," which issued a facsimile of the original in 1984 (Jackson, "Learning Texas History," 99).

22. Ward, "Introduction," [4].

23. Jackson, "Learning Texas History," 99 (first and second quotations), 100 (third quotation); *Texas History Movies,* rev. ed. (1954), 102 (first part of Fig. 3.8); *Texas History Movies* (TSHA, 1986), 41 (second part of Fig. 3.8).

24. *Texas History Movies* (TSHA, 1986), 15 (first and second quotations, first part of Fig. 3.9); *Texas History Movies* (1928 original and 1984 facsimile editions), 32 (third quotation, second part of Fig. 3.9). Note that the TSHA editors have also remodeled the Goliad presidio, replacing the incongruous Anglo American style "log fort" with something closer to the Spanish style, though the result resembles the modern Alamo more than the presidio at Goliad. The "horseshoes" panel did not appear at all in the 1954 revised version of *Texas History Movies.*

25. "Forward [*sic*]" by Jack Patton and John Rosenfield Jr., *Texas History Movies* (1928 original and 1984 facsimile editions), [1] (quotations).

26. Jackson, "Learning Texas History," 100.

27. For an example of such a use of these images, see James E. Crisp, *Sleuthing the Alamo: Davy Crockett's Last Stand and Other Mysteries of the Texas Revolution* (New York: Oxford University Press, 2004), 1–25.

28. *Texas History Movies,* rev. ed. (1954), 65 (Fig. 3.10). See John David Smith, *An Old Creed for the New South: Proslavery Ideology and Historiography, 1865–1918* (Athens: University of Georgia Press, 1991).

29. Eugene C. Barker, *The Life of Stephen F. Austin, Founder of Texas, 1793–1836: A Chapter in the Westward Movement of the Anglo-American People* (Austin: University of Texas Press, 1969), 208–11. See also Randolph B. Campbell, *An Empire for Slavery: The Peculiar Institution in Texas, 1821–1865* (Baton Rouge: Louisiana State University Press, 1989). For William Goyens, see Alwyn Barr, *Black Texans: A History of African Americans in Texas, 1528–1995,* 2d ed. (Norman: University of Oklahoma Press, 1996), 4, 5, 7, 10.

30. Eric von Schmidt, "The Alamo Remembered—From a Painter's Point of View," *Smithsonian* 16 (Mar. 1986): 57.

31. For a more detailed account of the mystery as well as the larger context of the slashing of this painting, see James E. Crisp, "An Incident in San Antonio: The Contested Iconology of Davy Crockett's Death at the Alamo," *Journal of the West* 40 (Spring 2001): 67–77; and Crisp, *Sleuthing the Alamo,* 139–78.

32. Crisp, *Sleuthing the Alamo,* 139–78; von Schmidt, "The Alamo Remembered," 57–58. For the popularity of the Otto Becker lithograph of *Custer's Last Fight,* see Michael Kammen, *Mystic Chords of Memory: The Transformation of Tradition in American Culture* (New York: Vintage, 1993), 186.

33. Brian W. Dippie, "'What Valor Is': Artists and the Mythic Moment," *Montana: The Magazine of Western History* 46 (Autumn 1996): 52; see also Crisp, *Sleuthing the Alamo,* 161–62.

34. Sam DeShong Ratcliffe, *Painting Texas History to 1900* (Austin: University of Texas Press, 1992), 39 (first quotation); Emily Fourmy Cutrer, "'The Hardy, Stalwart Sons of Texas': Art and Mythology at the Capitol," *Southwestern Historical Quarterly* 92 (Oct. 1988): 307, 308 (subsequent quotations).

35. "Comment by Ruben [*sic*] M. Potter, United States Army, retired, on McArdle's painting of the Battle of the Alamo," Nov. 18, 1874 (manuscript copy), 4, Henry McArdle Files, Daughters of the Republic of Texas Library at the Alamo, San Antonio, Tex.

36. Cutrer, "'The Hardy, Stalwart Sons of Texas,'" 308.

37. I have addressed these questions in Crisp, *Sleuthing the Alamo,* 165–78, and Crisp, "An Incident in San Antonio," 67–77.

38. David Montejano, *Anglos and Mexicans in the Making of Texas, 1836–1986* (Austin: University of Texas Press, 1987), 104 (quotations), 105, 159–161. The associations between the Alamo as an image and the changing face of Texas during this period are more explicitly analyzed in Flores, *Remembering the Alamo*. See also Richard R. Flores, "Mexicans, Modernity, and Martyrs of the Alamo," in *Reflexiones 98: New Directions in Mexican American Studies,* ed. Yolanda Padilla (Austin: Center for Mexican American Studies Books, University of Texas Press, 1999), 1–19.

39. Montejano, *Anglos and Mexicans,* 220–23, 224 (quotations), 225.

This chapter is dedicated to the memory of
Jack Edward Jackson — 1941–2006

Chapter 4

"MEMORIES ARE SHORT BUT MONUMENTS LENGTHEN REMEMBRANCES": THE UNITED DAUGHTERS OF THE CONFEDERACY AND THE POWER OF CIVIL WAR MEMORY

KELLY MCMICHAEL

The small talk and gossip that filled the Hauschild Opera House in Victoria, a prosperous community about 120 miles southwest of Houston, in May 1896 hushed as Kate Wheeler approached the podium to welcome the "band of sisterhood" present at the first United Daughters of the Confederacy (UDC) state convention. In her remarks, Wheeler, representing the local UDC chapter, urged the members of all five chapters in attendance to build Confederate monuments because they stood for the "imperishable remembrance in our hearts." Quoting a poem, Wheeler said that southern soldiers were "slain for us; and the years may go, but our tears will flow o'er the dead who have died in vain for us."[1]

Most Daughters believed that despite losing the war the southern soldier and the cause he fought for were worthy of honor and deserved to be memorialized in stone. One of the state UDC's most popular presidents, Cornelia Branch Stone, claimed, "The history of a people and their monuments measure their consequence as a nation, and the character of their intelligence, their morals, religion and civilization." An often reprinted quotation written by a UDC member argued that "a people who have no monuments erected to perpetuate heroism and virtue have no history, and we must have our shining shafts of marble pointing to the fadeless stars, fit emblems of their [the Civil War generation's] lofty aspirations."[2]

The UDC engaged in many Confederate-related activities but pursued the building of monuments most vigorously. Virtually every UDC chapter in almost every city or county in Texas at some time considered and attempted to raise the funds necessary to commemorate the Civil War through statuary. Why did the women of the UDC take up the work of creating a public memory of a war lost? War memorials are fundamentally public art, but it is art imbued with a political and cultural purpose. The women who erected them intended for their aesthetic appeal to be appreciated, but by their very nature, monuments dedicated to commemorate a war are expected to convey a message. When a memorial is erected, the stakes are always high. Who erects the memorial and why become vital questions because monuments carry cultural power. Not only do the statues serve to remind an individual of his or her own lived experience of an event, but the memorial creators intend them to offer a lesson to future generations. Monuments and the process of choosing, fundraising, building, and unveiling provide a select group with the opportunity to shape society's memory of an event.

The collective memory created through activities such as monument erections and dedications brings a shared remembrance, and those memories lend a group a sense of the past and an aspiration for the future. Creating memory—controlling memory—constitutes real societal power, and historians of memory have assumed that men have dominated the memory production for communities. As the traditionally recognized source of power in patriarchal cultures, men have used memory to solidify authority, forming a top-down approach to guiding the masses.

If memory creation through monument construction represents such cultural power, how is it that *women* seized this opportunity for power in Texas, erecting more than fifty of the sixty-five large, public monuments to the Confederate generation in the state? Assuming that creating and perpetuating a specific past brings power to the creator, did the erection of monuments represent true power for women in society? And if it did represent power, what did women choose to do with their strengthened position? Since women have historically been classed below men socially, did the UDC's memory creation represent a "bottom-up" approach to guiding society?[3]

Though always claiming that monuments were an "object lesson in history," UDC members engaged in monument building for a host of reasons in addition to memorializing southern soldiers. The Daughters understood the potential power in memory construction and used it to project the morals they valued, morals such as honor, sacrifice, and patriotism. They also believed that their mothers had worked in complementary roles with their fathers during the war—positions that were absolutely essential to the region's cause—and they wanted their mothers' efforts remembered. Much of the Daughters' monument work in Texas attempted to guarantee that women were recognized and remembered for their efforts through word, art, and symbol. In the ideal, the monuments represented an acceptable public and culturally powerful position for women.

Men appeared content to allow women to grasp this power, power such as speaking in public in front of thousands of Texans at dedication ceremonies. The authority women achieved, however, may have been illusory. Although men did not push for the creation of monuments, they did use the women's work for their own ends, finding materialistic benefits in the monument dedication parades that drew thousands to their hotels, restaurants, and businesses. Prominent male sculptors and marble companies owned by men grew wealthy, vying to win bids as UDC chapters competed to build larger and outwardly more impressive monuments. Although the Texas Daughters recognized and sought the power that could potentially be achieved by memory-making, the power they actually achieved was greatly diffused.

Memory by its very nature is highly individualized and subjective. No two people remember the same event the same way. A simple child's game of passing a phrase from person to person around a circle inevitably results in laughter and teasing, the verbiage changing significantly from the first to the last individual. How much more diverse, then, would be a people's memory of something as profound and enormous as a four-year civil war? The individuals whose homes Sherman burned perceived the war differently than did those who were hundreds of miles away from the action. And while it is true that wars are experienced on a personal level, they are also experienced by groups of people. These groups, whether defined by families, communities, or entire regions, seek a consensus in their experience—some means of unifying their collective memories that brings meaning or closure or understanding to the events through which they have lived.[4]

Collective memory creation is not just a simple act of recalling the past but an intricately contrived means of forming a particular social identity based on a largely invented story. The creation of the myth of the Lost Cause fits perfectly this pattern of an invented, collective memory. The tradition evolved out of the defeat, poverty, and dislocation following the Civil War. Many historians have argued that the memory of the South's defeat in the war remained central to the southern character for decades, and American literature of the period reinforces this perception. Mark Twain provides only one example in *Life on the Mississippi:*

> There [the South], every man you meet was in the [Civil] war; and every lady you meet saw the war. The war is the great chief topic of conversation. The interest in it is vivid and constant; the interest in other topics is fleeting. Mention of the war will wake up a dull company and set their tongues going, when nearly any other topic would fail. In the South, the war is what A.D. is elsewhere; they date from it. All day long you hear things "placed" as having happened since the waw; or du'in' the waw'; or befo' the waw; or right aftah the waw; or 'bout two yeahs or five yeahs or ten yeahs befo' the war or aftah the waw. It shows how intimately every individual was visited, in his own person, by that tremendous episode. It gives the inexperienced stranger a better idea of what a vast and comprehensive calamity invasion is than he can ever get by reading books at the fireside.[5]

Certainly there was a tendency in the South to relive and memorialize the war, a preoccupation that people in the North did not share to the same degree, perhaps because they had emerged the conquerors and not the conquered, and as a conquered people, there was a "crisis in the local community." The myth of the Lost Cause grew out of this sense of crisis.[6]

The myth emerged as a psychological defense against defeat immediately following the Civil War. It first appeared in the writings of Edward A. Pollard, an outspoken secessionist, journalist, and writer of the book *The Lost Cause* (1866). By the 1880s the myth of the Lost Cause had lapsed into a nostalgic celebration. The phrase "Lost Cause" originated with Sir Walter Scott's accounts of the lost cause of Scotland and served to romanticize both events; in the South it created a sentimentalized tale of a Confederate ideal, an ideal that declared the region's secession from the Union just and legal. Proponents of the Lost Cause interpreted the conflict as a war fought for constitutional rights, the principle of secession, and the preservation of the homeland. The South lost because of overwhelming odds—the North had too many soldiers and its factories turned out too many materials. Robert E. Lee, Thomas "Stonewall" Jackson, and Jefferson Davis were heroes and perfect role models for contemporary society, not traitors.[7]

Men have traditionally been attributed with the creation of the myth of the Lost Cause. Starting with Virginia veterans groups, led by men like Jubal Early and Fitzhugh Lee, and then with the United Confederate Veterans and the all-male Southern Historical Society, influential political and financial male leaders invented a story of the war that created a sense of stability in the region. One historian likens the myth to a civil religion, invented by men and distributed by men, that served the postwar needs of all southerners, providing a "sense of identity" and cultural distinctiveness. The story assumed a role for all: kind masters, valiant soldiers, genteel wives, and faithful slaves. If the people of the South found defeat unbearable, they could retreat into a made-up past that honored a civilized culture—the Lost Cause memory enabled the region to take pride in itself.[8]

Historians assumed women to have had only a cursory role in the myth creation, usually mentioning how ladies passed out cookies at the old soldiers' meetings. More recently women's position within the creation of the Lost Cause myth has been reevaluated. For example, in "Woman's Hand and Heart and Deathless Love," W. Fitzhugh Brundage noted that women were considered at the end of the nineteenth century as the "custodians" of culture, especially the "preservation of links with the past." Today historians of the South are beginning to recognize the crucial role women played as memory caretakers and creators of the Lost Cause tradition.[9]

The United Daughters of the Confederacy are now recognized as the main force in promoting and funding monuments in the South. This proposition was certainly true in Texas. Kate Alma Orgain, an officer in the Texas UDC, explained why she believed the women of the United Daughters of the Confederacy were so interested in and successful at monument building when she said, "It is natural and appropriate that women should engage in commemorative work. When death comes to our homes and takes the loved ones, it is the woman, the wife, the mother who lays away the old worn hat, the baby slipper, the broken toy. It is the women who keep the grave and cultivate the flowers around it." Orgain believed, as did most of her contemporaries, that women by their very biological nature were more inclined toward remembrance. A letter printed in *The Southern Tribute* in 1898 by the UDC's committee on anniversaries explained to its members that "to cherish the memory of the illustrious dead is a sacred privilege, this loving duty being the special province of woman since the days when Mary brought fragrant spices to the tomb of the world's Redeemer." Texas UDC members believed that it was their sacred duty to commemorate those they loved, and this duty found expression in Confederate monuments.[10]

It appears that most men agreed about this sacred duty, at least to the point that they allowed women to lead in this type of work, but their agreement may have had less to do with their belief in women's natural talents and more to do with the fact that they were busy pursuing other interests. Charles B. Emanuel summarized men's attitudes in a speech he delivered at the Rusk, Texas, Confederate reunion in 1901. Emanuel argued that men's work ended with the war, and the next task, that of "preserving the memories of the gallant heroes who fell in defense of our native land," was left to the women. In other words, southern men had moved on and were engaged in more profitable, and in their opinion, more important matters—such as rebuilding the region and making money. If men became involved, explained J. W. Graves in the *Houston Chronicle,* it was because as "commercial men, even putting the question on its lowest plane, we believe that our commercial prestige would be enhanced and our material standing elevated in the minds of the whole world by an exemplification of finer feeling and nobler sentiments, as such a movement [to build a Texas monument at Vicksburg, Mississippi] would prove." Memorial work, while appreciated by veterans, was not of primary importance, and because men gave it such low priority, the task of memorializing the Confederacy could be and was taken up by women.[11]

UDC members, unlike their male peers, embraced the work and were empowered by their ability to raise funds to create monuments when others had given up. Some men may have seen only the commercial prospects in monument building, but the Daughters saw Confederate memorials as one of the best means to remind Texans of their obligations and duties as citizens. The UDC believed that each time an individual passed a lone soldier cast in marble on a courthouse lawn or at a public park, he or she would comprehend and internalize the beliefs and values the organization associated with the Old South. Such assimilation would, according to the Daughters, encourage correct social order by stressing patriotism, duty, and honor.[12]

The UDC chapter in Sherman, located in north-central Texas, erected the first Confederate monument on a courthouse lawn in Texas in 1897. The Sherman chapter did not want its memorial simply to honor the dead but to serve as a visual reminder to the city's citizens of the sacrifices and values the chapter associated with the Civil War generation. The monument's inscription states the Daughters' objectives for the memorial: "[S]acred to the memory of your Confederate dead, true patriots, they fought for home and country, for the holy principles of self-government—the only true liberty, their sublime self-sacrifices and unsurpassed valor will teach future generations the lesson of high born patriotism, of devotion to duty, of exalted courage, of southern chivalry."[13]

The Sherman chapter unveiled its monument on April 21, 1897, the day set aside to commemorate the Battle of San Jacinto, to an estimated crowd of five thousand. A huge procession led citizens to the courthouse in a parade that consisted of local bands, military organizations, college students, Masonic and other secret societies, veterans, UDC members, and schoolchildren. The city's streets were decorated with red, white, and blue bunting, and the *Dallas Morning News* stated that the ceremony represented that grand type of "Americanism, the southern soldier." When the monument was in the planning stages, the *Sherman Daily Register* had referred to it as a "permanent tribute to the loyalty and patriotism of southern sons and daughters."[14]

These monuments did not merely offer a history lesson to Texans. Their unveilings also provided UDC members with a chance to focus public attention on women. Chapters seized every possible opportunity to promote and emphasize southern women's strength and independence. One of the Daughters' first attempts to erect a large monument in the state, a tribute to Albert Sidney Johnston, reflects the potential power available to women in monument construction. The memorial drive was filled with setbacks, but the Daughters eventually succeeded, and when they did, the women of the Texas UDC realized that they could do far more than just memorialize the soldiers; they could gain power and prestige for themselves with such projects.

The Albert Sidney Johnston Chapter of the UDC organized in Austin in 1897 and reported that their "grand objective" was to "erect a monument over the grave of Albert Sidney Johnston, that gallant commander, who when dying, begged that his body might be laid to rest in Texas soil." The chapter soon realized that it could not raise sufficient funds to create a fitting tribute. That same year, the state UDC secretary, Sarah Fontaine Sampson, said that she knew "every chapter in the state is probably contemplating the erection of a monument" but that it would be wiser for the organization to "unite their efforts and produce one great work, that of the Albert Sidney Johnston monument in Austin." This proposal was brought before the division at the 1897 convention, but the ladies did not even consider it. Most of the Daughters preferred to work toward the raising of monuments in their local areas, but the Texas division's president, Benedette Tobin, agreed with Sampson that a single great monument would better represent the state than several smaller ones.[15]

President Tobin and the Albert Sidney Johnston Chapter of Austin then began in earnest to raise the funds necessary to create a monument. Tobin organized a monument committee of thirty-four women, who then presented a petition to the regular session of the Texas legislature in 1898 asking for a state appropriation to build the monument. The legislature denied the UDC's petition. Tobin then increased the committee to fifty women and asked Sen. R. N. Stafford of Mineola for suggestions and advice. Though

Tobin died in 1900, her successor, Eliza Sophia Johnson, continued to pressure the state for money to build an Albert Sidney Johnston monument. Following Stafford's instructions, Johnson organized a media campaign to influence the state legislature, stressing the importance of remembering Texas' and the South's war heroes. She and the UDC monument committee sent a copy of the petition to all the leading state daily newspapers. They also mailed twenty-six hundred copies of the petition to prominent men of the state with a personal letter asking each of them to sign the petition and return it to the governor. The committee sent an additional two hundred copies to all the United Confederate Veterans camps in Texas. The UDC tried again in 1901 to secure an appropriation at the state legislature's regular session but failed. Not discouraged, Johnson made one more attempt. She sent circulars and personal letters to all of the Texas legislators and wrote every newspaper in Texas seeking support. Finally, at a special session of the legislature in the autumn of 1901, she brought the petition before the house once more and, "after having first aroused a healthy sentiment over the state for its passage," received a ten-thousand-dollar appropriation.[16]

After three years the UDC had succeeded in securing the funds to build a Confederate monument, but by soliciting help from the state government the Daughters sacrificed control of the monument. The legislature organized a committee to direct the monument's construction, and while Johnson served on the committee, she was the only representative of the Daughters of the Confederacy to do so. Still, the Daughters considered the monument's completion a success, and many of the women realized that they held great power potentially if they banded together and pressured their state or local governments and their local newspapers.[17]

The majority of UDC members, however, found city or county monuments more appealing, requiring less cash to build and allowing local chapter members' greater control in determining a monument's style and location. Some chapters erected monuments rather quickly. The Dallas UDC chapter, known as "Dallas Chapter #6," took only three years to erect a sizable and expensive monument. On the other hand, the Huntsville chapter saved for fifty-seven years to unveil a small stone monument to the Confederacy. Regardless of the length of time, all UDC chapters struggled to raise the necessary funds. Some chapters simply gave up; others chose to make their monuments points of pride. Viola Bivins, lifetime president of Longview's UDC chapter and a state UDC president, summarized the Daughters' purpose for erecting monuments in 1911 in an address to Longview's citizens at the local monument unveiling: "Men's memories are short. This bond of sisterhood is keeping the fires of patriotism kindled by these gatherings. It is our absolute duty to observe these ceremonies with public and dignified exercises by which the young, ignorant and the careless should be instructed and thrilled to a higher patriotism."[18]

Dallas Chapter #6, under the direction of Katie Cabell Currie Muse, erected the second and one of the largest Confederate memorials in Texas. The Dallas chapter began immediately upon organization in 1894 to save money to erect a monument in the city. Three years after the project's inception, the monument was unveiled on April 29, 1897, to an estimated forty-thousand people, one of the largest gatherings in Dallas's history to that time. Parades, a "love feast," banquets, and a ball marked the two-day celebration, and thousands of Texans attended the ceremonies. These same citizens cheered for the women of the UDC, who had marked in a conspicuous place on the monument that the piece had been "erected by the Daughters of the Confederacy."[19]

Though the monument was dedicated to the common soldier and consisted of a single tall column topped by an eight-foot bronze image of a private soldier, surrounded by four smaller columns with the likenesses of Jefferson Davis, Thomas "Stonewall" Jackson, Robert E. Lee, and Albert Sidney Johnston, the Daughters were adamant that an inscription to southern women accompany the memorial. They "pointed with pride to the tribute they had placed there in memory of the mothers of the Confederacy: this stone shall crumble into dust before the deathless devotion of the southern women be forgot."[20]

Dallas Chapter #6 never wanted the public to forget that Dallas women were responsible for erecting the Confederate monument in their city. Though the Daughters argued that they erected Confederate monuments purely to venerate the old soldiers and instruct southerners, the organization and individual women consistently made sure that the public knew who raised the funds and organized the campaigns, and what memory of the war they were creating. Katie Cabell Currie Muse, the individual most responsible for Dallas's monument, basked in the recognition she received at the grand ball held at the Oriental Hotel in Dallas the night before the unveiling. She claimed that she was totally surprised when she was led onto the dance floor, proclaimed "the daughter of monuments," and presented with a diamond, ruby, and sapphire brooch on behalf of the local UCV camp.[21]

In San Antonio the Barnard E. Bee Chapter's lifetime president, Sallie Moore Houston, did not shy away from the recognition she received as the individual responsible for her city's first public monument, unveiled in 1900.

Not wanting to take all the credit, Houston recognized the efforts of Mrs. J. P. Nelson with a "beautiful medal" of appreciation for her single contribution of five hundred dollars. These women and the other chapter officers sat prominently on the stage in front of the estimated crowd of six thousand to ten thousand people gathered for the monument's unveiling. These "representative women of San Antonio whose lives are full of social duties, of business and home cares" were responsible for the erection of their monument, and with this responsibility came the opportunity to exercise power.[22]

The Daughters realized that by erecting monuments to the Confederacy, they had also found a means of becoming public memory caretakers. Historian H. E. Gulley writes that southern women erected monuments as an "expression [of their] devotion to Confederate veterans . . . to reassure these men of the value of their wartime sacrifices," but Gulley's argument is too limited. Though Texas women did not hold high government positions or other means of exerting official power, they were not so subordinate that they did not conceive of expanding their own influence. Male soldiers may top monuments across Texas, but an equal number reflect in inscription or dedication female participation in the Civil War and in the South's recovery.[23]

The UDC did not merely ensure that southern women were properly remembered in the Lost Cause celebration; they also took the lead in organizing and speaking at the festivities. The Daughters preferred to have full control of their monuments and the accompanying ceremonies and hesitated before allowing male intervention. The William P. Rogers Chapter of Victoria dedicated a monument in De Leon Plaza called *The Last Stand* on June 3, 1912. An entirely female committee planned the day's events, including a parade consisting of a silver cornet band and the local UCV, UDC, Sons of Confederate Veterans (SCV), and Grand Army of the Republic (GAR). Kate Wheeler was responsible for the monument's erection but died before the unveiling. Her daughter Katie was honored by being chosen to pull the cord to reveal the statue.[24]

The Barnard E. Bee Chapter in San Antonio chose a woman's design for their monument. Virginia Montgomery of New Orleans, daughter of one of the chapter's members, became the first female designer of a monument erected in the United States. Such an opportunity was rare, though, and more often Texas women were honored by a monument's inscription. Gainesville's courthouse monument reads, "To the women of the Confederacy, whose pious ministrations to our wounded soldiers and sailors soothed the last hours of those who died far from the objects of their tenderest love;

and whose patriotism will teach their children to emulate the deeds of their revolutionary sires."[25]

In one quick motion, Gainesville's Daughters had established both the importance of their participation in the Civil War and the validity of their new role as instructors of patriotism and memory-makers. Mrs. J. M. Wright, president of the Lou Dougherty Chapter, spoke to Gainesville's citizens in 1908 at the city's unveiling ceremony and said, "In the sixties [1860s] woman by sacrifice and practical management made possible the maintenance of an army to defend country and rights. Now by sacrifice and practical management she made possible the erection of monumental stones that perpetuate the principles for which that army fighting died or fighting lived and endured. The mission of woman was to inspire. Now the mission of woman is to commemorate, and in commemorating inspire future generations to be like the mothers of the South."[26] The Daughters set themselves to the task of creating memory, drawing strength potentially from the power of culture building, especially the creation of a memory of women.

Confederate monuments across Texas bear inscriptions to and about Texas' women. Bastrop's UDC chapter carved the words "erected by the United Daughters of the Confederacy of Bastrop" on their monument's foundation stone and presented the stone to the "citizens and county as a tribute of gratitude of Southern women to the devotion and chivalry of Southern men." The UDC columnist for the *Houston Daily Post* wrote that the unveiling of the "spirit of the Confederacy" by the Daughters in Sam Houston Park marked more "than the rearing of another Confederate monument in a southern city—it marks the reward that crowns long and faithful and consecrated service of self-sacrificing womanhood."[27]

In 1910, Mary Hunt Affleck spoke to the large crowd gathered in Austin for the unveiling of the Hood's Texas Brigade monument, which sits on the capitol grounds. She was only one of the numerous women who took on prominent roles in the public ceremonies that accompanied the erection of Texas' Confederate monuments. In cities across the state, Texas women stood before large crowds of men and women and spoke eloquently about war, patriotism, and the capabilities of women. While they spoke for themselves, they also carefully chose prominent men to address the crowds, men who would deliver speeches the Daughters deemed appropriate.[28]

W. R. Hamby spoke after Mary Affleck in Austin and claimed that the memorial represented "American valor, American citizenship, and American patriotism," all values that the UDC intended their monuments to reflect, but he continued by reminding the audience that "in the race for success in life, in the eager rush for commercialism, do not forget the great principles for which the South fought and to which your fathers so bravely and faithfully consecrated their young hopes and aspirations."[29]

The creation and erection of memorials honored woman's traditional role in society and expanded on it, ensuring these women a form of meaningful work, independence, and a prominent place in their communities. Women seized the opportunities that came with memory construction, defying the image of the southern women as quiet, acquiescing belles. But while cultural power seems inherent in their activities, the Daughters were only too aware that power was relative.

Judge W. L. McKee's speech in Hillsboro in 1925, at the city's combined unveiling ceremony and annual Confederate reunion, summarized the many possible ways in which the UDC's cultural power might be illusory. He examined the various ways Texans might interpret monuments and the reasons they might have for attending the unveiling ceremonies beyond the simple function of assimilating and joining in the Daughters' created memory of the war. McKee asked, "Why? What is it that has drawn them [Texans] together? The greater number, no doubt, [have] the purest motives," said the judge, but he wished "to high heaven that it [their pure motive] was universal." Thousands of Texans attended the unveiling ceremonies of Texas' Confederate monuments but most came to meet friends, socialize, and enjoy a rare day out. The majority of citizens did not attend because they agreed with or accepted in an unquestioning manner the created myth of the Lost Cause or the Daughters' constructed memory. Bonham's newspaper clarified why its citizens might attend their local monument's unveiling: It encouraged Fannin County's population to "take a few days off, wash up the children, get your wife a new dress, fill your baskets full and then hitchup [sic] old Jack and Beek and come down to the county seat for a few days of jollification. It will do you good, your family good, and allow your team to get a little rest."[30]

Texans enjoyed the varied activities associated with a monument's unveiling. Some cities, like Hillsboro, chose to dedicate their memorials during the annual Confederate reunion as a means of ensuring a large attendance. Others hosted elaborate parades, barbecues, and balls to raise money and increase citizen participation; fiddlers' contests proved especially popular. Tyler's Mollie Moore Davis Chapter of the UDC hosted one in the city's opera house, and Edward W. Smith Jr. reported that "it was fine, and the people enjoyed it ever so much. It set one's heart busy with memory, and the good old days from the dust of recollection trooped before the mind's eye." Tyler raised two hundred dollars at its fiddling contest, but such a successful fundraising event was unusual.[31]

UDC chapters across the state struggled to raise the funds necessary to build monuments, a telling indication of the general public's lack of interest in monument erection. Most Texans were simply not interested in contributing financially to the Daughters' visual history lessons. Laura Elgin, known as the "mother" of Marshall's monument, chastised the crowd gathered at the memorial's unveiling in 1906. She said in her speech, "'Tis true there has been lagging with some of us, but thank God this monument to those noble heroes stands like a 'stone wall' to commemorate their many virtues and bravery until time shall be no more." The UDC and UCV in the nearby town of Jefferson could not interest their citizens in building a monument until after their rival city, Marshall, the seat of Harrison County, unveiled one. Many Jeffersonians attended Marshall's ceremonies and afterward began to plan a monument and program that would "surpass those of Harrison County."[32]

Every UDC chapter that attempted to build a monument found it difficult to raise the necessary funds. Unless there were other motivations, many Texans did not care enough about commemorating the Confederacy to contribute money. Perhaps this parsimony was because money remained scarce, but more than likely it was because the public did not demand the erection of monuments; instead the monuments represented the interests and concerns of a small minority. The Daughters were a select group of self-appointed memory-makers who assumed that the citizenry would respond wholeheartedly to their projects, but such was not usually the case.[33]

The Daughters in Corpus Christi commissioned a celebrated Italian sculptor, Pompeo Coppini, to create their monument, which would be the first piece of public art in the city. Coppini conceived of something radically different from the "stereotyped memorial," but the local chapter could raise only a thousand dollars, despite using "every means of turning an honest penny." The chapter held rummage sales and waffle suppers, and members served as clerks at furniture stores for percentages of the profit. Such limited funds forced Coppini to create the work in cast stone that looked like granite, instead of the more costly bronze he had intended to use. Though the chapter hosted a dedication celebration in 1915 that included an opera singer, the crowd that gathered along the seawall where the monument was placed was estimated at just over one hundred people. Few of Corpus Christi's residents showed any interest in funding or seeing their local Confederate monument.[34]

Dr. Blocker - a & adams - Wm Heartsill - Mrs. Elgin.
Tom Elgin - E. f. Fry - Tom Whaley.
Statue unveiled Jan 1906.

FIG. 4.1. Laura Elgin with veterans on Marshall's monument erection day in 1906. Courtesy Harrison County Historical Museum, Marshall, Texas.

That same year Llano's Daughters planned to build a memorial by voluntary subscriptions "but met with indifference as the people thought it was too great an undertaking for the Daughters." The project became more appealing, though, when the Daughters announced that they had secured Gov. James E. Ferguson to be the keynote speaker at the unveiling. Local historian Wilburn Oatman said of the event, "Llano as a town benefited in more ways than one on that gala day. First, by the monument itself as it adorns the public square; second, that it was honored by a visit of the State's highest officer who had passed an invitation to speak at a banquet of a large city in order to come to our little town, and but for this occasion, many might never have had this opportunity of seeing and hearing the Governor; and third, Llano gained publicity in the large daily newspapers of the State, which carried the news of the dedication, a publicity it could not have gained otherwise."[35]

Unlike Llano, Palestine's business owners saw little advantage to themselves if they aided their local UDC chapter in building a monument to native Palestinian John H. Reagan, postmaster general in the Confederate government. The local chapter tried for years but could not raise the necessary funds. A monument was finally unveiled in 1911, but only because the Michaux Park Land Company donated $2,950 to the project—the money they had made from selling about eight acres to the city to create a park. The Palestine UDC chapter did not plan any activities or celebrations to accompany the Reagan monument unveiling, so few people attended. Only UDC members and their sons and daughters, city commissioners, and a handful of local veterans and their families were present to hear Georgia Crawford, president of the local UDC chapter, speak.[36]

Perhaps it did not really matter to the Daughters that the general public was basically disinterested in erecting Confederate monuments. Though the bulk of Texas' citizens might not help or contribute money for the erections, local UDC chapters continued to believe that they could impart particular values and lessons by erecting monuments and holding large celebrations.[37]

Along with memorializing soldiers and honoring women, the Daughters meant for the monuments to physically represent particular values, one of which was the rejection of the "New South" emphasis on economic materialism in favor of a return to the seemingly more genteel and less competitively capitalistic antebellum southern economy. Instead, the erection of memorials fostered a huge industry that pushed UDC chapters and their cities into competitions to see who could raise the biggest and most impressive monuments, a competition fueled by aggressive dealers who used sentimental language to encourage the building of even more monuments. For example, the sculptor Pompeo Coppini wrote extensively about the commercialism that sprang up around the building of Confederate monuments. He wrote, "It is easy to influence small communities to give parks or other utilitarian projects for memorials, as the small masses are not educated to art appreciation." Coppini added that some unscrupulous men appealed to the Confederates "with sentimental hypocritical devotion to their cause, that as the Confederate Army wore the gray uniforms, that their Memorials should be built of gray granite, even if it came from Yankee states to make Yankee manufacturers rich."[38]

FIG. 4.2. Pompeo Coppini provided a unique Confederate sculpture to each UDC chapter with whom he had a contract. Victoria's William P. Rogers Chapter dedicated Coppini's *The Last Stand* on June 3, 1912. The monument is considered one of Coppini's best. Courtesy Local History Collection, Victoria College, Victoria, Texas.

Coppini saved his most scathing comments for his toughest competitor in the erection of Texas' monuments. Though the largest and eventually wealthiest monument dealer in the South was the McNeel Marble Company of Marietta, Georgia, Texas had its own sculptor, Frank Teich of Llano, who made an enormous amount of money peddling and producing Confederate monuments. Coppini said that Teich was responsible for developing the gray granite industry in the state because he had "worked that gag [building monuments out of Confederate gray] with the Confederates and the State politicians for all it was worth and with a handsome profit." Coppini stated that there was "no question about it, he was a good salesman. He could talk the language of those that know nothing of the value of the thing they were to buy, by misrepresenting himself as something he never was." Teich Monumental Works, claimed Coppini, was responsible for the "lowgrade commercial distribution of shameful public monumental monstrosities" in Texas.[39]

Certainly from an artistic standpoint, Coppini's monuments are more sophisticated than those produced by Teich, but many UDC chapters chose to buy mass-produced memorials rather than wait five, ten, or even fifteen years to attempt to raise enough money to hire a sculptor. Fort Worth's Julia Jackson Chapter contacted Coppini in 1921 to request a catalog of designs ranging from five thousand to twenty thousand dollars. The sculptor sniffed that "artists have no catalogs because each monument is individually made." Coppini claimed he would meet with the Fort Worth chapter and discuss plans, but he could not "compete with the cold blooded and mercenary stone dealers, who love no art and build monuments simply to sell stones." The UDC in Fort Worth could never raise sufficient funds for such an ambitious project. They eventually erected a small stone to the Confederacy on the courthouse lawn in 1938.[40]

The United Daughters of the Confederacy seemed to accept the reality that some individuals became wealthy from the sale of monuments because the women believed that the value of the monuments outweighed any negatives associated with the construction. And while the Daughters loved to be praised for their efforts (for example, Longview's mayor, G. A. Bodemheim, claimed that "no tongue can do justice to their heroism, no pen can tell what they suffered and endured, but this much may be said for them, that they never gave up, and that some of them are fighting to this good day"), most UDC members were adamant that they did not want *men* to erect a monument in stone to Confederate women. It was not that Texas' women did not want their men to praise them or remember them or that they did not want stone dealers to make even more money, but rather most women feared the type of message that men might memorialize about them.[41]

The United Daughters of the Confederacy built monuments to instruct citizens, especially children, in the values they deemed appropriate, but in addition to teaching patriotism and honor, the UDC built monuments with inscriptions that represented the heroic characteristics of women's personalities. They feared, and later found their concerns justified, that men who wanted to commemorate them would deliver a vastly different message. A letter in the *Confederate Veteran* in 1897 suggested that a monument be built to southern women that cost no less than fifty thousand dollars because the women were "unfailing" in their "devotion to their loved soldiers, a devotion which amounted to heroism of the highest type." Another correspondent in 1903 claimed that "if the Southern soldier made the Confederate armies immortal and covered all this Southland and their respective States with imperishable glory and renown, it is due to the fact that he sprung [sic] from such motherhood. We will prove ourselves unworthy of such motherhood if we do not perpetuate in some endearing memorial the . . . virtues of our women."[42]

It was exactly this type of commemoration that Texas women wanted to avoid. The men who discussed building a woman's monument spoke of portraying females as the helpmates and mothers of men, as though women achieved heroism only vicariously through the support and birth of males. UDC members viewed their mothers, and in turn themselves, as individuals who were worthy of praise for their own actions and not simply for their support of men's actions. Organization members believed that the war years had "evolved a special type of Southern womanhood," one that had fought bravely to the end and then had endured great hardship afterward, not as mothers but as "southern women." The Daughters strongly suggested that if the men wanted to remember them, they should do so in a way that recognized their equal sacrifice and their continued need—by building an industrial school or a university for women. Southern women did not object to being honored, but they knew that funds were limited, and they preferred that the money available be used to help white women in a more concrete and permanent way.[43]

In 1900 several proposals were offered across the South, including one in Texas, to use any funds made available for commemoration purposes to build a school "as a more enduring and useful monument than marble or brass." Other women's organizations, such as the Southern Industrial Educational Association (SIEA), petitioned the veterans' camps and the Sons of Confederate Veterans to defer to the wishes of southern women and their "universal objection to a 'shaft.'" The SIEA president begged the veterans "that the proposed monument will not be a shaft, but that it may take the form of an industrial college." She argued that "such a monument, with its great purpose and lasting results, would challenge the admiration of the world." In addition, the building and maintenance of a college would signify southern men's recognition that southern women had proven their loyalty during and after the war years and would address women's continued need for training so that they could support themselves and their families. The men interested in building a woman's monument ignored their requests.

Perhaps an industrial college called attention too publicly to the need for white women to care for themselves without male support.[44]

By 1910 the United Confederate Veterans had accepted a monument's design that the Daughters immediately protested. The *Confederate Veteran* described the memorial, claiming that the design represented a "wounded and dying Confederate soldier supported by Fame [a female allegorical symbol]. Just as his spirit takes its flight to his god a typical Southern woman crowns the soldier with laurels, and it is then that Fame crowns the woman for her patriotism and devotion." A photo of a preliminary sculpture of the monument reveals a cast of three with their heads bowed. The "typical Southern woman" appears downtrodden and largely enveloped in Fame's robes. Her posture and appearance speak of defeat.[45]

The UDC's Texas Division president, Katie Black Howard, formally rejected the proposal and accepted resolutions against the monument because the design was

> wholly inadequate to represent the matchless women whose memory it is designed to perpetuate. Nay, more, we believe that the design gives an utterly false idea of the women of the war. It was a period that called for immediate action, not for timid shrinking and fearfulness of spirit. Our mothers met the call of the hour courageously, undauntedly, and when Appomattox came, faced defeat as proudly as once they exulted in success. This monument is supposed to commemorate the women of '61–'65—a period of years that evolved a special type of Southern womanhood—but the design has singled out one feature, Appomattox alone, wholly ignoring the long, brave days of self-less, loving endeavor that made shine survivors of that epoch which proved the worth of Southern women, one with them both by blood and tradition, it is but just that we should have a voice in deciding what we think fitly hands down their memory to the future.[46]

Howard said that if this sculpture was to be simply a state monument, the Daughters would not protest, but since it was to represent the entire South, the organization would not tolerate the monument's adoption. Theirs was not a protest against the "chivalrous compliment of the Confederate veterans . . . but of the unmeaning, unrepresentative design adopted by them."[47]

The Daughters' protests did not stop the veterans, but the old soldiers' inability to raise sufficient funds did. No single regional monument to southern women was ever erected (though several monuments to Confederate women were dedicated in individual states) nor did the veterans ever offer the UDC the money they raised to build an industrial school for women. Texas has only one monument erected by men specifically to women. A veteran in Texarkana contributed the greatest part of the ten thousand dollars required to erect in the city a monument to "southern mothers." The monument represents a reduced representation of the female participation in the war, portraying a Confederate private above a square formed by four marble pillars on which a female figure sits representing the mothers of southern soldiers. Texarkana's 1918 monument reads, "O great Confederate Mothers, we would paint your names on monuments that men may read them as the years go by, and tribute pay to you, who bore and mustered hero-sons, and gave them solace in that darkest hour, when they came home, with broken swords and guns." The monument recognizes women as the mothers of sons who conducted war, celebrating the republican mother image and revealing how fleeting women's cultural power through memory-making could be.[48]

Men's memories of women's wartime participation differed markedly from women's perceived remembrances of their own roles, and the potential creation of a regional monument had as much to do with solidifying gender relationships as it did memorializing women's actual role in the war. Men's insistence on representing women as helpmates revealed their desire to re-shape the memory of women's war efforts as men wanted them to be remembered rather than as an actual representation of events, a representation and image of the female role that women sharply disagreed with, both for their present and for the future. The erection of a regional monument based on a "mothering image" would have allowed men to validate their understanding of what it meant to be men and potentially devalue women's true wartime participation, a lesson that the Daughters did not want taught to the public or to later generations.[49]

Confederate monuments represented more than just rhetorical space on the southern landscape. For the United Daughters of the Confederacy, memorials provided a physical location where Texans could gather and learn particular values. Although it is difficult to determine whether the monuments or the speeches delivered at the unveiling ceremonies taught anyone lessons like patriotism or honor or to remember the active role that women played in the war years, it is obvious that the women of the UDC enjoyed their participation in the festivities and believed they were claiming cultural power. Women understood that memory creation through activities like monument building could offer a bottom-up opportunity to guide society.

The reality, however, proved less than ideal for women. Though men took an essentially hands-off approach to most of the monuments that the Daughters organized, funded, and erected, they used the dedication ceremonies and parades for their own commercial and business interests. Texans reluctant to donate money for a statue's construction gladly attended the festivities, partaking of the watermelon and barbecue if not, perhaps, internalizing the messages. Even the veterans, when they discussed the erection of a monument to southern women, continued to view women as simply the vessels that produced great manhood rather than recognizing women as agents of their own lives.

Viola Bivins argued at Longview's monument dedication ceremony that "memories were short but that monuments could lengthen and solidify the remembrances." The United Daughters of the Confederacy eagerly accepted the challenge of creating a Civil War memory for Texans, recognizing the cultural power potential. But in the end, the power proved elusive.[50]

NOTES

1. United Daughters of the Confederacy (UDC), *Minutes of the First Annual Convention of the Texas Division of the United Daughters of the Confederacy* (Galveston, Tex.: Clarke and Coats, 1898), 22.

2. UDC, *Proceedings of the Fourth Annual Convention of the Texas Division of the United Daughters of the Confederacy* (Tyler, Tex.: Sword and Shield Publishing, 1899), 17; *Southern Tribute Magazine* 1 (May 1898): 289; *Confederate Daughter* 1 (Jan. 1900): 1.

3. For more information on the numbers and types of monuments erected by the UDC in Texas, see Kelly McMichael, "Sacred Memories: A Guide to the Civil War Monuments of Texas" (manuscript currently under review for publication by the Texas State Historical Association); and Kelly McMichael Stott, "From Lost Cause to Female Empowerment: The Texas Division of the United Daughters of the Confederacy, 1896–1966" (Ph.D. diss., University of North Texas, 2001).

4. For background on history and memory, see Pierre Nora, "Between Memory and History: Les Lieux de mémoire," in *History and Memory in African American Culture,* ed. Geneviève Fabre and Robert O'Meally (New York: Oxford University Press, 1994); David Paul Nord, "The Uses of Memory: An Introduction," *Journal of American History* 85 (Sept. 1998): 409–10; Jacquelyn Dowd Hall, "'You Must Remember This': Autobiography as Social Critique," *Journal of American History* 85 (Sept. 1998): 439–65; John Bodnar, *Remaking America: Public Memory, Commemoration, and Patriotism in the Twentieth Century* (Princeton, N.J.: Princeton University Press, 1991).

5. Mark Twain, *Life on the Mississippi* (1875; reprint, New York: Signet, 1980), 257.

6. Robert Wiebe, *The Search for Order, 1877–1920* (New York: Hill and Wang, 1967), 76–110; Thomas L. Connelly and Barbara L. Bellows, *God and General Longstreet: The Lost Cause and the Southern Mind* (Baton Rouge: Louisiana State University Press, 1982), 119.

7. Rollin G. Osterweis, *The Myth of the Lost Cause, 1865–1900* (Hamden, Conn.: Archon Books, 1973), x, 11; Connelly and Bellows, *God and General Longstreet,* 2; Gaines M. Foster, *Ghosts of the Confederacy: Defeat, the Lost Cause, and the Emergence of the New South, 1865–1913* (New York: Oxford University Press, 1987), 125; Charles Reagan Wilson, *Baptized in Blood: The Religion of the Lost Cause, 1865–1920* (Athens: University of Georgia Press, 1980), 11; Joan Marie Johnson, "'Drill into Us . . . the Rebel Tradition': The Contest over Southern Identity

in Black and White Women's Clubs, South Carolina, 1898–1930," *Journal of Southern History* 66 (Aug. 2000): 525–63.

8. Osterweis, *The Myth of the Lost Cause,* x, 11; Connelly and Bellows, *God and General Longstreet,* 2; Foster, *Ghosts of the Confederacy,* 125; Wilson, *Baptized in Blood,* 11.

9. W. Fitzhugh Brundage, "'Woman's Hand and Heart and Deathless Love': White Women and the Commemorative Impulse in the New South," in *Monuments to the Lost Cause: Women, Art, and the Landscapes of Southern Memory,* ed. Cynthia Mills and Pamela H. Simpson (Knoxville: University of Tennessee Press, 2003), 64–82. For another example of the importance of women to the creation of the myth of the Lost Cause, see Karen L. Cox, *Dixie's Daughters: The United Daughters of the Confederacy and the Preservation of Confederate Culture* (Gainesville: University Press of Florida, 2003), 12–13.

10. UDC, *Proceedings of the Fifth Annual Convention of the Texas Division, United Daughters of the Confederacy* (Ennis, Tex.: Hal Marchbanks, Printer, 1900), 7; *Southern Tribute* 1 (Apr./May 1898): 307. For sources that discuss the UDC and monument erections, see Melody Kubassek, "Ask Us Not to Forget: The Lost Cause in Natchez, Mississippi," *Southern Studies* 3 (Fall 1992): 155–70; and Foster, *Ghosts of the Confederacy,* 129. The national UDC formed in Tennessee in 1894. Local organizations calling themselves "Daughters of the Confederacy" were already forming in Texas and quickly joined with the national division. The first annual convention of the Texas Division of the UDC was held in 1896, and Texas UDC membership increased quickly: 31 chapters with 2,047 members in 1898, 56 chapters with 3,381 members in 1902, 105 chapters with 5,046 members in 1904, 146 chapters with 6,242 members in 1907, and 154 chapters with 7,641 members in 1913 (UDC, *Proceedings of the Third Annual Convention of the Texas Division of the United Daughters of the Confederacy* [n.p., 1899], 12; UDC, *Proceedings of the Seventh Annual Convention of the Texas Division of the United Daughters of the Confederacy* [Fort Worth, Tex.: Press of Humphreys and Carpenter, 1902), 16; UDC, *Proceedings of the Ninth Annual Convention of the Texas Division of the United Daughters of the Confederacy* [Fort Worth, Tex.: Speer Printing, 1905], 18–20; UDC, *Proceedings of the Twelfth Annual Convention of the Texas Division,* 22–24; UDC, *Proceedings of the Eighteenth Annual Convention of the Texas Division of the United Daughters of the Confederacy* [Austin, Tex.: Von Boeckmann-Jones, 1914], 22–25; "Report of the President-General to the 35th Annual Convention of the United Daughters of the Confederacy, 1928," Texas Collection, Baylor University, Waco, Tex.). Membership was based on heredity; the widows, wives, mothers, sisters, nieces, and lineal descendants of those who served or gave material aid could join, as could women and their lineal descendants who gave proof of aid during the war. Membership increased rapidly during the early years, although always with an eye on the "character and lineage" of the applicant.

11. *Confederate Soldier* 1 (Oct. 1901): 14; *Houston Chronicle,* June 13, 1909.

12. Stott, "From Lost Cause to Female Empowerment," 1–9.

13. Mattie Davis Lucas, *A History of Grayson County, Texas* (Sherman, Tex.: Scruggs Printing, 1948), 202; *Dallas Morning News,* Apr. 22, 1897; monument inscription copied during personal visit. Although Sherman has laid claim to the first Confederate monument in Texas, Waco unveiled a monument on May 2, 1893 (Decoration Day), in its city cemetery. The Sherman monument is the first Confederate monument erected on a courthouse lawn. For a contemporary reaction to Sherman's claims, see the letter from Dr. J. C. J. King published in *Confederate Veteran* 5 (July 1897): 388. For a photograph of Waco's monument, see Ralph W. Widner Jr., *Confederate Monuments: Enduring Symbols of the South and the War between the States* (Washington, D.C.: Andromeda Association, 1982), 231.

14. *Dallas Morning News,* Apr. 22, 1897; *Sherman Daily Register,* Apr. 3, 1896.

15. UDC, *Texas Division Chapter Histories* (Austin: United Daughters of the Confederacy, Chapter 105, Albert Sidney Johnston, 1990), 8; UDC, *Minutes of the Second Annual*

Convention of the Texas Division of the United Daughters of the Confederacy (Galveston, Tex.: Clarke and Coats, 1898), 11–12; *Confederate Soldier and Daughter* 1 (Feb. 1902): 17–18.

16. C. W. Raines, *Yearbook for Texas, 1901* (Austin: Gemmel Book Co., 1902), 129; *Confederate Veteran* 10 (Jan. 1902): 10; *Confederate Soldier and Daughter* 1 (Feb. 1902): 17–18 (quotation). The monument to Albert Sidney Johnston, created by Elisabet Ney, consists of a life-size sarcophagus of Italian marble. The state placed it over his grave in the Texas State Cemetery in 1905 (Emily Cutrer, *The Art of the Woman: The Life and Work of Elisabet Ney* [Lincoln: University of Nebraska Press, 1988], 48).

17. *Confederate Soldier and Daughter* 1 (Feb. 1902): 18.

18. *Dallas Morning News,* June 4, 1911 (clipping), in vertical file: Confederate Monument, Longview Public Library, Longview, Tex.; Kelly McMichael Stott, "The Lost Cause in Dallas, Texas, 1894–1897," *Legacies* 12 (Spring 2000): 4–12.

19. *Dallas Morning News,* Apr. 28, 1897; *Dallas Times Herald,* Apr. 28, 1897; unidentified newspaper clipping in Scrapbook, Katie Cabell Currie Muse Papers, Dallas Historical Society, Dallas, Tex.; Stott, "The Lost Cause in Dallas, Texas," 4–12.

20. *Confederate Veteran* 6 (July 1898): 299.

21. Ibid.

22. *Confederate Veteran* 8 (June 1900): 261; *Confederate Daughter* 1 (Feb. 1900): 3.

23. H. E. Gulley, "Women and the Lost Cause: Preserving a Confederate Identity in the American Deep South," *Journal of Historical Geography* 19 (Summer 1993): 132.

24. William P. Rogers Chapter #44 Yearbook, Archives/Special Collections, University of Houston–Victoria College, Victoria, Tex.

25. *Confederate Daughter* 1 (June 1900): 8.

26. *Confederate Veteran* 16 (July 1908): 377 (quotation); Mrs. B. A. C. Emerson, *Historic Southern Monuments* (New York: Neale Publishing, 1911), 355.

27. *Confederate Veteran* 19 (Jan. 1911): 1; *Houston Daily Post,* Jan. 19, 1908.

28. *Confederate Veteran* 18 (Dec. 1910): 564.

29. Ibid.

30. *Hillsboro Mirror,* July 28, 1925; *Fannin County Favorite* (Bonham), July 13, 1905.

31. *Confederate Daughter* 1 (July 1900): 113.

32. Program, Jan. 1906, and unidentified newspaper clipping (quotation) in vertical file: Confederate Monument, Harrison County Historical Museum, Marshall, Tex.; Fred Tarpley, *Jefferson: Riverport to the Southwest* (Austin, Tex.: Eakin Press, 1986), 205.

33. For examples of women having trouble obtaining the public's support for building Confederate monuments, see Brundage, "Woman's Hand and Heart and Deathless Love," 69.

34. Mary A. Sutherland, *The Story of Corpus Christi* (Houston: Rein and Sons, 1916), 142; newspaper clipping, "Forgotten Historical Fountain May Soon Brightly Spout Again," vertical file: Historical Sites—Confederate Memorial, Special Collections & Archives Division, Bell Library, Texas A&M University–Corpus Christi, Corpus Christi, Tex. Though the number of veterans living declined sharply in the 1910s, the UDC reached its peak membership levels during the period. The Daughters renewed their interest in monument construction during the decade in reaction to the patriotism and nationalism engendered by World War I.

35. Wilburn Oatman, *Llano: Gem of the Hill Country. A History of Llano County, Texas* (Hereford, Tex.: Pioneer Book Publishers, 1970), 115.

36. Mary Kate Hunter Notebooks, vol. 1, 48, 59, Genealogy Room, Palestine Public Library, Palestine, Tex.

37. In *The Path to a Modern South* Walter Buenger argues that Confederate monuments anchored memories for Texans and that local townspeople formed such a "strong connection

between monuments and everyday life" that when a tornado toppled the memorial in Linden, "the city's failure to immediately repair the monument drew criticism." Buenger assumes that the individual who wrote to the local newspaper criticizing Linden's rulers represented the sentiments of the general public. In all likelihood, the comments were illustrative only of that person's opinion. Buenger points out the difference class made in accepting the prohibition of alcohol, illustrating that middle-class Texans embraced the idea while poorer whites "either opposed these measures or had no interest in them." Poorer whites likely took a similar stand on the erection of monuments. They had little interest in funding them but wholeheartedly enjoyed the accompanying free festivities and entertainment provided by their economic betters (Walter L. Buenger, *The Path to a Modern South: Northeast Texas between Reconstruction and the Great Depression* (Austin: University of Texas Press, 2001), 118, 124.

38. Pompeo Coppini Notebook, 111, 128, 172, in file 2, Coppini-Tauch Papers, Center for American History, University of Texas at Austin (cited hereafter as CAH).

39. Ibid., 111.

40. Pompeo Coppini to Mrs. W. P. Lane, Apr. 18, 1921, folder 20, box 6, Julia Jackson Chapter UDC Papers, Fort Worth Public Library, Fort Worth, Tex.

41. *Dallas Morning News,* June 4, 1911.

42. *Confederate Veteran* 5 (June 1897): 245; *Confederate Veteran* 11 (July 1903): 310. For more information on the women's monument drive, see Cynthia Mills, "Gratitude and Gender Wars: Monuments to the Women of the Sixties," in *Monuments to the Lost Cause: Women, Art, and the Landscapes of Southern Memory,* ed. Cynthia Mills and Pamela H. Simpson (Knoxville: University of Tennessee Press, 2003), 183–200.

43. *Galveston Daily News,* Jan. 23, 1911.

44. *Confederate Veteran* 5 (Aug. 1897): 420 (first quotation); *Confederate Veteran* 14 (Apr. 1906): 159 (second quotation); *Galveston Daily News,* Jan. 23, 1911 (third quotation); UDC, *Proceedings of the Fifth Annual Convention of the Texas Division,* 72 (fourth quotation). The state appropriated money for a women's vocational school, now Texas Woman's University, in 1902, but the UCV never contributed to its creation. For information on the founding of Texas Woman's University, see Joyce Thompson, *Marking a Trail: A History of the Texas Woman's University* (Denton: Texas Woman's University Press, 1982).

45. *Confederate Veteran* 18 (Mar. 1910): 97, 101.

46. *Galveston Daily News,* Jan. 23, 1911 (quotation); Cornelia Branch Stone Scrapbook, Vertical Files, Rosenberg Library, Galveston, Tex.

47. *Galveston Daily News,* Jan. 23, 1911.

48. Lela McClure, "Captain Rosborough and the Confederate Memorial: A Short History" (civic project of the Texarkana Chapter, UDC), Vertical Files, CAH. For more information on the regional drive to build a woman's monument and on individual state monuments to women, see Mills, "Gratitude and Gender Wars," 183–200.

49. For more on monuments as a "complex discourse about . . . gender relations," see Mills, "Gratitude and Gender Wars," 196–97.

50. *Dallas Morning News,* June 4, 1911.

Chapter 5

MEMORY AND THE 1920S KU KLUX KLAN IN TEXAS

WALTER L. BUENGER

During the early 1920s the Ku Klux Klan grew to enormous size and influence in Texas, but from the mid- to late 1920s it dwindled away. Usual explanations for the rapid rise and fall of the Klan describe its growth as an aftershock of World War I and connect it to changing gender roles, an upsurge in racial tension, class anxiety, increased urbanization, and concerns about lawlessness and licentiousness in the Prohibition era. In Texas the Klan also functioned as a fraternal organization and as a faction within the dominant Democratic Party that elected a U.S. senator in 1922 and almost elected a governor in 1924. It grew because of effective organization and advertising. It lost influence, the standard argument goes, when it lost elections, when leading newspaper editors and community leaders became increasingly critical of its violence, and when scandals exposed Klan leaders as hypocrites.[1]

In ways reminiscent of European fascism, however, the Klan also grew because it rested upon racialized myths and memories of the past that touched popular chords. It grew because among white Protestants these memories turned widely held but amorphous attitudes about Jews, Catholics, blacks, and non-English speakers into concrete action intended to defend America. Through symbols and images that drew upon regionalism, race, religion, and patriotism, promoters of the Klan attracted adherents and gave their organization focus and energy. In turn opponents of the Klan used countervailing myths, memories, symbols, and images. For them, the Klan stood opposed to memories of the founding fathers as advocates of freedom of religion and of Texans as rugged individualists who resisted the influence of the mob. But this clash of memories was more than a story of two competing sides using the best available weapons against each other. It was more than a contest for power in the present between factions trying to control what the community remembered and what it forgot. By using memories associated with Americanism, members of the Klan and opponents of the Klan further transformed themselves and their society from southern to American. Using memories has often been depicted as a reactionary act, a defense of entrenched ideas and established power. The Texas example suggests that memories also served as agents of transformation.[2]

Focusing on memory, then, adds to our previous understanding of the 1920s Ku Klux Klan and its long-term impact. In her perceptive study of the Klan in Indiana, Kathleen M. Blee makes the point that "deep-seated racism" and "xenophobic attitudes" did not automatically translate into membership in the Klan. The Klan espoused the normal range of ideas and opinions among white Protestants in the 1920s, but not all with those ideas and opinions joined the Klan. Klan membership drew out, heightened, organized, and focused racism and xenophobia, but the original level of racism and xenophobia matched that of the majority of white Protestants.[3] Memory served as a trigger mechanism that influenced people to join the Klan and helped members articulate and act on racism and xenophobia once in the Klan.

Four strains of myth and memory contributed to the rise of the KKK and to its ability to energize and direct its members. The most obvious of these were memories of the Civil War and Reconstruction. Indeed, the Klan first appeared in Texas at a reunion of Confederate veterans in Houston in October 1920.[4] The Klan, as that term implies, also drew upon romantic images of medieval England, where chivalrous Anglo Saxons defended the virtues of their race. This romantic image encompassed both race and gender, as members of the Klan defended the white race and established their own manliness in the process. The Klan also depended upon the religious primitivism of the time—an impulse to return to the imagined purity of the early Christian church. The Klan advocated an unadorned but muscular Christianity whose followers changed the world around them. Finally, the Klan preached "Americanism," devotion to flag and country, and adoration of the founding fathers.

Links to the Confederacy and Reconstruction appeared early in the history of the Texas Klan and persisted throughout its glory days. On October 8, 1920, a group marching in the Confederate Veterans Parade in Houston carried three messages: "We were here yesterday, 1866." "We are here today, 1920." "We will be here forever." This insistence that the 1920s Klan directly descended from the noble Klan of Reconstruction appeared repeatedly in Klan literature and distinguished the Texas Klan from Klans in the North and the West. Two examples give a flavor for the link to the Confederate and Reconstruction experience. In 1921 about four hundred members of the Houston Klan rode the train out to Brenham, Texas, to break up a celebration of Mayfest by the local Germans—Germans who in most cases had been born in Texas or resided in Texas for decades but still clung tenaciously to a distinctive language and customs, making them alien to Klansmen. Members of the Klan carried signs that read, "Our fathers were here in '61, and their boys are here in '21." Those who acted to protect their communities in 1861 were linked directly to those who acted to defend their communities in 1921. They were of the same type. Indeed they were of the same family. In another example of this link to the Confederate past, in 1922 the Klan paid for a group of veterans to attend the annual reunion of Confederate veterans, and the Klan newspaper editor commented, "The Ku Klux Klan of today is a continuation of the Klan that was born in the 'old South' which was composed of Confederate soldiers. We consider it a privilege to have the opportunity to help in such a noble cause." It was more than a privilege. It was savvy marketing of an image that struck a popular chord.[5]

This tie to the Civil War and Reconstruction worked to the advantage of the Ku Klux Klan because by the 1920s most white Texans remembered the original Klan as a force for good in trying times. J. T. Renfro, pastor of the First Baptist Church in Sinton, Texas, declared in a sermon on the Klan, "With pride, the historian tells of that noble, brave and patriotic band of men, who in the days of reconstruction in the latter sixties saved the civilization not only of the South, but of the entire Nation. And what man is there among us tonight who does not regard those men as our greatest heroes?" Historians such as Charles William Ramsdell and novelists like Thomas Dixon had so vividly depicted the plight of southern whites during Reconstruction and so glorified the virtue of their defenders that by the 1920s most did regard the first Klan as heroic. They agreed with another Texas minister, Walter Carl Wright of Waco, that the original Klan "saved the South from negro domination, protected the chastity of Southern womanhood from black brutes in human form, drove the carpetbagger-vultures from the bleeding carcass of an outraged people, swept away the ashes of ruined homes and built a new 'Dixie.'"[6]

Even opponents of the Klan admitted that "heroic measures" were needed during Reconstruction, and they felt obliged to deny any link between the old Klan and the new Klan. In tying itself to the first Klan, the 1920s Klan used memory to its advantage. It used memory as distinct from history, for as more modern historians would testify, the original Klan more closely resembled a terrorist organization than a band of noble defenders of the white race.[7]

Memories also linked this white race, and its self-appointed defender the Ku Klux Klan, to its ancestral origins among the Anglo Saxons of medieval England. As Reverend Renfro put it, "The Anglo-Saxon is the typeman of history. To him must yield the self-centered Hebrew, the cultured Greek, the virile Roman, the mystic Oriental." He went on to say that "the Ku Klux Klan desires that the control of America shall be of this all-conquering blood."[8] English history and English culture separated true Americans from the rest of humankind and gave them the habits and practices that allowed, indeed demanded, that they rule. Their remembered race gave Klansmen a unity found in nothing else. Their whiteness, more particularly their descent from the noble Anglo Saxons, gave them strength and purpose.[9]

Elaborate expressions of race pride, calls for chivalry, and insistence on white supremacy appeared in most Klan literature. Klansmen insisted that they did not so much oppose blacks, Mexicans, Germans, Catholics, Jews, and other groups but rather that they stood for their own race, a race defined by a metaphor from the past. They continued the ancient struggle between white and nonwhite. Tellingly, they defined whiteness as being Anglo Saxon, Protestant, and English speaking. In romantic language they gave their race and their order the characteristics of English knights and rested their entire movement on notions that Klansmen should act chivalrously. They should protect "pure womanhood." They should set an example for children and perform works of charity. They should lead in church and school. Acting on the ancient purposes of their blood, Klansmen conquered and commanded, and those who challenged this protocol challenged the designs of God and risked the degeneration of society.[10]

Klan symbols, especially the sword and shield, also drew on the crusading image evoked by links to Anglo Saxon knights. (Klansmen more or less ignored the Norman conquest and focused on Sir Walter Scott's heroic fictional character, Ivanhoe.) Klansmen were warriors. They defended their race against invaders. They carried on the tradition of their noble past. The point, of course, was to use the past to encourage men of the present to measure up and defend racial solidarity. Fanciful calls to preserve the historical purity of the race gave membership in the Klan a glorious purpose and helped turn rituals that seemed ridiculous to outsiders into symbolic actions of great moment. To wear the shield or carry the sword or speak out for the white race meant to carry on a thousand-year-old tradition.[11]

Emphasis on keeping the Anglo Saxon blood pure inevitably led to discussion of God and sex. God meant the blood to remain pure. God designed the system in which the Anglo Saxon led, and godly men must preserve it. As W. C. Wright said, "We avow the distinction made by the Creator between the races of men and are pledged to forever strive to keep the white Caucasian blood pure and undefiled." Miscegenation went against God's will and threatened the purity and purpose of the race. Thus, memory of the past encouraged efforts to police sexual behavior. God demanded that his valiant knights keep blacks and whites from having sex together and risking the purity of the white race. Not simply racism—fear and loathing of an allegedly inferior race—but a defense of the white race based on memories of the past demanded action against those who crossed the racial/sexual divide.[12]

Such depictions of the past confirmed idealized gender roles. There were many reasons why the group called themselves Knights of the Ku Klux Klan, but one of them was that they defended the damsel in distress in the best tradition of English chivalry. They were "tall men, sun'crowned, who live above the fog . . . real men, courageous, who flinch not at duty." They protected helpless women from those who would prey on them, which usually meant protection from Jews, Catholics, and blacks. It meant protection from the evils of society. It implied that women were weak, could not take care of themselves, and needed their knight. Memory of what a medieval knight should be underscored what a modern knight should be and, of course, what a modern woman should be.[13]

In an age of rapid change and, not surprisingly, fear of modernity, the Klan found its moorings in the past, a past of the Civil War and Reconstruction, a past where chivalrous Anglo Saxon knights protected fair damsels and engaged in crusades against the infidels, and a past in which the Christian church first took form. Across Texas the Klan drew heavily on Protestant churches for its members and leaders, and it continually stressed that it sought to uphold Protestantism. This Protestantism was not just any type but more often a Protestantism that stressed a return to the ways of the original church and/or a Protestantism that stressed a need to purify modern society. Occasionally, some Protestant denominations such as the Churches of Christ stressed the need to return to the early church but typically stayed within their own exclusive group, eschewing reform of the larger world. Most Protestant denominations in the South, however, stressed both the need to purify the larger society and to restore traditional religion. In any case, Protestantism based on memories energized the Klan.[14]

Strong anti-Catholicism fed this mix of primitivism, moral progress, and adherence to the KKK. Klan literature often devoted more space to attacks on Catholics than to any other topic. In one typical piece the editors of the *Texas 100 Percent American* argued that there were "two ways—the way of Christ and the way of Rome." Dismissing the development of the church from the fifth to the sixteenth century, adherents of the Klan argued that Catholics had perverted true Christianity. True Christians either returned to the early days of the church or continued the Reformation tradition. Anything that sprang from in between did not follow the ways of Christ. As the Klan manual argued, "Membership is restricted to those who accept the tenets of true Christianity, which is essentially Protestant." Klan spokesmen argued that Catholics interjected a man, the pope, between believers and God. They argued that the church hierarchy went against the traditions of the early church. They accused priests of taking sexual advantage of nuns and of holding them in slavery. Catholics taught children to obey a foreign power, the pope, instead of instilling loyalty to the U.S. government. They undermined public education. Catholics plotted to seize power in the government and conspired to subvert freedom and liberty.[15]

While these Klan pronouncements were standard fare for an anti-Catholic age, what gave them particular energy was the insistence that Catholics were un-Christian. That position flowed from the argument that only churches close to the early church in form and function could be Christian. Throughout the nineteenth century and into the early twentieth century, Baptists, Methodists, Cumberland Presbyterians, Disciples of Christ, Churches of Christ, Pentecostals, and others in smaller Protestant denominations sought a return to the primitive church. This return involved various practices, including particular forms of baptism, music, church structure, ecumenism, and education of the ministry. It also involved a rejection of science and modern analysis of the Bible. The key to understanding the link to the Klan was that it rested on a distinct memory of what the early church was like, a memory that made Catholicism unacceptable.[16]

By the 1920s some elements of restorationist theology emerged in the fundamentalist movement that was occurring in several Protestant denominations. Fundamentalists believed themselves the true adherents of restoration theology, the ones who truly sought a return to the first principles of Christianity and who fit prevalent images of what the early church was like. In Texas, J. Frank Norris led the fundamentalist movement, and he was

FIG. 5.1. "Hurrah for the Ku Klux Klan," from the cover of sheet music published in 1923 by Mrs. Harvey Thompson of Waller, Texas. Note the mix of Protestant and Klan imagery, including the anti-Catholic banner. Courtesy Cushing Library, Texas A&M University, College Station, Texas.

closely linked to the Fort Worth Klan. This link between conservative theology, fundamentalism, and Klan membership occurred across Texas, and it had much to do with the rejection of modernism—including the rejection of evolution, the use of history to evaluate the Bible, and the use of other forms of modern biblical criticism—but it also drew upon conceptions of what the church once was and again should be.[17]

While some believers in restorationist theology and fundamentalism rejected involvement in political movements, for many, calls to enforce prohibition laws underscored the need to return to a more perfect age and the identification of Catholicism as un-Christian. Prohibition rested on the belief that greater perfection was obtainable in the here and now. It simply required more Christ-like practices and returning to ancient principles. (Advocates of prohibition conveniently ignored common references to the consumption of wine in the Bible, including the miracle of Christ turning water into wine.) Catholics consumed wine. Immigrant groups such as the Irish and the Germans, who were often Catholic, opposed prohibition and defended the consumption of alcohol. The Klan took it on itself to defend society from those who violated prohibition laws, and a large percentage of Klan violence was directed against bootleggers and their customers.[18]

Klansmen believed that "the real opponents to illiteracy and enforcement of prohibition are the Catholic church and the Knights of Columbus." Indeed they seldom saw the need to distinguish between attacks on Catholics and defense of prohibition; the two accomplished the same thing. This advocacy of prohibition and link to anti-Catholicism fit easily with a type of millenarianism common to believers in restoration theology. Perfection might elude human beings on earth, but good government, great happiness, and prosperity lay within reach. You just needed to create a world like the early church. You simply needed sincere Protestant citizens who worked for Klan principles and all would be possible, according to Reverend Wright: "The supreme aim of the Klan is to develop a dependable Christian citizenship that will be patriotic in serving the country, both in times of war and in times of peace. The perpetuation of the government and the existence and safety of civilization depends upon the type and character of citizens we produce during the present age."[19]

Thus, affirming Protestantism and adhering to the Klan were acts of great patriotism for members. Here, too, Klansmen entered into the world of memory, particularly by stressing George Washington and the American flag. Ironically, for an organization whose other memories included the Confederacy, when it came time to build patriotism, its spokesmen turned to American images and symbols. George Washington earned special praise, and clearly the Klan displayed far more interest in the remembered Washington than the real Washington. In June 1923 the Klan newspaper in Texas accused historian Samuel Flagg Bemus of rewriting history when Bemus disputed one of the sayings attributed to Washington. Klansmen wanted a virtuous Washington who never told a lie and who conquered all, and they reacted vehemently to any chipping away at the icon. In fact, they saw a conspiracy in attempts to use the term "District of Columbia" instead of "Washington City." Klansmen felt obliged to point out that Columbus did not really discover America, Leif Erickson did. This article of belief, of course, fit nicely with anti-Catholicism and diatribes against the Knights of Columbus. It also reinforced their belief that northern and western Europeans—not Italians—accomplished all that was worthwhile. Thus, denigrating Columbus and elevating Washington completed a triple play. It pointed to the virtue of the race. It slammed Catholics, and it sanctified a founder of the nation.[20]

Klansmen repeatedly insisted that love of country compelled them to join the Klan and to act as they did. As Klansmen in Jefferson, Texas, put it, "We love our country and will save it. We salute one flag and will follow it and know one government and stand ready always and everywhere to die for it." They loved the American flag and adored American memories. In fact Texas Klansmen even accepted Abraham Lincoln as a true American hero and used him in their literature far more often than Confederates such as Jefferson Davis or Robert E. Lee. In the 1920s, at least, the Confederate flag never appeared as a prominent Klan symbol. Instead, in their promotional literature the American flag joined their other symbols: mounted knight, sword, shield, and cross.[21]

Flags evoked conflicting and often controversial memories as a 1921 incident in Houston illustrated. That year the local Ku Klux Klan, Sam Houston Klan Number 1, began donating funds for the purchase of American flags, and a local group called the War Mothers placed a large flag purchased with Klan money on the corner of Main and McKinney. A Houston priest on his way to perform the funeral service of a fallen soldier, disturbed that this patriotic Catholic would be excluded from the Klan, refused to salute the flag and said so in the service. According to the *Houston Chronicle* the priest explained, "No man or set of men can question the Americanism of that young man who sacrificed his life for those colors that shelter his casket, and we can only condemn and despise any organization that proclaims 100 per cent Americanism, yet excludes from its membership such men as he." A firestorm of protest followed. In one letter to the editor, a writer insisted, "The United States became the land of the free and the home of the brave through the bravery of George Washington and the legal talent of Thomas Jefferson and this beginning was cemented by Abraham Lincoln, and the basis of our government is the Holy Bible, giving freedom to every man who is sound in mind and members. The emblem of my country is the flag and it is entitled to all the reverence we can give it." Other letter writers went on to defend the Klan as a patriotic organization and the flag as always deserving of support no matter what. The flag called forth unthinking patriotism and forged a natural link with Washington, Jefferson, and Lincoln. No matter

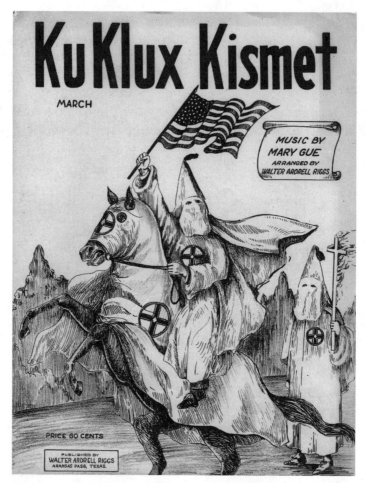

FIG. 5.2. "Ku Klux Kismet," from the cover of sheet music published in 1924 by Walter Ardrell Riggs of Aransas Pass, Texas. Note the American flag held high by the mounted knight with the fiery cross in the background. Courtesy Cushing Library, Texas A&M University, College Station, Texas.

what the Klan did, while it was clothed in the flag the Klan deserved support. In a country where memories of World War I remained fresh, patriotism increased membership and encouraged Klansmen to preserve and protect right attitudes toward the country and its symbols.[22]

This Americanism blended with the other memories undergirding the Klan, and that potent mixture of memories led to specific action. In the 1921 Mayfest incident in Brenham mentioned earlier, in addition to the signs reminding onlookers that their "fathers were here in '61," Klansmen also carried signs that read "Speak English or quit talking on the streets of Brenham."

The four hundred Klansmen from Houston (probably joined by numerous Klansmen from the Brenham area) went further and posted a proclamation that read in part, "Having pledged our allegiance to the Flag which protects our Nation, we maintain and insist upon 100 per cent Americanism, which includes speaking the English Language." Texas Klansmen targeted Germans because, just as their ancestors had done in 1861, they needed to defend their communities from a foreign threat. In this case it was an un-American threat and a non-Anglo Saxon threat. Germans also became targets because they were not restoration Protestants and because they drank home brew and bootleg whiskey at Mayfest and other community gatherings. Obviously America's recent war against Germany made attacking Texas Germans a defense of the flag. Both the selection of targets—Germans in this case—and the willingness to act depended upon memories and myths of the Civil War and Reconstruction, of Anglo Saxon knights, of restoration Protestantism, and of Americanism.[23]

German Texans in the Brenham area struck back at the Klan in a variety of ways. In other nearby areas in the Texas German Belt local residents got out their guns to meet Klan violence head on, but in Brenham Germans were content to use more peaceful means. They limited the public use of the German language, and they stressed their own Americanism. They pointed to the service of their sons in the recent war. They also used the ballot box. As was often true in Texas, the local sheriff, Burney Parker, belonged to the Klan. When he ran for reelection in 1924, he realized that German Texans had enough votes to defeat him and so he moved to disband the local Klan. On his motion in July 1924 the local Klan chapter, Klan Number 20, voted to disband and gave up its charter. Parker put out a broadside calling for reconciliation and highlighting his role in ending the Klan in Brenham and Washington County. It did not matter. He lost badly to Hoffman Reese and joked to the new German Texan sheriff that he had to keep his gun, saying, "Anyone who got so few votes in the election as I did needs a gun." Memories of the Civil War and Reconstruction, calls to preserve the Anglo Saxon race, commitment to restoration Protestantism, and an Americanism that stressed "English only" did not resonate with German Texans, and they organized around their own version of Americanism and their own appeals to ethnic solidarity based on memories of being German Texans.[24]

African Americans also faced action motivated by a complex set of memories, and they too resisted. In February 1922 near Texarkana, P. Norman, a black farmer, drove W. T. Jordan, the white deputy sheriff, from his neighbor's farm. A few days later Jordan arrested Norman for bootlegging, and four masked and robed men widely assumed to belong to the Klan murdered him while he was in Jordan's custody. In their eyes Norman's actions called for a violent defense of white supremacy.[25]

William A. Owens well remembered such defenses of white supremacy in Commerce, Texas. Once a week one fall in the early 1920s Owens went out to watch the Klan parade through the streets: "After the march there were speeches in the middle of town, mainly repetitions and enlargements on slogans I had lived with all my life: 'Keep the niggers in their place,' 'Give them a inch, they'll take a mile,' 'You watch out, they'll take the bread right out o' yo' mouths.'" Being a knight of the Ku Klux Klan called for defense of these principles, for a defense of the Anglo Saxon race. Such a defense was all the easier when the offending black who overstepped his place could be accused of bootlegging. Then calls for the new millennium and prohibition reinforced a defense of the purity and prosperity of the white race.[26]

Occasionally, African Americans also took to the ballot box to express their own ideas about Americanism and to limit the impact of the Ku Klux Klan. Although the white primary and the poll tax squeezed most blacks out of the political process in the 1920s, in the larger urban areas they still voted in municipal elections. In hotly contested elections even Klan sympathizers needed black votes and toned down their white supremacy rhetoric. Instead they based their appeals to black voters on the other mainstays of the Klan: knighthood, Protestantism, and Americanism. In 1923 Mayor E. R. Cockrell of Fort Worth, a Klan sympathizer if not a member of the Klan, appeared before a black audience at the Saint James Baptist Church. Appealing for their votes in the upcoming election, Cockrell declared, "When I was elected your mayor I told you I would stop certain practices of dirty, low down white men preying on your girlhood, and womanhood, and I have. There are some of those kind of men and in Fort Worth there is an organization known as the Ku Klux Klan, and I want the Klan to get those white men and take them behind the barn and spank them. If the Klansmen touch any unoffending negro, however, they will have to get me, too." Cockrell went on to attack bootleggers of all races and to claim that he delivered needed city services. Blacks too would be part of a progressive American city. Using Protestant themes for a Protestant crowd, Cockrell defended the Klan and his own involvement with it. His knighthood extended to defending black as well as white women. His idea of progress included blacks. Perhaps he was desperate, for an anti-Klan slate of city leaders soon dominated Fort Worth, but for a time the Klan worked to appeal to blacks along the same lines that they appealed to whites. White supremacy took second place to political survival as candidates appealed to black voters' Protestantism, knighthood, and Americanism.[27]

Ironically, Americanism proved to be the attacking wedge for opponents of the Klan who presented their own memories of the founders and their own conceptions of what it truly meant to continue the traditions of the past. Part of the problem for Klansmen was that the four memories that sustained the Klan often came into conflict. Obviously, it proved difficult to sustain both a claim to Confederate antecedents and to the tradition of Abraham Lincoln. Religious memories and Americanism led to action against German Texans, but Americanism that rested on democratic elections made such attacks suicidal in German-dominated counties. In like fashion, knighthood trumped white supremacy when a candidate needed black votes. On another level, however, the contest became a struggle over who got to define what being American meant—who achieved power by controlling what was remembered and what was forgotten. The opponents of the Klan won this struggle in Texas, and in the process both Klansmen and their opponents became less southern, less Texan, and more American.[28]

American memories used by opponents of the Klan also tended to fall into four categories. First, opponents claimed that no self-respecting Texan, the descendant of the quintessential Americans who won freedom during the Texas Revolution, would tolerate the Klan. Second, they pointed to the efforts of George Washington, Benjamin Franklin, Thomas Jefferson, and other founders to secure religious freedom. Third, they argued that the Klan undermined traditional reliance on the Constitution and the law. Fourth, they insisted on an inclusive and tolerant Americanism in the tradition of Abraham Lincoln.

The Klan so outraged A. V. Dalrymple of Fort Worth that in 1923 he published *Liberty Dethroned: An Indictment of the Ku Klux Klan Based Solely upon Its Own Pronouncements, Philosophy, and Acts of Mob Violence.* In this book, Dalrymple, a wealthy businessman and veteran of the Spanish American War, published a letter that read in part,

> I have faith enough in Texas to believe that the breed that died at Goliad and the Alamo, that plucked victory from the hazards and odds at San Jacinto, that gave a new republic to the world and a new pledge to human liberty, has not passed out of the Lone Star State. That band of heroes and patriots had men of many races and creeds. I know that the men who marched and fought with Houston[,] who counseled with Dallas and Burleson, who died with Travis, Crockett, and Bowie have not forgotten the deeds and principles of their fathers. . . . The men whose fathers drove a king from America and a dictator from Texas,

who cemented every stone in the Temple of American liberty with their blood, are not likely to tolerate the lawlessness and insolence of these secret society Santa Annas, either in Texas or elsewhere in free America.

The Texas Revolution against Mexico marked Texans as special, as both set apart from other Americans and as carrying on the unique American mission. The Klan could name its first organization in the state "the Sam Houston Klan" if it wanted. Yet for Dalrymple and the contributors to his volume, those who truly walked in the footsteps of the mighty Houston eschewed the lawlessness and prejudice of the Klan. No secret organization should be tolerated in a land consecrated by the blood of the heroic Texans of the revolutionary generation.[29]

Dalrymple also insisted that if George Washington and the other founders of the nation had not been sure that the U.S. Constitution protected religious freedom, they would have gone back and reworked the Constitution. Denying this basic freedom moved the Klan outside the pale. As the editor of the *Fort Worth Press* argued, "In this free country, where the right to worship God according to the dictates of one's own conscience is written into basic law of the land, no stigma attaches to adherence to Catholicism or any other faith, so far as those who think clearly, those whose minds are not warped by prejudice, are concerned." To be Catholic was to be American, to act in the best tradition of the founders. To oppose Catholicism was to be un-American and to act counter to the will of Washington, Jefferson, Franklin, and a host of other luminaries that designed the Constitution and the basic laws of the land.[30]

These same founders, according to opponents of the Klan, went to great lengths to establish the rule of law. Arguing that there was no need for the Klan, the editors of the *Dallas Morning News* insisted that "if freedom is endangered, it is by the redivivus of the mob spirit in the disguising garb of the Ku Klux Klan." In 1922 Judge P. A. Turner of Bowie County declared before the grand jury investigating Norman's murder that the Klan was "the most dangerous organization that has ever been organized in this country or that has been perpetuated in this country. It is the most dangerous organization I have ever known in my life to destroy law and order and government." Law, order, and government as designed by the founders stood imperiled by the Klan.[31]

In 1924 the Klan became the main issue of the Texas governor's race. The Klan candidate, Felix Robertson, led in the first primary and seemed destined to win. He failed, however, to secure enough votes to avoid a runoff. In the second primary he faced Miriam A. Ferguson, the wife of former governor James E. Ferguson, who had been impeached in 1917 and barred from holding state office. In a contest that set a record for turnout in any Texas election to that point, Jim Ferguson did most of the speaking. Loudly proclaiming that "our daddies set up a Republic and the voice of the people!" he insisted, "The klan would set up an empire and the voice of a grand gizzard. We are not going to bow to the voice of any dern gizzard that ever set on any dern throne." Besides poking fun at the title of Imperial Wizard, reserved for the head of the Klan, Ferguson demonstrated the common appeal of referring to the founding fathers and accusing the Klan of being undemocratic. It was a winning strategy. Despite her husband's impeachment and his opposition to prohibition, Miriam Ferguson won and served as the first woman governor of the state.[32]

Campaigning against Felix Robertson in 1924 drew together all the disparate elements who stood opposed to the Klan. The campaign's themes touched on being truly Texan and American. The Klan violated a growing sense that Texans' past made them modern Americans free from the irrational violence, visceral racism, and reactionary group behavior characteristic of a southern past, and it violated a carefully cultivated memory that Texans acted as honorable individuals instead of part of a mob. (These memories conveniently ignored a long history of white violence toward blacks in Texas, including gruesome lynchings attended by thousands of spectators.) Remembering an idealized past America, opponents of the Klan called for renewal. As the editor of the *Fort Worth Press* put it during the hotly contested 1924 gubernatorial election, "The people of Texas are coming back to a democracy of basic principles; a sound, rugged democracy as staunch as the heart of the oak. This democracy of basic principles pledges against discrimination on account of race, color or creed, and means what it says." Just as Klansmen called for a return to the old-time religion of the early church, their opponents called for a return to the founding tenets of American democracy and argued that Texas would be disgraced by the election of a Klan governor.[33]

Instead of a Klansman, Texans elected a woman. Given the elaborate gender roles associated with the Klan and their desire to protect womanhood, this outcome must have been particularly galling to the Texas Klan. In fact, it happened at about the same time as prominent women tried to get a Women of the Klan organization off the ground in Texas, and this Klan initiative may have been a response to the realization that, as in the case of blacks in Fort Worth, women voted. Miriam Ferguson actually played a clever game. She appealed for the votes of progressive women on the grounds that they needed to support their sex, and she appealed to more traditional men and women by representing herself as an old-style woman in a bonnet and plain farm dress. By appealing to memories of home and hearth she won votes.[34]

Voting for a woman, stressing both modernity and home and hearth, insisting on old-style American democracy—these things pointed to a key characteristic of opposition to the Klan. It was inclusive, not exclusive. It included all religious groups and all ethnic and racial groups—even African Americans in city elections. Attacks on the Klan as being un-American because of its exclusivity became common by the early 1920s. Dalrymple, for example, insisted that the Klan featured "religious intolerance, race hatred, thirst for political power, disregard of Constitutional government, contempt for the legal rights of others, and commercial craftiness through the boycott of not only Jews, Catholics, and the foreign-born, but all others who refuse to join the Klan." The Fergusons and other opponents of the Klan depicted themselves as the representatives of all the people. Here again opponents sought to harness memories of the past to achieve power in the present. They were inclusive after the pattern of Washington and especially Lincoln. For Dalrymple, "the Triple K constitutes a real menace confronting this nation, and that for our Union to endure there must be a firm belief in Constitutional Government OF THE PEOPLE, BY THE PEOPLE AND FOR THE PEOPLE."[35]

In enlisting Lincoln in their struggle to defeat the Klan, Dalrymple and other opponents of the Klan threw themselves into the midst of the intellectual shift from a southern mindset to an American mindset—because Lincoln, unlike Washington, signified a growing acceptance of a common national identity. Uses of George Washington in Texas persisted through the nineteenth and early twentieth century unabated and had entered the language of normal discourse. Even the Civil War did not lessen reliance on Washington, and if anything the need to prove they were more truly American than the North increased references to Washington in the South. The use of Lincoln, however, did not begin until the early twentieth century and signaled a new day, a shift in historical memory and self-identity among whites in Texas. By 1921 Lincoln had achieved a lofty place in Texans' minds as demonstrated by the quote used earlier: "The United States became the land of the free and the home of the brave through the bravery of George Washington and the legal talent of Thomas Jefferson and this beginning was cemented by Abraham Lincoln." Lincoln joined Washington and Jefferson as a type of short-hand reference to all that was right about the United States.[36]

Common reference to Lincoln indicated that the public mind had

shifted from the days when only Confederate images and Confederate symbols would do in Texas, a day when all the statues were of Confederates and
all the political speeches contained florid references to the Southland. I have
elsewhere argued that this shift began about 1910, and the evidence cited in
this essay indicates that the shift accelerated after 1920. Thus the Klan rose in
stature at a time when memories of the past stood roughly balanced between
southern and American images and symbols. It declined as the balance tilted
toward the American side. The question becomes: What did the Klan and
the memories that undergirded its proponents and opponents have to do
with this transformation?[37]

Interestingly, both support of the Klan and opposition to the Klan moved
Texans from Jefferson Davis toward Abraham Lincoln. Both defense and
criticism of the Klan nurtured an intellectual climate in which the past was
contested, not fixed. Change came easier in this fluid intellectual climate. In
addition, in constantly stressing their true Americanism both sides moved
away from easy references to a southern past. Repetition bred new habits of
mind. The intellectual transformation already under way influenced the outcome of the struggle over the Klan, but the influence went both ways. The
contest over who defined Americanism accelerated the transformation away
from a Confederate past.

Basically, from 1910 to 1936 Texans lived in a world with competing
memories and competing identities. A dialectic of types operated in society and culture.[38] Baldly put, on the one hand stood the Confederacy and
separation from the rest of the United States and on the other stood the
Texas Revolution and Republic, inclusion in the westering experience, and
American symbols such as Abraham Lincoln. Yet, as the Klan demonstrated,
this straightforward dialectic oversimplified what happened. It first appeared
in Texas at a Confederate gathering and depended heavily for its resonance
on memories of the Reconstruction Klan in the South. Klansmen sometimes named their chapters for Confederate veterans and certainly embodied
southern-style racism. Yet the 1920s Klansmen preferred the American flag to
the Confederate flag and made much of their claim to be 100 percent American. They too referred to Abraham Lincoln. The organization demonstrated
surprising strength outside the South, in Indiana, Pennsylvania, Oregon,
California, and elsewhere. Southern features and American characteristics
blended in the Texas Klan.[39]

This joining of memories and symbols followed a broader intellectual
pattern for the 1920s. Seeming opposites blended in one voice in a milieu
with a series of dialectics at work: romanticism and a fascination with the late

Middle Ages versus science and progress; nostalgia for a past America versus confidence in an emerging future; primitivism in religion versus the social gospel; coerced community versus unfettered individualism. Texas was a more extreme and in some ways an easier-to-analyze part of the whole—part of the whole United States and part of the whole of western Europe where fascism grew in a similar milieu.

In her detailed study of the Klan in Athens, Georgia, Nancy MacLean argues that members of the lower middle class, caught between labor and capital and always in danger of falling back from the hard-earned positions they had won over the past decade, used the Klan to express their frustrations and fears and to exert the power of their class. Ironically, attempts by the lower middle class to define society as classless led to focus on differences derived from "race, sex, and age." Although lacking the same detailed records available to MacLean, I would suggest that the impetus behind the Klan seemed broader in Texas. It was a moral crusade, as Charles Alexander long ago argued. It was a moral crusade that drew strength from the medium of expression—from memories and myths.[40]

MacLean, however, also includes a thought-provoking comparison of the American Klan and European fascist movements, and including memory in this comparison adds to its relevance. Reliance upon the emotions stirred by memories obviously resembled contemporary Italian fascism and the Nazi movement in Germany. The very term *fascism* came from the bundled rods used as a symbol of power in Roman times. Concepts of the Aryan race and attempts to purify and protect that remembered race animated Nazis. Memory did much the same thing for fascists and Klansmen. It drew them together and it focused them on particular targets. It encouraged actions. Yet the analogy should not be overdrawn. European fascist movements lacked the religious memories of the Klan. More importantly they lacked the emphasis on Americanism. They worshiped different ancestors, a crucial difference made clear by members of the Dallas Klan when they argued, "Klansmen love their country with that genuine zeal and devotion that invariably marks the highest type of American citizenship, and one of the highest and greatest aims of the organization is to preserve and maintain, at any cost, and hand down to succeeding generations, those splendid ideals, those fundamental principles of good and noble citizenship and those glorious traditions that have come to us as a priceless heritage from our forefathers and that distinguish the United States of America from any other country on the globe."[41] This worship of Americanism allowed the Klan to be attacked for violating a different collection of memories of what it meant to be American.

Violence, mob rule, the influence of secret societies, allegiance to a political boss, and the many other alleged crimes of the Klan drew criticism because they violated the American way—the old-time democracy lauded by opponents of the Klan.[42] In places without such memories of an American way of acting and places without widespread acceptance of the importance of Americanism, these charges had less impact. The resonance of these charges, the need to balance action with keeping inside the limits of acceptable American behavior, kept the Klan from drifting toward advocacy of authoritarian rule. Certainly the most hard-core advocates of the Klan had few scruples about compromising democracy or violating the rights of their victims. Unlike Klan politicians and their supporters, they cared little that their actions might get them voted out of office and probably held no qualms about violating the American way. They argued that their opponents simply misunderstood the Klan. For them their ends justified their means. Those on the margins of the Klan, however, like Sheriff Parker in Brenham or Mayor Cockrell in Fort Worth, held a more nuanced view. Whatever the mixed reasons for their original allegiance to the Klan—fraternalism, class, a hard-boiled attempt to gain votes and power, the pull of memory, or some other reason— Parker and Cockrell accepted the political process. They accepted the defeats that came to them because of their Klan affiliation. They remained within the American system.

You could add to this list merchants such as Marvin Leonard of Fort Worth, who probably joined the Klan at least in part to keep the business of Klansmen. Leonard clearly felt the pull of the religious memories of the Klan and identified with the calls for defense of prohibition. Yet Klan violence eventually led him to give up active participation. This withdrawal was relatively easy by the late 1920s, however, because there were fewer Klansmen to do business with. As the Klan began to decline, for those on the margins of the Klan Americanism was just as likely to help pry them away from the Klan as to keep them attached to it. For Leonard, Cockrell, Parker, and probably countless others in the Klan, the debate over Americanism proved the weakest link in their attachment to the Klan. Thus, in the end the broad shift from Confederate to American memories contributed to the rapid collapse of the Klan in Texas.[43]

But the story was more complicated than that—the competition to demonstrate that one side was more American than the other also contributed to the transformation in public identity. Arguments about Americanism between Klansmen and their opponents sharpened the focus on memories that all citizens could share and diminished the focus on what separated Texans and southerners from other Americans. Thus, continuous talk of Lincoln, waving the American flag, and the general emphasis on American citizenship further legitimized a non-southern identity. Southern images and southern memories did not disappear from Texas, but they did become less combatively un-American. In 1936, Franklin D. Roosevelt came to Lee Park in Dallas to unveil a new statue of Robert E. Lee on his horse Traveler. Confederate imagery continued in public life, but interestingly by this point the president and most of the rest of the country as well accepted Lee as a hero. At least in Texas the divide between North and South was disappearing. The Klan that began life in Texas as the child of the Confederacy and Reconstruction both reflected and assisted this process of transformation.[44]

Thus, memory played a vital role in the story of the Ku Klux Klan in Texas during the 1920s. Use of the past allowed Klansmen to attract new members and directed their actions. The past also served as a rallying point for opponents of the Klan. Memories shaped and focused the actions and ideas of Klansmen as well as their opponents. Some of what they did—the differences between bigoted Klansmen and equally bigoted non-Klansmen, for example—can adequately be explained only by the use of memory. Organized, focused, and ritualistic use of memory turned ideas into actions. These actions elicited opposition, and the opponents of the Klan proved equally adept at harnessing the power of memory. There ensued a pitched battle of sorts over true Americanism. The Klan grew weaker in Texas for many reasons, including this counterattack on the memory front. One historian recently described the use of memory as "the human quest to own the past and thereby achieve control over the present."[45] The Klan did not own the past unchallenged and therefore could not achieve full power in the present. As an unintended consequence of this struggle over Americanism Texans became less southern. This shift made memory a transforming and energizing force as well as a means of defending entrenched power. Past and present met in the 1920s to create a new Texas that by 1936 more nearly resembled the rest of the nation.

NOTES

1. Nancy MacLean, *Behind the Mask of Chivalry: The Making of the Second Ku Klux Klan* (New York: Oxford University Press, 1994), argues for the importance of race and class and that the Klan was an expression of reactionary populism that could be compared to European fascism. Kathleen M. Blee, *Women of the Klan: Racism and Gender in the 1920s* (Berkeley: Uni-

versity of California Press, 1991), argues that the Klan reflected the mainstream, middle-class Protestant view of the average white American in the 1920s. For a discussion of the literature see David A. Horowitz, ed., *Inside the Klavern: The Secret History of a Ku Klux Klan of the 1920s* (Carbondale: Southern Illinois University Press, 1999), 1–3, 153–54; Leonard J. Moore, "Historical Interpretations of the 1920s Klan: The Traditional View and Recent Revisions," in *The Invisible Empire in the West: Toward a New Historical Appraisal of the Ku Klux Klan of the 1920s,* ed. Shawn Lay (Urbana: University of Illinois Press, 1992), 17–38. For an introduction to the history of the Klan in Texas see Charles C. Alexander, *The Ku Klux Klan in the Southwest* (Lexington: University of Kentucky Press, 1965).

2. For good examples of historians' treatment of memory see John Bodnar, *Remaking America: Public Memory, Commemoration, and Patriotism in the Twentieth Century* (Princeton, N.J.: Princeton University Press, 1992); "The Uses of Memory: A Round Table," *Journal of American History* 85 (Sept. 1998): 409–65; W. Fitzhugh Brundage, ed., *Where These Memories Grow: History, Memory, and Southern Identity* (Chapel Hill: University of North Carolina Press, 2000); Michel-Rolph Trouillot, *Silencing the Past: Power and the Production of History* (Boston: Beacon Press, 1995); Richard R. Flores, "Memory-Place, Meaning, and the Alamo," *American Literary History* 10 (Fall 1998): 428–45; Kirk Savage, *Standing Soldiers, Kneeling Slaves: Race, War, and Monuments in Nineteenth-Century America* (Princeton, N.J.: Princeton University Press, 1997). For a Texas example of the use of memory in a conservative fashion see Walter L. Buenger, "'The Story of Texas'? The Texas State History Museum and Forgetting and Remembering the Past," *Southwestern Historical Quarterly* 105 (Jan. 2002): 481–93.

3. Blee, *Women of the Klan,* 157.

4. *Houston Post,* Oct. 9, 1920. On the growth and influence of the Klan in Texas see Norman D. Brown, *Hood, Bonnet, and Little Brown Jug: Texas Politics, 1921–1928* (College Station: Texas A&M University Press, 1984), 47–128; Alexander, *The Ku Klux Klan in the Southwest;* Charles C. Alexander, *Crusade for Conformity: The Ku Klux Klan in Texas, 1920–1930* (Houston: Texas Gulf Coast Historical Association, 1962); Max Bentley, "The Ku Klux Klan in Texas," *McClure's Magazine* 57 (May 1924): 11–21.

5. *Houston Post,* Oct. 10, 1920; *Brenham Morning Messenger,* May 21, 1921; *Texas 100 Percent American,* May 19, 1922.

6. J. T. Renfro, "The Invisible Empire, Knights of the Ku Klux Klan: A Sermon Delivered at Sinton, Texas," June 4, 1922, 3, Center for American History, University of Texas at Austin (hereafter, CAH); W. C. Wright, *Religious and Patriotic Ideals of the Ku Klux Klan: Being a Plain, Practical and Thorough Expositor of the Principles, Purposes and Practices of the Ku Klux Klan, a Textbook on Klancraft for the Instruction of Klansmen and the Information of the Non-Klansmen* (Waco, Tex.: n.p., 1926), 7. Also see Charles William Ramsdell, *Reconstruction in Texas* (New York: Columbia University Press, 1910); David Goldfield, *Still Fighting the Civil War: The American South and Southern History* (Baton Rouge: Louisiana State University Press, 2002), 15–42; Randolph B. Campbell, "Statehood, Civil War, and Reconstruction, 1846–76," in *Texas through Time: Evolving Interpretations,* ed. Walter L. Buenger and Robert A. Calvert (College Station: Texas A&M University Press, 1991), 191–96. For a good indication of the high standing of the Reconstruction-era Klan among early-twentieth-century Texas historians, see W. D. Wood, "The Ku Klux Klan," *Texas Historical Association Quarterly* (later the *Southwestern Historical Quarterly*) 9 (Oct. 1906): 262–68.

7. A. V. Dalrymple, *Liberty Dethroned: An Indictment of the Ku Klux Klan Based Solely upon Its Own Pronouncements, Philosophy, and Acts of Mob Violence* (Philadelphia, Pa: Times Publishing Company, 1923), 11. Also see Randolph B. Campbell, *Gone to Texas: A History of the Lone Star State* (New York: Oxford University Press, 2003), 281. For a northern example of deifying the original Klan while rejecting the 1920s version, see Ezra Asher Cook, *Ku Klux*

Klan Secrets Exposed: Attitude toward Jews, Catholics, Foreigners, and Masons: Fraudulent Methods Used, Atrocities Committed in Name of the Order (Chicago: Ezra A. Cook, 1922), 5–20.

8. Renfro, "The Invisible Empire," 5.

9. *Texas 100 Percent American,* Feb. 14, 1923. Also see Hiram W. Evans, *The Klan of Tomorrow, and, the Klan Spiritual* (n.p.: Knights of the Ku Klux Klan, 1924), 5–9. Evans, a Dallas native, became the Imperial Wizard of the Klan in 1923 (*Texas 100 Percent American,* Apr. 11, 1923).

10. For typical race-based justifications of the Klan, see *Jefferson Jimplecute,* June 14, 1922; *Texas 100 Percent American,* Apr. 21, 1922.

11. W. C. Wright, *The Seven Symbols of the Klan,* reprinted from the Dec. 29, 1920, issue of the *Fellowship Forum,* available in the CAH.

12. Wright, *Religious and Patriotic Ideals,* 44.

13. Klan self-description printed in the *Jefferson Jimplecute,* June 14, 1922.

14. For additional thoughts on the Klan and religion, see Walter L. Buenger, *The Path to a Modern South: Northeast Texas between Reconstruction and the Great Depression* (Austin: University of Texas Press, 2001), 206–209; David Chalmers, "Ku Klux Klan," in *Encyclopedia of Religion in the South,* ed. Samuel S. Hill (Mercer, Ga.: Mercer University Press, 1984), 396–97; Robert M. Miller, "A Note on the Relationship between the Protestant Churches and the Ku Klux Klan," *Journal of Southern History* 22 (Aug. 1956): 257–66.

15. *Texas 100 Percent American,* Apr. 27, 1923; Ku Klux Klan, *Ideals of the Ku Klux Klan* (broadside, no date or publisher, but with 1920s material). Every issue of the *Texas 100 Percent American* from 1922 to 1924 contained at least one anti-Catholic article.

16. For a straightforward introduction to a complex phenomenon, see Paul K. Conkin, *American Originals: Homemade Varieties of Christianity* (Chapel Hill: University of North Carolina Press, 1997), 1–56; Richard T. Hughes, "Restorationist Christianity," in *Encyclopedia of Southern Culture,* ed. Charles Reagan Wilson and William Ferris (Chapel Hill: University of North Carolina Press, 1989), 1303–1306. Also see Kenneth K. Bailey, *Southern White Protestantism in the Twentieth Century* (New York: Harper & Row, 1964); David Harrell, "Fundamentalism," in *Encyclopedia of Southern Culture,* ed. Wilson and Ferris, 1288–89; and Glenn T. Miller, "Modernism and Religion," in *Encyclopedia of Southern Culture,* ed. Wilson and Ferris, 1294–96.

17. On Norris and the Klan see *Fort Worth Press,* Nov. 7, 1924; July 23, 1926; John W. Storey, *Texas Baptist Leadership and Social Change, 1900–1980* (College Station: Texas A&M University Press, 1986), 39–69; C. Gwin Morris, "He Changed Things: The Life and Thought of J. Frank Norris" (Ph.D. diss., Texas Tech University, 1973). For other examples of the link between religion and the Klan, see *Paris Morning News,* Apr. 19, 1922; Renfro, "The Invisible Empire"; Wright, *Religious and Patriotic Ideals.*

18. *Fort Worth Press,* Mar. 29, 1923; *Paris Morning News,* May 3, 6, 7, 26, 1922; Buenger, *The Path to a Modern South,* 206; Alexander, *Crusade for Conformity,* 1–14; Brown, *Hood Bonnet, and Little Brown Jug,* 49–87.

19. *Texas 100 Percent American,* May 25, 1923; Wright, *Religious and Patriotic Ideals,* 37.

20. *Texas 100 Percent American,* June 22, 1923; June 16, 1922.

21. *Jefferson Jimplecute,* June 14, 1922. Also see *Texas 100 Percent American,* Feb. 8, 24, 1924; Wright, *Seven Symbols.* For an example of Klan women's use of an American flag in a parade, see *Fort Worth Press,* June 9, 1923.

22. *Houston Chronicle,* Sept. 2, 4, 1921. Also see Oliver Allstorm, *Poet and Priest: One Hundred Percent Americans and Not a Flag but the Flag, a Story of the Flag Incident at Houston, Texas, U.S.A.* (Houston: privately published, 1921).

23. *Brenham Morning Messenger,* May 21, 1921 (all quotations). Also see Wilfred O. Dietrich, "German American Pioneers in Washington County and Their Influence," *Journal of the German-Texan Heritage Society* 13 (Summer 1991): 123–25; clippings enclosed with W. F. Hasskarl Jr. to Walter Kamphoefner, May 12, 2003 (author's possession). For accounts of the incident see Thad Sitton and Dan K. Utley, *From Can See to Can't: Texas Cotton Farmers on the Southern Prairies* (Austin: University of Texas Press, 1997), 54; W. F. Hasskarl Jr. to Walter Kamphoefner, May 7, 2003 (author's possession).

24. W. F. Hasskarl Jr., "Brief History of County Lawmen," *Brenham Banner-Press,* Dec. 8, 2000. Also see Dietrich, "German American Pioneers in Washington County," 125; "Brenham Ku Klux Klan Disbands on Motion of Burney Parker," broadside enclosed in Hasskarl to Kamphoefner, May 12, 2003; Craig H. Roell, "Nordheim, Texas," in *The New Handbook of Texas,* ed. Ron Tyler et al., 6 vols. (Austin: Texas State Historical Association, 1996), 4:1032; *Brenham Banner-Press,* July 22, 1924.

25. *Paris Morning News,* Feb. 10, 22, 25, 26, 28, 1922.

26. William A. Owens, *A Season of Weathering* (New York: Charles Scribner's Sons, 1973), 21–22.

27. *Fort Worth Press,* Mar. 29, 1923. Also see *Fort Worth Press,* Aug. 21, 1924; Aug. 2, 3, 4, 1925.

28. For an example of Americanism harnessed to fight the Klan see Dallas County Citizens' League, "The Case against the Ku Klux Klan," June 1922 (pamphlet printed by the Venney Company, Dallas, Tex.), CAH.

29. Dalrymple, *Liberty Dethroned,* 68. For a similar linkage of opposition to the Klan and the heroes of San Jacinto, see *Paris Morning News,* Apr. 19, 1922.

30. *Fort Worth Press,* Aug. 21, 1924. Also see Dalrymple, *Liberty Dethroned,* 11, 55, 86–92; Dallas County Citizens' League, "The Case against the Ku Klux Klan."

31. *Dallas Morning News,* May 24, 1921; *Paris Morning News,* Feb. 22, 1922. Also see Dalrymple, *Liberty Dethroned,* 55; and a speech by O. B. Colquitt printed in the *Paris Morning News,* May 26, 1922.

32. Ferguson quoted in Brown, *Hood, Bonnet, and Little Brown Jug,* 219. Also see *Fort Worth Press,* Aug. 21, 1924; *Dallas Morning News,* Aug. 17, 23, 24, 1924; Ralph W. Steen, "Ferguson, James Edward," *The New Handbook of Texas,* ed. Tyler et al., 2:979–81; John D. Huddleston, "Ferguson, Miriam Amanda Wallace," *The New Handbook of Texas,* ed. Tyler et al., 2:981–82.

33. *Fort Worth Press,* Aug. 21, 1924. Similar themes appeared in the 1922 elections. See *Paris Morning News,* Feb. 22, 28, 1922; Mar. 4, 7, 9, 1922; and July 6, 20, 21, 1922. Also see the political advertisement for Miriam A. Ferguson in *Pittsburg Gazette,* July 18, 1924, 6. For details of a particularly gruesome lynching in Paris, Texas, see *Dallas Morning News,* Feb. 1, 2, 3, 1893; *Paris News,* Feb. 3, 1893.

34. Shelley Sallee, "'The Woman of It': Governor Miriam Ferguson's 1924 Election," *Southwestern Historical Quarterly* 100 (July 1996): 1–16. On the fierce struggle between rival women of the Klan organizations, see *Fort Worth Press,* June 28, 1924.

35. Quotations from Dalrymple, *Liberty Dethroned,* 11, 5, respectively (emphasis on the Gettysburg Address quote in the original). Also see *Fort Worth Press* issues from the summer of 1924.

36. *Houston Chronicle,* Sept. 4, 1921.

37. Buenger, *The Path to a Modern South,* 123–31, 253–60; Walter L. Buenger, "Texas and the South," *Southwestern Historical Quarterly* 103 (Jan. 2000): 308–24. Also see Gregg Cantrell, "The Bones of Stephen F. Austin: History and Memory in Progressive-Era Texas," *Southwestern Historical Quarterly* 108 (Oct. 2004): 145–78 (reprinted in this volume).

38. For an introduction to the broader cultural and intellectual change going on around them see Daniel J. Singal, *The War Within: From Victorian to Modernist Thought in the South, 1919–1945* (Chapel Hill: University of North Carolina Press, 1982).

39. For a brief introduction to the Klan outside the South see David J. Goldberg, *Discontented America: The United States in the 1920s* (Baltimore, Md.: Johns Hopkins University Press, 1999), 117–39.

40. MacLean, *Behind the Mask of Chivalry,* 74 (quote); for a full discussion see 52–74. Also see Alexander, *Ku Klux Klan in the Southwest.*

41. "Official Souvenir of Klan Day at the State Fair of Texas, Dallas, October 24, 1923" (pamphlet printed in Dallas by the Standard American Publishing House, 1923). Also see MacLean, *Behind the Mask of Chivalry,* 177–88. For an introduction to European fascism see Arno J. Mayer, *Why Did the Heavens Not Darken?: The "Final Solution" in History* (New York: Pantheon Books, 1988), 90–109; George L. Mosse, *Nazi Culture: Intellectual, Cultural, and Social Life in the Third Reich* (New York: Grosset & Dunlap, 1966); George L. Mosse, *The Crisis of German Ideology: Intellectual Origins of the Third Reich* (New York: Fertig, 1981); George L. Mosse, *The Fascist Revolution: Toward a General Theory of Fascism* (New York: Fertig, 1999); Roger Griffin, ed., *Fascism* (New York: Oxford University Press, 1995); Roger Griffin, *International Fascism: Theories, Causes, and the New Consensus* (New York: Oxford University Press, 1998); Robin W. Winks and R. J. Q. Adams, *Europe, 1890–1945: Crisis and Conflict* (New York: Oxford University Press, 2003), 125–60.

42. For a convenient abstract of anti-Klan sentiments see *Fort Worth Press* entries related to the Ku Klux Klan in the Works Project Administration's "Guide to Fort Worth," which can be viewed on microfiche in the Fort Worth Central Library. For a long list of alleged Klan crimes see the editorial in the *Paris Morning News,* May 26, 1922.

43. Victoria Buenger and Walter L. Buenger, *Texas Merchant: Marvin Leonard and Fort Worth* (College Station: Texas A&M University Press, 1998), 62–67; Miranda Leonard, interview by Victoria Buenger and Walter Buenger, Oct. 27–28, 1996, transcript in Jenkins Garrett Library, University of Texas at Arlington.

44. On the Lee statue see Carol Morris Little, *A Comprehensive Guide to Outdoor Sculpture in Texas* (Austin: University of Texas Press, 1996), 161.

45. David W. Blight, "Southerners Don't Lie; They Just Remember Big," in *Where These Memories Grow: History, Memory, and Southern Identity,* ed. W. Fitzhugh Brundage (Chapel Hill: University of North Carolina Press, 2000), 349.

Chapter 6

JUNETEENTH:
EMANCIPATION AND MEMORY

ELIZABETH HAYES TURNER

Maj. Gen. Gordon Granger, Union commander of the Department of Texas, arrived at the port of Galveston on June 19, 1865. His first tasks were to secure the coast and take command of the eighteen hundred Union troops in Texas after the formal surrender of Confederate Lt. Gen. Edmund Kirby Smith on June 2, 1865. On the day of his arrival, General Granger allegedly went to the antebellum home known as Ashton Villa in the center of town. There, from the balcony, he read General Orders No. 3 and announced to the slaves of that city and of Texas that they were free. His orders came as a proclamation from the "Executive of the United States." The *Galveston Daily News* carried a printed notice two days later that read in part, "The people are informed . . . that all slaves are free. This involves an absolute equality of personal rights and rights of property, between former masters and slaves, and the connection heretofore existing between them, become that between employer and hired labor."[1] History and memory record the moment of emancipation in Texas with the reading of the General Orders. Former slaves in Texas referred to the day of their freedom as Juneteenth, and they and their descendants retained June 19 as a time of celebration. Emancipation carried with it the solemn expectation of life without chains, whips, sales, separations, rapes, and forced labor; it offered the promise of a future based on legal equality.

The meaning and the memory of Juneteenth are intertwined in accounts both historical and contemporary. No one can doubt the importance of the event, especially now that it is commemorated in celebrations all over the world and has been granted official holiday status in Texas and in Oklahoma.[2] As a result of the energy committed to this event, the memory of emancipation has emerged as a powerful and empowering force. The annual reminder of slavery's end in Texas cannot be understood as merely the recollections of a minority people; whites and many ethnic groups share this common history stemming from the event itself or from the yearly celebrations.

Yet memories of emancipation and its meaning among white Texans bring a different focus, demonstrating that their remembrances of the aftermath of the Civil War shaped a dominant cultural response in contrast to that recalled by African Americans. White recollections denied the importance or the wisdom of emancipation. Most white Texans after the Civil War believed that freedpeople had been happier in slavery, that their freedom had not led to material gain, that, in fact, they had been better off as slaves, cared for by benign masters even into old age.[3] As segregation took hold in Texas, Juneteenth and its message of freedom struggled to be heard or appreciated by whites. Yet Juneteenth celebrations, which began in 1866 and have been observed ever since, have always held meaning and historical memory for blacks. The fact that annual observances did not cease, even in the days of the civil rights movement when they disappeared from newspapers but not from private gatherings, is trenchant testimony to the strength of an emancipationist memory.

This chapter purports to explore the meaning of the historical event—the announcement of freedom in Texas in June 1865—and participants' memories of it. Ultimately, freedom's promise succumbed to the realities of postwar life, but June 19 became associated with yearly gatherings. Without doubt Juneteenth celebrations changed over time; they often began with solemn religious observances followed by parades, dignified programs, park gatherings, and feasting. Toward the turn of the twentieth century, committees planned the events, and by the 1920s through the 1940s commercialism as well as disillusionment with unfulfilled promises of equality found expression in Juneteenth observances. By the 1960s, Juneteenth disappeared from public spaces in cities like Houston and Dallas and in smaller places such as Gainesville to reemerge in new form by the 1970s. The new Juneteenth holidays spread from one to several days and included African American artistic expression along with memories of the past.

Admittedly, emancipation's memory took on new significance against a backdrop of racial and economic discrimination in a region hostile to the rising expectations of African Americans. The annual celebrations and the emergence of collective memories that followed year after year offered a reminder that freedom is a national treasure, a symbol and a reality worth cele-

brating, and that emancipation offered an entrée into American citizenship
and identification with American ideals. Juneteenth served as a potent life-
giving event, a means by which freedpeople could develop a joyful retort
to messages of overt racism. It represented a public counter-demonstration to
displays of Confederate glorification and a counter-memory to the valorization of the Lost Cause.[4]

For a time in the late nineteenth and early twentieth centuries in Texas
and across the South, the United Daughters of the Confederacy and the
Sons of Confederate Veterans worked diligently to memorialize their heroes
and with unprecedented energy pressed libraries and school boards to stock
shelves and adopt texts favorable to a white southern viewpoint. They raised
funds for the erection of statues to Confederate heroes and persuaded the
legislature to create state holidays honoring Jefferson Davis and Robert E.
Lee.[5] Confederate cultural hegemony once reigned via marble, stone, and
bronze statues, in official state holidays, in marches, reunions, pageants, and
in histories written from the vantage point of the defeated.[6] Today, Texas no
longer pauses to honor Davis and Lee; there are no parades to the memory
of the Confederacy; the cold icons to fallen Confederate soldiers rest mutely
on courthouse lawns, on esplanades, and in cemeteries, their message as dead
as their builders. And while a neo-Confederate, rebel flag–waving white con-
stituency exists today, it struggles with marginalization and loss of authority.[7]

By contrast, Juneteenth has survived—a living, energetic testimony to
the power of subversion. And while Texas legislators are just now planning
to build a monument to Juneteenth, there is the event itself, an anniversary
and official state holiday that reminds Texans and the nation that freedom
from slavery is a memory never to be eclipsed.[8] Juneteenth is part of African American commemorative culture. Historically it punctuated an oppositional perspective, produced a community of celebrants and observers,
and offered a counter-memory to those who could not or would not bow to
power represented by white memories and commemorations.[9]

Soon after the declaration of emancipation on Galveston Island, the news
spread quickly, but the official announcement did not result in the day of
jubilee slaves had expected. The former Confederate mayor rounded up black
"runaways" and held them for return to their owners. The Union army's
provost marshal went along with this action but did so for the purpose of
holding them as laborers for the military. Freedmen who entered the town
after that found themselves pressed into military service.[10] Although the
announcement had come, for many, freedom still seemed elusive.

William Pitt Ballinger, a prominent Galveston attorney and slave owner, found three of his slaves gone the day after they heard the news. Two of the three fled to New Orleans and made their way to freedom, but one, Henry, returned to the Ballinger household, where, according to Ballinger, he told a tale of misery away from home. For some whites the essential meaning of African American freedom came slowly. Although urged by his wife Hally to go after the other two former slaves and bring them back by force, Ballinger demurred, saying, "They were free to do as they pleased—the law was with them. I don't believe anyone, even our Negroes[,] truly understand what it [freedom] all means."[11] Ballinger sadly expressed his fears for the uncertainties of the future, but two of his slaves by their actions courageously faced the future with the intention to put slavery behind them.[12]

For the African American population of Galveston, freedom came first with Union occupation of the island; for the rest of Texas, history records a ragged version of emancipation. Unlike other southern states where the war had raged, emancipation evolved differently in the Lone Star state. More often former slaves' remote situation gave them no opportunity to learn of the Emancipation Proclamation that declared them free after January 1, 1863, or to act on it. Thus there were few if any examples of slaves "freeing" themselves before war's end by seeking refuge behind Union lines, working for the Federal armies, or gaining a bit of experience with freedom under the so-called protection of Union troops.[13] Some Texas slaves did not wait for the news of June 19 but took off for army posts as soon as Union soldiers passed by. Others did not hear the news for weeks or months. When they did get the news and attempted to act on it by leaving, their immediate joy succumbed to despair as white vigilantes punished former slaves for preferring freedom to labor exploitation. Uncertainty mixed with high expectations for the future. The size of the state, the long distances between farms, the thin lines of Union protection, the remoteness from urban areas and from the heart of the defeated Confederacy conspired to bring emancipation more slowly into the interior of Texas.[14]

Civil War scholars estimate that thirty-eight thousand former Confederate soldiers in the Trans-Mississippi Department journeyed home, some of them ransacking and pillaging along the way. Austin, the capital of the Lone Star state, succumbed to rebel marauders who stole the state treasury. Union troops, at first numbering only eighteen hundred, found it difficult to patrol or keep order in such conditions and in such vast terrain. Thus, military concerns overwhelmed Union occupying forces, leaving few reserves for the safe passage of slaves into freedom.[15] Texas, moreover, was the last state to receive assistance from the Bureau of Refugees, Freedmen, and Abandoned Lands, commonly known as the Freedmen's Bureau. The bureau officers did not arrive until early September 1865, more than two months after the announcement of freedom in Galveston. The actual lawful manifestation of freedom for former slaves was further hindered by a ruling that freedpeople were not allowed to congregate in groups or travel on state roads without passes from their "employers" until bureau agents arrived.[16]

In Texas, either violence or continued slavery met many slaves as they learned of their freedom. There is much evidence to suggest that southern whites—especially Confederate parolees—perpetrated more acts of violence against newly freed bondspeople in Texas than in other states. The Joint Committee on Reconstruction, in hearings held from February to April 1866, discovered from military observers that between the Brazos and Nueces rivers former slave owners, disappointed by lack of compensation for their lost "property," used violence, even murder, against freedpeople. In the vicinity of Beaumont, Liberty, Brenham, Columbus, Austin, and San Antonio witnesses testified to murders of African Americans and the continuation of slavery, with owners still believing there would be gradual emancipation or payment from the government.[17] Likewise, between the Neches and Sabine rivers and north to Henderson, reports showed that blacks continued in a form of slavery, intimidated by former Confederate soldiers still in uniform and bearing arms. Freed slaves verified the extent of violence in North Texas. Susan Merritt of Rusk County reported that "lots of Negroes were killed after freedom . . . bushwhacked, shot down while they were trying to get away. You could see lots of Negroes hanging from trees in Sabine bottom right after freedom. They would catch them swimming across Sabine River and shoot them. There sho' is going to be lots of soul cry against them in Judgment."[18] Taking advantage of the announcement of freedom could spell death for those liberated without protection. The war may not have brought a great deal of bloodshed to Texas, but the peace certainly did.

The process of emancipation unfolded slowly; the vast spaces in Texas left slaves isolated, unable to ally themselves with other freedpeople, unprotected, and in some cases still in bondage. Susan Merritt recalled the day in September when she heard of her freedom. A "government" official came to her master's house with a "big book and a bunch of papers." He came asking why freedpeople were still working, and her owner responded that he wanted to get his crop out. The federal official had him call his workers to the house, where he told them they were free. But even after the "man read the paper telling us we were free, . . . massa made us work several months after that.

He said we got 20 acres land and a mule, but we didn't get it." Katie Darling, from Marshall, Texas, recounted that after the war she worked for her owners six years. Her brothers left to work on a neighboring farm, but she remained with a brutal mistress who "whip me after the war jist like she did 'fore." At length, her brother Peter rescued her and she finally claimed her freedom by exclaiming, "I'se so happy to git away from that old devil missy, I don't know what to do."[19] Many served their masters longer and in some cases unlawfully longer than did slaves in other states.

Those slaves who did find freedom learned of their emancipation in various ways. Many actually were called forth by their masters who then read the announcement; they listened in wonderment and drifted away to decide what to do next. Jubilation followed the news on some plantations, consternation on others. Felix Haywood recalled that "the end of the war, it come jus' like that—like you snap your fingers. . . . Hallelujah broke out. . . . Soldiers, all of a sudden, was everywhere—comin' in bunches, crossin' and walkin' and ridin.' Everyone was a-singin.' We was all walkin' on golden clouds. . . . Everybody went wild. We all felt like horses and nobody had made us that way but ourselves. We was free. Just like that we was free. . . . Right off colored folks started on the move. They seemed to want to get closer to freedom, so they'd know what it was—like it was a place or a city."[20] The message finally made its impact all across the state. When all slaves had received their notice, when all slaves had freedom of choice to seek independence on new ground or to stay on familiar terrain, the idea and identity of freedom began.

African Americans became the narrators of their own story and thus gave new meaning to the concept of emancipation. In the words of Felix Haywood, "We knowed freedom was on us, but we didn't know what was to come with it. We thought we was goin' to get rich like the white folks. We thought we was goin' to be richer than the white folks, 'cause we was stronger and knowed how to work, and the whites didn't and they didn't have us to work for them anymore. But it didn't turn out that way. We soon found out that freedom could make folks proud but it didn't make 'em rich."[21] Memories of emancipation recorded seventy some years later still resonated with energy and emotion. Keeping those thoughts alive, allowing them to remind generations of their meaning, preserving the tradition of jubilee against a nagging reality presented great challenges for black Texans.

In the biracial post-Civil War South, a contest ensued to establish a common version of the past. Whichever group managed to wrest power—in office holding, in economic ascendancy, in concepts of virtue and courageous endeavors during and after the Civil War—would be in a position to

create a usable past, one that shaped memory, defined value, required defer-
ence. Collective memories guarded and sustained by whites brought forth
a view of the past that altered the human landscape into opposing groups,
labeling one group as dominant, the other as subject to dominance. One is
worth remembering, the other best forgotten. Friedrich Nietzsche made this
observation when he wrote, "Forgetting is essential to action of any kind."
In the late-nineteenth-century South, white collective memory sanctified
a triumphant southern civilization based on slavery (forgetting its abuses),
glorified gallant and valorous military heroes (ignoring their failings), and
proclaimed white superior to black (despite universalities in the human condition). Sometimes labeled the Lost Cause, this pervasive collective memory
shaped a generation of southerners both white and black. The consequence
of this influence can be seen in the eventual exclusion of blacks from public
life in areas of voting, office holding, and, in some cases where whites held
economic power, in business opportunities.[22]

Despite the pervasiveness of this cultural dominance, there never was a
moment when it completely obliterated an oppositional perspective or wiped
away the collective memories of former slaves. Memories, collective memories, and history have waited for the appropriate set of circumstances before
revealing fully the extent of this opposition. The memory of emancipation
from slavery is both powerful and subversive—powerful because it kept faith
alive that freedom's realities would become more than just a dream, powerful because it united communities under a common identity with a noble
goal, and subversive because it contradicted, even in its reality, notions held
by many whites that the destruction of slavery weakened the South and its
"superior" civilization. The powerfully subversive collective memory that
former slaves and their descendants preserved found its way into public space
almost every year, a reminder to the nation that African Americans, while
sharing a common history with white southerners, did not bow to the icons
of Confederate bellicosity or deny that freedom was immensely preferable
to bondage. Juneteenth transformed collective memory into a formidable
action of dissent. In the words of Ira Berlin, "Because it touches individual
men and women with such power, memory becomes the driving force in the
search for social justice, the mortar that bonds the violations of the past to
the grievances of the present."[23]

It is in the power of the event itself, the locus of memory, that one finds
the true meaning of emancipation for the 250,000 slaves that had lived in
Texas.[24] The celebration of emancipation, as symbolized by Juneteenth, unfolded unevenly across time and space in Texas. It marked a profound change,

an irrevocable rupture. Freedom was a foreign land to those who had spent their lives in bondage; it required navigating through unfamiliar terrain. As a site of memory, Juneteenth allowed travelers between slavery and freedom to mark a point in their lives, a "red spot on the calendar" that bonded them together as a free people, as Americans. With identity established, the commemoration of this day trained children in the collective memories of their parents, grandparents, and relatives. It transmitted a particular history essential to collective identity in a region and in a nation that had often labeled itself white man's country.[25]

In actuality Juneteenth celebrations preceded Lost Cause concerns. In 1866, when Juneteenth celebrations began, there was no equivalent organized commemoration of the Confederate legacy in Texas. Yet there existed among whites a sense that freedom for slaves represented loss for slave owners; emancipation had been thrust upon an unwilling Texas majority. From a white perspective, Abraham Lincoln, then, was a destroyer of southern civilization. In venerating Lincoln and in rejecting Jefferson Davis, freedpeople presented an emergent dissenting view. Lincoln's Emancipation Proclamation epitomized the freedpeople's dissenting view.

Public Juneteenth celebrations in the nineteenth and early twentieth centuries included a ceremonial reading of the Emancipation Proclamation, and black newspapers carried printed copies along with a pen-and-ink etching of Lincoln, a white civic icon in an age of hostility toward people of color. Clearly freedpeople preferred to remember emancipation over slavery, but one may wonder why black Texans over time have chosen to read the Emancipation Proclamation issued on January 1, 1863, rather than the general orders read by Gen. Gordon Granger or the Thirteenth Amendment ratified in December 1865. Why did Texas former slaves extol the leadership of Abraham Lincoln, who by June 19, 1865, had succumbed to an assassin's bullet and was no longer alive to welcome them into the national body politic? In the developing emancipationist celebrations why not give General Granger or the radical abolitionist Frederick Douglass positions of honor? Douglass became the Union's national evangelist, one who saw the war and its outcome as "the nation's apocalyptic *regeneration.*" Why not celebrate emancipation in Texas on January 1, as many former slaves did in other states?[26]

Why did black Texans choose to venerate Lincoln, when his assumptions about race differences and his views on citizenship and voting rights for blacks were in question? The answers lie in the use of memory. After 1863 Lincoln's view of emancipation from slavery was never in question. Congress had abolished slavery in Washington, D.C., in April 1862 and in the territo-

ries in June 1862. It was Lincoln, however, who after assembling his Cabinet
on September 22, 1862, declared all slaves in regions still in rebellion "forever
free." When the proclamation went into effect on January 1, 1863, he had
earned the title Great Emancipator, as a father of the nation, as a synonym
for manhood.[27]

The action was more than symbolic. Although slaves in rebellious states
would have the most difficulty finding their way to freedom, and though
many would not hear the news of emancipation until after war's end, and
while those slaves in territories under Union occupation were theoretically
not free, the September 1862 proclamation nonetheless changed the purpose
of the war. Soldiers in the lower ranks who saw the important labor and aid
that runaway slaves gave to Federal forces supported it. These men in turn
advised their families in the North that slaves were valuable resources for the
Union side and should not be forced to continue contributing their labors
to Confederate goals; Union lives were at stake. Soldiers worked at persuading their superiors until finally Lincoln acceded that blacks should no longer
serve Confederate designs. The proclamation prevented foreign interference,
and the conflict became more than just a crusade to save the Union. Four
million lives came under the pen of the commander-in-chief of the army and
the navy. Slavery would not long stand once the nation had directed itself
toward freedom.[28]

Freedpeople were pragmatists; they chose as their symbol of heroism a
white leader of the nation, martyred by a rebel enemy, an enduring figure
whose name would never be lost from memory. Lincoln, too, was a pragmatist; he learned, according to David W. Blight, "to convert his instinctive
gradualism about social change and his racial prejudices into the courage to
use his power as president to free slaves in the midst of total war. Thus, he
used the freeing of slaves in rebel territory to save the nation he loved."[29] He
was the president of the United States when he announced emancipation to
the nation and the world. There could be no higher earthly figure to validate
the justice of this point. As the leader of the United States, he gave to African
Americans an unqualified inheritance, one that should have been theirs centuries before. He symbolically loosed the bonds of slavery and lifted an oppressed people to a place of potential equality among Americans. He called
forth black soldiers to arm, train, and go forward into battle for the nation,
thus enlisting them in the act of patriotic duty and endowing them with the
privileges and responsibilities of citizenship. He spoke of a "rebirth" of the
nation in his Gettysburg Address in November 1863.[30] Thus the memory of
Lincoln's Emancipation Proclamation, not General Granger's reading of the

orders or the Thirteenth Amendment, crowned Juneteenth celebrations with symbolic meaning. A president, not a general, had issued their emancipation; a president, not a constitutional amendment, however legal and proper, personified their liberation.[31]

While Juneteenth celebrations embodied higher meaning, they also allowed for earthly enjoyments. Juneteenth was a freedom event that had to be celebrated by gathering and remembering the day of the emancipation announcement. In 1866, former slaves celebrated in various places all over the state of Texas. The history of the day, as told to Charles Morgan, was nothing short of explosive: "The way it was explained to me, the 19th of June wasn't the exact day the Negro was freed. But that's the day they told them that they was free. . . . And my daddy told me that they whooped and hollered and bored holes in trees with augers and stopped it up with [gun] powder and light and that would be their blast for the celebration. . . . Be hundreds of people looking at it."[32] Freedpeople appropriated symbols and songs for their own uses. In an act of subversion that must have galled white southerners, freedwomen converted a Confederate favorite, "The Bonnie Blue Flag," to a freedom song. Maggie Whitehead Matthews recounts, "I remembah den how our first Nineteenth was celebrated on June 19, 1866, and de song we sang was

> *De Blue Bonnet Flag*
>
> Hurrah fo' de Blue Bonnet Flag,
> Hurrah fo' de home-spun dresses
> Dat de colored wimmen wear;
> Yes I'm a radical girl
> And glory in de name–
> Hurrah fo' de home-spun dresses
> Dat de colored women wear.[33]

From the beginning, Freedom Day celebrations included church services in which preachers and educators reminded freedpeople of the sacred solemnity of the occasion, of their duty as emerging citizens, and of their profound right to the pursuit of legal equality. William H. Wiggins Jr. calls this combining "elements from both the sacred and secular."[34] In 1892, the Reverend D. A. Scott printed an announcement in the *Sunday School Herald* preparing Baptists across the state for "a grand reunion of the old and young freedmen in the great Baptist ranks of Texas" to commemorate "the day when we were emancipated." The nineteenth of June in that year fell on a Sunday, and churches were to plan the day according to the directives given. At 5 A.M. "have the bell rang [*sic*] by the oldest member of the church for covenant

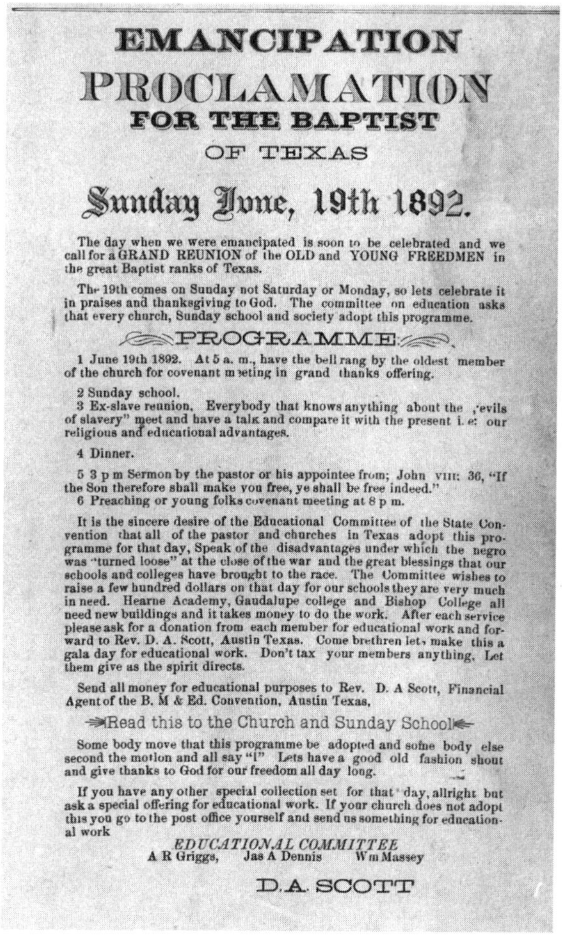

EMANCIPATION PROCLAMATION FOR THE BAPTIST OF TEXAS

Sunday June, 19th 1892.

The day when we were emancipated is soon to be celebrated and we call for a GRAND REUNION of the OLD and YOUNG FREEDMEN in the great Baptist ranks of Texas.

The 19th comes on Sunday not Saturday or Monday, so lets celebrate it in praises and thanksgiving to God. The committee on education asks that every church, Sunday school and society adopt this programme.

PROGRAMME.

1 June 19th 1892. At 5 a. m., have the bell rang by the oldest member of the church for covenant meeting in grand thanks offering.

2 Sunday school.

3 Ex-slave reunion. Everybody that knows anything about the "evils of slavery" meet and have a talk and compare it with the present i. e. our religious and educational advantages.

4 Dinner.

5 3 p m Sermon by the pastor or his appointee from; John VIII: 36, "If the Son therefore shall make you free, ye shall be free indeed."

6 Preaching or young folks covenant meeting at 8 p m.

It is the sincere desire of the Educational Committee of the State Convention that all of the pastor and churches in Texas adopt this programme for that day, Speak of the disadvantages under which the negro was "turned loose" at the close of the war and the great blessings that our schools and colleges have brought to the race. The Committee wishes to raise a few hundred dollars on that day for our schools they are very much in need. Hearne Academy, Gaudalupe college and Bishop College all need new buildings and it takes money to do the work. After each service please ask for a donation from each member for educational work and forward to Rev. D. A. Scott, Austin Texas. Come brethren let, make this a gala day for educational work. Don't tax your members anything. Let them give as the spirit directs.

Send all money for educational purposes to Rev. D. A Scott, Financial Agent of the B. M & Ed. Convention, Austin Texas,

Read this to the Church and Sunday School

Some body move that this programme be adopted and some body else second the motion and all say "I" Lets have a good old fashion shout and give thanks to God for our freedom all day long.

If you have any other special collection set for that day, allright but ask a special offering for educational work. If your church does not adopt this you go to the post office yourself and send us something for educational work

EDUCATIONAL COMMITTEE
A R Griggs,   Jas A Dennis   Wm Massey

D. A. SCOTT

FIG. 6.1. In 1892, the Reverend D. A. Scott printed an announcement in the *Sunday School Herald* preparing Baptists across the state for Juneteenth. *Sunday School Herald* (Austin), June 4, 1892. Courtesy Center for American History, University of Texas at Austin.

meeting in grand thanks offering." This gathering should be followed by Sunday school and a reunion for former slaves to compare slavery to the "religious and educational advantages" of the day. Then dinner would be eaten, a great feast no doubt, followed by preaching at 3 P.M. from John 8:36, with this text: "If the Son therefore shall make you free, ye shall be free indeed." Although Reverend Scott wished to turn the festivities into a fundraising day for educational institutions, his message nonetheless reminds readers of the "disadvantages under which the negro was 'turned loose' at the close of the war" and the advantages of freedom with their own schools and churches.[35]

Songs and hymns were always part of Juneteenth worship services and celebrations; spirituals were the heart and soul of Juneteenth, including "Free at Last," "Go Down Moses," and "Many Thousands Gone." Abolitionist songs, such as "John Brown," and patriotic songs, such as "America" and the national anthem, were among the choices. After 1927, celebrants began singing James Weldon Johnson's poem set to music, "Lift Every Voice," now known as the black national anthem.[36]

In towns and cities, Juneteenth celebrants marked the day with a parade, which gave African Americans an opportunity to enter public space. Even though Juneteenth celebrants rejoiced over their independence, they represented a confrontational presence, an emphatic expression of the right to use public space, which was often resented or feared by white observers. Because African Americans brought forth the memory of emancipation, because they celebrated freedom over the so-called benefits of enslavement often counseled by whites, their actions silenced momentarily a dominant voice.[37] In 1896, the year that the U.S. Supreme Court in *Plessy* v. *Ferguson* upheld the "separate but equal" principle, African Americans once again reminded citizens of the meaning of emancipation. In Austin that year one parade began at Metropolitan A.M.E. Church on West Ninth and proceeded down Congress Avenue to Sixth and on to Govalle Park for the festivities. According to a local newspaper report, "Marshals' decorated cockhats, streaming sashes and prancing steeds made their hearts leap for joy." The Austin Cornet Band, "rendering excellent music," led the parade marshal; the ministers and their wives in carriages preceded "the Goddess of Liberty and her maids all on a large decorated float." These were followed by "Singing Sunday School" children, orators, floats with Sunday school boys, and celebrants in their own buggies, hacks, and carriages.[38]

Another typical Juneteenth parade unfolded in Galveston in 1904, but preparations for the event had begun well before. A local newspaper reported that "the Women's Nineteenth of June Committee of Galveston is going right along getting things in shape to pull off a magnificent parade which is thought by many to excel the parade of last year." The parade would be a grand affair organized into five divisions: first, the mounted police and the Grand Marshal, heralded by the Island City Brass Band and supported by the Hawley Guards. In the following divisions would ride the assistant marshals, a young woman dressed as the Goddess of Liberty, and her maids of honor. Rolling floats "representing the race's progress in industrial, educational, commercial and laboring pursuits followed by other decorated vehicles, and the flower parade" would take up the rear.[39]

These same participants would gather to hear speeches and to solem-
nize the event at the end of the parade route, usually a park designated for
Juneteenth celebrations. In 1904, the Juneteenth program would begin when
two young women from Galveston opened the ceremony from center stage:
Laura Austin would read the Emancipation Proclamation while Everlena
Anderson represented the Goddess of Liberty. The keynote address by the
invited speaker, C. J. Williams, would be followed by another given by Miss
H. A. Richards, a Galvestonian who would speak on "Solving the Negro
Problem."[40]

Perhaps no one found it unusual that women took such prominent roles
in the presentations. In the 1895 Austin Juneteenth festivities, the Goddess
of Liberty held "the scales of liberty and justice." But what poignant themes
emerged from these renderings—a reading of the Emancipation Proclamation followed by the visual countenance of Liberty dressed in robes and wearing a crown? No kneeling slaves, no unfettered bondsmen, but instead Liberty, an American icon, served to illustrate the meaning of Juneteenth. The
Statue of Liberty, standing at the gates of New York City, was a gift from
America's ally, France. Commemorating the centennial of the nation's independence, it finally stood in New York harbor by 1886. By 1904 it had become a symbolic beacon to immigrants, representing freedom, opportunity,
and acceptance to all dispossessed. Liberty's torch sheds light over the future,
not the past. She heralds what is to come. Liberty's image evokes patriotism,
even political equality; but she gives her compassionate gaze to those fleeing
oppression and poverty. One wonders, did daughters of slaves see Liberty as
the emancipator of their people? "Or did she represent one of the few bea-
cons of hope in a racist age?" Did Liberty's gendered appearance "resonate
with special meaning for women who carried the double burden of race and
sex?" It is likely; yet Liberty tells another tale. Celebrants of the anniversary
of freedom preferred to dream of the future rather than to revisit slave memories from the past. For many, historical memory was shifting from slave
remembrances to national promises.[41]

Public space became a mighty ingredient in the forming of Juneteenth
memories. Not content to borrow or beg for public park space, most African
Americans made a point of buying land of their own for the purpose of celebrating their freedom day. The alleged promises of forty acres and a mule
never materialized for the former bondspeople after the Civil War, and therefore the purchasing of land and its ownership, even for community purposes,
took on a serious significance. It provided space, a site of their own free from
infringement by whites. In Houston, in 1872, the Reverend Jack Yates, pastor

of Antioch Baptist Church, and the Reverend Elias Dibble of Trinity Methodist Episcopal Church raised one thousand dollars among the leaders of the community to buy land—ten acres—at the corner of Dowling and Elgin Streets. Calling it Emancipation Park, this site proved the tenacity of freedpeople in their quest for independence. The park's trustees managed to pay the taxes on the land for the use of black citizens in Houston and Harris County. It saw years of celebrations and remained an independently owned park until 1916, when the city absorbed it into its park system. In Mexia at Comanche Crossing in 1898, a "Nineteenth of June Organization" bought ten acres of land next to the Navasota River and called it Booker T. Washington Park. In Galveston, the Women's Nineteenth of June Committee by 1904 had "accumulated nearly $200 for the purpose of buying a celebration grounds of their own in the corporate limits of the city."[42]

These sites constituted an advance in the extension of Juneteenth celebrations. "Weary of moving from 'pillow to post,'" it allowed black communities to establish a suitable place to reflect, to enjoy, and to collect memories—partly sad, of baneful slave days, partly joyful, in the celebration of emancipation. French philosopher/historian Pierre Nora argues that "memory attaches itself to sites," and by this statement he means sites marked by monuments. But in a world where no memorials to black emancipation graced courthouse lawns, the ownership of land anchored celebrants to a point on a map as well as a spot on the calendar.[43]

Afternoon festivities included a feast for all the participants. To a people deprived of plenty while in bondage, bountiful tables filled with good things to eat provided tangible evidence of the advantages of freedom over slavery. Barbecued meats, prepared in underground pits by the men, were tended through the night. Memories of the savory smell of roasted beef or pork resonates today with reminiscers, who add that there is no current equivalent to the all-night roasted meat from Juneteenth. Homemade dishes prepared most often by the women burdened tables that grew to become groaning boards. David A. Williams recalled, "In the early Juneteenth morning in our community, we could always smell the mixed aroma of food coming from every house. I remember that you could smell roast beef, spare ribs, fried chicken, collard greens, turnip greens, mustard greens, pork chops, purple hull and blackeyed peas, pastries, breads, roasted wild game, fish, and chitterlings."[44] Revelers even remembered the delights of red soda water: "Early celebrants claimed that they lived from one year to the next just waiting to drink red soda water on Juneteenth." If store-bought red soda water could not be obtained, red-colored lemonade sufficed. Some report the presence of watermelons as traditional to the Juneteenth refreshments. Afternoons were spent with games for children, baseball games for grown-ups, and dances well into the night for those old enough to stay.[45] In Galveston in 1904 and 1905, it was the men who organized the speeches and the feast following the parade, with free barbecue for former slaves and Union soldiers over fifty. Men brought to the festivities a fiddler's contest with cash prizes, fishing, crabbing, boating, bathing, and excursions to Galveston from San Jacinto Bay.[46]

The meaning of Juneteenth went beyond the celebration of emancipation and took on broader implications for citizenship. What did it mean to be free in a republic where responsibilities for self-governance prevailed? During the Civil War, free blacks and former slaves joined the Union army and fought for freedom. In the years following the close of the war, citizenship represented itself above all in acts of voting, in political party membership, in campaigning for candidates, and in holding office. Reconstruction governments demonstrated that the hypothetical notions of democracy could be carried out among a voting populace. Tied to this were examples of black legislators and Republican office holders across the South and in Texas. State constitutions reflected changes toward public education, public services, and multiethnic representation. Juneteenth celebrations also reflected these designs for a democratic society, based in part on the recollections of President Lincoln as the Great Emancipator. Juneteenth celebrants remembered their political activism by symbolically incorporating national symbols of liberty into their parades and by inviting respected Reconstruction office holders to address the audience. In 1905, when celebrating the fortieth anniversary of freedom, Galvestonians invited a venerable citizen to give the keynote address. Judge Richard Nelson, former justice of the peace appointed during Reconstruction, had created the first black newspapers in Texas: the *Galveston Spectator,* founded in 1873, and the *Freeman's Journal,* in 1887. His presence and authority stemmed from his active participation as citizen and as upholder of freedom of the press. The visual message was that African Americans remembered Reconstruction as a time when they were able to act on their newly won citizenship.[47]

Nelson's presence and address came precisely in the year when white Galvestonians were deciding to segregate their streetcars. One month after Nelson had addressed the citizens of Galveston, the editors of the black-owned *New Idea* protested against the white-owned *Galveston Tribune* for letting "the-Jim-Crow-white man" push for segregated streetcars. By December, black editors warned their readers to pay the poll tax in order to vote against city commissioners who want "to pass a JIM CROW STREET CAR LAW against you." In 1906, Galveston city commissioners voted 3-to-2 to implement the law.[48] This slap in the face to blacks was preceded by disfranchisement laws. Voting, a right gained over time and then reduced by white southern legislatures, jeopardized African American citizenship. When Texans ratified a constitutional amendment creating a poll tax in 1902, it was touted as a progressive law, as a way to elevate the electorate, eliminate undesirable voters, prevent fraudulent voting, and provide funds for education. It required voters to pay a tax of between one dollar and one dollar and a half. To their credit Texans never sanctioned a literacy test to qualify for voting, but they did create primary elections for whites only. The white primaries excluded blacks from voting in the only meaningful elections in the state. Although the poll tax challenged their acceptance as citizens and they were always aware of their minority position, for black Texans it became a point of pride to pay the tax, to maintain their tenuous hold on citizenship.[49]

The marginalization of Juneteenth celebrations in cities followed the increase in disfranchisement and segregation, the abandonment of blacks by the Republican Party, and the acceptance by the nation of the Lost Cause as its dominant Civil War memory.[50] Counter-memories, however, have powerful repercussions for those who are subjected to loss, whether it is the loss of equal opportunities for advancement, loss of voting rights, loss of manhood or womanhood, or even the loss of physical space in the convoluted separation of the races that permeated the South. Memories represent power to people who are oppressed, for while they cannot control much of what occurs in their lives, they can own their own memories. Memories are often teleological in nature, and this fact prevents them from becoming purely objective, rational thoughts. But memory and collective memory serve other purposes—identity and empowerment.

Texas African Americans saw themselves as American citizens, but from their perspective white southerners were slow to see themselves as American citizens. For example, most blacks in urban areas had long celebrated Independence Day, while white Galvestonians and many other Texans often had not. In San Antonio, celebrating the Fourth of July with parades and festivities gained appeal during Reconstruction and the Spanish American War but declined in the early twentieth century. According to the editors of the *City Times* in Galveston in 1905, "The fourth of July . . . the nation's 129th anniversary . . . was celebrated with two street parades, four picnics, and a horse racing contest." The only Independence Day parades that day were held by black citizens, and they announced that they "have discovered through the spirit of [Crispus] Attucks that their work was shared in the cause of independence." African Americans assumed the traditions of Independence Day not only for what it meant in their collective memories of freedom but for what it meant to belong to a nation that valued freedom enough to fight a long and bloody civil war. Blacks called it the Freedom War.[51]

Michael Kammen sees in the United States' cultural history a varied pluralism leading to particularistic traditions. He points out that immigrant groups at times eschewed national celebrations, memories, and traditions for ethnic allegiances, especially when associated with a particular religious heritage.[52] Examining the rich celebrations that African Americans invented, however, leads one to conclude that these events were much more national in ideology than were celebrations engineered by white southern proponents of the Lost Cause. "Freedom" and "liberty" are terms that resonate with Americans; they reverberate through memory from the bridge at Concord or the Battle of Saratoga. The terms "freedom" and "emancipation," as remembered by freedpeople and by most northerners, however, represented troublesome connotations for white southerners. In the evocation of Lost Cause rhetoric, freedom evinced an entirely different meaning: freedom from federal intervention, freedom of home rule, freedom to invoke local vigilante "justice." Thus, African Americans and white Texans danced 'round each other, infrequently joining one another in celebrations that evoked historical meaning.

An important testing time for American citizenship and for its expression came just as soldiers returned to Texas after World War I. In 1919, a horrific year by any standard, Houston city fathers seemed to subvert the solemnity, dignity, and importance of black sacrifices for the nation during war. This suppression did not lead to silence. The black editor of the Houston *Informer*, C. F. Richardson, took umbrage when the *Houston Post* attempted to define patriotism for the community as a whole.

It began with a quarrel over Decoration Day. Rather than honor the recently fallen in World War I, which could have included black soldiers, the city ignored Decoration Day, a national holiday celebrated on May 30 to honor the soldiers of past wars. The *Informer* reported that on that day Woodrow Wilson had delivered a "stirring speech" at a cemetery in France. Except for a closing of the U.S. Post Office, there was no observance of American sacrifices in Houston. Instead, on June 3, Houston closed its banks and its businesses to observe the birthday of Jefferson Davis. Richardson could not keep still: "Here was a man who sought to destroy the Republic and because he failed in his endeavor does not palliate his offense or extenuate his crime. . . . To keep the banks open on Decoration Day and then close them on Davis's birthday is a reflection upon such a species of patriotism and

Americanism."[53] By ignoring Decoration Day—a tribute to all soldiers who had fallen in battle—in favor of the leader of the rebellious southern states, Houston leaders had disregarded national norms of observance. Richardson reminded his readers that despite the actions by city leaders, each Texan belonged to the United States and African Americans prized their national citizenship.

Denying Decoration Day was one thing; relegating Juneteenth celebrations to the margins of Houston was quite another. By 1919, Juneteenth had become firmly established in Texas as a holiday for African Americans. It was so important that white employers routinely gave their workers the day off and so large that annual parades all over the state each ended with celebrations in parks. Even though 1919 proved to be a fateful year for black Texans, Juneteenth represented the greatest black cultural event in the state.[54] Thus it was with increasing resentment that blacks noted their celebration pushed increasingly to the edges of public space; Juneteenth day celebrations suffered under the control of powerful white forces. An angry C. F. Richardson wrote, "For the first time in the city's history the colored citizens of this community were refused a permit to route their Juneteenth parade over either Travis or Main Street, . . . but [were] shunted . . . from Milam to San Jacinto, a route never before employed by any parade. . . . The parade by all means could have used Travis Street, where quite a number of race men operate places of business, but we were black and that meant shunting us off to a back and out-of-way street. . . . We are citizens of Houston and as such shall not be discriminated against."[55]

Adding insult to injury, the *Houston Post* ran an editorial that, according to Richardson, belittled the meaning and the memory of the event and denied participants the importance of their recent heroic sacrifices. At the close of World War I, the Juneteenth speechmakers honored black soldiers and their sacrifices. Elderly former slaves and young soldiers in uniform together were proudly recognized and feted. Memories of freedom intertwined with the realities of national obligations; emancipation brought civil liberties, and citizenship in the United States meant military duty.

The editorialist for the *Post*, which proclaimed itself "one of the South's leading white daily newspapers," found a way to remind readers that blacks, after all, deserved few substantive rewards for their valor: "Every Negro soldier who fought in France should have been rewarded with a watermelon on Juneteenth for his individual use."[56] Richardson shot back, "The above utterance . . . shows the average white Southerner's idea of what our race deserves for its unparalleled and unprecedented record in the late world war. . . . The black man responded to the call, firstly because he was an American citizen; secondly, because he knew that the world could not be made and maintained safe for democracy without at least bursting asunder some of the fetters that bound his race in 'democratic' America. . . . The black soldier fought for democracy—and not for a little measly, mushy watermelon." It was an out-and-out battle of the pens for the power to interpret historical meaning and memory. The *Post's* editor drew sharp fire from the *Informer's*. "Take our creditable Emancipation Day celebration in this city June 19 and then see how the white papers endeavored to ridicule the race," Richardson griped.[57] He knew that the *Post's* readership was likely to see only the watermelon jab and not the soldiers in uniform or the angry but reasoned response representing black Houston.

Clashing images and conflicting memories seemed to plague Texans during the dangerous 1920s, when black pleas for the fulfillment of freedom's promises were drowned out by threats, police intimidation, and lynchings. Creating a past out of memory—exaggerating the wrongs of blacks who took part in Reconstruction politics and justifying disfranchisement—had worked well for dominant groups seeking political and cultural hegemony until 1920. White political leaders, town officials, and elite white club women tried to remove from consideration an emancipationist past, but this memory, a subaltern view, would not be forgotten. The day of jubilee reminded all who would remember that emancipation was part of history and memory. Whites grudgingly gave limited space for its celebration and condescendingly interpreted its meaning.[58]

By the 1920s and 1930s, Juneteenth celebrations, not unlike the society surrounding it, had taken on a commercial tone. Advertisements in African American newspapers invited celebrants to buy, buy, buy for the Juneteenth festivities. This advertising push created a commercial bonanza for shop owners and department store chains that had begun appearing in cities like Houston. Foley Bros. in Houston advertised dresses for $1.99, "just in time for June Nineteenth." C. F. Richardson echoed the advertising hype, citing just cause to feel pride in the record of achievement since liberation from "the shackles and fetters of slavery. . . . when called upon to defend and protect the interests of others, the black man has never faltered . . . and his record is well known on a thousand battlefields. Wouldn't it be a fine thing if that same spirit were injected into the commercial and economic life of the colored race?"[59] Juneteenth festivities also brought innovation: trained aviators flew overhead, stock car racing and swimming exhibitions were added, beauty pageants introduced young women to the community, and band concerts replaced the old-time fiddler contests. Sports played a role as black baseball teams competed with one another. Dallas's Steer Stadium hosted "one of the biggest 'Juneteenth' celebrations ever arranged," when the Dallas Black Giants and the Waco Black Cardinals encountered each other. Wrestlers and female boxers, "each tipping the scales [at] more than 200 pounds," matched each other at Juneteenth carnivals—such as those at Fair Park in Dallas—that invited families to celebrate amid the whir of rides.[60] Bars and juke joints—some of them on Hall Street and Deep Ellum in Dallas—tempted revelers to a taste of freedom. Juneteenth began to take on characteristics of mass entertainment as commercial events superseded the barbecues and picnics of older, simpler times.[61]

Two extraordinary events, however, countered the excessive commercialization. Folklorist J. Mason Brewer, collector of vignettes from slavery days entitled "Juneteenth," published his work in 1932. Then, two Dallas activists, A. Maceo Smith and Jesse O. Thomas, were instrumental in establishing a Hall of Negro Life at the Texas Centennial Exposition in Dallas in June 1936. The fifty-thousand-dollar hall was devoted to "Negro progress" since the year of emancipation and was dedicated on June 19, 1936. That day, 46,116 African Americans attended the Centennial Exposition. It remained open until December 1936 and displayed works of art by African American painters, including Hale Woodruff and Aaron Douglas.[62]

World War II brought more questions regarding full citizenship for African Americans, and the war's aftermath only intensified the drive for full equality. Ralph Ellison's words seemed to mock the event: "They called it Juneteenth . . . *[t]he celebration of a gaudy illusion.*" On Juneteenth 1941, concerns over the fate of the nation hung in the balance. "Today," the *Informer* lamented, "Negroes are not sure whether to be gay on 'Juneteenth' or to observe the day with sadness. They do not know whether they are actually free here. . . . With America on the brink of another war, Negroes are not certain just what their attitude should be. Unquestionably, they will join forces with the rest of the nation for defense against any of the foreign isms that threaten the development of democracy. But their big wonder is based on the realization that they have not been permitted to share in America's democracy for which they will have to spill their blood and give their lives. June Nineteenth should be observed with joy, and not with sadness."[63]

The coming test of democracy in Texas proved to be a great struggle. The week of June 15 and 16, 1943, an estimated two thousand plant workers and one thousand bystanders in Beaumont rioted against blacks, killing three persons, burning cars, and looting more than one hundred homes. Tensions due to the biracial war work at Beaumont's Pennsylvania Shipyard, the accusation of rape, the proposed assembly of the Ku Klux Klan, and preparations for Juneteenth celebrations brought the city to a point of explosion. Called the worst race riot in Texas history, it took a force of eighteen hundred guardsmen, one hundred state police, and seventy-five Texas Rangers to quell the riot. Yet that year Juneteenth celebrations continued in Houston.[64]

During the civil rights movement, there were even more discussions about the place and meaning of Juneteenth in the African American community. The movement highlighted the glaring inequalities and held up the promises of freedom against the drab realities of disfranchisement, segregation, and violence. The movement brought a temporary slowdown to public Juneteenth celebrations, which seemed out of step with the times or perhaps too old-fashioned or unsophisticated. Marjorie Allen remembers waiting eleven years to be able to dance all night at the annual Juneteenth celebration in Gainesville, but when she turned eighteen in 1950, the Juneteenth celebrations stopped. By the 1960s Emancipation Day was celebrated occasionally in theme parks but more often at private parties in individual homes. Public celebrations ceased in some cities altogether and were no longer reported in many black newspapers.[65]

The hiatus proved fruitful, for in the end the civil rights movement accomplished what all the years of Juneteenth celebrations could not; it legitimated black history, black rights, and black citizenship in the eyes of the nation. It acknowledged the right to own memories counter to those held by the powerful. The state-sponsored memory of a regional past produced only one version, complete with landscapes dotted in Confederate stone monuments. Juneteenth represented no such idealized memory. It asked only that the promise of democracy become reality. Public Juneteenth celebrations returned in 1973, when Houston pastor C. Anderson Davis, a civil rights activist and former president of the Houston NAACP, began a rebirthing process by organizing the National Emancipation Association. The Black Arts Center also revived interest in Juneteenth, and festivities expanded from celebrating Emancipation Day to glorifying black culture—jazz, blues, spirituals, and other music, plus art, crafts, and traditional designs.[66]

When state legislator Al Edwards (D-Houston), introduced House Bill 1016 in 1979 to make June 19 a state holiday, he did so as a beneficiary of the civil rights movement. With elimination of the white primary via *Smith* v. *Allwright* in 1944 and ratification of the Twenty-fourth Amendment to the

Constitution outlawing poll taxes in 1964, black Texans once again became voters and office holders without overt legal impediments. His campaign to make Juneteenth a legal state holiday continued for five months. During that time he received support from a contingent of black, white, and Tejano representatives and from citizens of other states. Paul Darby, a Juneteenth celebrant, said it best: "Even if the American people in the United States didn't really set that day aside for us, I believe they owe it to us anyway. . . . they ought to give the colored man a day for his freedom. It should be a red spot on the calendar and really took aside for."[67]

In 1979, Texas created the first legal state holiday honoring black emancipation, giving all Texans the right to celebrate an event that changed the course of history. Representative Edwards noted that "it's a time when white, brown, and blacks can celebrate freedom together." Edwards couched the victory in language mindful of the important place that memory has played in sustaining this event; the children, he said, need to know their history so they can find their "source of strength." Added to the festivities were also health and job fairs with the understanding that "freedom without proper health and employment doesn't mean much."[68]

The celebrations have only become grander since Texas made Juneteenth a legal holiday. In 1981, Juneteenth in Houston spread out over four days, and musicians who formed the Juneteenth Blues Festival performed at both the Miller Outdoor Theatre and Emancipation Park; two thousand people came to hear the renowned and the less well known share their musicianship with the public. In Austin in 1985, the Black Arts Alliance, an association designed to foster appreciation for black cultural arts, sponsored a four-day celebration called Juneteenth Bluezfest to honor local and state artists. Today, Juneteenth celebrations in many cities offer plays, concerts, "gospel explosions," festivals, art exhibits, dance performances, and all manner of food. Communities that never before held Juneteenth celebrations are starting them now.[69]

Some of the best of American culture resides in dance, jazz, blues, and other music derived from African roots. When Juneteenth returned as a celebration of freedom and the arts, it spoke to a universal audience. Memories of slavery and emancipation, even the joyful realization that a nation of people had been given their freedom, brought pain to some and joy to others, guilt to some, and feelings of resentment to others. But African American music and dance bring another message to all humanity regardless of race. It is this universalizing force speaking through black cultural heritage that has taken Juneteenth out of segregated parks and into communities in and beyond

Texas. Now celebrations are found all over the world, in part transported there by American troops, but enjoyed by an international audience. Now politicians of every stripe in Texas recognize Juneteenth as a time to court votes and gain approval by acknowledging the importance of this day to millions of Texans. Gov. Ann Richards was chief among many elected and appointed office holders who placed advertisements in black newspapers honoring Juneteenth. On June 19, 1991, she also signed into law Martin Luther King Jr. Day as a state holiday, giving added emphasis to the symbolic nature of Texas' emancipation day. According to one observer, "Remembering that day 126 years ago when Union General Gordon Granger stood before a similar mixed crowd at Galveston Bay and announced the emancipation proclamation [General Orders No. 3] the governor said it was appropriate that she sign the bill on the 19th of June. Governor Richards said that in doing so, she was not only honoring the memory of Dr. King, but also 'honoring a segment of the society in Texas that has often been overlooked and left out. . . . King's cause was an American cause, King's dream was an American dream.' [A]nd she vowed to work toward that day when we all cross over to the promised land of freedom and equality for all."[70]

Signing bills and holding immense public celebrations in recent times indicate that Juneteenth has evolved from the days when simple church services marked the opening of the day with prayer and thanksgiving, when Abraham Lincoln held a special place in the memories of black citizens as the Great Emancipator, when a young woman dressed as Liberty read the Emancipation Proclamation, when floats, bands, and black militia units paraded down streets lined with mostly black spectators, when picnics, games, contests, red soda, and barbecue marked the height of candor and amusement. From 1866 to the early twentieth century, black determination to celebrate emancipation in Texas proclaimed freedom from slavery a historic rite of passage, a counter-memory to the increasingly strident efforts at Confederate glorification. Once the Lost Cause memorialization frenzy abated sometime after 1915 with the fiftieth anniversary of the conclusion of the Civil War, Juneteenth revelers found that they faced other discouragements. Disfranchisement and segregation measures influenced white city officials to push Juneteenth parades to the margins in cities like Houston. White editorialists questioned black patriotism and citizenship rights. Riots, lynchings, and bloodshed mocked the meaning of African American wartime sacrifices. As the dislocations between reality and black expectations for dignity and rights became ever more obvious, Juneteenth celebrants attached citizenship, patriotism, and loyalty to the United States as part of their freedom memories.

In the Spirit of Juneteenth
We Are Working Together
to Build a New Texas
for All Its Citizens.

Paid for by the Ann Richards Committee, P.O. Box 12404, Austin Texas 78711

FIG. 6.2. Gov. Ann Richards was chief among many elected and appointed officials who placed advertisements in newspapers honoring Juneteenth. On Juneteenth 1991, Governor Richards signed the Martin Luther King Jr. Day into law. *Nokoa—The Observer* (Austin), June 21–27, 1991. Courtesy Center for American History, University of Texas at Austin.

By the 1960s slavery, however, presented a shadow shame, a memory best forgotten. Juneteenth celebrations seemed old fashioned and quaint by modern standards. The civil rights movement more adequately expressed black aspirations. Thus, Juneteenth celebrations went underground to reemerge in new form.

Juneteenth in collective memory today has new associations, with greater expression in artistic endeavors and less focus on recalling emancipation. Americans are chary of thinking too much about slavery; these memories, however essential to the celebration of freedom, serve as painful reminders of past sins. The former voice of subversion has transmogrified into a powerful celebratory sound. Today *Americans* gather together; a celebration of the arts, having neutralized the acid memories of pain, loss, and guilt, attracts a wider audience, including Asians, Mexican Americans, whites, and multiple ethnic groups. Collective memory is being molded by generations now born into a new era of post–civil rights freedom.[71]

The universalizing of Juneteenth since the late 1970s has allowed color lines to blur and barriers to come down. In the words of poet Lorenzo Thomas, "This commemoration of Emancipation Day in Texas reminds us that we all enjoy what our forerunners struggled to make a reality—that our efforts are not only for ourselves but for the future."[72] Counter-memories provided by Juneteenth celebrations kept alive the notion of emancipation and the promise of legal equality for a minority of the American population; collective memories of Juneteenth today are being created out of the universality of the human experience with new realities and new hopes.

NOTES

1. Because the military was a relatively weak presence in Texas compared to other departments in the South, Granger also made this announcement concerning future work patterns: "The Freedmen are advised to remain at their present homes and work for wages. They are informed that they will not be allowed to collect at military posts; and that they will not be supported in idleness either there or elsewhere" (quoted in *Galveston Daily News,* June 21, 1865). See also *War of the Rebellion: A Compilation of the Official Records of the Union and Confederate Armies,* 70 vols. in 128 (Washington, 1880–1901), series I, vol. 48, pt. I, 297–302; Robert W. Shook, "The Federal Military in Texas, 1865–1870," *Texas Military History* 6 (Spring 1967): 3–53, esp. 6; Carl H. Moneyhon, *Texas after the Civil War: The Struggle of Reconstruction* (College Station: Texas A&M University Press, 2004), 6–8; Alexander T. Pratt, "The Day the Slaves Got the News," *Broadsides* (Spring 1996): 20–21, 27.

2. On June 7, 1979, the 66th Texas legislature designated June 19 as "Emancipation Day in Texas," a legal state holiday (William H. Wiggins Jr., "Juneteenth: A Red Spot Day on the Texas Calendar," in *Juneteenth Texas: Essays in African-American Folklore,* ed. Francis E. Abernethy, Patrick B. Mullen, and Alan B. Govenar [Denton: University of North Texas Press, 1996], 237–52, esp. 247–50; William H. Wiggins Jr., *O Freedom! Afro-American Emancipation Celebrations* [Knoxville: University of Tennessee Press, 1987], xiii).

3. For an example of this belief, read William A. Owens' memory of 1913: "I began feeling sorry for him [a black neighbor]. He had been a slave with a good home and somebody to take care of him and the war had ruined everything for him. I knew what the war had done to the slaves. . . . 'You'd a been better off staying slaves,' I said. I knew I was right in saying it. All white people I knew said the same thing. Slaves didn't have to worry about anything. They got everything furnished when they needed it, and were taken care of when they got old" (Owens, *This Stubborn Soil: A Frontier Boyhood* [New York: Charles Scribner's Sons, 1966], 138). Remarks in 1905 by Judge Lewis Fisher of Galveston to a meeting of the Baptist Educa-

tional and Missionary Convention indicate a similar attitude. He noted that "Rastus," unlike "old slavery time darkies," was not prospering in freedom; it had provided him no home, no schools, but had left him with plenty of temptations: "He was greedy as a prairie colt turned into a feed house and he ate ignorantly of everything. As a result the race of today has become foundered as a horse, all the doctors of the race question are advising him and he has become a very sick . . . man" ([Galveston] *New Idea,* Oct. 14, 1905).

4. Counter-memories, which are collective memories held by those not among the dominant group in a society, exist among minority or dissident groups. Their collective memories manage to survive, sometimes in marginalized or in muted state alongside a dominant collective memory. African Americans and Mexican Americans in Texas have worked continuously to keep counter-memory alive. See, for example, Andrés Tijerina, "Constructing Tejano Memory," in this volume, and Ann Burlein, "Countermemory on the Right: The Case of Focus on the Family" in *Acts of Memory: Cultural Recall in the Present,* ed. Mieke Bal, Jonathan Crewe, and Leo Spitzer (Hanover, N.H.: University Press of New England, 1999), 208–17.

5. Kelly McMichael Stott, "From Lost Cause to Female Empowerment: The Texas Division of the United Daughters of the Confederacy, 1896–1966" (Ph.D. diss., University of North Texas, 2001); Fred Arthur Bailey, "Free Speech and 'The Lost Cause' in Texas: A Study of Social Control in the New South," *Southwestern Historical Quarterly* 97 (Fall 1994): 453–77. For the rise of the Lost Cause across the South see Gaines M. Foster, *Ghosts of the Confederacy: Defeat, the Lost Cause, and the Emergence of the New South, 1865 to 1913* (New York: Oxford University Press, 1987); Charles Reagan Wilson, *Baptized in Blood: The Religion of the Lost Cause, 1865–1920* (Athens: University of Georgia Press, 1980); Cynthia Mills and Pamela H. Simpson, eds., *Monuments to the Lost Cause: Women, Art, and the Landscapes of Southern Memory* (Knoxville: University of Tennessee Press, 2003).

6. The valorization of defeat is an anomaly, for most histories are written from the perspective of the victor. In the case of white southerners acting as advocates of the Lost Cause, recapturing their history was among the first steps toward legitimization within the Union. Eventually northerners adopted the southern version of valor in the face of defeat, of noble sacrifice rather than treason. Northerners mitigated the courage, valor, and sacrifice of those who had endured slavery or of black soldiers, who in some cases fought against former masters. Who, asked the freedpeople, were the true citizens of the newly united land? The studies of the South's cultural victory are numerous, but essential are Nina Silber, *The Romance of Reunion: Northerners and the South, 1865–1900* (Chapel Hill: University of North Carolina Press, 1993); David W. Blight, *Race and Reunion: The Civil War in American Memory* (Cambridge, Mass.: Harvard University Press, 2001); Karen L. Cox, *Dixie's Daughters: The United Daughters of the Confederacy and the Preservation of Confederate Culture* (Gainesville: University Press of Florida, 2003).

7. Contrast Texas to South Carolina, where state employees until 2000 had the choice of taking one holiday out of four different options: Jefferson Davis's birthday (June 3), Robert E. Lee's birthday (January 19), Confederate Memorial Day (May 10), or Martin Luther King Jr. Day (January 16). Martin Luther King Jr.'s birthday is now an official state holiday in South Carolina as well as in Texas. South Carolinians also made May 10, Confederate Memorial Day, a state holiday (K. Michael Prince, *Rally 'Round the Flag, Boys!: South Carolina and the Confederate Flag* [Columbia: University of South Carolina Press, 2004], 224, 239; James C. Cobb, *Away Down South: A History of Southern Identity* [New York: Oxford University Press, 2005], 297–301; David Goldfield, *Southern Histories: Public, Personal, and Sacred* [Athens: University of Georgia Press, 2003], 1–5; David Goldfield, *Still Fighting the Civil War: The American South and Southern History* [Baton Rouge: Louisiana State University Press, 2002], 29).

8. In 1997 the Texas legislature created the Texas Emancipation Juneteenth Cultural and

Historical Commission (Acts 1997, 75th Leg., chap. 563, sec. 1, effective Sept. 1, 1997). Its purpose is to "coordinate state and local activities relating to the . . . celebration of Juneteenth; . . . and to establish a Juneteenth memorial monument on the grounds of the State Capitol" (Texas Government Code, chap. 448: Texas Emancipation Juneteenth Cultural and Historical Commission). According to bids sent out by the State Preservation Board, the monument's granite base was to be constructed and ready for the placement of bronze sculptures by May 20, 2005. Estimates on the cost of the memorial were $1.2 million (*Houston Chronicle*, June 12, 2003). Plans were also being made for a monument to be placed at Ashton Villa in Galveston, the purported site of the reading of the Texas freedom proclamation (*Houston Chronicle*, Sept. 25, 2003; June 10, 17, 2004). Contrast these plans to the bronze statue dedicated to the "memory of the devoted Negro of ante-bellum days" and unveiled in Natchitoches, Louisiana, in 1927. It was erected "by the City of Natchitoches in Grateful Recognition of the Arduous and Faithful Service of the Good Darkies of Louisiana" ([Houston] *Informer*, June 18, 1927). See also Micki McElya, "Commemorating the Color Line: The National Mammy Monument Controversy of the 1920s," in *Monuments to the Lost Cause: Women, Art, and the Landscapes of Southern Memory*, ed. Cynthia Mills and Pamela H. Simpson (Knoxville: University of Tennessee Press, 2003), 203–18; Alwyn Barr, *Black Texans: A History of African Americans in Texas, 1528–1995*, 2d ed. (Norman: University of Oklahoma Press, 1996), 245; and Kirk Savage, *Standing Soldiers, Kneeling Slaves: Race, War, and Monument in Nineteenth-Century America* (Princeton, N.J.: Princeton University Press, 1997).

9. Elizabeth Janeway, *Powers of the Weak* (New York: Knopf, 1980); Geneviève Fabre, "African-American Commemorative Celebrations in the Nineteenth Century," in *History and Memory in African-American Culture*, ed. Geneviève Fabre and Robert O'Meally (New York: Oxford University Press, 1994), 72; Kathleen Clark, "Celebrating Freedom: Emancipation Day Celebrations and African American Memory in the Early Reconstruction South," in *Where These Memories Grow: History, Memory, and Southern Identity*, ed. W. Fitzhugh Brundage (Chapel Hill: University of North Carolina Press, 2000), 107–32; Kathleen Ann Clark, *Defining Moments: African American Commemoration and Political Culture in the South, 1863–1913* (Chapel Hill: University of North Carolina Press, 2005). See also Michel Foucault, "Nietzsche, Genealogy, History," in *Language, Counter-Memory, Practice: Selected Essays and Interviews*, ed. Donald Bouchard (Ithaca, N.Y.: Cornell University Press, 1977), 151–54.

10. Nancy Cohen-Lack, "A Struggle for Sovereignty: National Consolidation, Emancipation, and Free Labor in Texas, 1865," *Journal of Southern History* 58 (Feb. 1992): 64.

11. William Pitt Ballinger diary, July 16, 1865, vertical files, Galveston and Texas History Center, Rosenberg Library, Galveston, Tex., as cited in John Anthony Moretta, *William Pitt Ballinger: Texas Lawyer, Southern Statesman, 1825–1888* (Austin: Texas State Historical Association, 2000), 174.

12. As was the case with the Ballingers, all over the South slaves left their former masters, some permanently, others temporarily. The literature is now voluminous on the subject of master/former-slave relations in the immediate aftermath of emancipation, but reference should be made certainly to Eric Foner, *Reconstruction: America's Unfinished Revolution, 1863–1877* (New York: Harper & Row, 1988); Leon F. Litwack, *Been in the Storm So Long: The Aftermath of Slavery* (New York: Vintage, 1980); James L. Roark, *Masters without Slaves: Southern Planters in the Civil War and Reconstruction* (New York: Norton, 1977); Leslie Schwalm, *A Hard Fight for We: Women's Transition from Slavery to Freedom in South Carolina* (Urbana: University of Illinois Press, 1997). For primary documents see Ira Berlin et al., eds., *The Destruction of Slavery* (Cambridge: Cambridge University Press, 1985); Ira Berlin et al., eds., *The Wartime Genesis of Free Labor: The Lower South* (Cambridge: Cambridge University Press, 1990); Ira Berlin et al., eds., *The Wartime Genesis of Free Labor: The Upper South* (Cambridge:

Cambridge University Press, 1993); Ira Berlin, Joseph P. Reidy, and Leslie S. Rowland, eds., *The Black Military Experience* (Cambridge: Cambridge University Press, 1982).

13. Shook, "The Federal Military in Texas, 1865–1870," 3–53; Foner, *Reconstruction,* 3–4; Litwack, *Been in the Storm So Long,* 128, 164–66.

14. Cohen-Lack, "A Struggle for Sovereignty," 64.

15. James M. Smallwood, *Time of Hope, Time of Despair: Black Texans during Reconstruction* (Port Washington, N.Y.: Kennikat Press, 1981), 25; Barry A. Crouch, *The Freedmen's Bureau and Black Texans* (Austin: University of Texas Press, 1992), 12; Cohen-Lack, "A Struggle for Sovereignty," 62.

16. Crouch, *The Freedmen's Bureau and Black Texans,* 13.

17. Report of the Joint Committee on Reconstruction, House Executive Documents, 39th Cong., 1st sess., no. 30, 124; Crouch, *The Freedmen's Bureau and Black Texans,* 12–15, 17; Barr, *Black Texans,* 39–43; Shook, "The Federal Military in Texas, 1865–1870," 12–13.

18. Ronnie C. Tyler and Lawrence R. Murphy, eds., *The Slave Narratives of Texas* (Austin, Tex.: Encino Press, 1974), 121 (Merritt quotation); Ira Berlin, Marc Favreau, and Steven F. Miller, eds., *Remembering Slavery: African Americans Talk about Their Personal Experiences of Slavery and Freedom* (New York: New Press, in association with the Library of Congress, 1998), 270. See also James M. Smallwood, Barry A. Crouch, and Larry Peacock, *Murder and Mayhem: The War of Reconstruction in Texas* (College Station: Texas A&M University Press, 2003), 41.

19. Tyler and Murphy, *The Slave Narratives of Texas,* 121 (Merritt quotation); George P. Rawick, ed., *The American Slave: A Composite Autobiography,* vol. 4, *Texas Narratives,* parts 1 and 2 (Westport, Conn.: Greenwood Publishing Co., 1972), 280 (Darling quotation).

20. Berlin et al., *Remembering Slavery,* 266.

21. Ibid.; Tyler and Murphy, *The Slave Narratives of Texas,* 114.

22. Friedrich Nietzsche, *Untimely Meditations,* ed. Daniel Breazeale (Cambridge: Cambridge University Press, 1997), 62. The literature on the Lost Cause and segregation is voluminous: Leon F. Litwack, *Trouble in Mind: Black Southerners in the Age of Jim Crow* (New York: Knopf, 1998); Grace Elizabeth Hale, *Making Whiteness: The Culture of Segregation in the South, 1890–1940* (New York: Pantheon Books, 1998); Joel Williamson, *Crucible of Race: Black/White Relations in the American South since Emancipation* (New York: Oxford University Press, 1984); Katharine Du Pre Lumpkin, *The Making of a Southerner* (New York: Knopf, 1946), especially book 3, "A Child Inherits the Lost Cause."

23. Ira Berlin, "American Slavery in History and Memory and the Search for Social Justice," *Journal of American History* 90 (Mar. 2004): 1266.

24. Estimates for the number of slaves emancipated in Texas vary between two hundred thousand and four hundred thousand. I have chosen the most commonly used number. See Cohen-Lack, "A Struggle for Sovereignty," 59. She bases her estimate of four hundred thousand on the report of William E. Strong, Inspector Genl., to Genl. Oliver O. Howard, Jan. 1, 1866, in House Exec. Docs., 39th Cong., 1st sess, 1866, no. 70: *Report of the Commissioners of the Bureau of Refugees, Freedmen, and Abandoned Lands* (Serial 1256, Washington, 1866), 312.

25. Pierre Nora, "Between Memory and History: Les Lieux de mémoire," in *History and Memory in African-American Culture,* ed. Geneviève Fabre and Robert O'Meally (New York: Oxford University Press, 1994), 284–300; Paul Darby, Nov. 1972, "red spot" quotation from Wiggins, *O Freedom!,* xvii.

26. David W. Blight, *Frederick Douglass and Abraham Lincoln: A Relationship in Language, Politics, and Memory* (Milwaukee, Wisc.: Marquette University Press, 2001), 6–12 (quotation, 12). Michael Kammen writes that "the blacks' collective memory of slavery remained

vivid, . . . but what they chose to emphasize by means of traditional activities each year was the memory of gaining freedom" (Kammen, *Mystic Chords of Memory: The Transformation of Tradition in American Culture* [New York: Knopf, 1991], 123).

27. Blight, *Race and Reunion,* 25.

28. Ira Berlin, "Who Freed the Slaves? Emancipation and Its Meaning," in *Union & Emancipation: Essays on Politics and Race in the Civil War Era,* ed. David W. Blight and Brooks D. Simpson (Kent, Ohio: Kent State University Press, 1997), 105–21; Amy Grey, "Juneteenth: A Historical Perspective, 1991," Juneteenth vertical file, Center for American History, University of Texas at Austin (hereafter, CAH).

29. Blight, *Frederick Douglass and Abraham Lincoln,* 7. See also Blight, *Frederick Douglass' Civil War: Keeping Faith in Jubilee* (Baton Rouge: Louisiana State University Press, 1989), 219–39.

30. Blight, *Race and Reunion,* 13.

31. William H. Wiggins Jr., "'Lift Every Voice': A Study of Afro-American Emancipation Celebrations," *Journal of Asian and African Studies* 9 (July/Oct.1974): 180–91. Wiggins also notes that "tradition has also dictated that the reader of this precious document must be young, preferably in his [*sic*] late teens or early twenties, and a female, though young men have been selected with some success" (185).

32. Charles Morgan, interview by William Wiggins, Nov. 23, 1972, as quoted in Wiggins, *O Freedom!,* 35.

33. Maggie Whitehead Matthews, 1937, quoted in George P. Rawick, ed., *The American Slave: A Composite Autobiography,* suppl., ser. 2, vol. 7, pt. 6 (Westport, Conn.: Greenwood Publishing Group, 1979), 2625. Speculations on the term "radical" include its association with the radical wing of the Republican Party.

34. Wiggins, *O Freedom!,* xx. See also David A. Williams, *Juneteenth, Unique Heritage: An Historical Analysis of the Origin and Development of the 19th of June Celebration in Texas* (Austin: Texan African American Heritage Organization, 1992), 18; [Houston] *Informer,* June 18, 1938.

35. [Austin] *Sunday School Herald,* May 28, June 4, June 11, June 18, 1892.

36. Wiggins, "Lift Every Voice," 184–85; Izola Ethel Fedford Collins, interview by author, tape recording, Galveston, Tex., Jan. 4, 2005.

37. Shane White, "'It Was a Proud Day': African Americans, Festivals, and Parades in the North, 1741–1834," *Journal of American History* 81 (June 1994): 13–50; Mitch Kachun, *Festivals of Freedom: Memory and Meaning in African American Emancipation Celebrations, 1808–1915* (Amherst: University of Massachusetts Press, 2003), 233–35; Clark, "Celebrating Freedom," 109–13. See also Elizabeth Hayes Turner, *Women, Culture, and Community: Religion and Reform in Galveston, 1880–1920* (New York: Oxford University Press, 1997), 250–51.

38. [Austin] *Herald,* June 27, 1896. The newspaper also indicated that there were two parades and celebrations in Austin that year, the result of a division between those who called for a more sedate church-going celebration and those who wanted to enjoy a more raucous celebration.

39. [Galveston] *City Times,* June 11, 1904. For a description and analysis of Juneteenth parades in San Antonio see Judith Berg Sobré, *San Antonio on Parade: Six Historic Festivals* (College Station: Texas A&M University Press, 2003), 51–72.

40. [Galveston] *City Times,* June 11, 1904.

41. [Austin] *Herald,* June 22, 1895 (first quotation); [Galveston] *City Times,* May 28, June 11, 1904; Marina Warner, *Monuments and Maidens: The Allegory of the Female Form* (New York: Atheneum, 1985), 14–15; Turner, *Women, Culture, and Community,* 251 (subsequent quo-

tations). For a discussion of symbolic protest as a vital part of African American identity see James Oliver Horton, *Free People of Color: Inside the African American Community* (Washington, D.C.: Smithsonian Institution Press, 1993), 164.

42. Quotation from [Galveston] *City Times,* May 28, 1904; Patricia Smith Prather, "Juneteenth: A Celebration of Freedom," *Texas Highways* 35 (June 1988): 4–5; Lorenzo Thomas, "Texas Tradition," *Houston City Magazine* 5 (June 1981): 103–105; Doris Hollis Pemberton, *Juneteenth at Comanche Crossing* (Austin, Tex.: Eakin Publications, 1983), 205–12; Smallwood, *Time of Hope, Time of Despair,* 103–104.

43. Pemberton, *Juneteenth at Comanche Crossing,* 205; Nora, "Between Memory and History," 298. Nora's fuller statement is that "memory attaches itself to sites whereas history attaches itself to events" (298).

44. Williams, *Juneteenth,* 18; Izola Ethel Fedford Collins interview, Jan. 4, 2005; Marjorie L. B. Allen, interview by author, tape recording, Houston, Tex., Jan. 8, 2005.

45. Prather, "Juneteenth: A Celebration of Freedom," 4 (quotation); Sobré, *San Antonio on Parade,* 59; Marjorie L. B. Allen interview, Jan. 8, 2005; Izola Ethel Fedford Collins interview, Jan. 4, 2005.

46. [Galveston] *City Times,* May 28, 1904, June 11, 1904, June 10, 17, July 8, 1905, June 20, 1914, June 21, 1919; [Galveston] *New Idea,* Mar. 4, 1905.

47. [Galveston] *City Times,* June 10, 1905. The *Galveston Spectator* ran until 1885. The *Freeman's Journal* ran until 1893.

48. [Galveston] *City Times,* May 15, 1906; [Galveston] *New Idea,* July 15, Dec. 23, 1905, Mar. 31, 1906; *Galveston Daily News,* June 29, 1906.

49. Michael Perman, *Struggle for Mastery: Disfranchisement in the South, 1888–1908* (Chapel Hill: University of North Carolina Press, 2001), 271–81; J. Morgan Kousser, *The Shaping of Southern Politics: Suffrage Restriction and the Establishment of the One-Party South, 1880–1910* (New Haven, Conn.: Yale University Press, 1974), 203–208; Lewis L. Gould, *Alexander Watkins Terrell: Civil War Soldier, Texas Lawmaker, American Diplomat* (Austin: University of Texas Press, 2004), 151–52, 154–55. (Perman's study of disfranchisement is the best to date; Kousser's study is older but still provocative.) Editors of the [Galveston] *City Times* complained, "The colored citizens of voting age have paid as much poll taxes as the whites in proportion to their number. . . . The *Houston Daily Post* is in error when it tries to have the public believe that the Negro as a citizen is not interested in any public benefit, when he is asked to contribute toward such an end. . . . Over 35,000 Negroes have paid their poll taxes. Thousands of whites of Texas, who are better able to pay . . . refused to pay it, holding that it is an injustice to fix a price upon manhood suffrage"([Galveston] *City Times,* Oct. 29, 1904). By 1908, Galveston African Americans organized a "poll tax club" to rally the voters and qualify them for voting in the city commissioner election ([Galveston] *City Times,* Dec. 26, 1908; Barr, *Black Texans,* 79–88; Dewey W. Grantham, *Southern Progressivism: The Reconciliation of Progress and Tradition* [Knoxville: University of Tennessee Press, 1983], 123–27).

50. Blight, *Race and Reunion,* 354–62.

51. Tyler and Murphy, *The Slave Narratives of Texas,* 96; Lerone Bennett Jr., "Jubilee," *Ebony* 27 (Feb. 1972): 39; Sobré, *San Antonio on Parade,* 35, 38–50; [Galveston] *City Times,* July 8, 1905. Crispus Attucks was killed by British soldiers at the Boston Massacre in 1873. He is considered the first black martyr for American independence.

52. Kammen, *Mystic Chords of Memory,* 8.

53. [Houston] *Informer,* June 7, 1919.

54. [Galveston] *City Times,* June 21, 1919.

55. [Houston] *Informer,* June 28, 1919.

56. *Houston Post,* June 22, 1919.

57. C. F. Richardson, "Is Watermelon to Be Our Only Reward for Great Service in Democracy's Martial Conflict?" [Houston] *Informer,* June 28, 1919.

58. [Houston] *Informer,* Sept. 29, 1923. David A. Williams notes that from 1866 to 1979, Juneteenth was "called many things (coon-day, nigger-day, etc.)"(Williams, *Juneteenth,* 21).

59. [Houston] *Informer,* June 16, 1937 (first quotation, from advertisement); June 16, 1923 (second quotation, from Richardson editorial); also June 16, 1928; June 15, 1929; June 17, 1939; June 14, 1941.

60. "Juneteenth Observed by Negroes of Dallas," *Dallas Morning News,* June 20, 1929 (first quotation); "Plan Big Juneteenth Celebration at Ball Park; Game Features," *Dallas Morning News,* June 17, 1931 (second quotation). For advertisements to theme parks see [Houston] *Informer* June 14, 1947, June 18, 23, 1949, June 17, 1950, June 20, 1953, June 16, 1956, June 15, 1957. Sometime before 1960 black journalists began objecting to the obvious discrimination and exploitation practiced by segregated theme parks. In 1960, one wrote, "We have opposed Negroes accepting the one day at the fair in Dallas[,] . . . we have on previous occasions opposed Negroes accepting a one-day opening of Playland Park. It is almost a sacrilege for parents to be taking their kids to Playland Park on the 19th of June, their Emancipation Day, which at Playland is a one segregated day for Negroes" ([Houston] *Informer,* June 18, 1960).

61. [Houston] *Informer,* June 16, 1928, June 20, 1931, June 16, 1937, June 14, 1941; "Juneteenth Observance Delayed Because Sunday Is Not Workday Anyhow," *Dallas Morning News,* June 20, 1932; "Three Celebrations Regale Negroes for Juneteenth Holiday," *Dallas Morning News,* June 21, 1932; "Negro Nines Face in Juneteenth Go," *Dallas Morning News,* June 17, 1934; "Juneteenth Passes Quietly; One Killed, Twelve Jailed," *Dallas Morning News,* June 20, 1935.

62. "Negroes Stage Big Juneteenth at Centennial," *Dallas Morning News,* June 20, 1936; "Two Dedications," *Dallas Morning News,* June 20, 1936; "Centennial," *Dallas Morning News,* June 20, 1936; J. Mason Brewer, "Juneteenth," in *Tone the Bell Easy,* ed. J. Frank Dobie (Austin: Texas Folk-lore Society, 1932). On Brewer's scholarship see [Houston] *Informer,* June 16, 1932; Thomas, "Texas Tradition," 103–105; John David Boswell, "Negro Participation in the 1936 Texas Centennial Exposition" (master's thesis, University of Texas, Austin, 1969); Jesse O. Thomas, *Negro Participation in the Texas Centennial Exposition* (Boston: Christopher Publishing House, 1938); Michael Phillips, *White Metropolis: Race, Ethnicity, and Religion in Dallas, 1841–2001* (Austin: University of Texas Press, 2006), 112–16; W. Fitzhugh Brundage, "Whispering Consolation to Generations Unborn: Black Memory in the Era of Jim Crow," in *Warm Ashes: Issues in Southern History at the Dawn of the Twenty-first Century,* ed. Winfred B. Moore Jr., Kyle S. Sinisi, and David H. White Jr. (Columbia: University of South Carolina Press, 2003), 341.

63. Ralph Ellison, *Juneteenth: A Novel* (New York: Random House, 1999), 115 (emphasis in original); [Houston] *Informer,* June 14, 1941.

64. [Houston] *Informer,* June 26, 1943. In a column entitled "This Is FREEDOM Calling," H. A. Bullock wrote, "With Democracy taking a holiday, . . . 5,000 workers at the local shipyard left their jobs to go on a lynch hunt and a Gestapo party" ([Houston] *Informer,* June 19 1943). As if to emphasize the increasing politicization of postwar freedom celebrations, by 1947 the growing Houston chapter of the NAACP sponsored the Juneteenth celebration in Houston and advertised successful membership drives in the community's newspaper ([Houston] *Informer,* June 14, 1947).

65. *Dallas Morning News,* June 19, 1968; Thomas, "Texas Tradition," 103–105; Grey, "Juneteenth: A Historical Perspective, 1991," 12; Marjorie L. B. Allen interview, Jan. 8, 2005. David A. Williams writes that young African Americans involved in the struggle for civil rights felt that "Juneteenth was antiquated or inept . . . archaic" (Williams, *Juneteenth,* 20). According

to Patricia Smith Prather, "Austin blacks revitalized Juneteenth in 1976, after a 25-year hiatus" (Prather, "Juneteenth: A Celebration of Freedom," 7). From 1960 to 1967 no mention of June-teenth was made in the *Dallas Morning News.* Between 1961 and 1970 no Juneteenth celebra-tions were recorded in the [Houston] *Informer.* In the *Houston Negro Labor News,* however, radio station KYOK advertised that it was sponsoring a "Century of Progress" celebration on June 19 at Playland Park in Houston. The station advertised a similar Juneteenth celebra-tion in 1964 (*Houston Negro Labor News,* June 15, 1963, June 13, 1964). On June 26, 1971, the [Houston] *Informer* noted that "June 19 all across the nation was celebrated by small groups and families in all Negro communities. . . . In the early days big celebrations were held all over the states but now only smaller minority groups seem to stick with the old trend of barbecu-ing and drinking red soda water. . . . [T]he people seem to get further and further away from the celebration of June 19." See also Frances Imon, "No Plans Made: Emancipation Day Fete Fading Away," *Daily Oklahoman,* June 18, 1965. Evidence of the cessation of publicly adver-tised Juneteenth celebrations was determined by reading the summer issues of the [Houston] *Informer* from 1919 until 1973 and the *Dallas Morning News* from 1885 to 1977.

66. Prather, "Juneteenth: A Celebration of Freedom," 7; *Houston Post,* June 5, 1980, June 18, 1989.

67. *Houston Post,* May 21, June 5, 1980; Williams, *Juneteenth,* 26–29; Paul Darby, Nov. 1972, as quoted in Wiggins, *O Freedom!,* xvii. Gerrymandering continued to be a problem, leading to many subsequent legal battles.

68. Prather, "Juneteenth: A Celebration of Freedom," 8 (first two quotations); *Hous-ton Post,* June 20, 1989 (third quotation). According to the National Juneteenth Observance Foundation, "Juneteenth is now recognized as a state holiday or state holiday observance in Texas, Oklahoma, Florida, Delaware, Idaho, Alaska, Iowa, California, Wyoming, Missouri, Connecticut, Illinois, Louisiana, New Jersey, New York and also in the District of Colum-bia. Many more states, including Colorado, Arkansas, Oregon, South Dakota, Mississippi, Massachusetts, Pennsylvania, Montana, Maryland, Virginia, Michigan and Wisconsin have recognized Juneteenth through state legislative resolutions and Gubernatorial Proclamations. In 1997, a historic resolution was passed by the Congress of the United States through Senate Joint Resolution 11 and House Joint Resolution 56, recognizing the '*19th of June*' as Juneteenth Independence Day in America" (NJOF website, http://www.19thofjune.com/calendar/index .html [accessed Jan. 10, 2005]).

69. *New York Times,* June 19, 1989; *Austin Chronicle,* June 14, 1985; flier, "Emancipation Week, 1987, Organized by the Texas Association for the Study of Afro-American Life and History," "Juneteenth" vertical file, CAH. Disputes did arise over the manner and meaning of the celebration, however. By 1989 three organizations had emerged to sponsor Juneteenth celebrations in Houston alone: the National Emancipation Association, founded in 1973 by Rev. C. Anderson Davis; the Juneteenth Blues Festival under the sponsorship of SumArts, an underwriting organization for the arts in Houston; and Juneteenth USA, organized by Rep. Al Edwards (*Houston Chronicle,* Feb. 25, 1982). Davis is quoted as saying, "They've turned the day into a party when it should be an educational and pride-building experience" (*Houston Post,* June 18, 1989). See also *Houston Chronicle,* June 12, 19, 2003.

70. Carroll Parrott Blue, *The Dawn at My Back: Memoir of a Black Texas Upbringing* (Austin: University of Texas Press, 2003), 85. Blue recalls the criticism of Houston women in the 1950s who did not like art that "highlighted slavery, a period regarded by the women as being 'too dark.'" Also, "Governor Signs MLK Holiday Bill," [Austin] *Nokoa—The Observer,* June 21–27, 1991. Among the well wishers with advertisements in that issue of *Nokoa—The Observer* were Sen. Gonzalo Barrientos, Railroad Commissioner Lena Guerrero, Assistant City Attorney Iris Jones, Rep. Sherri Greenberg, Rep. Wilhelmina Delco, and Travis County

Judge Bill Aleshire, who wrote, "Juneteenth is a day more to *Remember* the call for Freedom than to *celebrate* it, because not all people are yet free." For a literary rendering of Houston's joyous Juneteenth celebrations after 1977 see Tracy Daugherty's short story "Burying the Blues," in his collection, *It Takes a Worried Man: Stories* (Dallas: Southern Methodist University Press, 2002), 150–200.

71. David Ellison, "Juneteenth Not for Blacks Only," *Houston Post,* June 15, 1986.

72. Thomas, "Texas Tradition," 105.

Chapter 7

CONSTRUCTING TEJANO MEMORY

ANDRÉS TIJERINA

The first years of the twenty-first century witnessed a number of statues erected across Texas under the leadership of Mexican Americans who were intent on honoring their heritage. This construction boom marks the first time that monuments have been raised to their memory in the state. In years prior Mexican Americans did not have exclusive authority over the institutions or funds that raised historical monuments or markers; therefore, their heritage with few exceptions has been almost systematically excluded in the public transcript of Texas history.

Members of the Ballí family were among the first to use private funds for such a monument by erecting in South Texas a statue of their ancestor, missionary Padre José Nicolás Ballí, in 1983. Padre Ballí was the eighteenth-century priest for whom Padre Island was named because he personally held title to the island.

In 1986, the state of Texas officially sanctioned a monument to General Ignacio Zaragoza, the commanding general who won the famous Battle of the Cinco de Mayo against a French army in Mexico in 1862. The monument was placed in Goliad, Texas, the general's birthplace. In 2000, amid ceremonies and a parade, a statue of José de Escandón was erected in Alice, Texas, by a private Mexican American committee. Escandón was the Spanish colonizer who sponsored hundreds of ranching families and settled them in present-day South Texas, where they established the great cattle kingdom of Texas longhorns and vast ranches. That fundraising committee was composed of descendants of the Escandón founding families who still live in South Texas.

On October 28, 2000, members of the Seguín Family Historical Society,

FIG. 7.1. Father José Nicolás Ballí, owner of the original land grant for what is now known as Padre Island, which was named in his honor. Courtesy Ballí family.

with privately raised funds, erected a bronze statue in Seguín, Texas, honoring their ancestor, Col. Juan N. Seguín. Seguín was a cavalry commander who served at the Alamo and at the famous Battle of San Jacinto in the Texas Revolution in 1836. Since the 1990s numerous other plaques and markers honoring Tejanos have been erected across the state.[1]

Perhaps the most grandiose of these monuments is the proposed Tejano Monument to be erected on the state capitol grounds. It was initially proposed by the Tejano Monument Committee, a private fundraising committee of Mexican American leaders. On May 17, 2001, the 77th Texas Legislature adopted House Concurrent Resolution (HCR) 38, authorizing the commit-

FIG. 7.2. The statue of José de Escandón was erected in Alice, Texas, by Mexican American descendants of the ranching families who settled the South Texas cattle kingdom. Courtesy Travel Division, TxDOT.

tee to erect the monument on the Texas capitol grounds to pay tribute to the contributions of Tejanos to the state of Texas. The Tejano Monument is proposed to be more than just a statue, however. The plan features a twenty-foot stone base with several statues and bronze relief plaques, making it one of the largest monuments on the capitol grounds. To date, it is the most ambitious project attempted by Mexican Americans in public monument raising. It is significant not only for its scale but also for its very name.

The significance is in the name "Tejano." It is not called the Mexican American monument, although Mexican Americans conceived it. It is not called the Latino monument, although "Latino" is the politically current label

FIG. 7.3. Col. Juan N. Seguín, Texas Revolution hero, honored by the Seguín Family Historical Society. Courtesy Seguín Family Historical Society, Albert Seguín Gonzales, Founder.

for the fastest growing Hispanic segment of the Texas population, mostly
Mexican and Central American immigrants. It is called the Tejano Monument because the term "Tejano" includes any Spanish-surnamed Texans
whose historical or cultural roots are in Texas. Tejanos have a history that can
be found in the land grants, the church records, and the archival documents
of Texas. Latinos have a well-documented history in the census records and
demographic growth of modern Texas cities. But in their search for a link to
the founders of Texas, Latinos and Mexican Americans have found a common memory in the Tejano—the native Mexican of Texas—the Texan who
was here before the first Anglo American immigrated to Texas. By using the

FIG. 7.4. The Tejano Monument proposed for the state capitol grounds. Courtesy Cayetano Barrera.

term "Tejano," Hispanics of various national origins can relate to a common heritage as Texans, even though they come from diverse national origins.

The Tejano memory is significant because it provides a comforting sense of historical belonging for Mexican Americans and even Latino immigrants in Texas. Memory is what James C. Scott calls a "public transcript" or a publicly held story of a people's past that binds them as a social and cultural group. It gives them a self-perspective of their heritage, just as memory serves Anglo Texans in their self-perception. To Tejanos, memory is the shared story of their common heritage—a story they have composed largely from sources such as traditional music and art, knowledge of historical sites, and, perhaps most importantly, legends and oral traditions passed down through the generations. Memory is not based exclusively on historical documents and facts any more than Anglo myths and memory are based only on historical facts. Much of the Davy Crockett story is myth, and much of the Tejano memory is not taken from recorded history. Memory may not be documentary, but it reflects the positive aspects that Tejanos prefer to attribute to their heritage. W. Fitzhugh Brundage argues that memory records only "selective knowledge." In *Where These Memories Grow*, Brundage states that a group's collective memory focuses only on select concerns. The selective memory cleanses otherwise uncomfortable historical realities and "purifies them, it makes them innocent, it gives them natural and eternal justification, it gives them a clarity."[2] The Tejano collective memory is the idealized story of the Hispanic past in Texas, cleansed of blemishes. It is in part through public statues and images that Mexican Americans have constructed their collective memories.

According to the idealized memory shared by today's Latinos, Tejanos were the first Texans of European lineage and culture. They were the only ones to have been on this land under all six flags over Texas. They were the colonizers who came with Don Domingo Ramón in 1718 or later with José de Escandón, the count of Sierra Gorda. Escandón was a nobleman, one of the sons of nobility or *hijos dalgos*. They were Spanish, white Europeans. They were the educated elite or the *gente de razón*. Their land grants were the original land titles of Texas granted under the Crown of Spain for their stalwart defense of the northern *frontera*. They brought the famous Texas longhorn into present-day Texas. These ranching families raised millions of cattle that were later driven north on the famous cattle trails—the Chisholm, the Goodnight-Loving, and the Western Trail—to such towns as Denver, Dodge City, and Sedalia. They were the first cowboys, the ones who perfected the riding and roping skills now exhibited in the modern rodeos of the West. Today's Mexican Americans proudly recite the lexicon of Tejano words that constitute the cowboy vocabulary—words like lasso, corral, rodeo, and barbecue. In the South Texas ranch country, they can still drive the back roads near Hebbronville and see an old eighteenth-century-style "Spanish fence" made of mesquite logs, stacked in a crisscross, log-cabin style. If they know just where to look through the dense chaparral, Mexican American fathers can show their children the old limestone block ranch houses built in the 1790s and early 1800s—still standing proof that the Tejanos were here long before Sam Houston ever thought of building an Anglo American–style log house. And the most notable signs of the early Tejano settlements are the missions—the Alamo, San José, and La Bahía—built in the early 1700s. These missions are the physical representations, the sites of memory to which modern Mexican Americans link their claim to Texas and its braggadocio. In their construction of this memory, Tejanos have sought what historians Jacques Le Goff and Pierre Nora would call "a whole history of human [Tejano] experience." In their book *Constructing the Past*, Le Goff and Nora describe the process by which groups like Tejanos seek a broad range of facts from which to construct their own story. Instructively, the Tejano memory is not one celebrated event or a single hero but an envisioned past in Texas that gives them—more than anything else—legitimacy as true Texans.[3]

Other major elements of this idealized memory are Tejanos' claims concerning Mexican independence from Spanish colonialism and their service in the Texas Revolution. Tejanos were among the first Mexican colonists to declare Texas to be free from Spanish rule. Bernardo Gutiérrez de Lara fought the initial campaign, albeit abortive, against a superior Spanish royalist army just outside San Antonio de Béxar. After the long and bloody war was consummated in 1821, Tejas was one of the first Mexican states formally to commemorate Mexican Independence Day, September 16, El Diezyseis. The Diezyseis is still celebrated in San Antonio every September. Likewise, Tejanos such as Juan N. Seguín fought for the independence of the new Republic of Texas from Mexico. Others such as José Francisco Ruiz, José Antonio Navarro, and Lorenzo de Zavala signed the Texas Declaration of Independence in 1836. Tejano memory serves to accommodate Mexican Independence Day, Texas Independence Day, and the Battle of the Cinco de Mayo in Mexico. In the rotunda of the state capitol in Austin every September 16, Mexican American citizens and Latino immigrants newly arrived from such places as El Salvador or Nicaragua gather to commemorate the Tejano commitment to independence and liberty.[4]

Tejano memory serves conveniently to place the modern Mexican American in the popular Texas story that resonates across all of American history. It reconciles the Tejano Spanish and Mexican past with the Anglo American memory of the Alamo, giving Tejanos a share in the glorious victory at the Battle of San Jacinto. Tejano memory also dissociates Tejanos from the Mexican general Antonio López de Santa Anna—the demon of Texas history. Tejano memory's value is in its linking modern Mexican Americans to all that is good about Texas, even if it glosses over minor inconsistencies. Indeed, the Tejano memory conflicts with and efficiently omits contradictory facts in history. Memory is like history in that way: It mixes fact with omission. Historian Michel-Rolph Trouillot describes history as an interplay between the facts that we choose to mention and the facts that we choose to silence in our narrative. Thus is memory composed of the "mentions and the silences" in the public transcript.[5] For example, Lorenzo de Zavala is the Tejano hero for whom the state library building in Austin is named. Zavala was a last-minute political refugee from Mexico City in 1836, however. He had no family or roots in Texas, but the Tejano memory usefully neglects to mention that he was not really a Tejano settler. Another inconsistency is the notion that Tejanos have been under "six flags" in Texas. Tejanos actually had no settlements in Texas when the flag of France flew over Texas soil in 1684. Also, most Tejanos were not white Spanish Europeans but a racially mixed *mestizo* of Spaniards and natives of Mexico, unlike their idealized self-image described above. The Tejano memory, like Anglo Texan memory, is not based on documented historical facts. It must be distinguished from the formal history of Latinos or of Mexican Americans in Texas.

A distinction between Tejano memory and Tejano history can be seen in the works of Américo Paredes, the dean of Mexican American writers. Paredes wrote that "the final element" in defining the Mexican American was the Treaty of Guadalupe Hidalgo of 1848. The treaty set the Rio Grande as the dividing line between South Texas and northern Mexico and put the Mexican American community at the mercy of an insensitive Anglo Texan government and a corps of abrasive Texas Rangers. But as he wrote his book, *With His Pistol in His Hand: A Border Ballad and Its Hero,* Paredes referred more to folklore than he did to historical documentation. Indeed, he wrote the book as an analysis of a border ballad in which an innocent Mexican American, Gregorio Cortez, eluded Texas Rangers and scores of law enforcement officers across South Texas. Paredes was forced to rely on Tejano memory because the dark side of the Texas Rangers had been silenced by ethnocentric historians such as Walter Prescott Webb, the dean of Anglo Texas historians. Paredes dedicated his book "to the memory of my father who rode a raid or two with Catarino Garza; and to all those old men who sat around on summer nights, in the days when there was a chaparral, smoking their cornhusk cigarettes and talking in low, gentle voices about violent things; while I listened."[6]

Thus, Webb had access to the records of the state archives for his book *The Texas Rangers,* while Paredes complemented his history with "those documented old men's tales called histories." Here, the term "histories" meant tales. Webb wrote about "one riot, one Ranger" while Paredes glorified Cortez, saying, "Ah, so many mounted Rangers just to take one Mexican!"[7] Each man related the glories of his community: one, the Anglo; the other, the Mexican American. Each used historical documentation, but Paredes openly admitted his reliance on the shared memory of his community. He was one of the first Mexican American writers to publish a major book articulating the Tejano memory.

A community uses both history and memory to define itself. Historians, on the other hand, craft their formal story by referring to documentation housed in archives. The community refers to scholarly history and adds its own emphasis, remembering only that part of history that is useful in constructing a desirable identity. In Texas, however, many formal histories and memory in the public discourse are anti-Mexican. The Texas creation myth integrates racist themes in its lessons on the ideological principles of freedom or democracy. In his book *Remembering the Alamo,* Richard Flores states that the popular memory of the Alamo serves only to formalize the "segregated, prejudicial, and devalued social relations between Anglos and Mexicans."[8] Thus, it is likely that Mexican Americans can be U.S. citizens and native Texans but find themselves racially excluded from the communal womb of Texas memory.

In Texas, scholarly history and Anglo memory have tended to define a negative identity for the Mexican American. The Mexican American was labeled as an outsider or condemned for associating with the enemy. The Anglo memory serves to alienate Mexican Americans even today. This act of alienation happens every year when seventh-grade Mexican American students attend the required Texas history class in the public schools across the state. They listen as the teacher recites the racially coded public text, and they are categorically distinguished from their Anglo classmates. Richard Flores writes that when he experienced this moment, his best friend nudged his elbow, saying, "You killed them! You and the other 'mes'kins'!"[9] Like a sacred rite of passage, the seventh-grade Texas history lesson means the birth of awareness, but for Mexican American students it represents a separating line in the socialization process. Before that class, they were simply Americans looking for their place in society. After the history lesson, they are "Mexicans in Texas," seeking to reconcile their place within a dominant society. Too often, if they want a positive identity they must seek it outside the Texas history classroom. This incongruence illustrates the use of memory as an alternative to the formal text. As in the example of Américo Parédes, he had to access a distinct source for his story: memory. For the subordinates in a society, memory may also grow as a "hidden transcript" of history. James C. Scott states that the powerless may safely criticize the dominant transcript of history in "sequestered settings" such as hush arbors. The old men in the story told by Paredes were in the dark chaparral and spoke in "low, gentle voices." Their story incorporated what Scott calls a "shared critique" of the public transcript.[10] Here Tejano memory germinated, and it offered them a proud identity. Likewise, modern Mexican Americans have sought memory to protect their rightful place in the Texas story.

To a great extent, they have constructed their own identity as a counter-memory to the part of Anglo memory that excludes positive references to the Mexican culture. In a shared critique of the exclusively Anglo memory, they have used the Tejano memory to legitimize their own role in formal Texas history as well. In reviewing the formation of Tejano memory, the following discussion will attempt to identify the negative interpretations and forces that have been imposed on Mexican Americans as part of the distortion and suppression in Texas history. Many of the abuses imposed in the last century on Mexican Americans are unknown to the general public as well as to historians. But the victims know the real history of abuse. They regularly drive past their lost lands. Mexican Americans wept when their grandfathers were murdered. They endured poverty and deplorable migrant labor on farmlands that once belonged to their ancestors. Much of this abuse has been rationalized in the Anglo memory, and formal history has silenced it. As an example of historical neglect, two of the most assertive Tejano historians give only a paragraph to coverage of the Peñascal Raid of 1874, which devastated the largest Tejano ranches between Corpus Christi and Harlingen. David Montejano's *Anglos and Mexicans in the Making of Texas* and Arnoldo De León's *They Called Them Greasers* both omit any mention of the even more devastating Refugio Raid of the following year. This statement is not a criticism of their works, but it may explain why Texas college history textbooks make little or no mention of these and other mass murders that left thousands of prominent Mexican American families landless and destitute.[11]

Neither memory nor history has been favorable to the Mexican heritage. Indeed, this glaring omission was the impetus for the Tejano Monument, according to an article in the *Laredo Morning Times*:

> One summer day, two years ago, Dr. Cayetano Barrera of McAllen made the rounds of the newly renovated Capitol in Austin when he suddenly noticed something he never had before. "I told my wife, 'I need to go around again.' I couldn't believe my eyes," said Barrera, who had walked the grounds dozens of times in the past. "Out of the 31 statues and monuments I saw inside and outside the Capitol, not a single one had a Spanish or Mexican name, and not one was dedicated to the Spanish or Mexican pioneers that have lived on this land since 1519." The family practitioner got on the phone and called his nephew Richard Sanchez, chief of staff for state Rep. Kino Flores of Mission, and asked, "Would you please go around the grounds to look because maybe I missed something?" When Sanchez called his uncle back with the response, Barrera set the ball rolling to undertake the "historic and long-overdue project."[12]

To Mexican Americans like Barrera, Texas memory has been like a distorted two-way mirror standing between them and the Anglo. From one side, Anglos see only a grandiose reflection of themselves. From the opposite side, Mexican Americans see the Anglos as they really are, yet they struggle to discern their own positive image. Like other Texans, Mexican Americans have had an ongoing need for a positive memory, but they also have a need for the public discourse to acknowledge their denied history.

For Mexican Americans, the Tejano memory has held a strong appeal to their need to legitimize themselves in Texas history. They have shared an acutely developed critique of the Anglo American perspective. Since the time of early Tejano writers such as José Antonio Navarro, who penned a series of newspaper articles between 1853 and 1857, Mexican Americans have argued that Anglo historians had suppressed the Tejano role in Texas history, which led to the distortion of the Mexican heritage in Texas. Navarro reacted strongly against Henderson Yoakum's 1855 *History of Texas,* saying that it was "plagued by a number of inexactitudes." He wrote that Tejanos were "disappearing, murdered in full view of a people who boast of their justice and excellence." Navarro was particularly sensitive that the distortion of history and culture had been used to rationalize land theft, labor controls, discrimination, and other tenets of Anglo American domination. The Tejano memory was one way that the Tejano community could attempt to refute the tenets of domination. These tenets rationalized that Anglos were justified in taking Tejano lands, that Mexican Americans could not be trusted with the vote, that they did not need or appreciate education, and that racial segregation was necessary to preserve order in society. As Jill Lepore argues in *The Name of War,* the victors "cultivated" a historical lexicon of their domination. In her study of the Puritan conquest of the Algonquins, Lepore says that the English settlers used their warfare to kill, to justify, and ultimately to create their own distinctive American identity.[13] Early Anglo Texans such as Henderson Yoakum wrote their own myth and memory of an exclusively Anglo American triumph in Texas. It incorporated not only the Anglo elements of myth but also the Anglo tenets of domination. Mexican Americans, in turn, used their collective memory to address all of these tenets and added their own legitimizing balm to Tejano memory.

The theme of "the founders of Texas" has been of primary importance to Mexican Americans. The Tejano statues mentioned above focus on reinforcing the idea that Tejanos are the original native Texans. This idea is strongly illustrated in the proposed Tejano Monument at the state capitol. Indeed, the mission statement presented to the state legislature by the citizens' Tejano Monument Committee cited three facts to defend their rationale that Tejanos were the original founders of Texas. One was the statement that Tejanos "established the first permanent colony in Texas." Another was that Tejanos "first established civil and criminal law to govern the colonies." The third claimed that Tejanos "established [the] first private ownership of land and the ranching industry in Texas."[14] In the formal resolution and in the design of the monument and statues, the strongest tenets of the Tejano mem-

FIG. 7.5. The statue of a Spanish soldier on the Tejano Monument, later revised to depict a Spanish explorer holding a royal land grant charter. Courtesy Cayetano Barrera.

ory are asserted. The Tejano Monument is not simply a statue but a series of statues on a large stone base or pedestal, high above ground level at the rear and sloping to ground level in the front of the monument. The bronze statues are placed along the top ridge of the stone base as a series depicting the chronological development of Tejano settlement. A Spanish explorer is at the rear. At top center is an equestrian statue of a mounted Tejano vaquero leading two longhorn cattle down the slope. At ground level in front of the stone base is a family group depicting a mother and father holding an infant in their arms between them. At ground level in front of the mother and father are two young children at play with smaller ranch animals. While the Tejano Monument has much symbolism in its statuary, its most striking statement is that Tejano heritage now asserts a major presence in the public space of the Texas capitol.

Nowhere is the claim of "the founders of Texas" more vividly seen than in the figure of a Spanish explorer at the top of the Tejano Monument. As one of the most prominent statues, this life-size bronze figure depicts a Spanish explorer reading a royal land grant charter.

The Spaniard symbolizes the Tejano claim that they were the first European explorers and settlers in Texas. This figure represents not only the Spanish nation but also the white European race. Although modern Latinos as a group have a mixed gene pool or *mestizo* background, Tejanos have frequently asserted their white European background in response to white supremacy in Texas history. The Spaniard is clothed as an explorer holding a land grant title, rather than a soldier wearing a helmet and carrying a sword. In this way, the statue suggests that the Tejanos came to Texas as settlers to establish a stable society for posterity, rather than simply to conquer and expropriate resources from the native population.

Another theme in the Tejano Monument is that of family. The central figure at ground level on the monument floor is the Tejano family group described above. The Tejano family statue was selected to symbolize the founding Tejano families, according to a statement given at a press conference in 2001 by Rep. Kino Flores of Mission, the sponsoring legislator. Representative Flores announced that he wanted to remind the public that the Tejano family was the pillar of society and that some of those founding families were represented at the press conference. Indeed, many of the members of the Tejano Monument Committee, including Dr. Cayetano Barrera, were direct descendants of the founding Tejano families who accompanied Count José de Escandón in 1750 and still live on the same family lands today. One modern writer, Daniel D. Arreola, argues in his book *Tejano South Texas: A Mexican American Cultural Province* (2002) that Tejano families today constitute "the largest ethnic subregion in the United States, a veritable Mexican American rimland enclave along the south-central border." Arreola asserts that these founding Tejano families are the "continuous community" of South Texas whether they still own their ancestral lands or have moved into modern Texas cities such as Houston, San Antonio, or Corpus Christi.[15] For modern Hispanic Texans, family is not only an important theme but also a major component of their Tejano memory.

The theme of family is obviously intended to indicate that Tejano memory embraces a fully developed society in early Texas, a civilization complete with law and order in which families could flourish. In Tejano memory, however, family is also directly associated with landownership. Land dispossession is one of the most sensitive issues in the Tejano memory. The Tejano claim to their lost lands is substantiated by their family land grants because family represents land. This relationship was established when the Tejano founders gave formal land titles to the founding families. As an example, José

FIG. 7.6. The central figure of the Tejano Monument is the Tejano family group at ground level in the center of the monument floor. Courtesy Cayetano Barrera.

de Escandón granted vast tracts of land to the founding families of South Texas that today are the "continuous community" that Daniel D. Arreola cites in his book. Some of the Tejano families still own their lands, some are in the courts suing to regain their lost lands, but all of them can subscribe to the memory that Texas land was rightfully theirs. Just as southern families remember their "Lost Cause," Tejanos remember their "Lost Lands." This loss is one of the unspoken themes in the growing genealogy movement among Hispanic Texans. They strive to prove their ties to the family tree, but the family tree chart is based on the land grant. The family group occupying the central ground on the Tejano Monument represents not only individual family land titles but also Tejanos' general claim or title to the land.

In stressing the theme of native Texans, the Tejano Monument Committee was reciting a popular argument made by early Mexican American writers. Through the years, Tejano writers have stressed that Tejanos were not simply immigrants to Texas but the original founding families. One of the earliest writers to defend Tejano nativity was Juan N. Seguín, the veteran of the Texas Revolution and former member of the Republic of Texas Congress. In 1842, Seguín complained that newly arrived Anglo American immigrants assumed a resentful attitude toward Tejanos who occupied some of the best lands in Texas. Calling himself "a foreigner in my native land," he was finally forced to leave his native San Antonio to escape numerous attempts on his life by resentful Anglo immigrants. He complained that "I have been the object of the hatred and passionate attacks of some few disorganizers, who, for a time, ruled as masters, over the poor and oppressed population of San Antonio."[16]

Many decades later, a well-read Mexican American writer, Jovita González, articulated the same theme. She wrote her master's thesis under J. Frank Dobie at the University of Texas in 1930 and was one of the few Mexican Americans to achieve that level of formal academic training in Texas at the time. As a teacher, González was acutely aware of the Anglo rationale behind the discriminatory policies in Texas schools. In the 1920s, state education officials issued policy statements that singled out the Mexican American students as foreign recalcitrants who refused to adopt Anglo American culture. The state superintendent of public instruction, Annie Webb Blanton, promoted a formal policy to make Texas schools teach "Americanization," a euphemism for Anglo conformity. In a blatant statement of opposition to Mexican American culture, she proclaimed, "If you wish to preserve, in our state, the language and the custom of another land, you have no right to this." Many Mexican American citizens, probably most, spoke Spanish, and her statement clearly made no distinction between them and newly arrived Mexican immigrants. School boards then began to follow a widespread practice of neglecting Mexican American student enrollment almost completely, a practice condoned by Superintendent Blanton.[17]

González was an early apologist for Mexican American culture in Texas, and her thesis, entitled "Social Life in Cameron, Starr, and Zapata Counties," became one of the most widely consulted unpublished sources of historical information. Generations of Mexican American writers, including Américo Parédes, turned to it for its accurate record of daily life. Her prefatory comment in that thesis became one of the most articulate statements of the Mexican American reaction to the Anglo sense of superiority over Tejanos:

> There exists in Texas a common tendency among Anglo Americans, particularly among Americans of one or two generations' stay in the country, to look down upon the Mexicans of the border counties as interlopers, undesirable aliens, and a menace to the community. Those among the last group named who have this opinion should before making a definite stand consider the following: First, that the majority of these so-called undesirable aliens have been in the state long before Texas was Texas; second, that these people were here long before these new Americans crowded the deck of the immigrant ship; third, that a great number of the Mexican people in the border did not come as immigrants, but are the descendants of the *agraciados* who held grants from the Spanish crown.[18]

In articulating the Tejano memory, González was only one of several women who spoke for the Mexican American community in the early decades of the twentieth century. As stated in her analysis of the Alamo myths, Holly Beachley Brear learned that gender plays a role in the preservation of memory. Society lets men design and produce the future, but keeping the past alive is "appropriately the domain of women."[19] Likewise, as the Daughters of the Republic of Texas cared for the Anglo memory, so did Mexican American women keep Tejano memory alive while the men were busy organizing the League of United Latin American Citizens (LULAC) in public forums during the late 1920s. None of these women was a trained historian, and all of them relied heavily on folklore, ballads called *corridos,* and their studies of the built environment of South Texas ranches. Their contributions were invaluable to those later researchers who accessed their master's theses, but their true gift was in their contribution to Tejano memory in their respective communities. These women were teachers, each writing the story of her respective region of the state. Fermina Guerra, a teacher in Laredo, wrote "Mexican and Spanish Folklore and Incidents in Southwest Texas" as a master's thesis at the University of Texas in 1941. Another schoolteacher, Emilia Schunior Ramirez, wrote *Ranch Life in Hidalgo County after 1850* about Tejano life in the Rio Grande Valley.[20]

Perhaps the most impressive of the Mexican American women to preserve Tejano memory was Elena Zamora O'Shea, who in 1922 became the first Mexican American to publish a novel in Texas, *El Mesquite.* O'Shea was the daughter of Porfirio Zamora, who commanded the Mexican cavalry unit for General Ignacio Zaragoza in the famous Battle of the Cinco de Mayo. O'Shea was the first Mexican American to be admitted to the Southwest

Texas Normal School in San Marcos, and when she taught school in Alice, Texas, one of her students was future folklorist J. Frank Dobie. In her novel *El Mesquite,* O'Shea lamented the fact that the "early historians do not mention" the Tejano pioneers who founded Texas. She addressed the suppression of Tejano history in saying that the sacrifices of the Tejanos "have been entirely forgotten."[21] She made it the focus of her book to rectify the omission. These Mexican American women were part of the generation that created the Tejano memory for the following generations who transformed it into statues and Tejano monuments of bronze. They were actively involved in community affairs across the state. O'Shea regularly communicated with LULAC founders, including J. Luz Saenz and state representative J. T. Canales.

Since the 1970s, Mexican American heritage organizations have assumed the role of memory stewardship. A small number of genealogy groups in the larger cities had organized during the early 1970s. In 1979 they all joined forces in the first statewide Hispanic genealogy conference in Austin. At the conference, they attended sessions on methodology, toured the archives and libraries of the state and the University of Texas, and hosted a book fair. The book fair featured historians Robert S. Weddle and Robert H. Thonhoff, who signed their recent work, *Drama & Conflict: The Texas Saga of 1776,* which documented the Tejano contribution to the American Revolutionary War effort. In October 2004 Hispanic genealogy groups from cities across the state commemorated the twenty-fifth anniversary of their first statewide conference. The growth of the Hispanic genealogy movement gave formal expression to private efforts that had always been popular among Mexican American families. The 1970s gave rise to organizations such as the Spanish American Genealogy Association (SAGA) of Corpus Christi and the Moya Family Association of Victoria, but it also created a forum for minor publications such as the privately published book, *Historia de la progenie de Rafael Solís y Cipriana Arismendes de Solís* (*Progeny of the Solis Family*), first printed in San Diego, Texas, circa 1905.[22] The groups proliferated across the state, even in small cities such as Zapata and Goliad. They took on names that hearken to their Spanish colonial roots. The San Antonio genealogy organization took the name Los Bexareños. San Antonio was named San Antonio de Béxar when it was founded under the Spanish Crown in 1718. The use of that name is a strong claim by the genealogy group to the founding of that colorful city. Another group in South Texas is named Las Porciones, which refers to the original land grants along the Rio Grande in the 1750s. The genealogy movement later manifested itself in Internet web pages on diverse heritage topics such as genealogy chat pages, family associations, and Tejano heroes.

An unspoken aspect to the genealogy movement is the use of the family tree for reclaiming dispossessed Tejano lands. The Ballí family organization created a model for using genealogy as a base for fundraising and initiating a lawsuit to regain lands taken from Tejano land grantees under questionable circumstances. One group, the Asociación de Reclamantes, based ·in San Antonio, openly recruits Tejano families for the express purpose of support-ing such lawsuits. And finally, publications such as *El Mesteño: A Magazine about Mexican-American Cultural Heritage in South Texas and Mexico (published by Homero Vera in Premont, Texas)* have begun to find increasing readership. While heritage is the unifying focus of these community efforts, all of them tend to direct part of their energy to legitimizing Tejano memory and de-veloping a shared critique of the traditionally Anglo perspective of Texas heritage.

One of the major criticisms that Tejanos seemed to share is the distorted version of Texas history often used by Anglo Texans to rationalize property claims against Tejanos. Anglo Texan memory portrays Anglos as the exclusive heroes of the Texas Revolution, thus providing them a rationale for owner-ship. Anglo land speculators often used fictitious lawsuits in an effort to sap the energy and legal resources of Tejano landowners. But for Tejanos, the historical rationale added insult to the injury. Throughout the twentieth century, the racialization of politics and the economy had continued to the point that Texas had what amounted to a caste system, with Anglo Ameri-cans in dominant positions and Mexican Americans generally in subordinate positions. Even as late as 1965, a federal study of Texas race relations stated explicitly that "Anglos have always been on top . . . and the Mexican Ameri-cans isolated on the bottom."[23]

A distorted historical transcript had been developed by 1900 that de-picted the Anglo American as the liberator of Texas from a heathen Mexican population. The historical transcript was articulated by policy leaders and the public in order to perpetuate the political and economic subordination of Mexican Americans. As an example, in a 1911 state vote on prohibition, state leader Thomas Ball in Brownsville rationalized the suppression of "the Mexican vote, which Texas in 1836 declared unfit to govern this country." Historians reinforced this negative view of Mexican culture by suppressing the positive role of Tejanos in history. Anglo Texans were gratified by the negative image of Mexicans and used it to rationalize discrimination and abuse. Although these comments made reference to history, the fact is that

these speakers were not historians, and they were not citing historical interpretation. Rather, they were making Anglo memory useful, obviously for
political purposes. This action is a function of memory. Another illustrative
example of the use of Anglo memory for economic advantage over Tejanos
was found in the statement of a poor Anglo sharecropper who used history
to elevate himself above Mexican Americans. Referring to his sense of history, he said, "The study of the Alamo helps to make more hatred toward
the Mexicans[.] . . . if a man . . slaughters your kinsman, . . I am in favor of
not letting Mexicans come over and take a white man's labor."[24] While most
Anglo Americans viewed this distortion as simply history, it was, in fact, a
blatant invoking of memory as rationale for economic advantage. Mexican
Americans were offended not only by the distortion of history but also by the
abuse of memory. Indeed, most modern studies still tend to gloss over the
political function of cultural suppression in Texas history, and no study has
previously inquired into the power and use of memory.

In response to the Anglo rationale for land dispossession and labor exploitation, Mexican Americans portrayed themselves as loyal American citizens. The largest Mexican American civic organization, LULAC, uses the
words "American Citizens" in its name, and its charter says it is to create
"perfect American citizens." The LULAC shield uses red, white, and blue
stars and stripes. Mexican American veterans groups regularly march in
U.S. military uniform, and many of them march as the color guard. On U.S.
Highway 16 south of Freer, Texas, a group of Mexican American veterans
of the U.S. Marine Corps maintains a replica of a Vietnam War military
camp called the Last Patrol. And the largest Mexican American veterans
organization is named the American G.I. Forum, which was founded in
Corpus Christi, Texas. These nationalistic symbols are a strong appeal to the
Mexican American claim of service to the nation as loyal citizens. Mexican
American combat veterans seek to portray the Last Patrol camp as evidence
of their service and loyalty. This detailed replica—hand built by the veterans
who lived in such camps in the jungles of Vietnam—is the place where their
memories grow. The Marine veterans periodically engaged in twenty-mile
double-time marches called "humps" to raise funds for their memorial. The
"humps" funded the memorial, and the memorial fed their memories.[25]

The Progressive era provides a major example of Anglo American political domination that injured the Mexican American sense of history in
Texas. Nationally, the Progressive reformers organized a moralistic campaign
against political, corporate, and financial corruption. In South Texas, "Progressive" meant anti-Mexican. Evan Anders's work on Progressives in South

Texas states that the Progressive "solution was the disfranchisement of most of the Hispanic electorate." David Montejano's work on South Texas states that the Good Government Leagues of this period sought disfranchisement of the Mexican Americans as "the proper place of the Mexican." Texas Progressives attacked political corruption by attacking the political bosses and their Mexican American constituents. By the turn of the century, Mexican Americans could find refuge only under the protection of political bosses who shielded them from Texas Ranger violence and Anglo American vigilante raids. In exchange, the bosses collected Mexican American votes for state and federal politicians. Texas history books state generally that the Progressives and prohibitionists intended to eliminate political corruption and intolerance. The Anglo ideologues and politicians of the era, however, more explicitly articulated their rationale to disfranchise what University of Texas professor William Leonard called the "dangerous" Mexican vote. During the 1914 gubernatorial race, for example, prohibitionist candidate Thomas Ball campaigned that with Progressive reforms, "liquor and Mexicans" would both "rest together forever in death."[26]

Education is another tenet of Anglo American domination that reflects historical distortion for racial advantage. Texas history books outline the development of public school systems in Texas. They indicate that a demand for schools was one of the grievances in the Texas Declaration of Independence. Rarely do the books mention that schools did not become a priority after independence or even with statehood. More significantly, the history books omit the manner in which the Texas government targeted Mexican American children for segregation and neglect. At all levels, the state government, counties, and local school districts rationalized gross discrimination. A South Texas school superintendent stated a frequently quoted sentiment: "So you see it is up to the white population to keep the Mexican on his knees in an onion patch or in new ground. This does not mix very well with education." A Nueces County superintendent said, "I always ask the board if they want the Mexicans in school. Here they told me to leave them alone. . . . If I got 150 Mexicans ready for school I would be out of a job." Mexican Americans could not look to formal Texas history for support. With less than three percent graduating from Texas high schools before the 1950s, the Mexican American community could hardly expect to challenge the formal writings of historians such as William Kennedy, Henderson Yoakum, or Eugene C. Barker.[27]

Labor is one of the most suppressed areas of Mexican American history in Texas as a field of study and as a field of endeavor. Not only was Mexican

American labor repressed, but the modern public has little or no knowledge of the extent to which it was exploited by Texas employers. Mexican Americans have had to quietly watch as an Anglo American employer became wealthy by exploiting their labor. Likewise, they watched quietly as public discourse systematically omits any mention of their suffering. As an example, history textbooks relate the standard issue of the "Black Codes" that were imposed on African Americans during Presidential Reconstruction. Few Texas historians before the 1980s acknowledged that Mexican American laborers faced vagrancy laws, county passes, armed guards, and violence imposed on them even in the twentieth century. Thus, it is not sufficient to simply relate the Mexican American memory without describing their labor suppression in Texas. To do so would only add to their frustration of an unacknowledged history.

Early in the twentieth century, Texas state and local officials began to relate labor control over the Mexican American population to social and political control. One South Texas school superintendent explicitly stated that state officials condoned minimal education of "the lower element" [Mexican Americans] specifically to control them in the labor force. "We don't need skilled or white-collared Mexicans. . . . There isn't a concerted effort against them but the white-collar man is not a common laborer." By 1927, Willacy County was implementing vagrancy laws enforced by the county sheriff, the justice of the peace, and the county attorney. They systematically arrested Mexican American laborers traveling in search of higher wages for not having the approved "county passes" signed by an Anglo employer or county official. These Mexican American workers were convicted and then paroled as "convict labor" to Anglo American growers.[28]

Texas Rangers, or "*los rinches*," were remembered by the Mexican American community for much more than simply voter intimidation or labor repression. Most Texans probably viewed the Rangers as defending Texas law, but Mexican Americans often thought of them as enforcing nothing less than Anglo domination. Walter Prescott Webb spoke vaguely about their violent methods. In his book, *The Texas Rangers,* Webb stated that the Rangers perpetrated a "reign of terror" that reached its peak after the turn of the twentieth century. He acknowledged that between five hundred and five thousand Tejanos died, "many of them innocent, at the hands of the local posses, peace officers, and Texas Rangers."[29] But Webb avoided citing any evidence or examples of the violence. With no more documentation than this bland statement, the story of their brutality has been suppressed for the better part of a century. Occasionally, a Mexican American writer such as Américo Parédes referred to the violence, but even then, much of it was related in general terms that could be dismissed by skeptics as hearsay or groundless resentment.

Recently released documents in the state archives reveal that Texas Rangers did in fact perpetrate a wave of violent repression that specifically targeted Mexican Americans. While the full story of their violent reign has never been published, a few notorious incidents have been exposed in disparate references in published and unpublished sources. By late 2004, three books had been published that indicated a new interest in the dark side of the Rangers.[30] The present discussion is not intended to suggest the scope of Texas Ranger violence against Mexican Americans; that could fill the pages of a full-length book. A few incidents can serve, however, to indicate not only the degree of inhumanity meted out by these law enforcement officials but also the great degree to which they are documented in the state archives. The focus of this discussion is not the horrific acts themselves but the gap between the reality of state law enforcement officials' oppression of law-abiding U.S. citizens and public awareness of this history. The documents were suppressed. The history was silenced. The bodies were buried. But the memory was kept alive in Mexican American "low, gentle voices about violent things" while children listened.

As mentioned above, Texas Ranger violence was used for labor repression, voter intimidation, and racial domination. One other use of Ranger violence was land acquisition. Anglo ranchers, land developers, and political bosses had traditionally used the Rangers for their own protection. Richard King of the famous King Ranch hosted the South Texas company of Texas Rangers on his ranch and allowed them to use it as their headquarters. An entire corps of informal Loyalty Rangers was appointed by the governor at the simple request of powerful Anglo ranchers such as Robert Kleberg, also of the King Ranch. Likewise, powerful Anglo American lawyers or politicians could use their personal relationships with Texas Rangers to pressure a Mexican American landowner, or they allowed the Texas Rangers to direct the violence to intimidate or neutralize Mexican American citizens. In one highly publicized hearing on Texas Ranger violence against Mexican American citizens in 1919, a witness, M. A. Muñoz, testified that a Mr. North was present at the interrogation of Mexican Americans by Ranger captain Hanson. North was the attorney of Ed C. Lasater, who was at that time acquiring Tejano land grants and using Texas Rangers to pressure Tejanos into the sale. The proceedings of these hearings were suppressed for decades by the state legislative committee. This history has been only vaguely mentioned in textbooks, but it has become a critical element in the Tejano memory of "*los rinches pinches,*" or the hated Texas Rangers.[31] In Tejano memory, the silencing of this violent suppression is an insult, and were it not for Tejano legends, the reality of this violence would have been buried forever.

One of the favorite abuses of this period was an extralegal death warrant referred to as a "black list." According to R. B. Creager of Brownsville, Texas Rangers did not randomly commit atrocities against Mexican Americans in the most violent year of 1915. "Rangers burned ranches, tortured suspects, and shot prisoners, leaving their bodies to rot," he testified in 1919 at the state legislative hearings on Ranger abuses, but the Rangers targeted specific Mexican Americans, often from a black list. He described a practice in which South Texas Anglo Americans of prominent standing "or even halfway standing" could add the name of a Mexican American to the black list for murder. The list was "circulated among officers and citizens," and the man would either learn of the list and abandon his home or he would suddenly "evaporate." Creager was a prominent longtime attorney and a Republican federal appointee in the Valley.[32] Indeed, there may be some doubt that the Rangers committed such atrocities or that their heavy-handed methods were inappropriate for the time. Certainly, the land developers and their employees benefited from the mass exchange of land that accompanied the intimidation. But for Mexican Americans, the wave of terror only reinforced their distrust of an insensitive state government and their misgivings of the public images that glorified the Rangers and vilified the often innocent victims as "Mexican bandits."

For the early Tejanos of the 1850s as for the Mexican Americans of the next century, Texas history held little relevance and even less credibility. For them, Texas history had proven its bias, which suppressed Anglo American vices as much as it neglected Mexican American virtue. Just as the early Texans created their own myth of the birth of Texas with the Alamo and San Jacinto, so did contemporaneous Tejanos work feverishly to weave their own role within that popular memory. The two most prominent Tejano writers were Juan N. Seguín and José Antonio Navarro. Their memoirs and their writings represent the initial development of the Tejano memory.

The wellspring in the construction of Tejano memory was the work of the early Tejanos as the native Mexicans of Texas. Their objectives were first to legitimize themselves as the original Texans, even more "original" than the first Anglo Texas settlers. They did this by identifying their Texas Revolutionary heroes, by celebrating their own independence from Spain as Mexicans, and finally by asserting their Mexicanness within the American state of Texas shortly after the Treaty of Guadalupe Hidalgo of 1848. Nineteenth-century Tejano writers Seguín and Navarro were followed by early-twentieth-century Tejanas Jovita González, Elena Zamora O'Shea, Fermina Guerra, and Emilia Schunior Ramirez. These women—all teachers—preserved Tejano memories in their master's theses and regional histories. Their writings were later used by Mexican Americans of Texas as arguments for statues, historical plaques, a Texas auto license plate, family associations, a web page, and even a U.S. postage stamp of Tejano heritage. By the 1990s, Mexican Americans had begun to develop an increasingly cohesive memory of Tejano images. Local community groups pressed for new schools, boulevards, and parks named after twentieth-century Mexican American war heroes and labor leaders such as César Chávez. While they are more numerous, none of these local markers approaches the broad appeal of the proposed Tejano Monument.

The proposed Tejano Monument speaks to many issues of Tejano memory, and its multifaceted interpretive features are intended to appeal to a statewide community across ethnic lines. It addresses "the founders of Texas" theme, the landownership issue, the pioneer, the distinctive Tejano identity, service to the nation, and other claims as well. In addition to the statues, the monument is designed with several bronze relief plaques, offering a textual narrative of the salient points of Tejano heritage. The plaques were drafted by a panel of Texas historians, including Félix D. Almaráz Jr., Gilberto M. Hinojosa, Carolina Castillo Crimm, and Jack Jackson. Although initially asked to write about Tejanos under the Six Flags of Texas, the professional historians chose instead to reject the Anglo periodization of Texas history. They proposed five phases of Tejano history based on the periods of Tejano development. Their phases referred to the interaction of Tejanos with native Americans in Texas, the Spanish and Mexican periods, the Mexican American identity, Mexican immigration, and the civil rights movement of the twentieth century. As a major installation on the state capitol grounds, the Tejano Monument proposes to represent the culmination of Mexican Americans' efforts to achieve legitimacy as true Texans. Children of the future may read revised history in new textbooks that depict the role of Mexican Americans, Latinos, and Chicanos. New books may finally portray Hispanic culture as an integral part of Texas. Whatever the formal history books say, the purpose of the Tejano Monument is to project a new vision of Texas heritage in the highest public setting of the state—the capitol—depicting Tejanos as true Texans. The Tejano memory is under construction.

NOTES

1. Emma L. Ballí Treviño and Pearl B. Ballí Mancillas, *Padre Island Trials and Tribulations: La Verdad* (Mexico City: Ballí Publishing, 1998), 7; Seguin Family History web page, www.seguinfamilyhistory.com (accessed Jan. 14, 2005).

2. W. Fitzhugh Brundage, ed., *Where These Memories Grow: History, Memory, and Southern Identity* (Chapel Hill: University of North Carolina Press, 2000), 4–5. For a full description of public and hidden transcripts in memory, see James C. Scott, *Domination and the Arts of Resistance: Hidden Transcripts* (New Haven, Conn.: Yale University Press, 1990).

3. Jacques Le Goff and Pierre Nora, eds., *Constructing the Past: Essays in Historical Methodology* (Cambridge: Cambridge University Press, 1985), 4.

4. Arnoldo De León, *Las Fiestas Patrias: Biographical Notes on the Hispanic Presence in San Angelo, Texas* (San Antonio: Caravel Press, 1978), vi; for general Tejano historical background, see Andrés Tijerina, *Tejanos and Texas under the Mexican Flag, 1821–1836* (College Station: Texas A&M University Press, 1994).

5. Michel-Rolph Trouillot, *Silencing the Past: Power and the Production of History* (Boston: Beacon Press, 1995), 48.

6. Américo Paredes, *With His Pistol in His Hand: A Border Ballad and Its Hero* (Austin: University of Texas Press, 1958), 3.

7. Ibid., 15.

8. Richard R. Flores, *Remembering the Alamo: Memory, Modernity, and the Master Symbol* (Austin: University of Texas Press, 2002), 10.

9. Ibid., xiii.

10. Scott, *Domination and the Arts of Resistance*.

11. David Montejano, *Anglos and Mexicans in the Making of Texas, 1836–1886* (Austin: University of Texas Press, 1987), 53; Arnoldo De León, *They Called Them Greasers: Anglo Attitudes toward Mexicans in Texas, 1821–1900* (Austin: University of Texas Press, 1983), 99. The single line in any textbook covering the atrocities is in Robert A. Calvert, Arnoldo De León, and Gregg Cantrell, *The History of Texas,* 3d ed. (Wheeling, Ill.: Harlan Davidson 2002), 299. For a full discussion of the vigilante raids, see Andrés Tijerina, *Tejano Empire: Life on the South Texas Ranchos* (College Station: Texas A&M University Press, 1998), epilogue. In each raid, law enforcement officials reported that hundreds of Tejano families were killed or fled in long caravans of carts. Texas Ranger L. H. McNelly telegraphed to Austin that "the acts committed by Americans are horrible to relate; many ranches have been plundered and burned, and people murdered or driven away; one of these parties confessed to me in Corpus Christi as having killed eleven men on their last raid" (quoted in Tijerina, *Tejano Empire,* 125–26).

12. Tricia Cortez, "Tejano Monument Planned for State Capitol," *Laredo Morning Times,* Aug. 11, 2002.

13. Navarro quoted in David R. McDonald and Timothy M. Matovina, *Defending Mexican Valor in Texas: José Antonio Navarro's Historical Writings, 1853–1857* (Austin, Tex.: State House Press, 1995), 24, 25; Jill Lepore, *The Name of War: King Philip's War and the Origins of American Identity* (New York: Vintage Books, 1999), 26, 27; Henderson Yoakum, *History of Texas from Its First Settlement in 1685 to Its Annexation to the United States in 1846, with an Extended Appendix* (1855; New York: Redfield, 1856).

14. "Mission Statement," Tejano Monument Committee Papers, Nettie Lee Benson Latin American Collection, University of Texas at Austin.

15. Press statement by Rep. Kino Flores, Aug. 23, 2001, Tejano Monument Committee

Papers; Daniel D. Arreola, *Tejano South Texas: A Mexican American Cultural Province* (Austin: University of Texas Press, 2002), 48.

16. Quoted in Jesús F. de la Teja, ed., *A Revolution Remembered: The Memoirs and Selected Correspondence of Juan N. Seguín* (Austin, Tex.: State House Press, 1991), 73.

17. Blanton quoted in Guadalupe San Miguel Jr., *Let All of them Take Heed: Mexican Americans and the Campaign for Educational Equality in Texas, 1910–1981* (College Station: Texas A&M University Press, 2001), 32.

18. Jovita González, "Social Life in Cameron, Starr, and Zapata Counties" (master's thesis, University of Texas, 1930), introduction.

19. Holly Beachley Brear, "We Run the Alamo, and You Don't: Alamo Battles of Ethnicity and Gender," in *Where These Memories Grow: History, Memory, and Southern Identity,* ed. W. Fitzhugh Brundage (Chapel Hill: University of North Carolina Press, 2000), 303.

20. Fermina Guerra, "Mexican and Spanish Folklore and Incidents in Southwest Texas" (master's thesis, University of Texas, 1941); Emilia Schunior Ramirez, *Ranch Life in Hidalgo County after 1850* (Edinburg, Tex.: New Santander Press, n.d.).

21. Elena Zamora O'Shea, *El Mesquite: A Story of the Early Spanish Settlements between the Nueces and the Rio Grande as told by "La Posta del Palo Alto"* (1935; reprint, College Station: Texas A&M University Press, 2000), preface.

22. See Robert S. Weddle and Robert H. Thonhoff, *Drama & Conflict: The Texas Saga of 1776* (Austin, Tex.: Madrona Press, 1976); *Historia de la progenie de Rafael Solís y Cipriana Arismendes de Solís* (San Diego, Tex.: La Libertad, n.d.), Nettie Lee Benson Latin American Collection, University of Texas at Austin.

23. U.S. Commission on Civil Rights, Mexican American Education Study, *Report 1: Ethnic Isolation of Mexican Americans in the Public Schools of the Southwest* (Washington, D.C.: Government Printing Office, 1971), 11.

24. Thomas Ball quoted in Evan Anders, *Boss Rule in South Texas: The Progressive Era* (Austin: University of Texas Press, 1982), 101; sharecropper quoted in David Montejano, *Anglos and Mexicans in the Making of Texas, 1836–1886* (Austin: University of Texas Press, 1987), 224.

25. "The Last Patrol," Veterans for America web page online, www.veteransforamerica.com (accessed Apr. 15, 2005).

26. Anders, *Boss Rule,* 241 (includes Leonard quotation), 283 (includes Ball quotation); Montejano, *Anglos and Mexicans,* 131, 145–47.

27. Quotations from Guadalupe San Miguel Jr., *Brown, Not White: School Integration and the Chicano Movement in Houston* (College Station: Texas A&M University Press, 2001), 12, 32. For an overall review of Texas historians through the years, see Laura Lyons McLemore, *Inventing Texas: Early Historians of the Lone Star State* (College Station: Texas A&M University Press, 2004); Montejano, *Anglos and Mexicans,* 192–93.

28. Quotations from Montejano, *Anglos and Mexicans,* 192–93, 205, 210–12.

29. Walter Prescott Webb, *The Texas Rangers: A Century of Frontier Defense,* 2d ed. (Austin: University of Texas Press, 1991), 176n, 462; Bruce S. Cheeseman, "Richard King: Pioneering Market Capitalism on the Frontier," in *Proceedings of Ranching in South Texas: A Symposium,* ed. Joe S. Graham (Kingsville: Texas A&M University–Kingsville, 1994), 88.

30. Benjamin Heber Johnson, *Revolution in Texas: How a Forgotten Rebellion and Its Bloody Suppression Turned Mexicans into Americans* (New Haven, Conn.: Yale University Press, 2003); Charles H. Harris III and Louis R. Sadler, *The Texas Rangers and the Mexican Revolution: The Bloodiest Decade, 1910–1920* (Albuquerque: University of New Mexico Press, 2004); Kirby F. Warnock, *Texas Cowboy: The Oral Memoirs of Roland A. Warnock and His Life on the Texas Frontier* (Dallas: Trans Pecos Productions, 1992).

31. Texas Senate, *In the Senate of Texas, D. W. Glasscock Contestant vs. A. Parr Contestee. Supplement to the Senate Journal; Regular Session of the 36th Legislature 1919* (Austin, Tex.: A. C. Baldwin & Sons State Printers, 1919), 74.

32. Texas Legislature, "Proceedings of the Joint Committee of the Senate and the House in the Investigation of the Texas State Ranger Force," typed transcript, 36th Leg., reg. sess., 1919, vol. 1, 355, Legislative Papers, Texas State Archives, Austin. For recently published descriptions of the atmosphere of violence at the time, see Johnson, *Revolution in Texas;* Harris and Sadler, *Texas Rangers and the Mexican Revolution;* and Richard Henry Ribb, "Jose Tomas Canales and the Texas Rangers: Myth, Identity, and Power in South Texas, 1900–1920" (Ph.D. diss., University of Texas at Austin, 2001).

Chapter 8

GENERATION VERSUS GENERATION: AFRICAN AMERICANS IN TEXAS REMEMBER THE CIVIL RIGHTS MOVEMENT

YVONNE DAVIS FREAR

In early October 2004, my stepdaughter and I sat down to view a Lifetime Television movie on a balmy Saturday afternoon. It was supposed to be our way of having some wind-down time from homework and chores. To my excitement a period piece was showing, *The Long Walk Home* (1990), starring Whoopi Goldberg and Sissy Spacek. The movie chronicled the relationship between a white housewife and her black maid during the turbulent events surrounding the 1955–56 Montgomery Bus Boycott. As a young civil rights movement scholar, I was ecstatic because I would be able to extract the historical points and share them with my stepdaughter, explaining to her my work and the significance of the movement. I was quickly taken aback when my stepdaughter asked to change the channel to something more interesting. I responded that the movie was a good movie and that she would like it, but she replied that she hates "those type movies." Intrigued by the "those type movies" remark and its curtness, I asked why. She informed me that the civil rights movement period in history was "so over" and that "we're past that." She continued that people her age are concerned with trying to build themselves up not by looking at the past but by focusing on the future. As a mother, I was impressed with the determined articulation of her argument, but as a historian, I was shocked by the casual disregard and apparent lack of respect for the memory of a period that was so important to my elders, me, and, even if unknowingly, to my stepdaughter.[1]

Initially, I had no idea that my stepdaughter had provided me with the basis for an argument for this essay regarding how African Americans in Texas remember the civil rights movement. I was more concerned with the pedagogical challenges that her instructors inadvertently forced me to consider regarding the teaching of such a challenging topic to pre-teens and teens. In the twenty-first century the memory of the civil rights movement is layered in an array of debates, interpretations, and inaccuracies. I believed that my stepdaughter's disregard for the significance of the movement, including subsequent actions, events, and stories, had more to do with her instructors having failed to teach the history of the civil rights movement through primary sources, oral histories, and films. And then it occurred to me that the problem was not the pedagogical negligence of her instructors but an individual assessment based on the least considered component—age.[2]

By coupling generational observations of how African Americans in Texas remember the civil rights movement with actual historical events and narratives, this essay seeks to reveal how the legacies of the civil rights movement are influenced by utilitarianism, or how different generations use collective memory to understand or acknowledge the past. It will explain how an individual's assessment of the usefulness of a memory becomes a device for understanding the legacies or benefits of the movement. The essay will also address how first-generation participants in the civil rights movement reconstruct their memories of events based on personal or internal knowledge of said events. It will also analyze how second- and third-generation beneficiaries of the civil rights movement, like my stepdaughter, remember and interact with the legacies of the movement such as integration, protests, and commemorative festivities, as a result of the selective memories or narratives woven by their elders in the first generation. With this essay, it should be clear that generational perspectives significantly influence the collective memory of the civil rights movement in Texas, because how one remembers the historical events is based on how one was affected by those events and their impact on the daily life of an individual.[3]

The manner in which history and historical events are interpreted often begins in the mind of an individual. The seemingly simplistic observation of a photograph, a gravesite, or even a high school yearbook invokes a historical memory that is often different from what is printed in history textbooks and scholarly monographs. If challenged about the validity of a particular presentation, an individual will comfortably rest on the authoritative nature of his or her interpretation and even reject the documented accounts of professional historians. In the end, the imagined past becomes the standard in which history and historical events are remembered and defined.

In the Lone Star State, young and old African Americans have interpreted received knowledge to build their own individual understanding of the modern civil rights movement in Texas. Although some scholars contend that accepting or incorporating individual and collective memories of minorities into historical recognition is problematic, the legacies of the civil rights movement require that these interpretations be passed down through generations and shared within communities. Other research has shown that older participants in the modern civil rights movement and the younger beneficiaries agree about the significance of the movement during the 1950s and 1960s, but the two groups disagree about the continuing significance of the movement and its legacies.[4]

Both first-generation and second- and third-generation African Americans in Texas have used their individual and collective memories to construct a formidable social memory of the civil rights movement. On the whole, the interpretations of both groups centered on a theme of utilitarianism in the sense that each generation processes its responses to the historical evidence based on how the group has benefited or on how intimate the images or statements involved influenced the individual. The utilitarianism or usability of the memory can be correlated by age—for instance, first-generation participants are approximately sixty years old or older and have a personal memory of the social change that occurred during the civil rights era. Second-generation beneficiaries, twenty-nine to forty-five years old, utilize memories of the movement differently than their elders, primarily because they are the first beneficiaries of the legacies of the movement and use the changes in the social and political arenas for their personal gain. Consequently, younger or third-generation beneficiaries, between twelve and twenty-five years of age, are not as personally affected by the legacies of the movement because their memories have been constructed through narratives, media, and social interaction shared with them by first-generation participants and second-generation beneficiaries. Third-generation beneficiaries appear least invested in the memories because they have not experienced the pains of protest, so they have no real use for the narratives or images of the movement.[5]

Historically, the civil rights movement in Texas was a manifestation of the larger national movement and the movements in Deep South states. In Texas, the intent was analogous to that of other areas of the country—to wipe out a system of segregation that had been prevalent for more than half a century. African Americans in Texas battled against entrenched segregation practices in an effort to gain the rights as outlined by the United States Constitution. In cities like Houston, Dallas, and San Antonio, social mobilization protests were organized and implemented as responses to racial oppression and segregation, codified by Jim Crow laws. Jim Crow laws shaped race relations throughout the state and the nation during the first fifty years of the twentieth century. It was Jim Crow's de jure segregation by law and de facto segregation by custom in politics, public accommodations, education, and housing that set the stage for African American leaders in the state. Leaders such as A. Maceo Smith, Lulu White, and Juanita Craft joined forces and orchestrated resistance to the bastions and despots of exclusion.[6]

Like their national counterparts in the movement, many of the leaders and participants in the civil rights movement in Texas were members of the National Association for the Advancement of Colored People (NAACP) because of its history of fighting inequality. In 1954, the NAACP and the United States Supreme Court set the stage for the modern civil rights movement and how it would be fought, moving from small, local battles in municipalities to defending such actions in federal courts. For fifty-eight years the doctrine of "separate but equal" had served as the basis for racial segregation in all things public or private. However, in 1954, the Supreme Court held in *Brown* v. *Board of Education* that mandatory racial separation contradicted the right to equal protection under the law guaranteed by the Fourteenth Amendment, thereby ruling that "separate but equal" was unconstitutional. By the late 1960s, the NAACP branches in Texas, along with assistance from national headquarters, were successful in ridding the state of the all-white primary, equalizing the pay of African American schoolteachers, desegregating schools, and convincing restaurants and the State Fair of Texas to serve and admit both blacks and whites.[7]

After a series of moderate successes statewide and the passage of national legislation in the form of the Civil Rights Act of 1964, which prohibited discrimination based on race and forbade discrimination in employment; the Voting Rights Act of 1965, which prohibited discrimination in voting rights and even placed federal officials at polling locations to ensure equality in the right to vote; and the Fair Housing Act of 1968, which addressed discrimination in housing and real estate, the elusive vision of integration seemed within reach. Many African Americans in Texas and the nation believed the movement to be over. The need for social protest had been replaced by the need to target issues relating to the poor and the displaced. This new politics of mobilization that focused on ending poverty also addressed the needs of those who were formerly segregated, but now integrated, in the early 1970s.[8]

It is this backdrop, the end of the civil rights movement, that produces an incongruity in the collective memory surrounding the movement. First-generation participants view the end of the movement as a success in many cases. The benefits derived from the Civil Rights Act of 1964, the Voting Rights Act of 1965, the Fair Housing Act of 1968, and the establishment of the Equal Employment Opportunity Commission (EEOC) provided the older cohort with the assurance of equality of opportunity and a national commitment to fairness in individual rights. Second- and third-generation beneficiaries view the end of the movement as either a failure, because of the inequality in school systems, job opportunities, and racial profiling, or as passé, because they take for granted the opportunity to attend integrated schools, participate in multiracial organizations, and maintain a plurality of personal friendships. For younger individuals the harsh reality of protests and racial segregation is from an era gone by. The paradox that is present for all generations is in the interpretation of the success of the movement based on the lingering images attached to an individual's memory—images that are personal because of observer-participant experiences or exposure to history books and movies that penetrate an individual's consciousness and become part of his or her personal experience.[9]

First-generation participants in the civil rights movement in Texas embrace a collective memory of the events, legislation, and images on a personal basis. Their memories of the protests, lunch counter sit-ins, and blatant discrimination by whites were painted from a black-and-white palette. That palette colored every encounter between blacks and whites, subordinating blacks in every social, political, and economic circumstance. For persons between the ages of sixty and eighty, the movement is an intimate component of their lives. In a *Dallas Morning News* article published in 1991, first-generation participants and Dallas NAACP members recalled their experiences in the civil rights movement in their city. Clarence Laws, NAACP member, former regional director, and volunteer campaigner against the poll tax in the 1960s, recalled that "there was nothing more important at the time than implementing equal opportunities for blacks in all aspects of American life." Clarence Laws and his wife, Ann German Laws, also recalled opening their home and sharing their dinner with civil rights leader Medgar Evers two weeks prior to his assassination in Mississippi. The Lawses' memory of their participation in the civil rights movement demonstrates the internal nature of their memories and how they respected the changes that grew from the movement. The Lawses even complained about inaccuracies in the memories of present-day African Americans who overlook the biracial nature of the Dallas NAACP in the civil rights era. Ann Laws remarked, "I resent people thinking that there were no whites actively involved in the NAACP in Dallas." She offered this explanation in response to praise being heaped upon Dallas NAACP branch president, Victor Smith, for appointing two whites, two Hispanics, and an Asian to the local branch's executive board. In the Lawses' view, the civil rights movement in Texas and throughout the nation was a traumatic time in history that culminated in positive results, and the memory of those results should not be forgotten simply because the original struggle had ended.[10]

Scholars are left to question how much of memory is fact and how much is imagined or constructed. One scholar has noted that "memory contains both facts and myths," suggesting that it is left to the listener or interviewer to determine the difference. In the cases of collective memory with first-generation participants in the civil rights movement, it is imperative to discern where fact ends and embellishment begins.[11]

This question of fact versus embellishment often clouded Thomas Cole's investigation into the story of integration in Houston in the 1960s. Cole's book, *No Color Is My Kind: The Life of Eldrewey Stearns and the Integration of Houston* (1997), is a participant account of the actions and reactions to segregation in Houston, Texas. It focuses on Eldrewey Stearns, a student activist at Texas Southern University who conducted many of the protests against segregation in the city in early 1960s. Cole was able to research the basic history of the movement through newspaper accounts and archival sources, but it was Stearns's memory of the events that provided Cole with the greatest challenge because during the research period, Stearns had been diagnosed with manic depressive illness and alcoholism.

According to the book, the city of Houston in the 1960s mirrored other southern cities in terms of de facto segregation. Although African Americans in Houston had "higher rates of per capita income and home ownership," they still experienced discriminatory restrictions in public accommodations.[12] After news of the lunch counter sit-ins in 1960 staged by students attending North Carolina Agricultural and Technical College spread across the South, students like Stearns grabbed the reins of action to initiate the peaceful sit-ins in their cities. Stearns was enrolled as a student in the Thurgood Marshall School of Law in Houston during the time he and other students began to organize a course of action to desegregate the lunch counter at the local Weingarten's, a Jewish-owned grocery store just minutes from the college campus in southeast Houston, a predominantly African American neighborhood. The student demonstrators met with resistance from Weingarten's officials after initial attempts at conciliatory talks. According to Cole, he possessed photographs that showed how the store had removed the seats from the lunch counter stools to dissuade student protesters, a plan Cole comically labeled "vertical integration." The student demonstrators expanded their protest plans to move beyond the community and into downtown Houston, specifically targeting Foley's department store. Unfortunately, their plan was interrupted by Foley's department store public relations and advertising director Bob Dundas, who carefully arranged a side deal with Texas Southern University president Sam Nabrit to recruit black students to integrate the lunch counter at Foley's and approximately seventy other supermarkets, department stores, and drugstore lunch counters. A peaceful arrangement that accommodated the white business leaders and the black community was accomplished without violence or media coverage, so as not to raise the ire of segregationists. According to Cole, on the surface the accommodationist arrangement appeared to be a shrewd political move, but for Dundas it ended the haunting recollections of the 1917 Camp Logan riots, during which he saw the bodies of sixteen slain whites at the morgue after the violent racial protests in downtown Houston.[13]

Cole carefully interweaves the success story of desegregating public accommodations in Houston with the lucid accounts shared by Eldrewey Stearns. According to Cole, however, when he first started interviewing Stearns in 1988, he realized that there were "other players in Houston's desegregation story." The memories recalled by Stearns and discovered by Cole are laced with clear and subtle personal sentiments regarding the movement, ranging from challenging the status quo, struggling for equality, and taking risks that demonstrate the very personal views of leadership and courage exhibited by Stearns in the sixties. Each of the memories recalled by Stearns and published by Cole are prime examples of how an individual's personal memory can contribute to collective memory by reconstructing some of the most significant moments in Houston's civil rights history. For both Cole and Stearns, the biography was a useful tool for reconstructing the past based on the social, political, and even cultural conditions of the period. Through the individual memories of Stearns, it is easy to understand how the courage of student demonstrators in the sixties effectively contributed to peaceful desegregation in Houston, thus contributing to the positive legacy of the movement.[14]

Memories of the civil rights movement in Houston are not limited by the explanations woven into biographical narratives. Houstonians had the privilege of making connections to the civil rights movement through the impassioned voice of a local civil rights leader, Rev. William A. Lawson. In early June 2004, Reverend Lawson announced his retirement as senior pastor of Wheeler Avenue Baptist Church, located in the Third Ward area of Houston. His announcement was not a shock to many church members and Houston elites, as it had been rumored that Lawson was preparing to step down. However, his announcement did cause some to wonder how his retirement would affect the ongoing effort to achieve political and civil rights in Houston. In the early 1960s, William Lawson was a key figure in the local civil rights movement. He helped to establish a local chapter of the Southern Christian Leadership Conference (SCLC), an organization formed by Martin Luther King Jr. and others in 1957 to promote nonviolent protest as a means of resistance to segregation, and he also organized Operation PUSH (People United to Save Humanity), a program that was instrumental in the desegregation of schools in Houston.[15]

In an interview with the *Houston Chronicle* in June 2004, Lawson offered his memories of the civil rights movement activities in Houston, specifically regarding the benefits of integration after the Supreme Court's ruling in *Brown* v. *Board of Education.* Lawson stated that whether or not integration harmed African Americans was a question that could not be answered in terms of "hurt or harm." He commented that although schools were segregated with minimal budgets and were "by nature inferior . . . , we had a sense of family." He continued that "segregation gave us inferior equipment, but it did not give us inferior care."[16]

The interview responses Lawson submitted to the *Chronicle* demonstrate that his memories of the past are almost accommodationist in tone. Lawson does not appear to be the outspoken civil rights activist that he was characterized to be in the sixties. His comments are personal and polished, which do not bring to mind the turbulence he experienced as he sought to achieve political and social change. Actually, his responses to the interviewer's questions are conservative and businesslike. Although his responses are formal in tone, when he speaks of trying to learn in a one-room school house with an inoperable furnace and torn books the harsh images are softened by the positive influence of a family that loved and cared for him.

Lawson's individual memory as presented in this interview, although utilitarian in form, does not seem representative of his previous experiences in the civil rights movement. Reverend Lawson's answers to the questions are evidence of how ideas shape collective memory. Lawson's ideas of how events of importance unfolded in the sixties tend to be more usable in his adult life. The Supreme Court's decision in *Brown,* the sit-ins, and the student demonstrations in Houston influenced Lawson's memory and his subsequent political outlook, which contributed to his community redevelopment efforts in Houston's Third Ward. As a participant-observer, Lawson's memories appear distant from the social protests of yesteryear, but they accentuate his political and community activism of today. As a grassroots activist during the height of the movement in Houston, Lawson's brief recollections about the effects of *Brown* and integration demonstrate how he, his church, and the Third Ward community in Houston benefited from the gains in the social, political, and economic arenas during the post–civil rights era.[17]

Second- and third-generation beneficiaries of the civil rights movement in Texas have a different posture regarding their collective memory of the movement. Like their elders, the younger generations follow a theme of utilitarianism in constructing and describing their social memories of the movement. What differs with the younger generation is their belief that the legacies of the civil rights movement provide a primary academic understanding of the necessity of civil legislation in contemporary society or that the movement is a distant series of historical events that are not related to present-day issues. The integration of second- and third-generation beneficiaries into mainstream schools, jobs, and organizations erodes the memory of past protests, sit-ins, and customary segregation based on the color of one's skin.

Easy access to historically significant movies on film, VHS, or DVD influences the shared memories of second- and third-generation individuals by offering them a glimpse of past events, dramatically reconstructed. Movies such as *A Raisin in the Sun, Guess Who's Coming to Dinner,* or *The Long Walk Home* attempt to chronicle a specific segment or period in the civil rights struggle in two hours or less, if television commercial time is included. In my assessment, the historical past is commercially dramatized so that younger viewers, those between twelve and twenty-five years old, can observe the horrors of racial segregation and discrimination that existed years prior to their being born. The re-created past also serves as a reminder to the older cohort that their past experiences will not be forgotten.

A Raisin in the Sun, Lorraine Hansberry's 1959 prize-winning play, was developed into a screen drama that portrayed African American experiences from an African American viewpoint, a relatively unique approach in 1960s Hollywood. The cast of characters provided a riveting portrayal of what it was like to be an African American family hoping to move into their first home in an all-white neighborhood. Throughout the movie, viewers learn about the racial discrimination that limited housing choices and constrained personal relationships The Academy Award–winning film *Guess Who's Coming to Dinner* addressed the controversial issue of interracial marriage head-on in its 1967 premiere. The director, Stanley Kramer, known for directing "message" films, presented viewers with an in-your-face storyline about social bias based on race in America. Although the movie had an optimistic ending, it presented a sobering story of why the actions and activists in the civil rights movement were needed to effect change in society, even though society was not willing to accept such socially liberal activism. A contemporary take on an actual event in the civil rights struggle is re-created in *The Long Walk Home.* The movie illustrated the modern struggle for racial equality that began with the Montgomery Bus Boycott in 1955, offering a more hopeful story to younger viewers because it portrayed a growing friendship between a white female and a black female. Unfortunately, their relationship is marred by segregation and violence, as the two women are forced to come to terms with the entrenched racism that existed in their everyday lives.

The availability of these movies allows second- and third-generation cohorts to construct radically different meanings about their lives based on the legacies of the civil rights movement. Collectively, the movies described above offer relatively accurate renditions of the issues that they attempted to address. However, as with any film, the story could always be more accurate or less offensive if certain gratuitous segments were left on the cutting room floor. Despite the minor inaccuracies, many individuals incorporate the themes of the movies into their arguments regarding pluralism and the efficacy of civil rights. Although some individuals are offended by the content of the movies because they show the violence inflicted on people because of the color of their skin, many individuals, like my stepdaughter, are simply not interested in reliving the past. This apathy is most likely seen in the responses from third-generation beneficiaries because they believe they are the least affected by the issues of the past, as they try to address the important questions in their present-day lives. If it were not for Black History Month in February of each year, many of the movies that chronicle the civil rights movement would remain safely stored away in airtight film canisters in Hollywood.[18]

The literature addressing the heroes of the civil rights movement also contributes to the memories embraced by individuals. Specifically, the works examining the accomplishments and experiences of Martin Luther King Jr. serve as convincing evidence of the nonviolent strides made in the early civil rights movement. Second- and third-generation beneficiaries have their first encounters with the literature of King in secondary and university-level education. Instructors generally include major works written by King himself, such as *Why We Can't Wait,* which analyze the events that fueled the civil rights movement in the early sixties. King presents his ideas about equality and why the fight to end racial discrimination is so important. He uses the early civil rights movement, especially those episodes in Alabama, as a backdrop to the story behind the struggle for civil rights in America. The short book provides a wealth of information for people of all ages about a sensitive issue in America's history. Advanced readers or university students are introduced to narratives centering on King's life in David J. Garrow's *Bearing the Cross: Martin Luther King, Jr., and the Southern Christian Leadership Conference* (1986) or Taylor Branch's *Parting the Waters: America in the King Years, 1954–63* (1988). Each of these books offers readers a detailed look into the life of Martin Luther King Jr. and his contributions to the movement that made him famous. In more recent years, African American literature and film professors, along with third-generation beneficiaries, are extending their knowledge of Dr. King to include the movie *Boycott* as a definitive explanation of Dr. King's purpose and involvement in grassroots activism with the Montgomery Improvement Association during the bus boycott in 1955–56. The individual memories of younger cohorts are influenced by the written literature because it allows them to develop a selective memory of the civil rights movement. The younger generations can use the information that they extract from the literature about Dr. King to formulate their own ideas about the racial injustices that were prevalent before and during the movement. At the same time, such individuals deprive themselves of a complete understanding of the years of racial inequality when they choose to ignore or simply remain unaware of historical events and persons that were also extremely important in the civil rights movement. In many cases, the younger beneficiaries construct in their conveniently selective memory the belief that they can gain a complete understanding of the movement and its heroes by reading any one work that centers on Martin Luther King Jr.[19]

Selective memories of the past are addressed in a *Texas Lawyer* special report, "Diversity and the Law" (2001). Genora K. Boykins, a second-generation beneficiary of the civil rights movement and a principal attorney for Reliant Energy, Inc., commented about diversity issues at her job. Boykins agreed with the reporter that there is a glass ceiling at Reliant Energy, and she blamed the presence of the ceiling on the industry, not the corporation. She stated that "the reality is it's still a white, male-dominated industry." Despite the gains of the civil rights movement, especially in the area of equal employment opportunity as a result of Title VII of the Civil Rights Act of 1964, which prohibits discrimination in employment on the basis of race, color, national origin, religion, and sex, Boykins found herself viewing the historic struggle with conflicted feelings. On the one hand she was thankful for the opportunity to attend integrated schools and secure a position with a top energy company, but on the other hand she was limited by the glass ceiling that was supposed to have been removed by her first-generation elders. Any exercise in remembering the achievement of Title VII of the Civil Rights Act of 1964 is clouded by the reality of opportunities for minority lawyers. Despite highly competitive résumés, it is still incredibly difficult for them to get a foot in the door because corporate legal departments prefer experienced attorneys and are less likely to hire individuals fresh out of law school, which in many cases restricts employment prospects for minorities and women.[20]

In the same special report, comments by LaMont D. Walker illustrated how the benefits of integration and racial equality at the end of the civil rights movement influenced his position as legal counsel at Dell Computer Corporation in Austin, Texas. Walker indicated that "he has not encountered any problems that he would blame on race or prejudice" and that "he's judged by the quality of his work at Dell and race isn't a factor." His idealistic comments are derived from the declarations by civil rights movement leaders like Martin Luther King Jr., who opined in his "I Have a Dream" speech that one day his four children would live in a nation "where they will not be judged by the color of their skin but by the content of their character." As a second-generation beneficiary of the movement, Walker implied in his comments that the struggles of African Americans who protested were not in vain but that the wrongs that they fought valiantly against have been righted. There are no visible hindrances to Walker's career in the legal field because of his minority status.[21]

The experiences of Boykins and Walker are representative of a diminishing collective memory of the civil rights movement and its legacies in Texas. The ability of these individuals to attend top-rated Texas law schools and to enter into mainstream careers validates the presence of diversity in upper-middle-class America. The necessity of civil rights legislation or mobilization protests is almost invisible in the comments they submitted for the *Texas Lawyer* special report. Neither Boykins nor Walker directly correlated their professional employment to the first-generation civil rights participants, but indirectly their comments make veiled references to the achievements and benefits gained from the movement. The statements from Boykins and Walker offer no evidence of their embracing a selective narrative handed down from their parents or of how shared memories from elders have influenced them to become more active in community or organizational settings that were opened up because of the movement. However, in editorial fairness to the attorneys, I should submit that the special report did not reference their pro bono or community activities that could indicate their participation in social or political networks that emanate from influences in the civil rights movement.

Third-generation beneficiaries have a different perspective when they "remember" the civil rights movement. Many youth and young adults between the ages of twelve and twenty-five are more cognizant of the failures of the movement. They believe that the lingering racial hatred based on a lack of tolerance stems from their parents' failure to continue the movement after it faltered in the early seventies. In late January 2003, Ted Koppel, then the ABC News *Nightline* anchor, traveled to Jasper, Texas, and hosted a special edition entitled, "America in Black in White: Two Towns of Jasper." The premise of the newscast was to see how the East Texas town of Jasper had healed, or not, since the dragging death of James Byrd in June 1998. Koppel entertained responses, comments, criticisms, and personal attacks from an array of individuals in the audience, from homemakers to business leaders, from preachers to sheriffs. However, his most poignant responses about race relations and civil rights in the town came from Jasper High School students in the audience. Zach, a Jasper High School student, said that the documentary had focused on the older generation and that "they have prejudices in their hearts because that's the way they were raised." Zach challenged Koppel and others in the media by saying that, when preparing a documentary, the producers needed to look at the whole picture to get a fair assessment of the subject. Conversely, Jeremy, a fellow classmate of Zach's, thanked Ted Koppel for enlightening him on the current events in Jasper and for illuminating the problem of racism in his town. Kathy, a female high school student, stated that the town hall meeting had been a learning experience for her as well, especially since she believed that students were color blind. She closed her remarks with the invitation "to learn to integrate ourselves in social areas, over time."[22]

In the final minutes of the newscast, Chelsea, a sophomore at Jasper High School, made a statement that related closely to collective memory and the civil rights movement in Texas. Chelsea commented that she thought the views of the black community were merely "reminiscences of the past and that she did not realize that many of the views embraced by the Black community were still prevalent today because of the views of the white community." Later in the broadcast, Chelsea confirmed for Koppel that despite the appearance of social segregation in the lunchroom and at football games, she and her friends did converse about issues of race and how it affected them. As third-generation beneficiaries of their elders' participation, Chelsea and her classmates had a nonexistent to minimal frame of reference for comprehending what life was like in Jasper, or even in the nation, just forty years prior to the newscast. For the high schoolers, the legacies of the movement were a continuum of freedoms and equality that they had always known. Prior to the town hall meeting, students did not see a need for memories of protests, sit-ins, or peaceful demonstrations because until their town hall meeting they did not have a tangible connection to the past. Their perspectives about the civil rights movement were presented in the pedagogy of the Texas educational curriculum or in apathy toward the movement because the past did not mean as much to them when they were busy trying to progress in life.[23]

"Generation versus generation" aptly describes the collective memory of the civil rights movement in Texas. First-generation participants embrace their knowledge of the movement in a personal or internal manner. In most cases, the memories of elders provided a connection to a usable past that was not dismissed as insignificant or passé. Second- and third-generation beneficiaries of the movement view its legacies as foundational, or as a failure, or possibly even nonexistent in their day-to-day lives. Unfortunately, the only theme the two groups share is that of utilitarianism. Memory consumes the cerebral psyche of each generation. It is how the generation consumes or processes the information that is important to the study of collective memory. It can be concluded that the collective memory of civil rights is greater and more usable for first-generation participants than for second- and third-generation beneficiaries. Older, or first-generation, participants embrace the critical events of the civil rights movement in their consciousness and their memory. On the other hand, second- and third-generation beneficiaries find the legacies of the movement ambiguous and less important to their present-day issues or concerns. Internalizing the struggles, turbulence, and even the gains is left to the older cohort who began the movement and want to hold on to the past.

My only hope is that the next time I sit down to watch a movie with my children and it is about civil rights, I will acknowledge the generational factors in what they will construe as historically important, as opposed to lording over them with my civil-rights-scholar scepter in a futile attempt to get them to accept the significance of the movement of which they are not only beneficiaries but also trustees. I also hope that I am mature enough to meet the same standard of excellence in preserving the integrity and memory of the civil rights movement that I expect my children to meet. I am equally responsible for making sure that the collective memory of civil rights in Texas does not disappear as I enter into the hallowed halls of academe. It is extremely important to shoulder the memories of my elders as they progress in years, because without their memories the legitimacy of events will be left to compressed curriculums and less than poignant pedagogy.

NOTES

1. The Lifetime Movie Network is a "sister service" of Lifetime Television for Women, a network dedicated to providing positive television for women. The movie, *The Long Walk Home* (1990), is a complement to the network's "critically acclaimed series," *Any Day Now*, which is a drama that chronicles the collective memory of two young adult women (one black, one white) who came of age during the turbulent civil rights era in Alabama.

2. My concern about how the civil rights movement is taught is addressed in several essays and reviews in the *History of Education Quarterly*'s special issue for the fiftieth anniversary of the *Brown* v. *Board of Education* decision, especially Jack Dougherty, introduction to "Teaching Brown: Reflections on Pedagogical Challenges and Opportunities," *History of Education Quarterly* 44 (Spring 2004): 95–97.

3. Avishai Margalit, *The Ethics of Memory* (Cambridge, Mass.: Harvard University Press, 2002), 14–16. Also, the terms *cohort* and *generation* are used interchangeably in this essay as a means of grouping. Specifically, I am referring to a group of individuals who were born during a particular period of time and have a common understanding of a historically relevant period such as the civil rights movement.

4. W. Fitzhugh Brundage points out that the question of inclusion of minorities, specifically African Americans and Mexican Americans, is historically contentious in regard to "public expressions of memory" because of "the legacies of discrimination and poverty as well as current race relations" (Brundage, ed., *Where These Memories Grow: History, Memory, and Southern Identity* [Chapel Hill: University of North Carolina Press, 2000], 18–19). James W. Pennebaker and Becky L. Banasik describe how historical events are included in the formation of collective memories if they significantly impact or validate a person's life (Pennebacker and Banasik, "On the Creation and Maintenance of Collective Memories: History as Social Psychology," in *Collective Memory of Political Events: Social Psychological Perspectives,* ed. James W. Pennebaker, Dario Paez, and Bernard Rime [Mahwah, N.J.: Lawrence Erlbaum Associates, 1997], 3–20).

5. The generational groupings presented in this essay are extracted from Howard Schuman and Jacqueline Scott, "Generations and Collective Memories," *American Sociological Review* 54, no. 3 (1989): 359–81. In their findings, Schuman and Scott extend Karl Mannheim's argument and generational breakdowns. Mannheim posits that the "up-to-dateness of youth consists in their being closer to the 'present' problems . . . the older generation cling to the re-orientation that had been the drama of their youth" (Karl Mannheim, "The Problem of Generations," in *Essays on the Sociology of Knowledge* [London: Routledge and Kegan Paul, 1952], 276–322). In essence, first-generation participants are more likely to express their memo-

ries of the civil rights movement in greater detail than their younger cohorts (second- and third-generation beneficiaries) because they have lived through the experience and understand the legacies of the turbulent period.

6. For a more detailed discussion of the battle for civil rights in Texas see Michael Gillette, "The NAACP in Texas, 1937–1957" (Ph.D. diss., University of Texas at Austin, 1984); Lewis W. Jones and Herman H. Long, *The Negotiation of Desegregation in Ten Southern Cities* (Nashville, Tenn.: Fisk University Press, 1965); Merline Pitre, "Black Houstonians and the 'Separate but Equal' Doctrine: Carter W. Wesley versus Lulu White," *Houston Review* 12 (1990): 23–36; Robyn Duff Ladino, *Desegregating Texas Schools: Eisenhower, Shivers, and the Crisis at Mansfield High* (Austin: University of Texas Press, 1996); W. Marvin Dulaney, "Whatever Happened to the Civil Rights Movement in Dallas, Texas?" in *Essays on the American Civil Rights Movement,* ed. John Dittmer, W. Marvin Dulaney, Kathleen Underwood, and George C. Wright (College Station: Texas A&M University Press, 1993); Ramona Allaniz Houston, "African Americans, Mexican Americans, and Anglo Americans and the Desegregation of Texas, 1946–1957" (Ph.D. diss., University of Texas at Austin, 2000); Amilcar Shabazz, *Advancing Democracy: African Americans and the Struggle for Access and Equity in Higher Education in Texas* (Chapel Hill: University of North Carolina Press, 2004); Carlos Kevin Blanton, *The Strange Career of Bilingual Education in Texas, 1836–1981* (College Station: Texas A&M University Press, 2004); Yvonne Davis Frear, "Battling to End Segregation in Dallas, Texas, 1945–1965: Race, Gender, and Social Mobilization in a Local Civil Rights Movement" (Ph.D. diss., Texas A&M University, forthcoming 2006).

7. In *Smith* v. *Allright,* 321 U.S. 649 (1944), the Supreme Court held that the white primary in Texas was unconstitutional, and within three years the number of African American voters in Texas increased from less than 100,000 to 645,000; in *Thelma Page et al.* v. *Board of Education of the City of Dallas, Texas, et al.* (1943) the United States District Court for the Northern District of Texas ruled that African American teachers would be granted increases in salary over a period of two years, until their salaries reached the same levels as their white counterparts; in *Sweatt* v. *Painter,* 339 U.S. 629 (1950), the Supreme Court justices ruled that the University of Texas law school had to integrate; in *Atkins* v. *Matthew,* Civil Action No. 1104 (E. E. Texas, 1955), a federal magistrate reversed a lower court's injunction prohibiting Joe Atkins from being admitted to North Texas State University and ruled that Atkins had to be admitted to the previously segregated school without delay.

8. Melvyn L. Fein, *Race and Morality: How Good Intentions Undermine Social Justice and Perpetuate Inequality* (New York: Kluwer Academic/Plenum Publishers, 2001); Orlando Patterson, *The Ordeal of Integration: Progress and Resentment in America's "Racial" Crisis* (Washington, D.C.: Counterpoint, 1997).

9. Ibid.

10. "Showing the Way—Veteran NAACP Members Recall Early Struggle," *Dallas Morning News,* Mar. 17, 1991, 20.

11. Glenace Edwall, "Comment," in *Memory and History: Essays on Recalling and Interpreting Experience,* ed. Jaclyn Jeffrey and Glenace Edwall (Lanham, Md.: University Press of America, 1994), 15. Edwall comments briefly from a psychological clinician's standpoint on the reliability and validity of memory in oral history as examined by historian and leading researcher in oral history Paul Thompson in his chapter, "Believe It or Not: Rethinking the Historical Interpretation of Memory," in *Memory and History,* ed. Jeffrey and Edwall, 1–13. Edwall argues that although Thompson is correct in saying that memory contains both facts and myths and that both are meaning structures, it is equally important to understand that the meaning behind the fact and the myth may not be equivalent. She concludes that the accuracy or fallibility would be essential in understanding the truths of one's perception.

12. Fritz Lanham, "The Silent End of Segregation," *Texas: Houston Chronicle Magazine,* June 15, 1997, 9.

13. Thomas R. Cole, *No Color Is My Kind: The Life of Eldrewey Stearns and the Integration of Houston* (Austin: University of Texas Press, 1997); Lanham, "The Silent End of Segregation," 9.

14. Cole quoted in "The Silent End of Segregation,"8. A more detailed discussion of the usability of memory as implemented by Cole in *No Color Is My Kind* is explained in Barbie Zelizer, "Reading the Past against the Grain: The Shape of Memory Studies," *Critical Studies in Mass Communication* 12 (June 1995): 214–39. Zelizer argues that "collective memory presumes activities of sharing, discussion, negotiation, and often contestation. . . . [R]emembering [has as] much to do with identity formation, power and authority, cultural norms and social interaction as with the simple act of recall" (214).

15. Sherina Miles-Miller, "Their Strength Was in Their Leadership: The Histories of Brentwood Missionary Baptist Church and Windsor Village United Methodist Church" (Ph.D. diss., Texas A&M University, forthcoming, 2006). Miles-Miller discusses the activist background of Rev. William Lawson in the early sixties as a springboard for the evangelical and progressive Baptist church under the leadership of his young protégé, Rev. Joe Samuel Ratliff.

16. "Retiring Reverend Shares Views on Redevelopment, Civil Rights," *Houston Chronicle,* June 13, 2004, 37A, 43A.

17. Ibid.

18. The movies discussed here are all available in VHS or DVD format. As a supplement to academic lectures or to stimulate discussion about the civil rights movement, the films offer a great springboard. For instance, the movie *Boycott* (2001) combines actual documented footage of the Montgomery Bus Boycott with fictional depictions. I believe, however, that the films must be appropriately coupled with historical evidence and explanation from scholarly sources/archives to properly juxtapose popular culture and real life.

19. For more detailed references surrounding the life and historical contributions of Martin Luther King Jr., see Martin Luther King Jr., *Why We Can't Wait* (1964; reprint, New York: Penguin Group, 1968); David L. Lewis, *King: A Critical Biography* (New York: Praeger, 1970); David J. Garrow, *Bearing the Cross: Martin Luther King, Jr., and the Southern Christian Leadership Conference* (New York: William Morrow, 1986); Taylor Branch, *Parting the Waters: America in the King Years, 1954–63* (New York: Simon and Schuster, 1988); Adam Fairclough, *Martin Luther King, Jr.* (Athens: University of Georgia Press, 1995); Taylor Branch, *Pillar of Fire: America in the King Years, 1963–65* (New York: Simon and Schuster, 1998); and Clayborne Carson, ed., *The Autobiography of Martin Luther King Jr.* (New York: Intellectual Properties Management in association with Warner Books, 2000).

20. Boykins quoted in Brenda Sapino Jeffreys, "More Diverse in-House Experiences," *Texas Lawyer* 17 (Mar. 26, 2001): 34–36.

21. Ibid., 36. For the text of "I Have a Dream," see Martin Luther King Jr., *The Peaceful Warrior* (New York: Pocket Books, 1968), or http://usinfo.state.gov/usa/infousa/facts/democrac/38.htm.

22. *Nightline:* "America in Black and White: Two Towns of Jasper," ABC News transcript, air date Jan. 23, 2003 (copy in author's possession), 10, 13.

23. Ibid, 14.

Chapter 9

LYNDON, WE HARDLY REMEMBER YE: LBJ IN THE MEMORY OF MODERN TEXAS

RICKY FLOYD DOBBS

My only memory of Lyndon Johnson just happens to be his last public event. I remember his funeral. The whole first grade sat (so-called "Indian-style") on the floor of our open classroom. We watched the televised goings-on in Washington; I watched the Hill Country burial at home with my mother. There wasn't much else on television back in those days. All three networks were all Lyndon, all day.

In retrospect, Johnson's obsequies seem muted, especially in comparison to the Reagan funeral extravaganza that consumed a whole week in June 2004. The most Texan of "Texan" presidents died on January 22, 1973. By afternoon on the twenty-fourth, the former president's body lay in state at the LBJ Library in Austin. An estimated thirty-two thousand persons paid their respects before its departure for Washington and the Capitol rotunda. Forty thousand more viewed the casket there, and a "Service of Tribute" celebrated LBJ's life of public service at National City Christian Church. The next afternoon, Johnson's body returned to Texas for interment on the former president's Gillespie County ranch.[1]

Johnson died only four years after leaving the White House. He had deceived the nation repeatedly about a far-off war. He had escalated American involvement in Southeast Asia, ignored advice to alter course, and saw the whole gamble come crashing down around him as America's cities burned and its youth rebelled. In 1973, not many were in the mood to forgive and remember. Johnson had died before his friends could properly build a memory of his accomplishments.

Even before his death, some suggested his legacy would be bigger than Vietnam. His personality alone, some claimed, would secure him a prominent place in American history and Texas memory. In 1969, journalist Marshall Frady described him as "an awesome phenomenon simply as a human being, with an epic ego, exuberances, glooms, ambitions, paranoias, generosities, will: a kind of ill-starred, left-handed Prometheus." Three years after his death, *Texas Monthly* remembered him as "a great original, a man whose energy and personality knew few bounds, the polar opposite both of Richard Nixon's rootless ambition and Gerald Ford's midwestern blandness." Eventually, time and his acolytes' advocacy restored Johnson's historical reputation. Paul Burka described 2000 as "a very good year" for Lyndon Johnson, "his best one since 1964." Historians reexamined Johnson's accomplishments, and the ongoing release of taped White House phone conversations strengthened his image. Johnson remains a hot property for students of the past.[2]

Unfortunately, the general public's memory of Lyndon Johnson has begun to fade. The scholarly attention LBJ has received over a twenty-year period cannot fully correct collective memory. Though historical sites and museums do a fine job of presenting the real Johnson, their ability to mold public perceptions is limited by the public's willingness to come through the door. Public school social studies curricula and textbooks might transmit scholarly understanding of the past, including insight into LBJ. But that is hardly their sole purpose, let alone their chief goal. The current generation's level of awareness of Johnson confirms this view. Lyndon Johnson no longer seems relevant to modern Texas, and he is best remembered for irrelevancies and failings rather than his contributions to the life of the state and nation.

A pleasure trip to the Hill Country in late July might be thought mad. During spring and fall, the Hill Country charms, but it is still Texas in the summer. Summer 2004 defied usual weather patterns, however. When I arrived for a tour and visit with National Park Service staff at the LBJ Ranch, it was overcast, mild, drizzling, and green. Even today, Johnson still looms over his particular patch of earth. It is the best place in Texas to get to know him and one of the few where his memory has yet to fade.

The LBJ ranch is a hybrid site. The National Park Service (NPS) administers the ranch complex and lands; the Texas Parks and Wildlife Department runs a state park across the Pedernales River from the Johnson place. Together, they share a visitor center on state land. NPS staffers describe the ranch as a "natural park" rather than merely a presidential historical site. Wildlife roams freely about. It is also a "working ranch," and descendants of its original Hereford stock lumber through the brushy country. Though LBJ is everywhere, interpretive exhibits in the visitor center might surprise those waiting for the NPS tour bus. These exhibits emphasize the cultural diversity of the Hill Country, making plain that Lyndon Johnson emerged from the region rather than the other way around. Indians, Tejanos, southern whites, African Americans, and Germans all made an impression on the place that molded a president.[3]

Thematically, the influence of "place" on Johnson, as well as his "complexity," drives the NPS interpretation of the LBJ Ranch. Throughout the nine-mile bus tour ranger comments and voiceovers reinforce these themes. Passing the river, a mention of the Hill Country's flash floods gives way to James Califano's disembodied voice describing the president's idea of a joke: driving a carload of visitors full-tilt into the river in his amphibious car. Luxury autos Johnson used to hunt deer and to fly down ranch roads sit on display, even as visitors come to terms with his boyhood experience of poverty and isolation. A one-room school Johnson attended later hosted the signing of the Elementary and Secondary Education Act (1965). Here rangers discuss his "mythic belief" in education as social leveler and cure-all. NPS interpreters consistently link Johnson's personality traits and beliefs directly to a place, building, or object. At the ranch's highest point, the bus stops and allows visitors to take in a wide vista. The voiceover is by LBJ himself, and the topic is the Hill Country's effect upon him.[4]

Park rangers know that many visitors don't care much for Lyndon Johnson. Even thirty years after his death, he remains controversial. Tour narrators point out a "duality" to LBJ's personality and ambition, making him at once "selfish" and "compassionate." No secret is made of his outsized ego or of his other failings. Concluding that Johnson "had many sides both positive and negative," Ranger David Shaffer bids visitors farewell and hopes they have gained new insight into a multifaceted leader. Throughout, the NPS rangers demonstrate professionalism and tact, but they also know their stuff. They converse easily not only about flora and fauna but also about arcane information on the Gulf of Tonkin incident and scholarly debate over Johnson's presidency.[5]

In Austin, official memory of Lyndon Johnson finds its zenith at the Lyndon Baines Johnson Library and Museum at the University of Texas. The university has grown spectacularly since the library opened in 1972. Still, the white stone edifice looms over the campus's eastern edge. Out here the university's trademark Spanish colonial architecture gives way to late-twentieth-century box. Former library director James Middleton and countless scholars have used the library's holdings to rescue Johnson's reputation. Its exhibits sanitize the truth now and then, but the museum usually remains true to the former president's "warts and all" dictum. For example, his eighty-seven-vote 1948 U.S. Senate victory over Coke Stevenson receives truthful, if not exhaustive, attention. For many people, the 1948 "landslide" represents LBJ's original sin, an indicator of innate depravity. Some leap from here to the Kennedy assassination to Vietnam, seeing emerging evil with facile clarity. Examined alongside his 1941 Senate defeat examined earlier in the museum, the 1948 vote typifies garden-variety Texas election theft, if only more historically significant. Context is the mortal enemy of memory.[6]

Later museum exhibits depict "Two Americas" as having existed before LBJ entered the White House. A comfortable, well-fed, prosperous America lived alongside a poor, marginalized one. Race separated still two other Americas. Fate thrust Lyndon Johnson into this circumstance. After experiencing the John F. Kennedy assassination in a darkened twenty-foot hallway, tourists walk out into exhibit space detailing efforts to right these wrongs. A wall adorned with the legend "The Thousand Laws of the Great Society" lists the Johnson administration's legislative victories in its war against racism and poverty. A few of these measures merit special attention with video terminals offering greater depth about Head Start, Medicare, and "A Broadened Concept of Freedom."

Johnson tried to bridge two Americas, but he helped create another division almost as huge as those he tried to heal: the rift over Vietnam. The museum captions offer factual information, but sometimes they are a little too generous. For example: "Only after he is given firm assurance that the attack occurred" did LBJ act after the 1964 Gulf of Tonkin incident. The truth is more complicated. The exhibit demonstrates Johnson's anguish over Vietnam and how he worked himself still harder in response to his inability to control the situation. The huge Texan's frustration with a small country leaps from White House photos of Johnson as commander-in-chief. In the modern context of another far-off war, a look back at a president plainly in over his head brings into question whether the will to forget can overwhelm both history and memory.

It is hard to peg either the ranch or the LBJ Library's impact upon collective memory. Measurement might seem a simple matter of statistics. Visitation at Lyndon B. Johnson National Historical Park has steadily declined since 1973, its best year. The year Johnson died, 579,200 visited, but a year later 200,000 fewer turned out. Attendance declined erratically until 1987 and then fell off sharply after 1989. The NPS reported its worst year ever at the park in 2003 when only 85,339 showed up. Anecdotal evidence suggests that traveling retirees make up a significant portion of tourists. Located some seventy miles west of Austin, the ranch is off the beaten path. One must go there deliberately. National Archives and Records Administration (NARA) figures for the Lyndon Baines Johnson Library and Museum in Austin also show decreasing visitation. In 1976, 701,472 persons visited, the most ever; 1973 came in second with 683,505 patrons. Since 1994, fewer than 300,000 have walked through yearly. After three particularly bad years, 2000–2002, when attendance fell below 200,000, numbers have rebounded, with 228,682 visiting in 2004.[7]

Can one construct a causal link between the LBJ ranch, the LBJ Library, and Texas collective memory? It would take a lot more imagination and facility with a graphing calculator than is present here. What's more, a hazard exists in looking too hard at numbers. If collective memory is partially chosen, not many have chosen the scholarly rendering offered by NPS and NARA. If collective memory might be imposed or absorbed, better places exist to find Texans' collective picture of LBJ. Peter Seixas, Peter Stearns, and Sam Wineburg suggested in 1999 that historians who study collective memory in "museums and through monuments" miss a more significant institutional contributor to society's understanding of the past—the schools. The LBJ Library claims 12,764,000 visitors since 1972. But, as Seixas, Stearns, and Wineburg point out, "the entire population" encounter and process "school accounts of the past during formative impressionable years."[8]

Multiple processes and actors produce the schools' influence upon collective memory. Authority over Texas textbook content inheres in elected officials and functionaries of the state bureaucracy. Locally elected school boards and their appointed administrators have some say in how that content is disseminated. In individual schools, other factors come into play: the principal's willingness to give teachers free rein, or not; a teacher's competence in the subject area; principals,' teachers,' and students' personal views about the relevance of history. Tracing out these local differences would be damnably difficult. The state education bureaucracy's influence upon collective memory is the most easily traced because it begins the process of shaping memory. That bureaucratic influence and the assumptions behind it merit attention. Lyndon Johnson's textbook persona offers some insight into that influence and those assumptions.

In 1916, the National Education Association (NEA) announced "the cultivation of good citizenship" as the "conscious and constant" justification of teaching "social studies." The NEA incorporated history into a group of disciplines individually unworthy of study and declared the past important only so far as it related to "the present life interests of the pupil." Such a utilitarian approach meant that texts and curricula would determine what memories were worth preserving and transmitting. That preservation and transmission had to serve present interests; learning about the past, like any other form of knowledge, had no value in and of itself. Texas schools have never adjusted well to modern ideas such as female linebackers, mandatory attendance, or proper funding. So it took time for this rationale for social studies to meld with or even overwhelm Texans' unnatural affection for their own past. However, a "culture war" now rages in the state's schools, and the utilitarian basis for teaching history predominates regardless of political orientation.[9]

Today's textbooks, for all grades and all subjects, must "align" with the state curriculum, which is called Texas Essential Knowledge and Skills (TEKS). TEKS is a lengthy, jargon-laden document crafted by bureaucrats to humor politicians who promised better schools to please constituents. Properly "aligned" texts prepare students for the state assessment of student progress, the Texas Assessment of Knowledge and Skills (TAKS). Checking this "alignment" is a power of the elected State Board of Education (SBOE). In 2000, the SBOE stipulated that new texts to be adopted in 2002 must promote "appreciation of democratic values and patriotism." Board members even drafted definitions of "patriotism," "free enterprise," and what it meant to properly "appreciate" them. The board's attempt to apply these definitions has drawn national attention to Texas' textbook adoption process.[10]

Appreciation of these concepts required students "to think well of; to understand and enjoy; to recognize and to be grateful for" them. Texas' primary and secondary schools' textbooks focus less upon history than operant conditioning. These books deliver approved information to enhance performance upon an arbitrarily created examination designed for "educational progress." In this, they differ little from other states' texts. However, given Texas' recent atypical presence on the cutting edge of "education reform," they carry greater weight. An examination of the texts, then, might also illuminate current collective memory of LBJ and also offer insight into its future.[11]

Factually, the textbooks tend to get it right. With respect to Johnson there are surprisingly few factual errors, though at times one can still find some half-truths or the occasional fabrication. Omission and overstatement appear frequently. Some things seem to happen for no apparent reason. The adoption process and utilitarian rationale of social studies instills a deadly factuality. But history is more than facts: It is context, interpretation, analysis, and connectedness. It is *life*.

So what of Johnson? How do the textbooks treat him? What memories of him are worthy of preservation? What follows is a composite summary of LBJ's life to 1960 patched together from the approved texts:

> LBJ grew up "in the dry Texas Hill Country." He was not poor, but he was not rich either. But, the Hill Country was a poor region and he saw poverty first-hand. After college he taught school briefly in Cotulla. He then headed the National Youth Administration in Texas and "made sure the agency provided jobs fairly." After leaving the NYA, he won a seat in the House and later, the Senate. Once in the Senate, he helped pass the Civil Rights Act (1957), and in his spare time, he got Felix Longoria buried at Arlington National Cemetery. LBJ was a colorful fellow, "a stereotypical Texas politician—loud and slightly crude." By employing the "Treatment" he became an effective Senate leader. In 1960, John Kennedy "shocked" his supporters by taking LBJ as his running mate as a "strategic choice." He helped the ticket "where Kennedy was not particularly popular."[12]

As is often the case throughout the textbooks, what is omitted is probably more damning of the process than what remains. Several books are coy about the type of school Johnson worked in at Cotulla. Those that offer descriptors tend to use the term "poor." But, there's more there. Johnson worked at the "Mexican" school in Cotulla and pressed white teachers there to take themselves and their charges seriously. None of the texts that mention LBJ's stint with the National Youth Administration bothers to explain how anyone could doubt the fairness of New Deal relief employment. In fact, Johnson's fair hiring and pay policies for blacks and Tejanos ran counter to New Deal employment relief throughout the South. The controversial 1948 Senate race gets only a cursory mention, perhaps because space does not allow greater detail. Some of the texts acknowledge that the liability of JFK's Catholicism was offset by Johnson's presence on the 1960 Democratic ticket. Most avoid or shade this issue and LBJ's significance to Kennedy's narrow victory.[13]

Once Johnson becomes president, textbook coverage becomes much more extensive, though not always more illuminating. The critical event in the Johnson narrative always happens in Dallas. Seventh-grade texts glide through the assassination quickly. It happened. Johnson became president. Most high school American history texts hint at conspiracy. *The Americans* is the worst; a whole paragraph entitled "Unanswered Questions" describes investigations since the Warren Commission, implying that the case is still

FIG. 9.1. Lyndon Baines Johnson takes the oath of office aboard Air Force One at Dallas's Love Field on November 22, 1963, with Lady Bird Johnson (*left*) and Jacqueline Kennedy looking on. This photograph is the first and most enduring image of LBJ as president. Disputes about the assassination and persistent questions about what might have been had JFK lived continue to overshadow Johnson's accomplishments as president. Courtesy LBJ Library, photo 1A-1-WH63.

open. A feature blurb tells readers that "newly declassified information has added some weight to a body of evidence that JFK was shot from the front," though it cautions that "no information has yet . . . conclusively disprove[d]" the Warren Commission's findings. *America: Pathway to the Present* explains that "some investigations support the theory" of Oswald's involvement "in a larger conspiracy." "Many Americans continued to believe" in a conspiracy despite the Warren Commission's report, says *American Nation*.[14]

The assassination dramatizes why collective memory is not history and should not be allowed to become history. "Many Americans" believe a lot of things that are not verifiable, true, or based on sound evidence. The Warren Commission's findings have not been "conclusively" repudiated because they probably represent the soundest account of events. It is a mistake to devote too much space to a single moment in time, no matter how tragic, and opening the door to that moment's most darkly dubious interpretations compounds that mistake. For Americans of a certain age, Kennedy's death represents a watershed event, a loss of innocence, or so they say. However, will it matter as much at the fiftieth anniversary in 2013? History must offer perspective here and now. The Kennedy assassination began the Johnson presidency. Any poetic uncertainty hovering over November 22 brings into question everything Lyndon Johnson did afterward.

All the texts correctly acknowledge that LBJ seized the moment to drive existing antipoverty and civil rights initiatives through Congress. But the books often reduce the Texan to a functionary—only a signer of the Civil Rights (CRA) and Voting Rights (VRA) Acts. Johnson had developed a real revulsion to the injustices of segregation and disfranchisement. His discomfort emerged as early as his teaching career. Neither John nor Robert Kennedy saw civil rights as America's great moral challenge from 1961 to 1963. They discouraged protests, bargained with segregationists, and authorized a program of FBI surveillance and harassment of the movement. Johnson certainly was not perfect. He periodically used the word "nigger," and he had not quite defeated his own ingrained racial attitudes. LBJ was a recovering southerner. He acknowledged that the South and the nation had a problem, and he fought it. He never quite beat it within himself, but he struggled on because it was the right thing to do. But the ambiguity and complexity of Johnson the Civil Rights Crusader is not present in these texts—only a man sitting behind a big desk signing bills.[15]

In pushing, signing, and believing in civil rights legislation Johnson performed a redemptive service for his region and state. This essentially thankless task is also missing from the textbooks. Some seventh-grade Texas history students learn that "some members of Congress" opposed the CRA and VRA but do not learn why. Others learn even less from their texts. One might think the reasons for opposition to these landmarks of legislation would be self-evident, but modern students labor to chronologically sort segregation and the stegosaurus. Dealing fully with civil rights issues means acknowledging that something now considered to be basically good and just could once have engendered serious opposition. As Yvonne Frear's essay in this volume demonstrates, many students already dispute the relevance of the past. When student skepticism combines with a bureaucracy's determination to inculcate patriotism through instructional materials, the mix kills history, renders it irrelevant, and creates collective memory, or forgetfulness, in its place.[16]

Now much maligned as a facilitator of poverty rather than its sworn enemy, Lyndon Johnson's own preferred legacy also suffers in the textbooks. Usually, both the War on Poverty and Great Society (and they are distinct, though often conflated in textbooks) appear with key components detailed in short descriptive paragraphs. These descriptions offer limited evaluation of effectiveness but bandy about dollar amounts as though mid-1960s costs have any relevance to today's students. Several explain that Johnson anti-poverty programs nearly halved the nation's poverty rate, from 21 to 11 percent between 1962 and 1973. Specific real-life examples of how these programs changed lives are few. Instead, LBJ emerges as a free-spending liberal driving the nation into debt. No wonder opposition arose so quickly to this largesse. High taxes, the belief that government aid created dependency, and fear that LBJ's program strengthened federal government at the expense of the states drove the criticism. Race apparently had nothing to do with it, according to textbooks. True, principled conservatives did fret over these issues, but the conservative backlash did not arise simply from anger at taxation. Taxes had been higher under Kennedy and Eisenhower. Civil rights and antipoverty efforts blended easily in many minds. None of the texts ventures that possibility.[17]

The Great Society was "a vast program of social welfare laws," intones a seventh-grade text. No, there's more to it than that. Visit an octogenarian relative and wonder at what might account for her longevity. Drive a country road and notice the hawks perched from time to time on telephone poles. Go see a play with your kids at a children's theater. Watch *Sesame Street* and learn the alphabet. Marvel at how a seatbelt keeps heads a comfortable distance from the windshield during fender benders. Send in a monthly payment on a government-insured loan that got you through college. All have ties to the Great Society. Sociologist James W. Loewen criticized texts for nearly always portraying the government in a favorable light, crediting it with progress forced by outside activism. When dealing with the federal government since 1933, Texas' modern textbooks often do the opposite: minimizing or over-looking the good done by government.[18]

Perhaps as a byproduct, the textbook Johnson lacks a political identity. Based upon his record against poverty and segregation, LBJ as president governed as a liberal. Students rarely get the news that bluntly, however. In *The American Nation in the Modern Era* we get a hint. "If you look at my record, you would know that I am a Roosevelt New Dealer," it has Johnson proclaiming, along with, "As a matter of fact, John F. Kennedy was a little too conservative to suit my taste." One Texas history text muddles the matter, claiming that by 1968 conservatives supported more aggressive measures in Vietnam, but "liberals wanted to withdraw entirely." Was Lyndon Johnson not a liberal? Here modern conceptions about the political ideology most willing to use force intrude upon a much more ambiguous past. What is not ambiguous, however, is Vietnam's influence upon LBJ's place in public memory.[19]

Like the assassination, but for better reasons, Vietnam won't go away either. Seventh-grade textbooks focus on Texas, so the narrative only touches upon the conflict. LBJ is passive throughout. High school American history books offer greater depth. Some play "what if." What if Kennedy had not been killed? "Shortly before his death, Kennedy had announced his intent to withdraw" from Vietnam, claims *The Americans.* On the contrary, JFK merely authorized advisors in private to plan for a withdrawal after the 1964 elections. Publicly, he made cryptic statements about the conflict being South Vietnam's to "win or lose." The tricky question of what Kennedy might have done weighs heavily upon Johnson's reputation. Kennedy's skepticism about Vietnam grew through 1963. Lyndon Johnson came into office skeptical as well but listened too much to holdover advisors, mistrusted his own instincts, and tried to score political points with toughness. The result proved disastrous for him and for the nation.[20]

Lyndon Johnson unquestionably misled the public about the Gulf of Tonkin incident in August 1964, paving the way for escalation in the years following. It is a truly blameworthy moment, and Texas high schoolers get the truth from their textbooks. That is, if they ever get to that point in history class. In 2002, as the SBOE scrutinized new texts, *Dallas Morning News* education reporter Joshua Benton interviewed some Dallas area teachers and discovered that the recent past got short shrift in most classrooms. Teachers explained their difficulties in getting past World War II. Benton predicted the social studies segment of the eleventh-grade TAKS would change all that. The TAKS would "force" more recent history into the classroom, "including the Vietnam war." Unlike previous years, a Texas Education Agency social studies official pointed out, "administrators are paying a lot of attention to social studies now." Indeed, administrators started preparing much earlier. Some lamented this changing emphasis. An associate dean of Texas A&M University's education school admitted, "Folks sure don't make it to the end of the book, but they don't make it because they're doing some very good things." Benton himself complained that things that "get kids fired up" about history "could be lost" in an attempt to cover the whole curriculum.[21]

Benton's prediction might not ring true three years later. After all, as a Carrollton–Farmers Branch Independent School District administrator told

FIG. 9.2. An exhausted President Johnson listens to a tape-recorded message from his son-in-law, Charles Robb, a Marine officer in Vietnam, July 31, 1968. Vietnam destroyed Johnson's ambitions for reelection in 1968 and undermined his reform agenda. These largely self-inflicted wounds dog his reputation to the present day. Courtesy LBJ Library, photo B-1274-16.

the reporter, "What gets monitored, gets done." Students first encountered the eleventh-grade social studies TAKS in 2003. In principle, the examination follows the TEKS curriculum. Therefore, exposure to the entire curriculum alone will produce satisfactory scores or actual knowledge, if that's what the state had in mind. The 2003 exam posed fifty-five questions that should have covered all twenty-six TEKS competencies for U.S. history since 1877. Of those twenty-six, only seven involve history, and only two dealt with American history since 1933. One specifically addressed the civil rights movement; the other is a catchall for everything else. Given these parameters, one could guess that 1963–69 might largely escape notice. On a sample test provided by TEA, ten of fifty-five questions dealt with either pre-1877 U.S. history or world topics ranging from the Black Death to the Aswan Dam. While preparation would have been uneven across Texas' thousand-plus school districts early on, TAKS results ought to allow some measurement of success in imparting the TEKS. We will know soon enough. Those earliest test takers enter colleges and universities in 2004 and afterward.[22]

I remember hearing almost nothing about LBJ in either seventh-grade Texas history or high school American history. Our junior high class stopped at 1845, drew the Alamo for fifty points on an exam, and did a lot of "definitions." That is, we defined chapter vocabulary terms in writing after scanning the textbook for the "definition" of Mirabeau Lamar or *Adelsverein.* Our teacher focused mainly on his playbooks and periodically bellowed "shut up" when we hormone-addled youths got out of hand. In high school, my teacher knew her stuff and worked to present it well and relatively truthfully. Still, we never got to LBJ. Perhaps we didn't have time. In the early 1980s, the Vietnam misadventure and the death throes of Jim Crow remained painfully recent. The era of Lyndon Johnson may have simply been too controversial. But, I also grew up in a benighted time: before Ross Perot and House Bill 72, George W. Bush and TEKS.[23]

If controversy once kept LBJ out of classrooms, chronological distance should have allowed his return, and students should know more about him, particularly given modern "standards." So I polled more than 100 students in university U.S. history survey classes. All seemed to know that Johnson was president once, but beyond that most claimed to know nothing. The survey was not scientific, but impressionistic. Of 159 students aged seventeen to sixty-five, 72 claimed to know nothing of his accomplishments, to have heard nothing of him that made an impression. A slender majority had some idea of the man, some impression of him, or knew of some event in his presidency.[24]

Most who had a mental image of LBJ viewed him negatively. Based on photographs, one student decided that he "didn't appear friendly" and looked "stern and strict." Others echoed this sense; he did not look likable. Modern politicians joke with David Letterman, appear on *Saturday Night Live,* and answer questions about their underwear to become more likable. Johnson came from a political tradition that felt the nation's business was above that sort of thing, and consequently, he never adjusted well to television. Some students know about the "Treatment," with one describing a leader who "would eat really bad smelling food then get right in your face in order to intimidate." Another had heard that he liked to urinate on Secret Service agents. Other negative impressions came back describing LBJ as a "good old boy," "wishy-washy," or a stereotypical politician. One student remarked that his dad thought Johnson a "crook," and still another claimed his family knew one of the president's mistresses.

Some had better, yet more vague, impressions of Johnson. He was a "good man," a "concerned" leader, or "someone the people loved." Occasionally, someone indicated LBJ's support for civil rights as the basis for their positive view. Only seven of eighty-seven offering detailed responses mentioned this portion of Johnson's legacy, arguably his most redeeming achievement. Plenty of students had mistaken impressions, such as believing that Johnson had resigned to avoid impeachment and removal from office. Several thought him a Republican; still others believed him "conservative." One even described him as a "mild mannered" sort. Three associations dominated these students' knowledge of LBJ: November 22, 1963, Vietnam, and Dallas's LBJ Freeway.

The assassination happened in Texas, in a political climate so charged that Dallas's leaders urged citizens to behave themselves prior to Kennedy's visit. Conspiracy theories abound, and people still go for them. These theories often ensnare Vice President Johnson as instigator, accomplice, or dupe. In 2003, just before the fortieth anniversary of the assassination, an ABC News Poll showed that 65 percent of Americans believed that questions remained unanswered regarding the crime, and 70 percent believed in a conspiracy beyond Lee Harvey Oswald. A media ruckus ensued when the History Channel trotted out eleven hours of documentaries collectively styled "The Men Who Killed Kennedy." History Channel promotions of one episode, "The Guilty Men," tantalized with the hook, "The roots of the crime lie buried deep in the heart of Texas and revolve around Lyndon Baines Johnson and high powered supporters of the assassination who felt their fortunes threatened by JFK's presidency."[25]

Blood, Money & Power: How LBJ Killed JFK, a book by former Austin lawyer Barr McClellan, spawned the History Channel documentary. McClellan claimed that Dallas football entrepreneur Clint Murchison, former vice president Richard Nixon, FBI director J. Edgar Hoover, and Johnson met at Murchison's Dallas residence the night before the assassination to finalize plans to kill President Kennedy. Former Johnson aides Bill Moyers and Jack Valenti, among others, brought sufficient pressure to force the network to air a panel discussion of professional historians who then eviscerated McClellan's yarn. *Blood, Money & Power* is only the latest attempt by a Texan to link Johnson to practically every evil imaginable. Its refutation is cold comfort for those who want collective memory to resemble history. ABC's poll showed that Americans aged eighteen to thirty-four are even more likely than their elders to believe a conspiracy was behind JFK's assassination.[26]

Twenty-six of eighty-seven detailed responses in the student survey mentioned the assassination and/or LBJ's succeeding Kennedy. More students knew this fact than any policy initiative or personality trait. Antipoverty efforts, Medicare, and Job Corps received no mention at all. Instead, the assassination overshadows all else. A handful mentioned Johnson as a possible conspirator. Had the survey directly brought up the assassination, more students likely would have gone this direction. It disheartens one that they know so little else, a single moment in a decade of change and upheaval. Perhaps, with time, the circumstances of Lyndon Johnson's move to the White House will fade in relation to his own accomplishments, as with Theodore Roosevelt. But, frankly, William McKinley was no Jack Kennedy.[27]

American history survey students at least appear keenly interested in Vietnam. It is always late in the semester when class attendance counterintuitively tapers off before finals. Advance notice that there will be two days of lecture on Vietnam fills the classroom. It was their parents' (sometimes grandparents') war, and it frequently pops up online, in movies, television, books, and periodicals. Reminders of America's involvement in Southeast Asia abound in modern Texas. Dat Nguyen, once a Texas Aggie standout, recently retired from the Dallas Cowboys. Vietnamese and Cambodian immigrants have thriving communities within the state's major cities, and the Fox television network's *King of the Hill* features an upwardly mobile Laotian family as Hank Hill's next-door neighbors. Interestingly, the war's presence in our lives does not mean its deeper lessons register with today's college students. Vietnam helped ensure the insulation of most from the ongoing war in Iraq, a topic one almost never hears in students' hallway conversations. This protective insulation was Lyndon Johnson's (inadvertent) doing because his handling of the war helped doom the draft. Still, few students seem to have thought it out that far.

However, ask what LBJ did or what his greatest failure was, and Vietnam leaps easily to mind for many. Twenty students elaborated on their survey forms about America's longest war. Their responses ran the gamut from incorrect, to speculatively incorrect, to insightful or ambivalent. One student counted Johnson's ending Vietnam as his greatest achievement; still another cited simply "Vietnam" as an achievement. (One encounters students unaware that the United States lost the war.) One guessed that he might have made some good decisions with respect to Vietnam, but that student did not elaborate. While blaming LBJ for the Indochina morass, a student judged him poorly equipped to deal with the situation. Vietnam, for another, was part of fixing "Kennedy's mess." None blamed Johnson or any other politicians for America's defeat, an otherwise perennial complaint. Instead, a number criticized his determination to stay when the U.S. should have left. Winning and losing mattered less than having wasted the nation's resources.

Tied with Vietnam in students' minds is the Lyndon B. Johnson Freeway (I-635). The proximity of my own teaching institution, Texas A&M University–Commerce, to Dallas certainly accounts for this response. At first glance, one could dismiss these twenty responses as having a bit of fun with the professor. However, they came evenly distributed across seven survey sections with four different instructors in three different academic sessions. Reference to a freeway might be the testing reflex kicking in—desperation to put something remotely true in a blank space. Some insisted, in the absence of any other evidence, that Johnson could not have been "that bad" with such a large stretch of road named after him. For Dallas area residents younger than fifty, this notion likely makes perfect sense, viz President George Bush Turnpike.

Surprisingly, Dallas did not wait until Johnson died to name I-635 after him. In October 1961 a unanimous city council decision honored the vice president. Considering that a well-heeled right-wing mob attacked LBJ and Lady Bird at the Adolphus Hotel barely a year earlier, the timing is surprising. Bickering broke out in early 1962 about whether the naming was appropriate or even legal. Was it a federal or city responsibility? No bids had been made on right-of-way acquisition for the project. *Dallas Morning News* writer Mike Quinn remarked, "This is conservative territory and how they will like seeing LBJ's name at 8 A.M. on the way to work is anybody's guess." When the first $100 million length opened from Stemmons Freeway (I-35E) to Marsh Lane in March 1967, Johnson was president and American combat forces were bogged down in Vietnam. The opening attracted protestors. A northwest Dallas mothers' group came to demand the pedestrian walkway at Marsh Lane be covered completely to prevent accidents or childish tomfoolery. The event is now long forgotten, certainly for modern students, rather like everything else Lyndon Johnson did. It is the way of all flesh for politicians. You rise, have things named for you, and then you are forgotten except as an address. Lyndon B. Johnson, meet Marvin D. Love.[28]

Why is there such a gap between the Lyndon Johnson of history and the Lyndon Johnson of Texans' collective memory? Two answers offer themselves. First, modern Texans associate Lyndon Johnson with unpleasant aspects of state identity. Second, he does not fit well with the modern political climate.

"What is the ape to men?" Nietzsche's Zarathustra asked. "A laughing stock or a painful embarrassment" was the answer. Embarrassment over LBJ started early for some Texans. Larry McMurtry bemoaned Johnson in *In a Narrow Grave.* In that collection of essays on Texas published in 1968, McMurtry ridiculed Johnson's ranch, his boorishness, even his ears. Thirty years later, while writing a biography of Lady Bird, native Texan Jan Jarboe Russell listened to him on newly released tapes. The voice brought back memories of childhood. "Everything about him—his body, his ranch, his Lincolns, his bear hugs, but most of all his voice—seemed ridiculously out of proportion," she wrote. "Johnson was the last of the really big hicks." Texans respond the forty-third president's accent with a wink and a nod. We know the truth. Crawford ranch aside, George W. Bush is no agrarian. He's a city boy. Just like most of the rest of us.[29]

Modern Texas is urban and predominantly middle class. Johnson's style, his accent, and the things he cared about emerged from a very different Texas. His Texas was rural, backward, segregated, and poor. Many present-day Texans would rather not think on such things, even if they know about them. Modern automobile license plates feature the space shuttle, a cowboy, a cactus, and an oil rig. Where's the cotton? The lynching tree? The soup line? Before World War II, most Texans lived in a netherworld of barely getting by. Hope for better times and opportunities for getting out were few. From suburban living rooms it might all seem bucolic, like the ubiquitous Hill Country landscape over the sofa. But it was hell. Past poverty and past realities might be too big an embarrassment, and perhaps Johnson himself, his style and his accent, represents too painful a reminder. These might explain many modern Texans' ambivalence toward Johnson.

And, of course, Texas has changed politically as well. The change first emerged in the last two decades of LBJ's career. In 1952 and 1956, Texas went for Republican Dwight Eisenhower despite Senator Johnson's best efforts. A Republican, John Tower, replaced him in the U.S. Senate in 1961. In 1971, former Texas governor John Connally joined the Nixon administration as treasury secretary, and a few months after LBJ died in 1973, his former protégé switched parties. Today, Texas state government, its congressional delegation, and its electorate are solidly Republican. Lyndon Johnson doesn't fit Texas anymore. He was a Democrat; he had liberal inclinations throughout his career. He believed government could do good for citizens. He tried to expand economic opportunity so more Americans could enjoy life within the Great American Middle Class. He spoke of social justice and racial equality. And he acted upon his words. Many twenty-first century Texans often complacently see poverty and racism as things of the past or of overactive imaginations. They don't want to hear Lyndon's voice anymore.

Some will question this essay's focus upon a single man. After all, haven't historians finished with the Great Man as the center of history? This essay is a project in collective memory—the residue that remains in the public mind after historical truth has either been forgotten or rejected. For such a project, the Great Man is a particularly apt figure of study. He provides a benchmark from which to examine the overall durability of historical truth. If that is true, then history had better watch out. Texans increasingly have trouble remembering so obvious a figure as Lyndon Baines Johnson.

NOTES

1. Press release, "President Lyndon B. Johnson's State Funeral and Burial," June 2004, Lyndon Baines Johnson Library and Museum, Austin, Tex. (hereafter LBJ Library). This short press release was prepared to answer questions on Johnson's funeral in light of the 2004 services for Ronald Reagan.

2. Marshall Frady, "Cooling Off with LBJ," *Harper's* (June 1969): 66; Judith Benson, ed., "Remembering LBJ," *Texas Monthly* 4 (Jan. 1976): 86; Paul Burka, "The Man Who Saved LBJ," *Texas Monthly* 28 (Aug. 2000): 118, 136–37, all three articles contained in Vertical File, LBJ Library. Renewed attention to LBJ among biographers has produced two multivolume works. Recent historical debate revolves around these contrasting understandings. Robert A. Caro's *The Years of Lyndon Johnson: The Path to Power* (New York: Knopf, 1982), *Means of Ascent* (New York: Knopf, 1990), and *Master of the Senate* (New York: Knopf, 2002), take Johnson's story as far as 1957. Historian Robert Dallek's *Lone Star Rising: Lyndon Johnson and His Times, 1907–1960* (New York: Oxford University Press, 1991), and *Flawed Giant: Lyndon B. Johnson, 1960–1973* (New York: Oxford University Press, 1998), offer a scholarly if less minutely detailed an examination of Johnson's life. Caro's first two volumes generated acclaim and controversy, with critics arguing that the journalist so plainly disliked LBJ that vitriol oozed from his work. *Path to Power* shows a young Johnson without redeeming characteristics conniving his way into power by selling his favors to George and Herman Brown. *Means of Ascent* centered upon the controversial 1948 Senate race with Coke Stevenson. To highlight Johnson's perfidy, Caro recast Stevenson as a heroic man on a horse. *Master of the Senate* tempered its treatment of LBJ somewhat, concentrating upon his role in crafting and passing the Civil Rights Act of 1957. Dallek's two volumes present a much different portrait of Johnson. A man of great complexity of motive and method, Dallek's Johnson has flaws, plenty of them. But he is also capable of great vision and compassion, executed with uncanny political skill and tenacity. In the end, Vietnam brings the man and his better angels down, jeopardizing his legacy.

3. Gus Sánchez and David Shaffer, NPS rangers, interview by the author, Stonewall, Tex., July 27, 2004.

4. David Shaffer, NPS ranger, tour narration, Stonewall, Tex., July 27, 2004.

5. Ibid.

6. Johnson's first race for U.S. Senate came in a special election in 1941. He made the run-off but was defeated by then-governor W. Lee "Pappy" O'Daniel amid suspicious circumstances. In 1948, three major candidates contended for the Democratic U.S. Senate nomination: Johnson, former governor Coke Stevenson, and George Peddy. The first primary eliminated Peddy, and in the run-off most suspected that Stevenson had the advantage. Certainly both sides engaged in illegalities, but LBJ managed to eke out a close win. Recent studies suggest that Stevenson's own supporters did not turn out, making the vote close enough that the election could be stolen. See Dale Baum and James L. Haley, "Lyndon Johnson's Victory in the 1948 Senate Race: A Reappraisal," *Political Science Quarterly* 109, no. 4 (Fall 1994): 595–602; Burka, "The Man Who Saved LBJ." A thirty-minute film shown at the LBJ Library detailing Johnson's life describes a "suspiciously lopsided" trend for W. Lee O'Daniel in the last-minute vote counting in 1941; it also describes a "suspiciously lopsided" trend in favor of LBJ in 1948. The parallelism is probably deliberate, but also instructive.

7. U.S. Department of the Interior, National Park Service, National Park Statistics, Lyndon B. Johnson NHP, accessed at www2.nature.nps.gov/NPstats/dspAnnualVisits.cfm (accessed Jan. 19, 2005); Sánchez and Shaffer interview, July 27, 2004; National Archives and Records Administration, Lyndon Baines Johnson Library, Visitors Statistics, in Robert Hicks to author, facsimile, Jan. 19, 2005.

8. Peter Seixas, Peter Stearns, and Sam Wineburg, "History Memory, Research, and the Schools: A Report on the Pittsburgh Conference," *AHA Perspectives* 37, no. 3 (Mar. 1999), www.historians.org/perspectives/1999/9903/9903TEC2.cfm (accessed Nov. 1, 2004).

9. Regarding the advent of social studies and professional historians see Peter Novick, *That Noble Dream: The "Objectivity Question" and the American Historical Profession* (Cambridge: Cambridge University Press, 1988), 185–93. Novick argues that history was not "completely displaced" by social studies. However, modern school history texts do show marked symptoms of infection nonetheless.

10. Texas State Board of Education, "Proclamation 2000 of the State Board of Education, Advertising Bids on Instructional Materials, March, 2002," www.tea.state.tx.us. If you are unclear on the definition of patriotism or free enterprise, you may consult this document for clarification. Materials relating to the SBOE and textbook approval may be found on the same Texas Education Agency website.

11. In 2002, Texas' 4.1 million students needed $345 million worth of social studies texts for 2003. Texas' influence upon the publishing industry may be academically unsound, but it is an economic reality. Given that what plays in Texas will play in Peoria, one can assume that Texas' U.S. history textbooks and their failings influence social studies teachers across the nation (*Christian Science Monitor,* July 22, 2002). Ironically, a budget crisis forced the Texas legislature to cancel the 2003 social studies textbook order.

12. Quotations come from the following books in this order (grade levels are indicated by MS for middle school and HS for high school): Gerald Danzer, J. Jorge Klor de Alva, Larry S. Krieger, Louis E. Wilson, and Nancy Woloch, *The Americans: Reconstruction to the Twenty-first Century,* Texas edition (Dallas: McDougal Littell, 2003) (HS), 686; T. R. Fehrenbach, Stanley Siegel, and David Crowley, *Lone Star: The Story of Texas* (Glenview, Ill.: Prentice Hall, 2003) (MS), 415; Paul Boyer and Sterling Stuckey, *The American Nation in the Modern Era,* Texas edition (Austin, Tex.: Holt, Rinehart and Winston, 2003) (HS), 639, 624. Johnson's early life and career can also be found at the following locations in these texts: Andrew Cayton, Elizabeth Israel Perry, Linda Reed, and Allan M. Winkler, *America: Pathway to the Present,* Texas edition (Glenview, Ill.: Prentice Hall, 2003) (HS), 744–45; Joyce Appleby, Alan Brinkley, Albert Broussard, James McPherson, and Donald Ritchie, *The American Republic,* Texas edition (New York: Glencoe McGraw-Hill, 2003) (HS), 733; Adrian Anderson, Ralph Wooster,

Arnoldo De León, William Hardt, and Ruthe Winegarten, *Texas and Texans* (New York: Glencoe McGraw-Hill, 2003) (MS), 505–506, 527, 543–44; Larry Willoughby, *Texas* (Austin, Tex.: Holt, Rinehart and Winston, 2003) (MS), 579; Rodolfo Rocha, Ann Fears Crawford, Archie P. McDonald, and Gary Elbow, *Celebrating Texas: Honoring the Past, Building the Future* (Dallas: McDougal Littell, 2003) (MS), 483, 520–21.

13. Julie Leininger Pycior, *LBJ and Mexican Americans: The Paradox of Power* (Austin: University of Texas Press, 1997), 7–22; Monroe Billington, "Lyndon Johnson and Blacks: The Early Years," *Journal of Negro History* 62 (Jan. 1977): 28–31; Robert Dallek, *An Unfinished Life: John F. Kennedy, 1917–1963* (Boston: Little, Brown, 2003), 267–70.

14. Danzer et al., *The Americans,* 682–83; Cayton et al., *America,* 740–41; Boyer and Stuckey, *The American Nation in the Modern Era,* 636–37.

15. Boyer and Stuckey (*The American Nation in the Modern Era,* 656) and Appleby et al. (*The American Republic,* 755–56) do contrast Johnson's determination on civil rights with that of the Kennedys. However, no book deals effectively with LBJ's apparently sincere belief in the cause itself. Cayton et al. (*America,* 718–19) and Danzer et al. (*The Americans,* 711–14) present Johnson mainly as executor of Kennedy's wishes. The seventh-grade texts reduce him primarily to a passive signer of legislation (Fehrenbach et al., *Lone Star,* 438; Anderson et al., *Texas and Texans,* 560–62; Willoughby, *Texas,* 592; Rocha et al., *Celebrating Texas,* 520–21).

16. Quote from Fehrenbach et al., *Lone Star,* 438. Regarding the evolution of LBJ's racial views see Dallek, *Lone Star Rising,* 519–20.

17. General coverage of the War on Poverty and Great Society: Danzer et al., *The Americans,* 689–93; Cayton et al., *America,* 745–50; Boyer and Stuckey, *The American Nation in the Modern Era,* 639–44; Appleby et al., *The American Republic,* 734–38. Seventh-grade Texas history books are most likely to degenerate into listing without analysis: Fehrenbach et al., *Lone Star,* 434; Anderson et al., *Texas and Texans,* 560; Willoughby, *Texas,* 588; Rocha et al., *Celebrating Texas,* 521.

18. Fehrenbach et al., *Lone Star,* 434; James W. Loewen, *Lies My Teacher Told Me: Everything Your American History Textbook Got Wrong* (New York: Touchstone, 1996), 215–16.

19. Boyer and Stuckey, *The American Nation in the Modern Era,* 639; Rocha et al., *Celebrating Texas,* 521.

20. Rocha et al., *Celebrating Texas,* 521; Willoughby, *Texas,* 588–89; Anderson et al., *Texas and Texans,* 562; Fehrenbach et al., *Lone Star,* 448–49; Danzer et al., *The Americans,* 734; Dallek, *An Unfinished Life,* 668–77. Dallek argues that Kennedy might have eventually withdrawn from the Southeast Asian conflict but cautions that "a plan was not a commitment" (Dallek, *An Unfinished Life,* 668). On LBJ's skepticism about Vietnam, see Dallek, *Flawed Giant,* 239–41.

21. Joshua Benton, "Recent History Often a Mystery to Students," *Dallas Morning News,* May 14, 2002. In *Lies My Teacher Told Me* James Loewen gives a national perspective on this same problem in a chapter called "Down the Memory Hole: The Disappearance of the Recent Past" (239–53). For the high school texts' coverage of the Gulf of Tonkin incident, see Danzer et al., *The Americans,* 734–35; Cayton et al., *America,* 796; Boyer and Stuckey, *The American Nation in the Modern Era,* 712; Appleby et al., *The American Republic,* 778–79.

22. Benton, "Recent History Often a Mystery"; Texas Administrative Code, Title 19, part II, chap. 113, Texas Essential Knowledge and Skills for Social Studies, § 113.32, High School. Sample TAKS online at www.tea.state.tx.us/student.assessment/resources/release/taks/2003 (Jan. 20, 2005). The 2003 administration showed that 78 percent of all students tested at or above the recommended passing standard. However, the SBOE altered the passing standard for 2003 to two standard errors of measurement below the recommended standard, raising the pass rate to 90 percent. In bureaucratese, students know the material because they passed

the exam and have obviously assimilated American history since 1877. That the examination provided by TEA does not thoroughly or meaningfully cover the period is of no consequence. See Texas Education Agency, "2003–2004 Academic Excellence Indicator System [AEIS] Report," available at the TEA website, but keep in mind that the AEIS report is somewhat misleading since it does not disclose adjustment of the passing standard to two standard errors of measurement; to see those figures in bar graph form, see www.tea.state.tx.us/student .assessment/taks/standards/710003_handout3.pdf.

23. In 1984, Gov. Mark White appointed a blue-ribbon panel headed by Dallas billionaire H. Ross Perot to investigate Texas' public schools and suggest reforms. House Bill 72 encapsulated most of these proposals. The controversial legislation mandated a variety of reforms, of which the most (in)famous was "no-pass, no-play." Under HB 72, the minimum passing grade increased to 70, and students who failed to meet the standard in any course became ineligible for extracurricular activities until they received a passing grade, meaning that a student who received a failing grade would be benched for a minimum of six weeks. The hue and cry from HB 72 helped drive White from office and led to the watering down of "no-pass, no play" under Gov. George W. Bush in 1995.

24. Students had no information other than the survey's purpose. They responded based on what they had learned *prior* to their university studies, either in school or from hearing the views of others. All were students in HIS 122 at Texas A&M University–Commerce during the summer and fall of 2004 and spring of 2005. Of the total sample, 128 respondents were traditional-age students, seventeen to twenty-two; 26 ranged in age from twenty-three to forty; the remaining 5 were older than forty. I am grateful to colleagues Kevin Delange, Robert Kisselburgh, and Frank von Neuhaus for their assistance.

25. ABC News Poll, "Who Killed JFK?" Nov. 9, 2003, www.abcnews.go.com/sections/ wnt/US/JFK_poll_031116.html (accessed Jan. 16, 2005); Bruce Weber, "Moyers and Others Want History Channel Inquiry over Film That Accuses Johnson," *New York Times,* Feb. 5, 2004. Former president Gerald Ford, the only surviving member of the Warren Commission, and his successor Jimmy Carter joined the protest (Howard Kurtz, "LBJ Aides Push History Channel for Probe of Show," *Washington Post,* Feb. 5, 2004).

26. Weber, "Moyers and Others Want History Channel Inquiry." One of the earliest published Johnson smears was J. Evetts Haley's *A Texan Looks at Lyndon: A Study in Illegitimate Power* (Canyon, Tex.: Palo Duro Press, 1964). Haley's accusations are in retrospect rather tame, claiming that Oswald, as an "agent" of "international communism," had killed Kennedy and that LBJ created the Warren Commission to cover for the liberals whose tolerance of communism had brought the country to such a pass. Instead, liberals used the assassination as a cudgel to attack conservatives in Texas and elsewhere. The commission's creation prevented the truth from coming out and created in turn public skepticism about its findings (Haley, *A Texan Looks at Lyndon,* 205–10). See also ABC News Poll, "Who Killed JFK?" Nov. 9, 2003. The historians on the panel were Robert Dallek, Stanley Kutler, and Thomas Sugrue. The History Channel issued an apology to aggrieved parties for the broadcast (Bruce Weber, "History Channel Apologizes," *New York Times,* Apr. 7, 2004). Dallek, foremost scholarly biographer of both Kennedy and Johnson, dismisses conspiracy theories and attributes them to the public's inability to accept the notion of a "nobody" killing the president (see Dallek, *An Unfinished Life,* 699–700, 701).

27. The survey question was: "Whether you are old enough to remember Johnson or not, what do you know or think you know about the type of person he was?" The survey was brief, open-ended, and intended to draw the broadest array of responses without seeking to directly elicit correct ones.

28. "LBJ Road Approved by City Council," *Dallas Morning News,* Oct. 4, 1961; Mike

Quinn, "LBJ Road Folk: 'Drive on the Right,' *Dallas Morning News,* Mar. 14, 1962; Maryln Schwartz, "Praise, Protest Greet Freeway," *Dallas Morning News,* Mar. 24, 1967. Dallas's habit of naming freeways after people befuddles newcomers and visitors. Marvin D. Love Freeway is U.S. Highway 67. Love is so obscure he's not even in the *Handbook of Texas.*

29. Friedrich Nietzsche, *Thus Spake Zarathustra,* trans. R. J. Hollingdale (New York: Penguin, 1982), 41–42; Larry McMurtry, *In a Narrow Grave: Essays on Texas* (Albuquerque: University of New Mexico Press, 1987), xviii, 71–72, 84, 129 (these pages represent a sampling of references to Johnson); Jan Jarboe Russell, "LBJ Sounds Off: The Fulminations and Bluster of the 36th President," *Slate,* Aug. 24, 1997, www.slate.com/id/2460 (Jan. 15, 2005).

Chapter 10

MISSION STATEMENT: THE ALAMO AND THE FALLACY OF HISTORICAL ACCURACY IN EPIC FILMMAKING

DON GRAHAM

The Alamo is the oldest Texas story that keeps getting retold for mass audiences in that form of national memory known as the movies. Yet despite repeated versions from the earliest days of filmmaking into the twenty-first century, no Alamo film has ever captured the national imagination to the extent that other ventures in historical epic movie-making have. Hollywood historical epics appeal to their audience not only because they entertain but also because they resonate with the collective memory of that audience, *Gone with the Wind* and *Red River* being cases in point. Each sold a version of America that Americans wanted to believe in. Such films reinforce shared values and a shared identity. Makers of Alamo movies have tried in various ways and with varying degrees of success to address this vast, amorphous national audience.

Indeed, the Alamo's epic proportions appealed to Hollywood even before there was a Hollywood.

The first effort to film the drama of the old mission and its famous battle was *The Immortal Alamo,* shot on location in San Antonio in 1911. All that remains from that effort are still photographs. Four years later came the second effort, *Martyrs of the Alamo.* Directed by W. Christy Cabanne and influenced by D. W. Griffith, it projected the familiar narrative in quite broad strokes of racist rhetoric, and it reinforced white supremacy at the zenith of Jim Crow. It looked and felt a lot like *The Birth of a Nation* (1915) and in fact exploited the connection with a subtitle, *The Birth of Texas.* Re-released in the 1920s under the title *The Birth of Texas,* the film sparked boycotts by Mexican Americans angry at its obvious racial stereotyping. None of the early Alamo films, however, enjoyed the popularity or impact of Griffith's opus, the first successful film to dramatize history for mass audiences. Griffith's epic thrilled viewers nationwide, and President Woodrow Wilson, who sponsored a screening of *The Birth of a Nation* in the White House, is reputed to have said, "This is history written in lightning." From then on, many Americans preferred their history in the dark instead of on the page. Today, many seem not to care about American history in any form.[1] Another silent-era Alamo film was the first to bring Davy Crockett front and center. Anthony Xydias's production of *With Davy Crockett at the Fall of the Alamo* (1926) portrayed Crockett as a slaveholder. The Alamo continued to draw the attention of filmmakers in the succeeding decades. In *Heroes of the Alamo* (1937), also produced by Xydias, the story line focused on two unusual figures: Almaron and Susanna Dickinson, the only Anglo married couple at the Alamo. On the night before the final assault, the Dickinsons and other Alamo defenders sing a "darkie" version of "The Yellow Rose of Texas" ("She's the sweetest rose of color/that Texas ever knew"). Probably few who saw the film were bothered, if they knew, that the song was anachronistic, that it had not been written until 1858. In the 1950s there were three Alamo movies. In *The Man from the Alamo,* Glenn Ford, wearing western cowboy garb, played Moses Rose as a hero. In the wildly popular Disney version, *Davy Crockett: King of the Wild Frontier* (1955), Fess Parker enshrined the coonskin cap image in every child's heart. In *The Last Command* (1956), filmed in Texas at Brackettville, Sterling Hayden gave a wooden-Indian portrayal of Jim Bowie.

John Wayne's paean to patriotism, *The Alamo,* released in 1960, became the landmark film by which to measure any future Alamo ventures. Although Wayne's publicity machine cranked out story after story about how accurate and authentic the film was, moviegoers and critics had a field day spotting errors. The geography was undeniably a bit wobbly: In the film the Alamo is located alongside the Rio Grande instead of the San Antonio River and Goliad is said to be north of San Antonio instead of southeast. But surely Frank Thompson, the author of numerous works on Alamo films and popular culture, overstated the case when he claimed that "not a word, not a deed, not an image corresponds with historical reality in any way, shape or form." However, according to Wayne, his version made plenty of sense. "I think it's the greatest piece of folklore ever brought down through history, and folklore has always been the most successful medium for motion pictures," he said in an interview at the time.[2]

The Alamo films of the 1950s came at the height of the cold war, when Americans presumably needed to be reminded of the stark contrasts between freedom-loving Americans and freedom-hating foreign despots. Historical epics like these do not create collective memory so much as they reflect and make use of existing memory. They also, in the memory, acquire the kind of mythical misrepresentation of the facts that history also acquires. Here is how journalist Jan Jarboe Russell misremembers Wayne's film: "In the 1960 movie about the Alamo, Laurence Harvey, who played Travis, drew a line in the dust the night before the Alamo fell. . . . That's the legend." In point of fact, in the film Harvey's Travis *does not draw a line* in the dust. Wayne declined to replicate this famous and undocumented gesture. But he gets blamed for following the legend anyway.[3]

A COALITION OF THE WILLING

Like those films of the cold war, the latest incarnation of the Alamo story, Disney's Buena Vista production of *The Alamo* (2004) has its roots in national, even global politics, specifically, the aftermath of September 11, 2001. Responding to the national crisis, Disney executive Michael Eisner declared that the film would "capture the post–Sept. 11 surge in patriotism." Whereas the cold war seems at times like a static weather front that lasted for decades, 9/11 produced a different kind of war, a different kind of weather, and with the speed and immediacy of media and Internet communications, the formation of a solid consensus of public opinion seems to have been more difficult to maintain. Patriotism in the wake of 9/11 could shift to splintered factionalism very quickly, and did, so that a film capturing the "surge in patriotism" would have to be brought out very quickly indeed. And speed of delivery was definitely not the means by which *The Alamo* would reach the public.[4]

The story of how the newest Alamo film got made is a long and complicated one and begins before the catastrophic events that catapulted it to the point of production. It begins with screenwriter Leslie Bohem, whose credits include such high-minded efforts as *A Nightmare on Elm Street 5: The Dream Child* and *Dante's Peak*. In the mid-1990s Bohem, at one of the annual meetings of the Austin Film Festival, had a conversation with Randall Wallace, author of the script for *Braveheart*. Wallace had driven down to San Antonio to visit the Alamo but said he did not intend to do anything with the story, whereupon Bohem decided that he would. He spent four years on the project, relying closely upon historical sources.[5]

The idea for a new Alamo movie was hardly a new one. According to Frank Thompson, there were "a lot of Alamo projects floating around Hollywood." Novelist Stephen Harrigan (*The Gates of the Alamo* [2000]) has made the same point in conversations with me. But the falling World Trade Center towers lent a new urgency to the idea of a movie about Americans taking a stand. The new century's newest disaster called for a patriotic response. In May 2002, director Ron Howard and Texas governor Rick Perry held a joint news conference to announce that a new Alamo film was in the works.[6]

Disney brought in John Sayles, a distinguished screenwriter and director whose film *Lone Star* had addressed racial issues in present-day South Texas, to rework Bohem's script. Sayles's version went to great lengths to be historically accurate. This effort is the beginning of one of the major problems that would plague the project from beginning to end: an obsession with historical accuracy. Sayles's script has been described by those who read it as either (1) brilliant or (2) unfilmable. In any case it was much too long to be a usable script. Disney hired Stephen Gaghan (*Traffic, Phone Booth*) to rewrite Sayles's version.[7]

Early on, Howard got an inkling of what might lie in store for him for having taken on the Alamo project. In a satirical open letter to Ron (Howard) and John (Sayles) published in *Texas Monthly* early in 2002, the author (myself) explained where the Alamo was, how to recognize the colors of authentic Tex-Mex food (brown and yellow as compared to the blues and greens of New Mexico and California), what the weather had been like during that fateful late February and early March of 1836 (nasty), and so on, all the salient atmospherics needed for an Alamo undertaking such as the one the team of Howard and producer Brian Glaser had set for themselves.[8]

More importantly, Howard received a thorough review of the problems an Alamo film might face when he came to Austin in May 2002 to meet with a group of historians and Alamo experts for a brainstorming session that lasted well into the night. The historians present for that meeting were Stephen L. Hardin, Alan Huffines, Frank Thompson, Jesús de la Teja, James Crisp, Andrés Tijerina, and Bruce Winders; the novelist Stephen Harrigan was also present. Apparently no one kept a record of the meeting, but Thompson has said that he and the other historians "urged Howard for as accurate a retelling as possible."[9]

According to press accounts, Howard wanted to shoot the new Alamo film in the style of Sam Peckinpah, the Goya of western film violence. Peckinpah's bloody masterpiece *The Wild Bunch* (1969) set the gold standard for last-ditch heroics and is still, emotionally and cinematically, a very powerful rendering of violence and sacrifice for a moral principle. But to follow Peckinpah's exemplary model, Howard would need about $125 million and the film would get an R rating. Howard's own standing had been recently enhanced by an Academy Award for directing *A Beautiful Mind,* and he intended to cast Russell Crowe in the role of Sam Houston. In retrospect, this move would seem to have been a mistake. Crowe possessed the star power and the ability to carry the film and, perhaps more importantly, had the international clout to bring in overseas viewers when the film was released abroad—often a profitable undertaking even when a film has failed domestically. But the figure of Sam Houston was never going to be important in a film about the Alamo because Houston was peripheral—he was not there— and Crowe in such a role would have been wasted.[10]

Differences between Howard and Disney soon surfaced, however. Disney balked at the cost, the violence, and the R rating and went ahead with new plans. In July 2002 Howard left the project to direct *The Missing,* an offbeat, interesting, and underrated western. Crowe had already left in favor of *Master and Commander: The Far Side of the World,* another all-male historical adventure film.

With Howard gone, Disney reduced the budget for *Alamo,* as it was still being called, by $50 million; the target audience was changed to get the tamer PG-13 rating; and the studio tagged John Lee Hancock, a native Texan, to rewrite the script and direct. Hancock, who grew up in Texas City, had made his mark writing screenplays (*A Perfect World, Midnight in the Garden of Good and Evil*). His only previous directing credit was *The Rookie,* a small, family-oriented film starring Dennis Quaid that had proven a surprise hit for Disney.[11]

EMBEDDED HISTORIANS

As a Texan, Hancock knew from the first how contentious a reception a poorly researched Alamo movie—or a well-researched one, for that matter—would likely receive in Texas. A responsibility to history was very much on Hancock's mind when I spoke to him on October 2, 2003, as he was putting the final touches on the film. The film was scheduled to premiere on Christmas Day—a standard big opening for a big-budget film, geared toward holiday box-office income and the upcoming Academy Awards in 2004. Things would change drastically before the month was out, but nobody knew any differently then. Hancock, however, certainly knew what the stakes were:

"I think that when you're doing something like this, when it's a story as important as it is to me anyway, you're always going to feel the burden of history."[12]

A director undertaking to tell the story of the Alamo faces daunting problems. The story already has built-in expectations because it has been filmed so many times and because there has been so much written about the Alamo. Starting out, Hancock was acutely aware of the mass of material: "So much has been written in the last thirty years that I really wasn't privy to, I read as much as I could, and like every other kid in Texas took how many years of Texas history, and knew all of that but there had been so much written in the last thirty years that I really hadn't read and catching up on that I said I'm just gonna find the most interesting stories." The reading continued right through the making of the film, and by the end the production office crew had assembled a small library of Alamo volumes, some twenty-one titles in all, ranging from the comic-book format of Jack Jackson's *The Alamo: An Epic Told from Both Sides* to Walter Lord's *A Time to Stand: The Epic of the Alamo.* Faced with all of the conflicting versions and arguments, Hancock held to his own convictions: "I think you have an obligation not just to whatever it is that historians currently believe—or can agree on. That's a small cross-section, by the way. What they believe and what they can agree on are two different circles and they don't intersect by much."[13]

Hancock's strategy involved him more fully than any previous director of an Alamo film with the direct and continuous input of Texas historians. He drew upon their expertise to try to get the facts right and, one has to believe, in the process, to co-opt and defuse criticism from these same historians. One has to wonder, however, when the opinions of historians ever affected the success or failure of a film.

At the beginning Hancock called upon Jesús F. de la Teja (*A Revolution Remembered: The Memoirs and Selected Correspondence of Juan N. Seguín*) and Andrés Tijerina (*Tejano Empire: Life on the South Texas Ranchos*) to review the script to verify the Mexican background. Two other historians, Stephen L. Hardin (*Texian Iliad*) and Alan Huffines (*Blood of Noble Men: The Alamo Siege & Battle*), played the most important advising roles. In September 2002, Hancock hired the two to serve as film historians and advisors. Thus they were actually embedded in the production. On most days of shooting, they were on the set. Shooting ran for 101 days, from January to June 2003, and consumed more than a million feet of film.[14]

The duties of the embeds ranged from vetting the script to giving on-the-ground advice. They turned in a seventy-five-page document listing recommendations. Huffines said of their function, "We sit behind John Lee and look at what the camera sees and try to find mistakes." Sometimes Huffines was astride a horse. In one scene the two historians suggested that Travis would have doffed his hat at a family he passed by on the road; in another they suggested that a particular flag should be flying in that scene. They helped choreograph the two battles (Alamo, San Jacinto).[15]

The striving for historical accuracy extended to the kinds of detail that few viewers would be able to distinguish—linguistic variations among the members of Santa Anna's army, for example. Hancock sought the expertise of Arnold Ventu, a University of Texas professor of Spanish and Portuguese, to get it right because, Hancock explained, "It's not just period Spanish, it's the caste system being in place, several different types of Spanish being spoken"—and he also brought in a "Cherokee specialist to monitor our Cherokee." In the finished film the non-English dialogue was rendered in subtitles, though it is hard to imagine anybody except an expert like Ventu noticing the subtle nuances of caste and class.[16]

Sometimes there were necessary compromises. The decision to film the Battle of San Jacinto at Lost Pines Nature Ranch near Bastrop instead of where the battle actually took place prompted Hardin to observe, "Does it look exactly like San Jacinto? No. San Jacinto is a swamp. We have all this dust here—but it looks great on screen." Huffines was equally enthusiastic: "People will be agog when they see this." He said it was the best nineteenth-century combat ever seen in a movie.[17]

On the question of the embeds, Hancock stated in the press that he was pleased with the results of their contributions. "It worked out really well," Hancock said. "They were great." But he added, "They get down into tiny details. The military manuals of the day—I certainly don't carry them around." In my October 2, 2003, interview with Hancock, he pointed to an inevitable difference of opinion between filmmaker and historian: "There's always going to be those moments when they point out, gosh, that guy has the wrong shoes on, and you tell them, well, he's about a thousand people back and no one will ever see that."[18]

Reports in the press before, during, and after filming emphasized the concern for historical accuracy; it became the mantra of the movie, and at times it is as though everybody connected with the film was working from the same talking points, as though it were a political campaign. Daniel Orlandi, the costume designer, stressed the authenticity of such details as the very buttons on the uniforms of the Mexican *soldados:* "We had to have buttons, why not do the right ones? It has to be right. It's pointless to do a movie like this unless it looks right." And so, he said, "Uniform buttons were forged from castings on the original uniforms."[19]

And always there were historians to affirm the overriding concept of historical accuracy. In March 2004, after a pre-screening of the film for the press, Bruce Winders, curator of the Alamo, declared that "it's probably the most accurate portrayal of the Alamo story to date. That's not saying it couldn't be more accurate, but it goes far beyond the John Wayne film."[20]

One of the things that just about everybody agreed upon on was that the set, built on Reimer Ranch near Dripping Springs, Texas, was the most accurate Alamo set ever constructed. Designer Michael Corinblith, another Texan who visited the Alamo when he was a child, oversaw the construction of the Alamo and environs on a site covering fifty-one acres, reputed to be the largest set ever built in the United States. (Alamo films, like the state, thrive on superlatives.) Harrigan, among others, praised Corinblith's scrupulous devotion to detail: "The set is almost brick for brick, San Antonio de Bexar in 1836." The set won admiration from nearly everybody who visited it, and Frank Thompson stated, "I think we all want to be able to visit it once a year for the rest of our lives."[21]

The fixation on the set's accuracy is a kind of metaphor for the preoccupation with historical accuracy. In a good film, the set may not be all that important. Take, for example, the Coliseum and Rome as represented by digital enhancement in *Gladiator.* Everybody can see that the sets are fakes, but the acting and story are so engrossing that nobody cares. In fact, one can interpret the transparently fake set in another way, as being a metaphor for the idea of Rome, not the actual Rome, and go on from there to considerations of the necessary artifice of any film purporting to be set in ancient Rome as inherently metaphorical rather than literal. The filmmakers and those who still defend *The Alamo* fetishized the realistic-looking set into the major element of the film.

BOOTS ON THE GROUND

To make a film about the Alamo, a director has to make choices. In the October 2, 2003, interview I asked Hancock about three tough ones concerning boots on the ground: the line in the sand, the yellow Rose of Texas (Moses Rose, not the song), and the death of Davy Crockett. "How do I answer this and still be smart?" he laughed. Then he added, "I don't have Rose in it. And I don't have Travis drawing the line." With regard to Travis, Hancock explained that the "Travis arc"—that is, the character's development, his "learning curve"—is to "let him become his own kind of man and a hero and a leader and has little to do with the heroic gesture."[22]

The question of Crockett's demise is one of the touchiest subjects for a contemporary director to deal with. Hancock did not want to talk about it, partly, it seems, in order not to give away that part of the plot. Said Hancock, "I guess when you talk about the line in the sand and Crockett's execution, I guess the best answer would be, I know those are hot-button issues and I hope that people come to the theater to see for themselves." In the interview with me Hancock only mentioned Crockett's "execution" in passing.[23]

The title page of the shooting script reads, "ALAMO by Les Bohem, John Sayles, Stephen Gaghan; current draft by John Lee Hancock, January 27, 2002—shooting script." The original title, *Alamo,* seems to have been modeled on such one-word hits as *Titanic* and *Gladiator,* but somewhere along the line it was decided to change the title to *The Alamo.* The reason, according to Hancock, was that in ordinary speech, everybody always put the article in front of the Alamo anyway.

I read the script before the film was released, and with regard to how Davy died, a burning question in Alamo circles, the film follows exactly what is in the script, which in turn follows the revisionist staging of a surrender and execution taken from José Enrique de la Peña's controversial *With Santa Anna in Texas.* According to de la Peña, Crockett and a handful of other defenders surrendered, only to be executed shortly thereafter on direct orders from Santa Anna.

The script's handling of Crockett's death scene brings together two of the major characters of the story in direct conflict. First, there is Santa Anna himself (played by Emilio Echevarría). Hancock wanted to make Santa Anna more complex though certainly no less brutal than in previous films about the Alamo. As Hancock explained to me, "If you're going to have an antagonist like Santa Anna, it's not very interesting if he just stomps around and plays dictator; that's kind of more cartoonish, and I needed to kind of understand politically what was going on, and the more I read about the coterie of generals around him the more fascinating the whole Texas campaign became to me from the Mexican side." Hancock used one of these officers, General Manuel Castrillón, to "ask the hard questions of Santa Anna" so that the dictator won't come off as "just a one-note kill-'em-all" monster.[24]

Crockett's brief confrontation with Santa Anna reveals a kind of postmodern awareness on Crockett's part, the knowledge that he is in many respects the prisoner of his own fame, that history is in fact forcing him to become the legend depicted in such popular media as *The Lion of the West* and the Crockett almanacs.

EXIT STRATEGY

The Alamo defenders had no exit strategy. Indeed, historians cannot even agree on whether the death-to-the-end defense of the Alamo was the right course of action or not. In an article on the Alamo for *Texas Monthly* historian H. W. Brands declared the Alamo "an exercise in martial folly" and stated that "the defense of the Alamo was woefully misguided." On the other hand, Thomas Ricks Lindley in *Alamo Traces: New Evidence and New Conclusions* (2003) has strongly defended the necessity of the strategy, arguing that the Alamo defenders always believed that help was on the way. The men at the mission would have been cut to pieces if they had tried to escape, except perhaps one at a time, and that was an implausible plan. So they stayed. They were not stupid or even foolhardy, but they were incredulous that reinforcements did not arrive in sufficient number. Small units dribbled in during the course of the buildup and the siege, but Travis, Bowie, and Crockett and all the rest were counting on major support from Col. James W. Fannin, who had nearly four hundred men under his command at Goliad. Although Fannin started to come to the aid of the Alamo, he turned back, discouraged by difficulties in crossing the Guadalupe River. He would remain in Goliad, where he and his command would be wiped out later, after the fall of the Alamo, on Santa Anna's orders, on Palm Sunday, March 27, 1836.[25]

Then there was Houston, the most paradoxical figure of the Texas Revolution. Houston could have rallied men and brought them to the Alamo if he had wanted to. But Houston never believed in the necessity of a defense of the Alamo. Indeed, it was he who had ordered James Bowie, on January 17, 1836, to blow it up and withdraw into the Anglo settlements in southeast Texas, part of Houston's strategy of luring Santa Anna's army closer to the border with the United States. When Bowie arrived at the Alamo, he changed his mind and, in a memorable turn of phrase, stated that "we will rather die in these ditches than give it up to the enemy." When Houston realized that his order had been countermanded, first by Bowie, then by Travis, he slipped off to East Texas on a dilatory mission to make a peace treaty with the already peaceful Cherokees. What he actually did for a month is anybody's guess.[26]

The conviction held by Travis and others in the Alamo that help was on the way seems to have remained firm right up until the last day or two of the thirteen-day siege, when Travis tried to surrender. He knew by then that unless reinforcements arrived the game was up. But Fannin wasn't coming, nor was anybody else. The last reinforcing batch of defenders, from Gonzales, arrived on March 3. Here is more news from Lindley's book: The Gonzales defenders have always been thought to number 32 volunteers who arrived earlier, on March 1. But Lindley has found evidence that there was a second Gonzales contingent, on March 3, that they numbered 52, and that it was none other than Crockett himself who left the Alamo, rode to Gonzales, and returned with the new men. (Here is an example of new facts being made known even as the Alamo movie was already completed, testifying further to the difficulty, if not downright impossibility, of ever getting everything absolutely right.) Lindley, by the way, ups the total of Alamo defenders to approximately 250, considerably more than the usual number of 187. In a story full of if's—if Fannin had brought his 400 and if Houston had brought hundreds more, the Alamo might have turned out quite differently. In any event Travis and his men lost the Alamo only to achieve immortality in the battle that never dies.[27]

Hancock's *The Alamo* does not end at the fall of the old mission, as most Alamo movies do. Here, and at the opening of the film, Hancock sought to broaden and enlarge the story of the Alamo, to explain how the men came to be at the old mission, especially the major figures, to present the political contexts of Texas independence, and to dramatize what happened following the fall of the garrison.

For the men who came to the Alamo, Texas offered, in Hancock's interpretation, a second chance. Travis fled debts and a wife and child, Bowie had a distinctly unsavory background as slave trader and frontier brawler, and Crockett wanted a fresh start in a new place far from Washington. The Alamo gave them all a shot at redemption, though they each would have much preferred to walk away from it victorious to fight another day.

To Hancock, the Alamo itself was "not just a building but an idea and representative of a lot of things, to Texans. . . . I think of it as not only a building, a fortress, a shrine, but also an idea." For if his movie were going to succeed, it must finally, Hancock believed, "capture some of the drama and emotion" of that long-ago event, not just convey a preoccupation with period authenticity. In the end it would matter less whether a Mexican soldier's uniform was 100 percent accurate than whether the emotion of the assault on the fortress would stir the audience. What "happened over the course of a month" in history may be compressed into one scene in the film. The large story—the epic—gets told as a "character drama." It's both a "big story and a small story at the same time."[28]

The difficulties of pulling the film together became a matter of public speculation when Disney, on October 28, 2003, announced its exit strategy from the original plan to release the film during the holiday season. Now, said Disney, the film would open in April. The kitschy headline in *Variety* was "Mouse Pushes 'Alamo' to Spring." In the film industry delaying a release is usually a sign of trouble, and the move did not bode well for the future according to most professional movie people. But there are always exceptions—*Titanic,* after all, had been delayed several times and went on to enjoy phenomenal box-office success—maybe the same would be true for *The Alamo.* But nobody really believed that except John Lee Hancock's coalition of the willing. In a press release Hancock offered this explanation: "The Alamo has, from a very early age, been the most important story of my life, so when I agreed to rewrite and direct the film, I set the bar very high, both for myself and the finished product. Post production on an epic ensemble piece takes time and no deadline, no prestige release date, no awards season is worth more to me than the movie being fantastic."[29]

Reactions to the changing of the release date were plentiful and almost all negative. Bob Polunsky, a movie critic in San Antonio, speculated that "maybe somebody caught them in an error that was really going to get somebody upset, and they have to redo quite a bit of the movie. Six months is a long time." Other commentary had more to do with filmmaking than with historical accuracy. The obsession with historical accuracy seems to have been of all-consuming interest chiefly in Texas and almost exclusively among "Alamo-heads," as Steve Harrigan calls them, and history buffs.[30]

One of the signs of real trouble with the film trickled out into the daily press from Harry Knowles's influential website "Ain't It Cool." According to Knowles, responses to an early screening used phrases such as "overly arty," "badly directed, shot and edited mess," and "clichéd and melodramatic" to describe the film. Dennis Quaid was pronounced to be "just pathetic." Another response from an early screening complained that the movie was "overly long and that the characters were forced."[31]

Knowles himself had some solid ideas about what the film ought to be. He pointed out, "You can tell the story of the Alamo from the Mexican or the Texan side, but you can't do both at the same time. You have nobody to root for." Knowles also intriguingly argued that the film should have been shot entirely inside the Alamo as a siege movie with intense psychological drama. In his view Santa Anna should never even be seen at all but only represented by the sound of a bugle.[32]

Knowles speaks for the mainstream audience, the people who buy the tickets and want to be entertained. They are the audience that made *Braveheart* a blockbuster hit. Scarcely anybody who saw that film had ever heard of William Wallace, but they knew what freedom was and they knew tyranny and injustice when they saw it on screen. In that film, there was certainly somebody to root for, and there was a revenge motif as well—for the rape and murder of Wallace's wife. Few in the audience knew anything about that period of Scottish history, but the themes were so powerfully and effectively presented that the audience "got" it. History may try to tell both sides of the story, though much of early triumphalist Texas history does not, but film has different goals such as entertaining, instilling patriotism, and creating emotional "truths" if not literal ones. Or it may do the opposite, as in a Michael Moore opus, and deride patriotism, but film lives or dies by its ability to marshal the emotions of its audiences in favor of one side or another. *The Alamo* 2004 waffled around on every side and refused, unlike the actual defenders of the Alamo, to take a stand. Thus only those historians who care deeply about the accuracy of the Mexican uniforms really loved the film. Their number is not large.

Interest in what the delay of the film might mean remained a matter for press speculation, with articles continuing to appear in the months from December onward. Billy Bob Thornton, among others associated with the film, did his best to counter the doubts and conventional wisdom—that delay meant disaster. Thornton said April was a better time to release the film because nobody wants to watch "189 people get slaughtered at the Alamo on Christmas Day." Perhaps April, the month of Christian sacrifice, would prove to be more profitable. And it would, for another film about another sacrifice: *The Passion of the Christ*.[33]

The embedded historians did their bit, too, to put a good face on the delay. On March 6, 2004, a month before the release of the film, Frank Thompson presided at a session titled "John Lee Hancock's Alamo Movie" at the annual meeting of the Texas State Historical Association, held in Austin. Michael Corinblith, the set designer, addressed the question of "Building Bexar: The Art and Research of Production." Alan Huffines's topic was "Getting It Right: The Challenges of a Technical Advisor." Stephen Hardin's was "Historical Authenticity in a Movie? The Impossible Role of the Historical Advisor." To a packed audience, the panel members testified that the film was going to be big. Alan Huffines stated that a few weeks earlier he had seen the final cut and that it was "great."[34]

Huffines insisted that there were no false scenes, only rearrangements. He stressed the accuracy of the uniforms, especially of the Mexican army. Uniforms and flags seem to have been the most compelling points of interest for the historians. Hardin pondered the conflict between historical accuracy and cinematic effectiveness and lamented that many of the costumes were not right, as compared to the perfection of the costuming in *Master and Commander: The Far Side of the World*. Everybody praised Corinblith's set for its unprecedented accuracy, and Corinblith said that his responsibility was for everything on the screen "that's not breathing." Frank Thompson ridiculed the inaccuracies in Wayne's *The Alamo*. The panel members were unified in their admiration for Hancock's film and for its unprecedented accuracy. Clearly they staked everything on that main principle—historical fidelity.

One thing they all lamented was that a five-minute scene between Sam Houston and Chief Bowles, the Cherokee leader who was a good friend of Houston's, had been eliminated. Filmed entirely in Cherokee (with subtitles) and starring a Cherokee actor, Wes Studi, as Chief Bowles, this scene's being cut was met with universal sadness by members of the panel. Indeed, producer Mark Johnson said in the press that Hancock himself was "near tears" when he had to tell Studi that his role had been completely dropped from the film.[35]

Yet from a cinematic viewpoint, it is hard to imagine what possible value such a scene could have. In fact, as would prove to be the case with most viewers, all the scenes involving Sam Houston could have been cut. The Houston story is peripheral to the Alamo—not only was Houston not there but he opposed the battle; part of the time he was off in East Texas pow-wowing with his Cherokee friends, and he was probably drinking heavily much of the time. The coda of the victory at San Jacinto seems just more wasted film time as well, though including it was doubtless meant to show that things were not so gloomy after all. The filmmakers seemingly bowed to the collective memory of their audience, a memory that (they believed) required the battle to be cast in heroic—and thus victorious—terms. They probably modeled the coda after the Disney epic, *Pearl Harbor,* a big, ponderous, unwatchable, youth-oriented hit that tacked on a retaliatory U.S. air raid to show those youngsters in the audience that America would go on to win World War II in spite of the disaster at Pearl Harbor.

There are some who would posit a chasm between history and historical cinema: History does not demand a happy ending, the argument goes, but popular entertainment does. I don't think this is altogether true. *The Wild Bunch* has a quiet coda but hardly a happy ending. All the characters we care about the most are dead at the end. *Braveheart* ends with the disembowelment and death of Mel Gibson's character. Even *Gone with the Wind* can hardly be said to end happily, or *Titanic,* the most successful moneymaker in the history of cinema. Audiences can take less than happy endings if the artistry of everything—plot, acting, emotion, and so forth—is strong enough.

OLVIDATE DEL ALAMO

Another audience sector that Hancock had to worry about was that of minorities, namely, Mexican American/Hispanic/Latino audiences. In his interview with me, Hancock stated the problem in this manner: "If you're making a movie about the Alamo, then it's a racist movie." Anticipating criticism on this score, he said, "We tried to make it as historically correct and dramatically correct as we could. . . . Our actors from Mexico and Spain and stuff certainly felt like it was more than fair, and I was happy to hear that." But, he conceded, "Everybody is going to have their ax to grind, and I know I'm right in the cross-hairs."[36]

In San Antonio on March 6, 2004, the anniversary of the day the real Alamo fell, the *Express-News* carried an article dealing with the paintings of Ramon Vásquez y Sánchez. One of his works is titled *Olvidate del Alamo,* or "Forget the Alamo." The artist explained his view thus: "It's all this negativity that Mexicanos feel about the Alamo." And he added, "The truth is, these people were defending their country." Another indication of how the film would likely be received by Mexican American audiences can be seen in the views expressed by Dagoberto Gilb, a creative writing professor and writer at Texas State University. According to Gilb, who had not seen the film, "For Mexican-Americans, the Alamo, even at its best, is about 'them,' not us, about how heroic 'they' are, in the land where we both still live. Celebrating the victory against Mexico is, for us, like someone reveling in the story of our drunk, abusive stepfather."[37]

The memory of the Alamo in the Mexican American community is never going to be the same as that of the Anglo community. The histories are different; ergo, the memories are, too. The same thing occurs with regard to the War of 1846–48, which goes by different names in the two countries.

There is one other demographic harbinger that should be mentioned—the likely tepid response of women to the film's subject matter. Discounting the Daughters of the Republic of Texas, the Alamo story does not hold much interest for many women. The best expression of this viewpoint appeared in a *New York Times* piece written by journalist Mimi Swartz in November 2003, months before the film was released. To Swartz, who grew up in San Antonio, "It [the Alamo] seemed to stand for everything I hated about San Antonio, most notably its fixation on a glorious, valorous past for which I had no use." Also, she pointed out, "part of the problem was that the Alamo story was mostly a boys' story. . . . Such heroics were lost on me."[38]

APRIL IS THE CRUELEST MONTH

After premiering in San Antonio on March 27, 2004, the film finally opened nationwide on April 9, 2004. Reviews were mixed but predominantly negative. On the positive side, William Arnold in a Seattle publication called it a "no nonsense western epic that zips us through the famous siege and the birth of Texas with style, verve and impressive historical accuracy." Paul Clinton, for CNN, rated it a "brilliant epic" and "that rare breed: an epic that's also a character study." John Anderson of *Newsday* praised it as a "grandiose but historically savvy account of Crockett's Last Stand," calling Crockett the "country's first prisoner of his own celebrity." Bruce Westbrook, in the *Houston Chronicle,* concluded that the film might be "flawed, but it tells a tale that still has the power to stir our souls." In the *Austin American-Statesman,* which had run numerous pre-release pieces on the film, reviewer Chris Garcia pronounced the film "surprisingly good," calling it "a jangly and compelling mix of legend, hype and historical record." Garcia also thought the star of the film was "newbie Patrick Wilson as Travis."[39]

What solace that might be found in those reviews was not enough to overcome a chorus of negative ones. Liam Lacey in *The Globe and Mail Review* called it a "dry history lesson that plays like a worthy movie-of-the-week, or fat-budgeted historical pageant." Like many other reviewers, he concluded that the "sole character of the group who possesses any pizzazz is Davy Crockett." Robert Wilonsky, writing in the *Dallas Observer,* assessed the film's entirety: "The result is something that feels very much like an overachieving made-for-TV movie—a history lesson dolled up like an action movie, with the action relegated to the final third, and even then, the battle is over before it really begins." He went on to say, "We like our heroes larger-than-life in

the movies; here, they shrink to the point of invisibility." But what bothered him the most was the tack-on of the victory at San Jacinto, turning the
Alamo story into a happy ending. The San Jacinto coda, incidentally, had
first been used in *Martyrs of the Alamo,* back in 1915.[40]

The always anticipated *New York Times* review did not bring good news
either. Manohla Dargis, in a review with the inevitable title, "Forget This
'Alamo,'" wrote that "the filmmakers never make the case why we should
remember the Alamo, especially now." She also roundly criticized two of the
lead performances, noting that "[Jason] Patric and especially [Dennis]
Quaid . . . affect the kind of grim determination often found in laxative com-
mercials." As if one were not enough, a second review in the *Times* on the
same day was equally dismissive. Elvis Mitchell pronounced it an "oppres-
sively solemn film" and one in which the audience is "left with figures who
are less than mythic but also less than human." Mitchell went on to make a
point about the movie's fidelity to period history: "This movie is awash in
minutiae like the gilt-edged bone china that the dandy Santa Anna . . . uses
for his coffee while fashioning his battle plan." In sum, the film was "more of
a schematic success than a dramatic one," in his view.[41]

In another inevitably titled review, "Houston, We Have a Problem," Geoff
Pevere of the *Toronto Star* tried to establish a connection between the film
and the present day, writing that "this somber, conscience-stricken re-staging
of *The Alamo* acquires added metaphorical baggage for corresponding with
the apparent collapse of American consensus over the war in Iraq." Finding
the characters "stricken with doubt," he made an important point about the
film's meaning: "It's a movie that ultimately can't convincingly get behind the
idea of sacrifice—the very idea that transformed the story of the Alamo from
history to myth in the first place."[42]

In a review in the *San Francisco Chronicle* Carla Mayer reached a conclusion similar to that of Pevere. She stated the case very clearly: "The brave
men who fought and perished at the Alamo believed fervently in their cause.
For 'The Alamo' to work, the audience must believe as well. That never
really happens." She also recognized a point made in different ways in several
reviews: "'The Alamo' covers all the bases, but in doing so dilutes its message
of sacrifice for a greater good."[43]

Whatever the message that *The Alamo* was supposed to convey, it was
not coming through. David Edelstein in *Slate* declared the film "a definitive
Hollywood muddle," but then seemed to reverse himself, writing, "This is a
careful and reasonably nuanced retelling, its canvas broad, its heroes imper-
fect, its key minor—at times even dirge like, in a post-9/11 sort of way." The

reviewer for the *Wall Street Journal* criticized both message and structure in unmistakable terms, calling the film a "long, muddled version" and a "misshapen semi-spectacle" with an "ill-conceived coda." The only thing that stuck in the critic's memory was "a sort of 19th century battle of the bands" with Crockett playing a fiddle to counterpoint the "ominous drum rolls." "The scene," the critic said, "may be pure Hollywood hokum, but here's to hokum when it provides some desperately needed flamboyance in a production that's at war with its earnest, rambling self."[44]

$22 MILLION

The film earned $22 million, enough to qualify it, in popular rhetoric, as a "bomb." The bad news happened fast. On the first weekend it finished in fourth place, earning $9.1 million compared with *The Passion of the Christ,* which earned $15.2 in its seventh week. Something called *Hellboy* came in second for the second week. Perhaps most cruel of all, the comedy *Johnson Family Vacation* defeated *The Alamo,* earning $9.4 for the first week. That film cost about $20 million compared with the $100 million plus spent making *The Alamo*. Gitesh Pandya, analyst for www.boxofficeguru.com, pointed to three reasons for the poor showing: the subject matter, lack of star power, and the staying power of *The Passion of the Christ*. Said Pandya, "The core audience for 'The Alamo' is basically adult men." Perhaps this statement should be amended to say that the core audience is the membership of the Texas State Historical Association and the Daughters of the Republic of Texas, teachers of Texas history (including those in the public schools [including coaches] and colleges and universities), and history buffs around the state. It is not a demographic to die for. In three weeks the film grossed $19.7 million, compared to *Kill Bill: Vol. 2,* which took in $25.1 million in its first weekend. By May 13, *The Alamo's* earnings had climbed to $22 million. The press was now reporting that the film had cost, including publicity, $120 million.[45]

The press was also offering a menu of reasons why, as one headline put it, "Armies of U.S. Moviegoers Fail to Storm the Alamo." According to well-known film maven Leonard Maltin, such a project was doomed from the beginning: "The younger demographic already doesn't like the western," Maltin wrote. "It has no interest in history, especially American history. Today's moviegoers don't care about 'The Alamo.' Even if Disney had made a great movie, they would have faced the same problem. It's less to do with the quality of the film than a lack of appeal of its subject. If they'd had a real box office star, perhaps that would have helped." Screenwriter Larry Gross (*Geronimo*) weighed in with a colorful and devastating explanation: "'The Alamo' is a feathered fish. It's neither grittily revisionist nor is it popcorn heroic. It's high-quality TV. It's not a David Lean epic-size visual spectacle."[46]

Patrick Beach, writing in the *Austin American-Statesman,* attributed the film's problems to a lack of romance, the slaughter inherent in the material, and the tack-on of San Jacinto. Beach also made the interesting observation that "Hancock's sin appears to be attempted fidelity to what little is certain about the Alamo."[47]

Brendan Miniter offered another view in the *Wall Street Journal,* arguing that the main problem was inherent in the concept of "inclusiveness." According to Miniter, "Nearly all points of view are understood to have an equal claim on the truth, and heroism is but an invention of either side. What 'inclusive' history often lacks is the moral judgment that a reading of the record demands."[48]

Perhaps not surprisingly, attempts to market the film in Mexico also failed. Isabel Valdés, a member of PepsiCo's Latino advisory board, stated some obvious reasons: "'The Alamo' is such an open wound among American Hispanics and comes at a time of growing resentment against immigrants that one has to wonder what they were thinking."[49]

Both the producer and the director offered their own opinions as to why the film failed. Mark Johnson, producer of *The Alamo,* found the reason for the failure in the audience: "Disney believed in this movie, and gave us the time to get it right. But the American audience doesn't have much interest in history."[50]

John Lee Hancock, on the other hand, blamed the media: "The national press was miraculously able to convince the left that this was a film that was pro-Bush, pro-war in Iraq, and convince the right that it was anti-American."[51]

At the end of 2004 when all the totals were in, *The Alamo's* $22 million stood in sharp contrast with the top three box-office leaders: *Shrek 2* ($437 million), *Spider-Man 2* ($373 million), and *The Passion of the Christ* ($370 million). Compared with historical epics released in 2004, *The Alamo* again fared badly. *Troy* (riding on the strength of Brad Pitt's buff body) earned $133 million, and even Oliver Stone's much maligned *Alexander* managed to pull in $12 million more than *The Alamo.* There were far fewer defenders of the film than there were defenders at the real Alamo in 1836. One who stood firm was Stephen Harrigan. "I like the movie," he told the *Austin American-Statesman.* At year's end the only person who remembered *The Alamo* as the best film of the year was Austin actor/author Turk Pipkin. Perhaps it should be pointed out that Pipkin appears on screen for a few moments in the film.[52]

LAST STAND

One arena for fighting and refighting *The Alamo* is the release of the DVD edition. DVDs are an interesting new form in the process of memory. They tell us what the filmmakers thought they were doing. In the case of critical and commercial failures like *The Alamo,* they provide exculpatory evidence; they tell us, if we care to attend, what we missed, what we did not understand, why, in short, we were wrong. They are the newest form built around the proposition, familiar in literary criticism, of the Intentional Fallacy. Put briefly, the Intentional Fallacy is the mistake made by the reader, in this case the viewer, of believing what the teller tells us rather than what the tale itself reveals. If given a chance to explain their intentions, all artists are great, because they can tell us, as our students like to, what they *were trying to do.* It is a chance for the artist to justify the purity of his or her intentions, to rectify a failure, to recuperate misunderstood or unperceived greatness, to explain something that the film was not able to. The author of every failed novel would love the opportunity to explain what he or she was trying to do.

And so it is that on the DVD edition of *The Alamo* (2004), most of the principal architects of the film are on hand to talk about it. Apart from the actors, all of whom formulate perfectly plausible statements of their intentions, we hear from director John Lee Hancock, set director Michael Corinblith, costume designer Daniel Orlandi, and the familiar circle of historically minded insiders—Stephen Hardin, Alan Huffines, Frank Thompson, Stephen Harrigan, Paul Andrew Hutton, and Bruce Winders—all testifying to the film's historical accuracy. Of special interest, perhaps, are scenes not seen in the film, ones deleted in the editing process. Most of the six minutes and twenty-six seconds of such scenes deal with Santa Anna's "wedding." Hancock muses upon their virtues and, in some but not every instance, laments their absence, but any disinterested viewer would be hard-pressed to say how the scenes could possibly add anything to the film. They seem leaden and beside the point. Of special interest is what is not here: the scene beloved of the Texas historians, the one with Sam Houston conducting, in Cherokee, a meeting with his friend Chief Bowles. Its absence is especially puzzling in light of Hancock's statement in April 2004: "It's fantastic and I'll put it on the DVD."[53]

The most significant commentaries on the film's failure occurred in the pages of the magazine *True West* and on the website, www.thealamofilm.com, where a small group of hard-core fans and non-fans of the film continue to battle it out. In July 2004 Allen Barra asked in an article in *True West,* "Why Did *The Alamo* Flop?" His answers ranged over a wide spectrum of reasons. "First off," he wrote, "there were no male action stars and no hot babes, so there goes the action and sex-comedy crowds." He also suggested that the culture of film reviewing had something to do with the negative press reception, arguing that if a famous director such as Martin Scorsese had made the film (e.g., *Gangs of New York*), it would have received more respectful notices. Other reasons offered by Barra are that the early promotional statements about post-9/11 patriotism seemed self-serving and that no Alamo film had ever really succeeded so why expect this one to (the earlier Disney film being an exception because of all the interest in Davy Crockett created by the TV series). But Barra's most interesting reason has to do with what he considers the failure of certain demographic groups to support the film, that is, "older men and perhaps a few women who know something about the history and lore of the subject." Instead of coming to the defense of *The Alamo,* "Alamo nerds" attacked the film, finding fault with all the little details in the film that were not historically accurate. "Once again," Barra concluded, "we see that curious phenomenon where the most historically accurate film on a subject is the one most brutally hammered by those you'd expect to appreciate it the most."[54]

But Barra's thoughtful article had nothing like the effect of an earlier piece on *The Alamo* in *True West.* Back in May 2004, in an interview with Alan Huffines, the editors of *True West* asked the film's military advisor questions about several phases of the film. The one reply of Huffines's that seems most problematic is this one: "There are no invented characters or scenes in the movie." In August 2004 *True West* published a response from Thomas Ricks Lindley, who retorted, "All the scenes in the movie were invented by writers." Lindley also pointed out in his letter that "Travis was the garrison's voice" but that in the film his voice had been replaced by Crockett's. Here is how Lindley described Billy Bob Thornton's portrayal of Crockett: "a scared rabbit, afraid to fight, afraid to kill and afraid of his public image. What a crock of bull." Lindley threw down the gauntlet in his closing words, declaring the 2004 effort "the worst Alamo film ever made."[55]

Lindley was the first to challenge *The Alamo* on its most defended grounds, those of historical accuracy. Indeed, Lindley scoffed at the frequent claims made on its behalf as being the most historically accurate of all the

Alamo films ever made. On July 17, 2004, Lindley's letter was posted on thealamofilm.com, and the fight took on new proportions.[56]

On August 10, 2004, Lindley defended himself from various negative responses from "Alamo heads" writing to the website. The piece is very long, in two parts, and runs to several thousand words. Lindley objected to the film on both structural/aesthetic grounds and on factual ones as well. He felt, for example, that the "pacing was too slow" and the point of view too split up to be effective. He also faulted the excessive use of flashback scenes, which he labeled as "lazy writing." But most of the critique is taken up by a point-by-point rebuttal of the claim of historical accuracy. Here are just a few examples: "Crockett and Houston did not meet in Washington in early 1835"; "Houston could not have offered Crockett land for serving in the Texas militia at that time. Land bounties did not exist until November"; "Seguin did not speak English"; "Travis was not against drinking. He was against drinking to excess." The list of such rebuttals is quite lengthy and detailed. He spends a good deal of time pointing out errors in the geographical representation of San Antonio and notes a number of discrepancies in the Alamo set itself. He even claims that the Mexican uniforms, the sine qua non of the Alamo advisors, "are not right."[57]

On larger issues, Lindley is equally forceful. He criticizes Travis's big speech in the film as an "example of moral relativism, a PC philosophical fad on university campuses today—that nothing is wrong—that all values are equal." Lindley, who advised Steve Harrigan on historical details for Harrigan's novel *The Gates of the Alamo,* cites numerous other historians who doubt the veracity of Crockett's death by execution.[58]

Finally, in a capsule statement that indicates his overall argument with Hancock and the embeds, Lindley states, "We don't remember the Alamo defenders because they were all too human. We remember and honor them because all of them, not just Travis, Bowie and Crockett, were by their actions during those 13 days, bigger than life."[59]

The next month, on August 15, thealamofilm.com posted a letter from none other than John Lee Hancock himself. Clearly stung by what Lindley had said, Hancock did not defend the film but instead launched an ad hominem attack against Lindley. Hancock began by saying how "incensed" he was by the criticism of Huffines and Hardin. Then he claims that Lindley's "feelings were hurt" when he was not invited to the "round table" discussion (of May 2002). Calling Lindley "a pretty sad fellow," Hancock complains that alone among all of those who visited the set, only Lindley was guilty of "rudely" chastising Michael Corinblith's set design. He accuses Lindley of attacking the film at every opportunity, of trashing the script in a Dallas newspaper, and of being the only historian who was not a "gentleman."[60]

POST-MORTEM

They could never have gotten it right. Consider, for example, the memorable (and made-up) scene of Billy Bob Thornton as Houston playing a fiddle atop a wall of the Alamo. The tune he is fiddling is the "Mockingbird Quick Step," a version of "Listen to the Mockingbird." The problem, however, is that the song was not composed until 1855 (and is thus as anachronistic as "The Yellow Rose of Texas" in the 1937 Alamo movie)—exhibiting once again the danger of using historical veracity as the main yardstick of merit. And then there is this disturbing side note: The tune was used as a theme song by the Three Stooges.

Also there is this problem: Maybe Crockett did not die by being executed; maybe de la Peña's account is fraudulent. Some Alamo historians, including most notably Thomas Lindley, believe so. And new documents from the republic period keep turning up, the latest being a "Lecture on Texas," which appeared in the *New York Daily Tribune,* November 11, 1842, and was reported on in the *Dallas Morning News* of February 6, 2005. In this talk by a San Jacinto veteran named James Hazard Perry, Crockett's death is related as having occurred outside the walls, on an attempt to dash toward the city of San Antonio. According to Perry, Davy went down fighting, not being executed after surrendering. Perry, incidentally, wanted to lay to rest the "story sometimes circulated that Crockett was still living in the mines of Mexico." At least we can all let that one go.[61]

And yet even as this document surfaced, a new argument in defense of the authenticity of the de la Peña document, James E. Crisp's *Sleuthing the Alamo: Davy Crockett's Last Stand and Other Mysteries of the Texas Revolution,* was published in February 2005. The battle over who fell when, where, and how at the Alamo goes on with no signs of a consensus being reached anytime soon.[62]

But in the film Crockett dies à la de la Peña, and in doing so he is given a strange last utterance: "I'm a screamer." This line recalls the stage Crockett in the play *The Lion of the West.* Early in the film, Crockett attends a performance of the play and sees "himself" enacted on stage by a bad actor wearing a huge coonskin cap (in fact, it looks as if he is wearing the whole 'coon). The actor gives a typical speech in the tradition of southwestern humor and says, among other things, "I'm a screamer." One can sense the pleasure of the screenwriter(s) in tying those lines together as part of the postmodern, self-conscious, ironic mode at the end. But one problem for some viewers, for me anyway, is that the line plays like real-life comedy: "I'm a screamer," uttered by an actor formerly married to Angelina Jolie.

Obviously, if the cinematic illusion had been established that Crockett is Crockett and not just Billy Bob Thornton playing him, then the line would have a better chance of working—perhaps. But the whole feel of Thornton and all the actors, and especially the background, group figures, is that of a reenactment, which is among the lowest forms of human activity.

The Alamo 2004 is more of an expensive reenactment than a movie. The makers, starting with Ron Howard, should never have sought advice or suggestions from Texas historians because the historians were going to harp on historical accuracy from beginning to end. The filmmakers should have just made a movie. And that movie should have been about something that moviegoers could connect with: whether patriotism or pathos, tragedy or melodrama. In some respects *The Alamo* was like another recent failure in the historical epic genre, the Civil War opus *Gods and Generals* (2003), which, at four hours, seemed to last nearly as long as the war. It too was unfocused, divided in its loyalties, and marred by an obsession with the accuracy of re-creating battles. It too felt at times like a reenactment.

There is an insuperable difference, of course, between history—what happened—and a movie, which is a dramatic interpretation of what happened, or what the filmmaker believes happened, or, as in the case of Oliver Stone's *JFK,* what the conspiracy-minded director wishes had happened. Such films are exploitations of public memory. Interestingly, in the case of the Kennedy assassination, the actual event was caught on film at the time (the Zapruder home movie), as was the attempted assassination of Ronald Reagan, but even when we have the home movie or TV camera version of the event happening—and rehappening before our eyes in replays—there still remain large holes in our understanding of sequence, motive, and, in the Kennedy instance, of the identity of the shooter.

Perhaps *The Alamo* failed, apart from numerous problems in acting, structure, tone, and pacing, because its preoccupation with accuracy and fairness clashed with everybody's collective memory of the Alamo siege. The Anglo audience had trouble accepting its premises of flawed heroes, and the Mexican American audience found fault (sometimes even without seeing the film) with its inevitable evocation of Anglo heroes. Historical epics can fail, too, when they try to get too much history into the story line. The 2004 version of the Alamo story certainly could have done without the complicated politics so crudely dramatized in the scenes with Sam Houston (again, the stupefied acting of Dennis Quaid was a problem) and the other politicians busily and noisily writing the Texas Declaration of Independence at Washington-on-the-Brazos. At this point in the film the viewer's eyes glaze over. History, to be successfully presented in the genre of the historical epic, needs to be streamlined, the narrative organized to drive home a viable "lesson"—if one too simplified to satisfy the historian, so be it.

Somewhat ironically, the collective memory attempted by *The Alamo* 2004 will certainly find its way into the collective memory of thousands of Texas schoolchildren who, for the foreseeable future, will be viewing the film in history classes all over Texas on those Fridays when there's a home game and the coach/history teacher is preoccupied with more important matters than the past and screens the film instead of teaching history.

NOTES

1. For accounts of Alamo films, see Don Graham, "History Lesson," in *Cowboys and Cadillacs: How Hollywood Looks at Texas* (Austin: Texas Monthly Press, 1983), 41–53; Don Graham, "Remembering the Alamo: The Story of the Texas Revolution in Popular Culture," *Southwestern Historical Quarterly* 89, no. 1 (July 1985): 35–66, reprinted in Don Graham, *Giant Country: Essays on Texas* (Fort Worth: Texas Christian University Press, 1998), 235–58; and Frank Thompson, *Alamo Movies* (East Berlin, Pa.: Old Mill Books, 1991). For a very brief but succinct overview, see Paul Andrew Hutton, "Alamo Movies," *Wild West* (Feb. 2004): 46–47; and for another by Paul Hutton, see "Remembering the Alamo Movies: Hollywood Posters from Bygone Days," *True West* 51, no. 4 (May 2004): 56–59. President Wilson is quoted in Louis Menand, "Gross Points," *New Yorker,* Feb. 7, 2005, 86.

2. Thompson, quoted in Jane Sumner, "'Alamo' Film Has a Date with History," *Dallas Morning News,* Mar. 6, 2003; Wayne, quoted in *San Antonio Light,* Sept. 28, 1958. For an account of the making of Wayne's *The Alamo,* see Don Graham, "Wayne's World," *Texas Monthly* 28 (Mar. 2000):108–13, 145–46.

3. Jan Jarboe Russell, "'The Alamo' Remembers Spirit of True Heroism, Second Chances," *San Antonio Express-News,* Mar. 28, 2004. For commentary on the cold war atmospherics of Alamo movies in the 1950s, see Graham, *Cowboys and Cadillacs,* 42–43; and Hutton, "Alamo Movies," 47. Hutton, for example, describes *The Man from the Alamo* as a "fascinating anti-McCarthyism period piece" (47).

4. Don Graham, "Alamo Heights," *Texas Monthly* 31 (Dec. 2003): 132.

5. Ibid.

6. Thompson quoted in Arnold Garcia Jr., "Hype, Hollywood Have Distorted Truth Surrounding Alamo," *Austin American-Statesman,* Nov. 23, 2002.

7. Graham, "Alamo Heights," 132.

8. Don Graham, "Mission: Impossible," *Texas Monthly* 30 (Feb. 2002): 83–85.

9. Thompson quoted in García, "Hype, Hollywood Have Distorted Truth Surrounding Alamo."

10. Graham, "Alamo Heights," 132.

11. Ibid., 144.

12. John Lee Hancock, telephone interview with author, Oct. 2, 2003. This interview was the basis for much of the article "Alamo Heights," *Texas Monthly* 31 (Dec. 2003): 130, 132, 139, 144, 214, 216, 218, 220, 234. I am grateful to *Texas Monthly* for permission to use this material.

13. Hancock interview.

14. Pamela LeBlanc, "Aiming for Accuracy," *Austin American-Statesman,* June 6, 2003; "Gung Ho Alamo," *True West* (May 2004): 61.

15. Huffines quoted in LeBlanc, "Aiming for Accuracy."

16. Hancock interview.

17. Quotations in LeBlanc, "Aiming for Accuracy."

18. Ibid. (first, second, and third quotations); Hancock interview (fourth quotation).

19. Quotations in Pamela LeBlanc, "Wearing History," *Austin American-Statesman,* May 16, 2003.

20. Quotation in Amy Dorsett, "Movie Gets a Little Closer to Reality," *San Antonio Express-News,* Mar. 27, 2004.

21. Harrigan and Thompson quoted in Graham, "Alamo Heights," 216.

22. Hancock interview.

23. Ibid.

24. Ibid.

25. H. W. Brands, "The Alamo Should Never Have Happened," *Texas Monthly* 31 (Mar. 2003): 90, 142; Thomas Ricks Lindley, *Alamo Traces: New Evidence and New Conclusions* (Lanham, Md.: Republic of Texas Press, 2003), 152; Clinton P. Hartmann, "Fannin, James Walker, Jr.," *New Handbook of Texas,* ed. Ron Tyler et al., 6 vols. (Austin: Texas State Historical Association, 1966), 2:944–45.

26. Bowie quoted in Brands, "The Alamo Should Never Have Happened," 141; Lindley, *Alamo Traces,* 1–36.

27. Lindley, *Alamo Traces,* 52, 139, 142–43, 148.

28. Hancock interview.

29. Carl Diorio, "Mouse Pushes 'Alamo' to Spring," *Variety,* Oct. 29, 2003; Press Release, Touchstone Pictures, Oct. 29, 2003, announcement made on Oct. 28 www.variety.com/index .asp?layout=bio&peopleID=1571 (accessed Oct. 29, 2003) (first quotation); Biz.yahoo.com/ prnews/031028/latu145 1.html (accessed Oct. 29, 2003) (second quotation).

30. Polunsky quoted in Max Fernandez, "Studio Delays Release of 'Alamo,'" News 9 San Antonio, Oct. 30, 2003, news9sanantonio.com/content/top_stories/default.asp?ArID=6263 (accessed Oct. 30, 2003).

31. Knowles quoted in Chris Garcia, "Forget about 'The Alamo' until Spring," *Austin American-Statesman,* Oct. 30, 2003 (first, second, third, and fourth quotations); Richard Verrier, "Disney Delays 'Alamo' Release," *Los Angeles Times,* Oct. 29, 2003 (fifth quotation).

32. Knowles quoted in Garcia, "Forget about 'The Alamo' until Spring."

33. Thornton quoted in Chris Garcia, "Billy Bob's Crockett: 40 Years in the Making," *Austin American-Statesman,* Nov. 21, 2003.

34. Quotes and information in this and the following paragraph are from the author's notes of the March 6, 2004, sessions at the Texas State Historical Association annual meeting.

35. Chris Garcia, "Director Hancock Fighting Siege of Bad Press, Rumors," *Austin American-Statesman,* Apr. 9, 2004.

36. Hancock interview.

37. Vásquez y Sánchez quoted in Elda Silva, "Artist: Forget the Alamo: Exhibit Views Battle from a Mexican Viewpoint," *San Antonio Express-News,* Mar. 6, 2004; Dagoberto Gilb, "Alamo Story Overlooks Other Side," *San Antonio Express-News,* Apr. 18, 2004.

38. Mimi Swartz, "Remembering the Alamo (Whatever Happened)," *New York Times,* Nov. 2, 2003.

39. William Arnold, "Against All Cinematic Odds, 'The Alamo' Is a Glorious Victory," Apr. 9, 2004 http://seattlepi.nwsource.com/movies/168284_alamo09q.html (accessed Apr. 20, 2004); Paul Clinton, "Review: A Rousing, Triumphant 'Alamo'" cnn.entertainment.printthis .clickability.com/t/cpt?action=cpt&title=CNN.com+-+$. (accessed Apr. 20, 2004); John Anderson, Newsday.com, Apr. 8, 2004 www.newsday.com/entertainment/movies/ny-thealamo-movies ,0,7432602,print.stor. (accessed Apr. 20, 2004); Bruce Westbrook, "Realistic 'Alamo' Is Worth Remembering," *Houston Chronicle,* Apr. 9, 2004; Chris Garcia, "This Rousing Retelling of the Big Battle at a Tiny Church Should Defeat Doubters," *Austin American-Statesman,* Apr. 9, 2004.

40. Liam Lacey, "Pioneer Texans' Patriotic Act," *The Globe and Mail Review,* Apr. 9, 2004 www.theglobeandmail.com/servlet/ArticleNews/moviePrint/MOVIEREVIEWS/200. (accessed Apr. 20, 2004); Robert Wilonsky, "Messin' with Texas: *The Alamo* Gets What It Always Needed—a Happy Ending!" *Dallas Observer,* Apr. 8, 2004.

41. Manohla Dargis, "Forget This 'Alamo': John Lee Hancock's Version of the Historical Battle at the Texas Shrine Has Little to Offer Beyond the Acting of Billy Bob Thornton," *New York Times,* Apr. 9, 2004; Elvis Mitchell, "A Mythic Last State Stripped of Fantasy," *New York Times,* Apr. 9, 2004.

42. Geoff Pevere, "Houston, We Have a Problem," *Toronto Star,* Apr. 9, 2004.

43. Carla Meyer, "Only Thornton Emerges Unscathed in 'The Alamo,'" *San Francisco Chronicle,* Apr. 9, 2004.

44. David Edelstein, "Remember the Alamo? Disney Doesn't. This Is the Texas Battle's Most Confused Treatment Yet," *Slate,* Apr. 8, 2004 http://slate.msn.com/toolbar.aspx?action= print&id=2098492 (accessed Apr. 20, 2004); "The Texas Movie Massacre: Forgettable 'Alamo' Script Weakens a Historic Drama," *Wall Street Journal,* Apr. 9, 2004.

45. Pandya quoted in Larry Ratliff, "'Alamo' in Struggle for Box-Office Legs," *San Antonio Express-News,* Apr. 16, 2004; Patrick Beach, "What Made 'The Alamo' Fall So Fast?" *Austin American-Statesman,* May 3, 2004; Frank Ahrens, "Disney 2nd-Quarter Profit Up," *Washington Post,* May 13, 2004.

46. Larry Ratliff, "Armies of U.S. Moviegoers Fail to Storm 'The Alamo,'" *San Antonio Express-News,* Apr. 13, 2004; Maltin and Gross quoted in Anne Thompson, "'Alamo' Is Latest Casualty in Disney's Losing Battle," *Washington Post,* Apr. 19, 2004.

47. Beach, "What Made 'The Alamo' Fall So Fast?"

48. Brendan Miniter, "A Famous Fort under Siege, and History Too," *Wall Street Journal,* Apr. 9, 2004.

49. Valdés quoted in Simon Romero, "A Marketing Effort Falls Flat in Both Spanish and English," *New York Times,* Apr. 19, 2004.

50. Johnson quoted in Anne Thompson, "'Alamo' Is Latest Casualty in Disney's Losing Battle," *Washington Post,* Apr. 19, 2004.

51. Hancock quoted in Beach, "What Made 'The Alamo' Fall So Fast?"

52. William Booth, "Follows the Leader: Sequels Topped '04 Box Office," *Washington Post,* Jan. 8, 2005; Harrigan quoted in Beach, "What Made 'The Alamo' Fall So Fast?"; "Nine

Local Film Lovers List Their 10 Favorites of the Year," *Austin American-Statesman,* Dec. 28, 2004.

53. Hancock quoted in Chris Garcia, "Director Hancock Fighting Siege of Bad Press, Rumors."

54. Allen Barra, "Why Did *The Alamo* Flop?" *True West* 51, no. 6 (July 2004): 48, 49, 51.

55. Huffines quoted in "Gung Ho Alamo," *True West* 51, no. 4 (May 2004): 61; Thomas Ricks Lindley, "Alamo Characters: Pure Fiction," *True West* 51, no. 7 (Aug. 2004): 12.

56. thealamofilm.com/forum/viewtopic.php?t=3627&start=0&sid=adb7b4cf3c771d7d7f b04aea0eaaf171 (accessed Aug. 15, 2004).

57. thealamofilm.com/forum/viewtopic.php?t=3751&start=0&sid=a63c556576d50ae8591 96e100ed1ca8a (accessed Dec. 23, 2004).

58. Ibid.

59. Ibid.

60. thealamofilm.com/forum/viewtopic.php?t=3627&start=0&sid=adb7b4cf3c771d7d7 fb04aea0eaaf171 (accessed Aug. 15, 2004).

61. Kent Biffle, "The Legend Dies On," *Dallas Morning News,* Feb. 6, 2005.

62. See Mike Cox, "Defending the Alamo Diary," *Austin American-Statesman,* Feb. 13, 2005. Cox's conclusion is worth noting: "[B]y March 6 next year we will likely have a new book from someone claiming that Crisp has it all wrong."

Chapter 11

HISTORY AND COLLECTIVE MEMORY IN TEXAS: THE ENTANGLED STORIES OF THE LONE STAR STATE

RANDOLPH B. CAMPBELL

The past lives in the present as both history and memory. History, at least as the discipline is generally understood today, is the written account of the past provided by scholars who base their works primarily on archival sources. History is a form of entertainment, but most regard it also as a means of informing and instructing the present by examining the past. Memory, which may be both individual and collective, is the deliberate recall of past events and developments. Every individual has a memory of personal experiences that serves as a key part of his or her identity. Individuals constantly interpret and evaluate their personal memories of the past as a basis for understanding and acting in the present. Individuals, however, also share collective memories received from families, schools, churches, museums, historic sites, works of art, and purveyors of popular culture such as magazines and movies. For example, no living person in the United States experienced the Civil War, but most share memories of that conflict with their fellow Americans. And those collective memories influence their view of the nation and themselves in the present.[1]

Collective memory is in some respects indistinguishable from popular myths about the past—both, for example, depend more on emotional and cultural needs than on fact. It seems, however, that collective memory is less grand in origin and scope than myth. The famed Texas Myth, for example, depends on a generalized belief in the Lone Star state as an exceptional place in the world, the home of self-reliant individuals who take advantage of the bountiful opportunities provided by a new American Eden. Nothing makes a person more special than being a Texan; indeed, even many who live in the state cannot qualify. This Texas Myth clearly draws from collective memories—the story of the Alamo and the cowboy legend, for example—but it is bigger and broader than all the memories of all the great events of Texas history combined.[2] By contrast, collective memories generally focus on remembering particular events, such as secession, the Civil War, and Reconstruction. Perhaps this distinction is overdrawn, but for purposes of analysis, collective memories may be thought of as key components of overarching myths.

Over the years, history and memory generally have appeared complementary rather than antagonistic in any significant way. Historians employ individual memories, especially in the form of memoirs and oral histories, as one of their array of sources, and they analyze collective memories for insight into popular views of the past. Memory stimulates popular interest in history. Granted, that interest may be expressed more by visiting museums and historic sites and watching the History Channel than by reading the works of academic historians; nevertheless, until recently, in the words of one historian, "History and memory seemed unproblematically cozy with each other."[3]

This seemingly cozy relationship has been challenged during the last two decades by scholars from outside the discipline of history, especially by French social scientist Pierre Nora. In seven volumes entitled *Les Lieux de mémoire* (the sites of memory) and an article, "Between Memory and History: *Les Lieux de mémoire*" that appeared in translation, Nora argued that history and memory do not complement each other but instead are in basic conflict. Nora bears quoting at length because his work stimulated scholarly interest in the concept of memory, and historians generally cite him as the intellectual godfather of this "memory surge," possibly without considering all the implications of his argument.

Memory and history, far from being synonymous, appear now to be in fundamental opposition. Memory is life, borne by living societies founded in its name. It remains in permanent evolution, open to the dialectic of forgetting and remembering, unconscious of its successive deformations, vulnerable to manipulation and appropriation, susceptible to being long dormant and periodically revived. History, on the other hand, is the reconstruction, always problematic and incomplete, of what is no longer. Memory is a personally actual phenomenon, a bond tying us to the eternal present; history is a representation of the past. Memory, insofar as it is affective and magical, only accommodates those facts that suit it; it nourishes recollections that may be out of focus or telescopic, global or detached, particular or symbolic, responsive to each avenue of conveyance or phenomenal screen, to every censorship or projection. History, because it is an intellectual and secular production, calls for analysis and criticism. Memory installs remembrance within the sacred; history, always prosaic, releases it again. . . . Memory is absolute, while history can only conceive the relative. . . . History is perpetually suspicious of memory, and its true mission is to suppress and destroy it. . . . History's goal and ambition is not to exalt but to annihilate what has in reality taken place.

To strengthen his case, Nora pointed with pleasure to how postmodernist historians were dropping their discipline's hopeless infatuation with objectivity and confessing to the "intimate relation" they had with their subjects. "Better yet," he concluded, the new historian is "ready to proclaim it [a personal involvement with the subject], deepen it, make of it not the obstacle but the means to his understanding."[4]

Even allowing for what historian Bernard Bailyn called Nora's "rhetorical exuberance," his attack on history in the name of memory defined the issue clearly: Advocates of collective memory saw it as the emotional, value-bearing, living remembrances of real people, whereas they regarded history as the valueless, sterile product of empiricists wearing white lab coats.[5] The idea of memory as opposed to history, Nora wrote in 2001, "acquired the prestige of a popular protest movement and resembles the revenge of the underdog and outcast, the history of those denied history. Hitherto, if history did not have truth, it at least had loyalty [patriotic identity with particular nations] on its side. But the last century's sufferings incited demands for a truth more 'truthful' than history, the truth of personal experience and individual memory."[6]

American historians, given our tendency to embrace any concept or interpretive paradigm freshly minted in the more theoretical disciplines, generally welcomed the idea of memory—the *Journal of American History*, for example, published a special issue on "Memory and American History" in 1989.[7] Most of those who wrote on the subject during the next fifteen years seemed to agree with Nora that somehow memory preserved living truths that history obscured. Ira Berlin, for example, in his presidential address to the Organization of American Historians in 2003, described how a conference in 1998 that focused on a massive new slave trade database attracted both academic historians and numerous African Americans. The scholars delighted in how the data allowed them to analyze the slave trade, but the African Americans, remembering the fundamental nature of slavery, expressed disgust at how the scholars ignored the immorality involved in buying and selling humans. "At base," Berlin concluded, "history and memory do not mix well. They speak past one another. Their dialogue is uncomfortable and rarely respectful."[8]

Berlin did not condemn the historians for their failure to appreciate the emotional needs of memory. Instead, he called for uniting the two: for history to appreciate memory and thereby gain increased relevance to the lives of ordinary people and for memory to accept history lest it become merely a means of present-day wish gratification with "little weight beyond assertion."[9] This position seems perfectly reasonable when the subject is slavery or the slave trade or any issue similarly freighted with undying moral implications.[10] However, memory is often invoked to challenge history on subjects that many champions of the former concept might find disconcerting. To use a personal example: I grew up in Virginia with a set of standard southern memories—slavery was a benevolent institution that had little to do with the Civil War except as an excuse for Yankee aggression, the Ku Klux Klan restored order and decency after Reconstruction, and so forth.[11] After years of studying history, I reached the conclusion that these memories were to a large extent misleading and reactionary. They needed revision on the basis of critical history written from archival evidence. Now, however, when reading appeals for placing memory on an equal footing with history, I realize just how much hope there may still be for the old Confederate soldier pictured on a bumper sticker with the message "Forget, Hell!" Historians cannot honestly "privilege," to use a word currently fashionable in the profession, the memories of African Americans about slavery and at the same time discount those of unreconstructed southerners, unless, of course, they make critical use of data and archival sources.

So, memory, for all of its current popularity, is a difficult, and in some respects, threatening concept, and historians are certainly correct in seeing the need to wrestle with it. Few are likely to accept Pierre Nora's contention that they are trying to kill memory. Instead, they recognize that memory, rather than being a separate entity, is inseparably entangled with history. The problem is how to deal with the tangle and present a story of the past that judiciously incorporates the living nature of memory with the source-based critical analysis of history.[12] The mere suggestion of such an ideal probably seems foolishly naive, especially since it hints at the quaint notion that there is such a thing as "truth." Also, this suggestion may seem to hint at the equally quaint notion that historians should strive for "objectivity"—a goal that, because it cannot be achieved absolutely in any interpretation, some say is outmoded and foolish. What, however, is the alternative if historians wish to maintain any semblance of integrity and relevance as the voice of the past and herald of the future? Would a history written with the same lack of concern for evidence and objectivity that is necessary in the case of collective memory be of any use to anyone other than the person writing it? Would such a history, in the words of Professor Berlin, carry "little weight beyond assertion?"

The "memory surge" of recent years obviously challenges Texas historians as well as those of the United States at large. In light of Pierre Nora's emphasis on a conflict between history and memory, how should those who write about the Lone Star State's past deal with the issue of memory? The answer is twofold, and the first part, which deals with individual memory, is obvious. Texas historians should continue, as they always have, to find every record of individual memory in existence—memoirs, narratives, oral histories, and so forth—and use them critically, as they would any other historical source. Where possible, they should collect individual memories themselves, provided that they have some expertise in oral history. The second part of the answer deals with collective memories and presents far greater difficulties. Above all, Texas historians must remember that the state's people have more than one collective memory. The dominant collective memory since the early nineteenth century has been Anglo American in nature, but there is also an African American collective memory, and a Mexican American collective memory. It would be reasonable, of course, to argue that equal consideration should be given to the collective memories of Germans, native Americans, and other smaller groups, but the point is clear: Texans do not have *a* collective memory; they have collective memories.

Texans still draw their most important collective memories from the nineteenth century, so the years before 1900 provide the key places to look for the entanglement of memory and history in Texas. For example, Anglos remember their arrival in Texas as a chapter in the march of civilization as settlers from the United States arrived in an unpopulated province, bringing progress and prosperity to the wilderness. To Anglos, the term "Manifest Destiny," which did not appear until the 1840s, manifested itself in Texas some two decades earlier. The famed "Texas History Movies," a comic strip version of the state's past that appeared in the *Dallas Morning News* in 1926–27, commented on reaching the 1820s: "Now begins the chronicle of the Anglo-American colonization of Texas, the event that made us all what we are today."[13]

Mexican Americans with roots in early-nineteenth-century Texas often remember the arrival of Anglos very differently. For example, according to Abel Rubio, a descendant of the Becerra family of South Texas, the opening of immigration by Stephen F. Austin brought land grabbers who stole the property of families such as his. The land grabber, he wrote, "was powerful and ruthless, cunning as a weasel, and often a supposedly respected member of the region where he lived. His respectability was only an illusion. To me, he was in fact *el diablo,* the devil. . . . The land-grabber resorted to fraud, murder, intimidation, persecution, and manipulation of the law. The unfortunate souls who fell victim to these unscrupulous villains were in most instances unsuspecting Mexican Americans."[14]

African Americans remember collectively that their people came to Texas first as the property of Anglo colonists. Their memory is one of subjugation and struggle rather than Manifest Destiny or the loss of lands. A black Texan named Paul Darby expressed this remembrance perfectly in 1972 when commenting on the movement to have Juneteenth, the African American commemoration of June 19, 1865, the day the Emancipation Proclamation became effective in Texas, declared a state holiday: "They [white Texans] owe the 19th of June to us, in a way of speaking. I don't care what they might say that it is a nasty spot, but it isn't. It's true, it really did happen. They really did have slaves. They did do that. And since they celebrate their day for they freedom, then they ought to give the colored man a day for his freedom. It should be a red spot on the calendar and really took aside for."[15]

No event, of course, is so central to collective memories in Texas as the siege of the Alamo in 1836. The Anglo memory, which dominated all forms of popular culture well into the twentieth century (and perhaps still dominates into the first decade of the twenty-first century), pictured heroic lovers of freedom fighting to the death against overwhelming odds. With only one exception (a veteran of Napoleon's army named Louis "Moses" Rose), the heroes stepped across a line drawn in the sand by Col. William Barret Travis, knowingly signed their death warrants, and fought to the last man against hordes of murderous Mexicans. In Anglo collective memory, the Alamo became the ultimate story of sacrifice in the name of liberty. Henry A. McArdle captured this memory perfectly in his famous painting, *Dawn at the Alamo,* which depicted an especially vicious-looking Mexican preparing to bayonet Travis in the back as the Texan commander stood on the wall firing at the attackers. Most historians write that Travis was one of the first defenders to die, shot in the forehead as he looked over the wall at the oncoming Mexicans, but that image is far less heroic than the one presented by McArdle.

As might be expected, Mexican American memories of the Alamo differ. Richard R. Flores, an anthropologist at the University of Texas, remembered visiting the Alamo on a school field trip and being told by one of his Anglo friends as they left, "You killed them! You and the other 'mes'kins!'" Flores's first thought was to deny having ever killed anyone. In fact, he said, his grandfather, the oldest Mexican American he knew, had not killed anyone either. Later, as he grew older, Flores discovered that many of his Mexican American friends, rather than being defensive, were hostile to the place called the Alamo and the story associated with it. Memories of the Alamo, he concluded, had become a key to establishing the identities and power relationships between racial/ethnic groups in Texas and beyond.[16] Abel Rubio argued in a similar vein that "early biased accounts of the battle of the Alamo have been very damaging to native Mexican-Texans and have resulted in prejudicing our position in this society, a society which we have defended since we became a part of it in the early nineteenth century."[17]

In recent years, historians have injected a great deal of archival-based information and interpretation into the story of the Alamo, in many cases challenging the Anglo collective memories. Most now argue, for example, that Travis did not draw a line in the sand and that the Alamo defenders expected relief from other Texians almost until the end. Worst of all for those who hold to the traditional memory of the Alamo, historians accepted evidence that David Crockett did not go down swinging "Old Betsy" at a horde of attacking Mexicans but instead surrendered or was overpowered, only to be killed on orders from General Antonio López de Santa Anna. A handful of other defenders met the same fate. The case made by historians has proven convincing enough that even novelists and filmmakers have paid attention. For example, the story of drawing the line in the sand does not appear in Stephen Harrigan's *The Gates of the Alamo* or in John Lee Hancock's 2004 movie, *The Alamo*. And in the film, Crockett dies as a captive bound and on his knees before Santa Anna.

Collective memory is resilient, however. Hancock's movie, in spite of much advertising fanfare, drew limited interest from the public and plummeted at the box office within weeks of its release. There are many possible explanations for the movie's seeming failure, of course, but a likely one is that advance publicity led the public to expect a "revisionist" story. In fact, the film, although it made the story more complex than usual and incorporated new interpretations, was, in the words of one of my academic colleagues, more "triumphal" than expected. For many Texans, however, any revisions remain unacceptable. As Bryan Woolley, a staff writer for the *Dallas Morning News,* explained it, the story of the Alamo that he had received from his grandmother was good enough for him. "The line, say the experts, isn't history. It's myth," he wrote. "But my world has room for myth. Myths often tell more truth than facts do. When I visit the Alamo, I still see Travis, in my mind's eye, drawing the line and the men carrying Bowie's bed across it. Even if it didn't happen, I'll always believe it."[18] Substitute "collective memory" for "myth," which I think is appropriate in this case, and the notion of history as being equally entangled with memory has taken another blow—warm memory trumps cold history.

The Civil War probably takes second place only to the Alamo in the collective memories of Texans, but in this case, because slavery was the issue, African American memories join those of Anglos on center stage. Anglo Americans tend to remember slavery as a relatively unimportant institution in Texas, one involving such a tiny percentage of the state's people that it did not deserve an entry in the original *Handbook of Texas,* which was published in 1952. Moreover, to the extent that slavery did exist, Anglos say, it amounted to a largely paternalistic, benevolent institution.[19] Eddie Stimpson Jr., a black Texan born in 1929, received quite different memories from his family. He wrote in a book entitled *My Remembers,* "Although during my growing up days it was pretty tough to survive, yet it was still easier than what I would hear about how my grand parent and ther parent suffered. Not only from the blistering sun, and hour from dark to dark, with little food, no bed to lay in, no stove to cook on, no clothes to mount to anything, no doctor, and on top of all this, some one standing guard over you with a whip in one hand and a gun in other, day and night."[20] Stimpson exaggerated the conditions under which most slaves lived, but his memories held a basic truth: All slaves were property who could be treated the way his family had described it.

Anglo Texans like to remember the Civil War as a conflict caused not by slavery, especially since in their memory so few slaves lived in Texas, but by issues such as states' rights and the protective tariff. Once, when debating the causes of the war in a public symposium, I pointed out that the proportions of slaves and slaveholders in the population of Texas almost exactly matched those in Virginia, a state in which virtually everyone recognized the importance of slavery. I then quoted from the "Declaration of the Causes which Impel the State of Texas to Secede from the Federal Union" adopted by the Texas secession convention in 1861 to show that it featured the threat to slavery above all as a reason for leaving the United States. When I concluded, a member of the audience countered by asking me if I had seen the film *Gods and Generals,* which barely mentioned slavery as a cause of secession and war. I responded that I did not take my history from the movies, but there is no way of knowing how many of those present agreed with me as opposed to endorsing the opinion expressed by the member of the audience. Obviously, however, in at least one case, warm memory again trumped cold history.

Reconstruction in Texas after the Civil War is strongly embedded in Anglo American collective memory as a period in which a Republican co-alition of carpetbaggers, scalawags, and freedmen destroyed all honor and decency in government. The carpetbaggers, northern-born adventurer/politicians who came to Texas after the war, are remembered as the guiding spirits behind this tragic era in Texas. As one Texas politician put it well over a century later, carpetbaggers "came in the dark of night, looted the liberties of Texans for a number of years, then finally . . . were kicked the heck out of Texas."[21] In 1994, for a presidential address to the Texas State Historical Association, I built a database of all major office holders in the legislative, executive, and judicial branches of the Texas government during the period of Republican control during Reconstruction and found that carpetbaggers constituted at most only 20 percent of those office holders. Putting these data in tabular form, I argued that the memory of carpetbagger domination during Reconstruction had no basis in fact. Following the presentation, several of my graduate students reported overhearing a conversation between two members of the audience. One asked what the other thought about my argument, and the reply was, "Oh, I could have argued with him all night. All he did was talk about that stupid table."[22] Once again, with at least one listener, cold history fell victim to warm collective memory. I can only hope that some members of the audience were persuaded by historical evidence.

The twenty-five or so years following the Civil War and Reconstruction, the period from the mid-1860s to the late 1880s that marked Texas' entry into the Cattle Kingdom—an era of cattle drives to railheads that connected with northern markets and the conquest of West Texas by cattle ranchers who soon made ranching a settled business—provided the setting for yet another collective memory of nineteenth-century Texas. According to this way of remembering Texas, heroically individualistic ranchers and cowboys successfully braved nature, defeated the Indians, and civilized the plains and prairies west of the one-hundredth meridian. This memory emphasizes all things western and allows Texans to escape from their essentially southern heritage. Being western may create problems for those who worry about such things as destroying the buffalo and dispossessing the Indians, but this western past is still far more appealing than a southern past that involves slavery, secession, Civil War, and defeat.

The memory of Texas as western has some basis in fact, making that western aspect more of a real part of the state's past than the beliefs that slavery was unimportant in Texas and that carpetbaggers dominated politics during Reconstruction. Texas, however, is far more southern than western and has been so for nearly two hundred years. The great majority of Anglo settlers who arrived in Texas before the Civil War were from the Old South, and many were slaveholders. By 1860, more than three-quarters of Texas households were headed by natives of the South, more than one-quarter of those households had at least one slave, and slaves constituted nearly one-third of the state's people. Although there were pockets of Unionism, more than three-fourths of Texans voted for secession, and the state contributed heavily to the Confederacy from 1861 to 1865. Texas emerged from defeat in the war and the Reconstruction era with attitudes typical of the South for the next century and a half: opposition to racial equality (reflected by segregation, disfranchisement, and lynching before a second Reconstruction by the federal government forced change), dislike of government (shown especially in insistence on the lowest possible level of taxation), and support of one-party conservative politics (indicated by overwhelming support for the Democratic Party until the last third of the twentieth century, when the Republican Party took over the mantle of conservatism and began to receive equally strong support).[23]

Thus, when modern Texans in cities such as Houston put on their boots and Stetsons and head for the rodeo or hearken back to the days of movie westerns that portrayed their state as a land of cowboys, rustlers, and gunfighters, they are drawing on a collective memory that, although it has a basis in fact, is not the essence of Texas. The cold history of being southern is not as pleasing as the warm memory of being western.

In summary, then, historians are always challenged by collective memory (in Texas, and many other places for that matter, by collective memories) in their efforts to write accounts of the past that entertain, inform, and instruct but at the same time are critical, analytical, and true to the sources. Beginning in the 1980s or so, this challenge has been heightened by a "memory surge" from scholars in a variety of fields, including some historians themselves. The advocates of memory insist that critical, empirical history has lost its relevance and that the public is turning more than ever to creators and purveyors of collective memory for knowledge of the past.

Texas historians could respond to this challenge by giving in to collective memory. If Anglo Texans want to remember Texas as an exceptional place in the world, the home of the Alamo where selfless patriots fought to the last man for freedom, a noble defender of states' rights against northern aggression, a long-suffering victim of carpetbagger corruption, and in the end a place of heroic western virtues, then perhaps historians should simply give them that version of the past. As historian Laura Lyons McLemore pointed out in her study, *Inventing Texas,* giving the public what it wanted proved popular in the nineteenth century.[24] Undoubtedly, the approach that worked then will work now. But is hewing to the line of collective memory the historian's job? Obviously, I do not think so.

Texas historians know that the past comes to the present entangled as memory and history. They should beware, however, of accepting collective memory as superior to, or even equal to, history, even though the suggestion is *new* and comes with all sorts of exciting theoretical trappings. Writing history, even with all its imperfections, is a worthy rational endeavor. Historians of Texas should not give up their discipline to reactionaries or romantics—even the well-intentioned ones—speaking in the name of memory. Instead, they should continue, as they always have, to write histories that use individual memories as sources. Perhaps they should attempt to mediate between memory and history by writing carefully worded accounts that have the intention and hope of modifying popular remembrances of the past. Above all, they should take fully into account the power of collective memories and make those memories themselves a means of understanding Texas' past.

NOTES

1. Remembering generally involves a certain degree of forgetting as well. It is cumbersome, however, to mention forgetting in every reference to memory, so this essay uses only the latter with the assumption that readers are aware that most individuals and groups are as selective in what they forget as in what they remember.

2. For a good summary of the Texas Myth, see Laura Lyons McLemore, *Inventing Texas: Early Historians of the Lone Star State* (College Station: Texas A&M University Press, 2004), 94–100.

3. Thomas W. Laqueur, introduction to "Grounds for Remembering," special issue of *Representations* 69 (Winter 2000): 1.

4. Pierre Nora, "Between History and Memory: *Les Lieux de mémoire,*" *Representations* 26 (Spring 1989): 8–9, 18. For the original texts, see Pierre Nora, ed., *Les Lieux de mémoire,* 7 vols. (Paris: Gallimard, 1984–93).

5. Bernard Bailyn, "Considering the Slave Trade: History and Memory," *William and Mary Quarterly,* 3d ser., 58 (Jan. 2001): 249–50.

6. Pierre Nora, "The Tidal Wave of History," http://www.project.syndicate.org/commentaries/commentary_text (accessed Aug. 20, 2004).

7. See especially David Thelen, "Memory and American History," *Journal of American History* 75 (Mar. 1989): 1117–29. Other indications of the rising popularity of memory studies abound. For example, a 1996 collection of essays concerning the dropping of the first atomic bomb on Japan made the point that it "unites up-to-date scholarship by diplomatic historians with the recent interest in memory that has emerged as part of the new cultural history" (publisher's advertising copy for Michael J. Hogan, ed., *Hiroshima in History and Memory* [New York: Cambridge University Press, 1996]). In 2002 the Department of History at Indiana University renamed its Oral History Research Center, calling it the Center for the Study of History and Memory, http://www.indiana.edu/~cshm/ (accessed Sept. 28, 2004).

8. Ira Berlin, "American Slavery in History and Memory," *Journal of American History* 90 (Mar. 2004): 1266–67.

9. Ibid., 1268.

10. Probably the historical event most responsible for the rise of interest in memory is the Holocaust. Survivors have tended to criticize historians for destroying the true meaning of the Holocaust through analysis rather than simply remembering. The journal *History and Memory,* which began publication in 1988, originated primarily as a result of this dispute.

11. Personal anecdotes are used, with due apologies, to make several points in this essay because collective memories are difficult to document. When everyone *knows* what happened in the past, there is little need to put it on paper in any organized fashion. Collective memories are most likely to pop up in conversations and debates in which things that are said may be taken as more generally believed.

12. The argument that history and memory are "entangled" is stated clearly in Marita Sturken, *Tangled Memories: The Vietnam War, the AIDS Epidemic, and the Politics of Remembering* (Berkeley: University of California Press, 1997). Sturken argues that "indeed, there is so much traffic across the borders of cultural memory and history that in many cases it may be futile to maintain a distinction between them. Yet there are times when those distinctions are important in understanding political intent, when memories are asserted specifically outside of or in response to historical narratives" (4).

13. John Rosenfield Jr. with Jack Patton, *Texas History Movies* (Dallas: P. L. Turner Company, 1928), 71.

14. Abel G. Rubio, *Stolen Heritage: A Mexican-American's Rediscovery of His Family's Lost Land Grant,* ed. Thomas H. Kreneck, rev. ed. (Austin, Tex.: Eakin Press, 1998), xx.

15. Darby quoted in William H. Wiggins Jr., "Juneteenth: A Red Spot Day on the Texas Calendar," in *Juneteenth Texas: Essays in African-American Folklore,* ed. Francis E. Abernethy, Patrick B. Mullen, and Alan B. Govenar (Denton: University of North Texas Press, 1996), 251.

16. Richard R. Flores, *Remembering the Alamo: Memory, Modernity, and the Master Symbol* (Austin: University of Texas Press, 2002), xiii.

17. Rubio, *Stolen Heritage,* 74.

18. *Dallas Morning News,* Apr. 10, 2004.

19. For a summary of the standard Anglo view of slavery in Texas, see Randolph B. Campbell, *An Empire for Slavery: The Peculiar Institution in Texas, 1821–1865* (Baton Rouge: Louisiana State University Press, 1989), 1.

20. Eddie Stimpson Jr., *My Remembers: A Black Sharecropper's Recollections of the Depression* (Denton: University of North Texas Press, 1996), 152.

21. State senator Ted Lyon of Rockwall quoted in *Dallas Morning News,* Jan. 12, 1992.

22. The text of this presidential address (for what it was worth) is in *Southwestern Historical Quarterly* 97 (Apr. 1994): 587–96.

23. The essentially southern nature of Texas since the early nineteenth century is documented in Randolph B. Campbell, *Gone to Texas: A History of the Lone Star State* (New York: Oxford University Press, 2003), 207, 242–44, 287–89, 325–26, 419–29, 457–63, 469–70.

24. McLemore, *Inventing Texas,* 94–100.

Contributors

W. FITZHUGH BRUNDAGE

W. Fitzhugh Brundage is the William B. Umstead Professor of History at the University of North Carolina, Chapel Hill. He received his Ph.D. from Harvard University and is the author of *The Southern Past: A Clash of Race and Memory* (2005), *A Socialist Utopia in the New South: The Ruskin Colonies in Tennessee and Georgia, 1894–1901* (1996), and *Lynching in the New South: Georgia and Virginia, 1880–1930* (1993). He also has edited collections on lynching, historical memory, and Booker T. Washington.

WALTER L. BUENGER

Walter L. Buenger is professor of history at Texas A&M University, where he also serves as department chair. He received his Ph.D. from Rice University in 1979. His most recent book is *The Path to a Modern South: Northeast Texas between Reconstruction and the Great Depression* (2001), which won the Coral H. Tullis Award for the best book on Texas history. He is the coauthor with Victoria Buenger of *Texas Merchant: Marvin Leonard and Fort Worth* (1999), and, with Joseph A. Pratt, of *But Also Good Business: Texas Commerce Banks and the Financing of Houston and Texas, 1886–1986* (1986). He also authored *Secession and the Union in Texas* (1984), and coedited, with Robert A. Calvert, *Texas through Time: Evolving Interpretations* (1991). He is a fellow and member of the board of directors of the Texas State Historical Association.

RANDOLPH B. CAMPBELL

Randolph B. "Mike" Campbell is Regents Professor of History at the University of North Texas. He received his Ph.D. from the University of Virginia in 1966. He is the author of *Gone to Texas: A History of the Lone Star*

State (2003), *Grass-Roots Reconstruction in Texas, 1865–1880* (1997), *Sam Houston and the American Southwest* (1993), *An Empire for Slavery: The Peculiar Institution in Texas, 1821–1865* (1989), and *A Southern Community in Crisis: Harrison County, Texas, 1850–1880* (1983). He also is coauthor, with Richard G. Lowe, of *Planters and Plain Folk: Agriculture in Antebellum Texas* (1986), and *Wealth and Power in Antebellum Texas* (1977). Professor Campbell's professional honors include the Coral H. Tullis Award, the H. Bailey Carroll Award, the Summerfield G. Roberts Award, the Charles W. Ramsdell Award, the Friends of the Dallas Public Library Award, and the Philosophical Society of Texas Book Award. He is currently editor of the *Southwestern Historical Quarterly.* He is a fellow and former president of the Texas State Historical Association.

GREGG CANTRELL

Gregg Cantrell holds the Erma and Ralph Lowe Chair in Texas History at Texas Christian University. He received his Ph.D. from Texas A&M University in 1988. He is the author of *Feeding the Wolf: John B. Rayner and the Politics of Race, 1850–1918* (2001), *Stephen F. Austin, Empresario of Texas* (1999), and *Kenneth and John B. Rayner and the Limits of Southern Dissent* (1993). He is coauthor, with Robert A. Calvert and Arnoldo De León, of *The History of Texas,* 3d ed. (2001). Professor Cantrell's professional honors include the Coral H. Tullis Award, the Kate Broocks Bates Award, the Summerfield G. Roberts Award, the Presidio La Bahía Award, the Ima Hogg Historical Achievement Award, the T. R. Fehrenbach Award, the H. Bailey Carroll Award, and the Philosophical Society of Texas Book Award. He is a member of the board of directors of the Texas State Historical Association and serves as series editor of Texas Christian University Press's Texas Biography Series.

JAMES E. CRISP

James E. Crisp is associate professor of history at North Carolina State University, where he is also assistant department chair. He received his Ph.D. from Yale University in 1976. He is the author of *Sleuthing the Alamo: Davy Crockett's Last Stand and Other Mysteries of the Texas Revolution* (2004), as well as numerous articles and book chapters. He also wrote the new introduction for the expanded edition of José Enrique de la Peña's *With Santa Anna in*

Texas: A Personal Narrative of the Revolution (1997), which includes Crisp's translation of newly discovered portions of this controversial work. Professor Crisp's professional honors include the Beinecke Dissertation Prize, the H. Bailey Carroll Award, and the Best Presentation Award at the Cities under Siege Conference in Montalcino, Italy.

RICKY FLOYD DOBBS

Ricky Floyd Dobbs is department head and associate professor of history at Texas A&M University–Commerce. He received his Ph.D. from Texas A&M University in 1996. He is the author of *Yellow Dogs and Republicans: Allan Shivers and Texas Two-Party Politics* (2005). His essays have appeared in the *East Texas Historical Journal, Baptist Heritage and History,* and *Papers on Language and Literature.* He also maintains an active interest in public school history instruction, contributing to textbooks and lobbying for improvements in public education.

YVONNE DAVIS FREAR

Yvonne Davis Frear is assistant professor of history at Sam Houston State University. She receives her Ph.D. from Texas A&M University in 2006. Her dissertation is "Battling to End Segregation in Dallas, Texas, 1945–1965: Race, Gender and Social Mobilization in a Local Civil Rights Movement." Her essays on African Americans in Texas have appeared regionally and internationally in *Major Problems in Texas History* and *Schriftenreihe des Fachbereichs Betriebswirtschaft der HTW.* She is currently working on a project that examines the legal and social implications of the civil rights movement in Texas.

DON GRAHAM

Don Graham is the J. Frank Dobie Regents Professor of American and English Literature at the University of Texas at Austin. He received his Ph.D. from the University of Texas in 1971. He is the author of *Kings of Texas: The 150-Year Saga of an American Ranching Empire* (2003), which won the Carr P. Collins Prize; *Giant Country: Essays on Texas* (1998); *No Name on the Bullet:*

A Biography of Audie Murphy (1989); *Texas: A Literary Portrait* (1985); and *Cowboys and Cadillacs: How Hollywood Looks at Texas* (1983). His edited works include *Lone Star Literature: From the Red River to the Rio Grande* (2003) and *South by Southwest: 24 Stories from Modern Texas* (1986). Professor Graham is past president of the Texas Institute of Letters and a writer-at-large for *Texas Monthly.*

LAURA LYONS MCLEMORE

Laura Lyons McLemore is head of Archives and Special Collections at Louisiana State University–Shreveport, Louisiana, and teaches online courses in United States history at Grayson County College in Denison, Texas. She received her Ph.D. from the University of North Texas in 1998. She received the Texas State Historical Association's John H. Jenkins Research Fellowship. She is the author of *Inventing Texas: Early Historians of the Lone Star State* (2004), as well as several articles and book reviews related to Texas history and archival practice.

KELLY MCMICHAEL

Kelly McMichael is visiting lecturer at the University of North Texas, conducting a grant-funded experimental study in pedagogical techniques across face-to-face, online, and blended classes as part of a university-wide initiative to improve undergraduate education. She received her Ph.D. from the University of North Texas in 2000. She is the author of *Waxahachie, Texas: Where Cotton Reigned King* (2002), *SparkNotes U.S. History 101, Colonial Period to 1877* (2005), and two manuscripts under review: "Sacred Memories: A Guide to the Civil War Monuments of Texas" and "Remember Our Southland: The Texas Division of the United Daughters of the Confederacy and the Construction of Social Memory, 1896–1927."

ANDRÉS TIJERINA

Andrés Tijerina is professor of history at Austin Community College. He received his Ph.D. from the University of Texas at Austin in 1977. He is the author of *Tejano Empire: Life on the South Texas Ranchos* (1998), *Tejanos and Texas under the Mexican Flag, 1821–1836* (1994), and *A War Remembered,* vol. 20 of *The Vietnam Experience* (1987). His edited works include Elena Zamora O'Shea's *El Mesquite: A Novel* (2000) and Andrés Saenz's *Early Tejano Ranching in Duval County* (2000). His professional honors include the Kate Broocks Bates Award, the Presidio La Bahía Award, and the T. R. Fehrenbach Award. Professor Tijerina has served as a state agency executive director of the Texas Good Neighbor Commission, and he is a fellow of the Texas State Historical Association. As a pilot in the air force, he flew more than one hundred combat missions in Vietnam, receiving the Air Medal and the Distinguished Flying Cross.

Elizabeth Hayes Turner

Elizabeth Hayes Turner is associate professor of history at the University of North Texas. She earned her Ph.D. from Rice University in 1990. She is the author of *Women, Culture, and Community: Religion and Reform in Galveston, 1880–1920* (1997), and the coauthor, with Patricia Bellis Bixel, of *Galveston and the 1900 Storm: Catastrophe and Catalyst* (2000). Her coedited works include *Clio's Southern Sisters: Interviews with Leaders of the Southern Association for Women Historians* (2004), *Major Problems in the History of the American South* (1999), *Beyond Image and Convention: Explorations in Southern Women's History* (1998), and *Hidden Histories of Women in the New South* (1994). Her professional honors include the Coral H. Tullis Award, the Ottis Lock Award, and the Certificate of Commendation from the American Association for State and Local History. Professor Turner is past president of the Southern Association for Women Historians, and from 1997 to 1998 she served as visiting managing editor of the *Journal of Southern History.* In spring 2003 she completed a Fulbright Scholar lectureship in Italy at the University of Genoa.

Index

Page numbers shown in *italics* refer to photo captions.

ISBN 978-1-58544-563-9

54500